THE WORLDWIDE GUN OWNER'S Guide

Every nation has gun rights!

A first-hand cultural and
comparative examination
of the world's gun laws

by *Larry Grupp*
with a foreword by Alan Korwin

BLOOMFIELD PRESS
Scottsdale, Arizona, U.S.A.

BLOOMFIELD PRESS

4848 E. Cactus #505-440
Scottsdale, AZ 85254
(602) 996-4020 Office
(602) 494-0679 Fax
1-800-707-4020 Order Hotline

gunlaws.com

ISBN-10: 1-889632-27-9
ISBN-13: 978-1-889632-27-8
Library of Congress Catalog No. 2011921614

Photographs by the author
Edited by Felicity Bower

ATTENTION
Clubs, Organizations, Libraries, Firearms Training Instructors, Schools, Educators, Think Tanks and all interested parties:
Contact the publisher for information on quantity discounts!

Visit our website for updates and new information!

Printed and bound in the United States of America
at Victor Graphics, Baltimore, Maryland

First Edition

TABLE OF CONTENTS

PHOTOGRAPHS

ACKNOWLEDGMENTS

If I tried to acknowledge everyone individually who helped with this book I would surely and unfairly miss some, embarrass or endanger others who live under regimes where this information is not supposed to be disseminated, and would have precious little space left for the contents of this tome! Let it suffice, my dear friends, confidants and secret sources, to proffer one huge indivisible thank you and deeply heartfelt sense of appreciation for the guidance and support you have afforded me, without which this book would have never come to be.

WARNING! • DON'T MISS THIS!

This book is not "the law," and is not a substitute for the law. The law includes all the legal obligations imposed on you, a much greater volume of work than the mere descriptions of national firearm rules contained in this book. You are fully accountable under the exact wording and current official interpretations of all applicable laws, regulations, policies, executive orders, dictates, court precedents, and more, when you deal with firearms under any circumstances.

Many people find laws hard to understand, and describing the main relevant ones for this many nations was a Herculean task. This book guides you through the maze of international gun laws, but is not a substitute for competent legal advice, in the native language, for any serious activity with firearms, including ownership, acquisition, possession, use, transfer and transport, among many other issues.

The laws and other regulations are discussed in regular conversational terms for your convenience. While care has been taken to accomplish this with a high degree of accuracy, **no guarantee of accuracy is expressed or implied, and the explanatory sections of this book are not to be considered as legal advice or a restatement of law.** In explaining the general meanings of the laws, using plain English, differences inevitably arise, so **you must always check the actual laws in their native languages**. The author and publisher expressly disclaim any liability whatsoever arising out of reliance on any information contained in this book. New laws and regulations may be enacted at any time by the authorities. **The author and publisher not only make no representation suggesting this book includes all requirements and prohibitions that may exist, we assure you that other requirements do exist, some of which may seem to be either traps or totally unjust**.

This book concerns the gun laws as they apply to law-abiding private citizens of the respective nations. It is not intended to and does not describe most situations relating to licensed gun dealers, museums or educational institutions, local or national military personnel, foreign nationals, the police or other peace officers, persons with special licenses (including collectors), non-residents, persons with special authorizations or permits, bequests or intestate succession, persons under indictment, felons, prisoners, escapees, dangerous or repetitive offenders, criminal street gang members, delinquent, incorrigible or unsupervised juveniles, judicial officers, government employees, or any other people restricted or prohibited from firearm possession.

Note that *The Worldwide Gun Owner's Guide* focuses on legal gun ownership, and avoids most issues related to deliberate gun crimes. This means many laws are excluded or not explained in the text. Some examples are: capital murder; homicide; manslaughter; gun theft; gun running; concealment of stolen firearms; enhanced penalties for commission of crimes with firearms, including armed robbery, burglary, theft, kidnapping, drug offenses, assault and priors; smuggling firearms into public aircraft; threatening flight attendants with firearms; possession of contraband; gun shoplifting, possession of a firearm in a prison by a prisoner; false application for a firearm; threatening and intimidating, accidental discharge, criminal street gang activity; removal of a body after a shooting; drive by shootings; retaliation; and this is only a partial list.

FIREARMS LAWS ARE SUBJECT TO CHANGE WITHOUT NOTICE. You are strongly urged to consult with a qualified attorney and local authorities to determine the current status and applicability of the law, in the native language, to specific situations you may encounter.

Guns are deadly serious business and require the highest level of responsibility from you. Firearm ownership, possession and use are rights that carry awesome responsibility. Unfortunately, **what the law says and what the authorities and courts do aren't always an exact match.** You must remember that each legal case is different and may lack prior court precedents. A decision to prosecute a case and the charges brought may involve enormous discretion from the authorities involved, with vast differences from nation to nation. Sometimes, there just isn't a plain, clear-cut answer you can rely upon. Abuses, ignorance, carelessness, human frailties and plain fate subject you to legal risks, which can be exacerbated when firearms are involved. Take nothing for granted, recognize that legal risk is attached to everything you do, and **ALWAYS ERR ON THE SIDE OF SAFETY.**

Pending Legislation

Governments worldwide continually consider new gun laws that might:
- Outlaw specific or classes of firearms by price range, melting point, operating characteristics, accuracy, type of safety mechanism, type of sights, point of origin, appearance, caliber and by name.
- Restrict the amount of ammunition a gun can hold, devices for feeding ammunition, allowable types of ammunition or reduce ammo shelf life
- Restrict the number of firearms and the amount of ammunition a person may buy or own, and implement burdensome storage requirements
- Change any proficiency testing or periodic licensing and expiration dates
- Register or change procedures for firearms and owners nationally
- Use taxation as a way to limit firearm and ammunition ownership
- Create new liabilities for firearm owners, manufacturers, dealers, parents and persons involved in firearms accidents
- Require firearms to be unloaded, locked away or otherwise inoperable
- Censor classified ads for firearms, eliminate firearms publications and outlaw any dangerous speech or publication
- Prohibit gun shows and abolish hunting
- Deny or criminalize firearm rights for government-promised security
- Adopt standards from countries that don't respect the right to arms
- Require technologies that don't exist or cannot be economically used

In contrast, governments typically pay less attention to laws that would:
- Mandate public-school-based firearm safety training and marksmanship
- Provide general self-defense awareness and training
- Encourage personal responsibility in resisting crime
- Protect and honor citizens who stand up and act against crime
- Guarantee people's right to travel legally armed for personal safety
- Fix the conditions that generate hard-core criminals
- Assure sentencing of serious criminals, increase the percentage of sentences that are actually served, provide more prison space and permanently remove habitual criminals from society
- Improve rehabilitation and reduce repeat offenses
- Close legal loopholes and reform criminal justice malpractice
- Improve law enforcement quality and efficiency
- Establish and strengthen victims' rights and protection
- Hold police and authorities accountable for abuse of citizens' rights
- Hold the rights of all citizens in unassailable esteem
- Provide for the common defense
- Recognize *democide*—murder by your own government—as the world's leading cause of preventable death, and help people resist this atrocity, which has led to the deaths of 180 million people in the 20th Century.

Some experts believe that easy-to-enact but ineffectual "feel good" laws are often pursued instead of the much tougher course of laws and social changes that would reduce crime and its root causes. Many laws aim at disarming citizens while ignoring the fact that gun possession by criminals is already strictly illegal and largely unenforced. Increasing attacks on civil liberties are threatening freedoms the world's inhabitants have or should have. You are advised to become aware of any new laws that may be enacted that affect you. Contact your legislators to express your views on proposed legislation.

Dedicated to all the gun owners
I met around the world,
and the great deal of camaraderie
I found and enjoyed there.

FOREWORD

The book you are now holding is a cultural and comparative window on gun law and gun culture around the world. Nothing like it has ever existed previously, and as you read on you will see this is a work of monumental scope. Unlike other guides published or distributed by Bloomfield Press, this is far from a legal-flavored description of gun laws in different jurisdictions. It reflects the journeys, explorations, research and insights of an incredible traveler who has accomplished what no other person has ever done before.

Obtaining the kind of information that allows you, with some legal certainty, to obtain, keep and bear arms outside the United States is notoriously difficult, as anyone who has tried it knows. Some governments make a concerted effort to hide the information from the public—all the better to keep the masses in the dark and under control. Language barriers, the expense, the distances, outright fear in indigenous populations and even official policies conspire to obscure the precious information. But that wasn't sufficient to deter author Larry Grupp from his self-selected task. His book is a virtual floodlight against the darkness.

Expedition outfitters have navigated the maze for their clients who hunt abroad, with cooperation from tourism-seeking, money-hungry governments who have little interest in arming their constituents. Going on an overseas safari with expensive, scoped, bolt-action big-game guns is hardly equivalent to traveling and bearing arms, or obtaining arms overseas, and it certainly does nothing for the natives.

Language barriers aside, local customs, "creative" bureaucracies, varying legal systems, routine corruption and favoritism within the legal systems, all conspire to keep the world's minions in the dark, when it comes to the freedom to keep and bear arms that too many Americans take too for granted. This accounts in large measure for why America is the freest nation on Earth, with people the world over struggling to get in here. We have so much gunpowder latitude we can barely see it. This book may change that understanding for you.

In developing the text, the author occasionally relies on phrases such as, "Nobody knows for sure," as a substitute for "Reliable information could not be found." It unpleasantly implies that the nation's own shopkeepers, gun owners and authorities, who were called upon for answers, are in the dark themselves.

Sometimes the country in question has designed it this way. Other times, the rules are flexible, unevenly applied, inconsistent, or different from one locale to another, leading to results that could differ literally from day to day and case to case. If you wish, like I do, that the world's gun laws could be more concrete, precise and knowable, well, maybe you can take that up with the UN in the interests of peace, freedom and equality for all humanity. Don't hold your breath.

What could we do to help ensure the accuracy of a book like this? It's not easy, but we took steps. I personally asked people overseas who could evaluate sections for their own lands, and repeatedly came up with approvals. I asked a Russian immigrant whom I know well and he approved of the Russian chapter, but did note that the information was weighted towards cities, and that in remote farm lands things were a good bit looser. We questioned the author repeatedly on points that seemed odd or at odds with each other, and he replied in detail, with logic, background and consistently. Will you spot a possibly needed change in the section on your homeland? Perhaps. If you do, be sure to let us know.

For the moment—and quite possibly forever—this is the best there is and the best there ever will be. The UN, standing steadfastly *against* arming the world's repressed masses, calmly watches obliteration of entire populations by governments, then sanctimoniously voices its concern. The bureaucrats and appointees there like this status quo. At least the UN issues sanction papers that make feel-good utopians feel good, and distract onlookers from massacres of unarmed societies.

Every nation studied has its own gun culture, a mass of gun buffs, at least some glimmer of understanding of the social utility of guns, a supply chain and places to shoot. In some places and in some respects, these exceed what we have in America.

The UN's approach is simple. Guns for government, in any quantity and configuration, no problem. Guns for the people? Just who do you peasants think you are? The much ballyhooed UN Universal Declaration of Human Rights starkly omits the right to self defense or to arms in any manner. This book, *The Worldwide Gun Owner's Guide,* should help counteract that. It is one small step in the direction of enlightening the world, educating the planet to the gun rights they do have intact, and gives us a road map to spread that knowledge.

Anti-rights types may be tempted to use this book to point out the massive restrictions so many governments enforce against their people, but that is balanced by the other side of the coin. While this book may be a list of restrictions, it is also a list of opportunities—to improve our own standing and to help remove the shackles from innocent people.

By carefully cataloging which populations are suffering under which restrictions across the globe, *The WorldWide Gun Owner's Guide* represents an index to where greater freedom is needed, where governments are particularly repressive, and which bans on peoples' rights are most odiously applied by regimes around the globe.

The United States is not the only place with a gun culture and gun laws—a key and stark conclusion borne out by the research. Every nation studied has its own gun culture, a mass of gun buffs, at least some glimmer of understanding of the social utility of guns, a supply chain and places to shoot. In some places and in some respects, these exceed what we have in America.

To the best of our knowledge, country-by-country gun-owner guides like we enjoy here do not exist in any other nation. Britain had one for a while, but it is so far out of date we can't pry one loose from any Brit who has even heard of it. If you should ever come across such a book, for the U.K. or anywhere else, let us know and we will make it widely available, with delight and without delay. Foreign gun stores, because they are frequently the main source of information for gun buffs, may have booklets available in their native language. We would love to see these. The stores, with easily revocable licenses to operate, are hard pressed to give good advice.

As far as I've been able to tell, until the first edition of *The Arizona Gun Owner's Guide* appeared in 1989, no gun owner even in America had such a book, and so could not precisely operate under "the rules." And it didn't much matter. No one ever really knew what the rules were! Police were tolerant, people were armed, this is America, have a nice day. As long as you didn't overtly commit crimes, gun ownership was as right as rain. Watch a western or an old black-and-white detective flick. That mindset existed, as near as I can tell, until the early 1960s, when political assassinations upset the apple cart.

Before the new era of fear, you got your first gun handed down from family, or by paying cash in a hardware store, or gas station, or gun store, or even by mail order (until the 1968 federal gun-controllers act), without paperwork. You bought it like any other private-property commodity, took it home, loaded it, and tried it out outdoors somewhere reasonably remote, or not. Neighbors didn't complain about the sporadic sound of gunfire. It was the sound of freedom.

The rules were something you got word-of-mouth, often from family, accuracy unknown. You acted out of common sense, and the common wisdom. A comparison of that information and the legalese in a law book somewhere was not made and was not known. Mr. Grupp has discovered that that's how most of the world works today.

It took a year of intense effort and research to get the first edition of the Arizona guide assembled and into print. The dark forest of rumors and the BS that substituted for knowledge was thick, obstinate and resisted chain saws of determination. More than a few locals proudly proclaimed they didn't need no stinking rules, because if you came into *their* house you were dead meat. The author of this worldwide guide book spent the better part of the last decade accomplishing the same thing that Arizona book did—but for planet Earth.

When I first got to Arizona in 1986, people bought guns and ammo in supermarkets. The Smitty's chain made more money per square foot on their gun counter in the back of dozens of stores than from any other square footage in the place, by far. To a young transplant from gun-repressed New York City this was pretty amazing. Run down to the store for some chop meat, a quart of milk, and a gun and ammo. Few foreign lands enjoy such liberty, with police gun-listing schemes instead occupying and employing countless bureaucrats, while delaying and tracking the innocent.

I distinctly remember going trepidatiously up to that counter and asking the counterman, "What do you need to get a gun?" He looked straight at me and asked, "How much money do you have?" Now *that* was counterintuitive. The Khyber Pass employs a similar technique.

"Well," I pressed on, "what are the rules?" Perplexed, he squinted at me and asked, "What do you mean, *rules*?" There was no Brady law back then, just freedom. No CCW permits. There weren't even many rules for kids. People just bought guns like they bought red meat, salt refined sugar or rat poison—everything's potentially dangerous, right? You get your goods, do with them as you will, you pays your money and you takes your chances. Government didn't regulate your safety. Our Constitution doesn't allow for such micromanagement by bureaucrats 2400 miles away—what's the question? Ah, those were glorious now bygone days.

That, it turns out, is what Larry Grupp has discovered about the rest of the world. You find out what the gun rules are by asking the people involved. They don't have the benefit of a plain-language description of the gun laws, like Arizona got in March of 1989 when the first book I ever wrote came out (I'm now up to my 13th book). They muddle through, operating on belief and good faith.

Criminals get guns despite any rules, and use them for evil. The rest of society gets guns under some vague notion of what's permissible, and use them accordingly. That essence is what *The Worldwide Gun Owner's Guide* captures. With details. And color. *And prices*, give or take an exchange rate or two and the passage of time.

It can't be another way. Each nation's laws are written in the native language. No one speaks that many tongues. No one has the money or interest in hiring lawyers in 60-plus states and having them unravel the mysteries of their gun laws in plain Urdu. Those peoples are destined to struggle under an impression of what the rules are, not what the rules are.

It has occurred to me over the years that *The Arizona Gun Owner's Guide* has had a bigger impact on American gun rights than is visible right there on the surface. The idea that you could actually know the laws, this was a novel concept. That book empowered the state's residents so they knew they were operating within the law. No guesswork, no unseen exposures, no legal traps for the unwary, no well-intentioned green baloney from the local cop (an info course that experience has repeatedly proven to be among the worst available). That wasn't the plan. But it seems it may have been a result.

People went from wondering and hoping they might be OK (which is where the rest of the world is apparently at, as you read through this book), to *knowing* they're right. As my co-author on *The Virginia Gun Owner's Guide*, Steve Maniscalco, liked to say, the government prefers that you're in the dark, or at least in some quasi-legal scuttlebutt limbo, because, "If you knew all your rights you might demand them."

That power shift empowered Arizonans. We started demanding our rights, because *at long last we knew what our rights were*. The nation, little by little, followed suit. We now have 29 states with gun-owner guides, to the best of our knowledge. Gun rights in this country have advanced dramatically in the ensuing decades, and we are poised to continue those gains. If your state doesn't have a gun-owner's guide, get cracking, find a suitable author, and spell out your state's gun rules in plain English. Bloomfield Press will help you, call us.

Once the Arizona guide appeared, cops couldn't just be woofin' and push you around, because you could flatly state, "Officer, thirteen thirty one oh two clearly allows loaded guns in a vehicle glovebox." Boy did it feel good to be able to say that! And watch the cop meekly withdraw, tail between his legs! That in some small way became a framework for the leadership position the Grand Canyon State has to some extent exerted on the nation. Gun-owner's guides that followed, my own and many many others, helped spread that power to the people, right on.

It is my sincere belief that *The Worldwide Gun Owner's Guide* can help empower the people of Earth to assume their rightful position as the power to be reckoned with in the human condition—and that governments only rule legitimately if they rule with the consent of the governed. That consent must be informed consent, which Larry's work and this book now helps provide.

We traditional Americans are pretty proud and completely convinced that we have the greatest gun laws, and the most robust right to keep and bear arms in the world. But do we?

The shooting sports are the number two participant sport in the country, behind exercise and ahead of golf.

Virtually any sane non-criminal adult here can go buy guns and ammunition to their heart's content. Indoor and outdoor shooting ranges are plentiful in most parts of the country, and shooting and hunting outdoors is a major American pastime. The shooting sports are the number two participant sport in the country, behind exercise and ahead of golf, according to the study undertaken by the National Sporting Goods Association, the industry trade group. They make and market the products. They need to know what sells, making their research particularly reliable.

The news media's often-denied bias on the subject of guns is self evident from the amount of coverage they give to golf, compared to the more popular shooting sports—a phrase you may never have even seen in the "news."

Americans buy between five and nine billion rounds of ammunition each year—and in 2009 the figures nearly doubled due to widespread concerns about Mr. Obama's well-known anti-rights positions on firearms. Those fears, visibly expressed through astronomical consumer arms sales, may have done a lot to convince the administration to stay away from the third rail of gun rights.

To listen to anti-rights activists though, we must have the worst gun laws in the world. That would include the obvious voices, like Sarah Brady and her now small and shrinking band of followers, who make their living seeking donations and funding to curtail the gun rights Americans do and have always enjoyed. The tiny Violence Policy Center with its minimal staff and extreme voice amplified loudly by a compliant, generally anti-gun-rights "news" media, works tiresomely hand-in-hand with the Bradys to vilify guns, gun owners, gun-rights-supportive legislators and the laws on the books.

The anti-rights groups periodically rate the states, giving failing grades to the states with the most vibrant rights, a badge of honor among enthusiasts. Unfortunately for that effort to denigrate firearms, the states with the highest Brady grades, meaning the most restrictive approach to the civil rights of gun ownership, correspond closely to the states with the highest violent crime rates.

When the honest are limited in their ability to keep and bear, criminals gain an advantage, and it shows. Arizona, vigorously seeking more robust rights, is striving for a perfect Brady score of zero out of 100; it currently suffers along with a two (and some locals are seeking an unprecedented negative score by enacting proactive gun rights and training measures).

And of course, the United Nations, skulking around secretively below the radar, hamstrung by bickering and rules concerning international treaties and national sovereignty, is an organization dedicated to containing the United States and its values. Judged solely by the UN's actions, it seeks to disarm innocent people worldwide. It denies this publicly, but anyone who knows anything knows it's true.

There is no civilian possession of firearms that the UN supports, and their so-called bill of human rights very conspicuously omits anything related to self defense, defense against tyranny or private possession and ownership of arms. From the UN perspective, it's preferable to see all power amassed in the hands of the "leaders" and elites of the world. Despots, tyrants, monarchs, dictators, usurpers, oligarchs, autocrats, bureaucrats and electeds all sharing equal honors, tells you something about the ruling class in its East River Manhattan high rise.

Perhaps surprisingly, even the comparatively free U.S. gun-rights enthusiasts bemoan a sorry state of affairs regarding RKBA here (the Right to Keep and Bear Arms). Except for five states, just carrying a firearm discreetly in most cases requires applications, approvals, testing, fingerprints, taxes called *fees*, a plastic-coated government permission slip and an expiration date on your "rights." You can't own anything that fires a cartridge over .50 caliber (a mere half inch), and a full-auto, the most basic general-duty weapon for any military person, is restricted worse than prescription drugs, with only a tiny supply available at all for civilians.

On the other side of that balance sheet though, we have some gun laws that are the envy of the free world. Only in America can guns be *legally* obtained in some places with absolutely no government involvement—while many foreigners can only accomplish this in their *sub rosa* economies. Though some of the states are obviously more restrictive, in others, private sales, paperless sales, limitless sales, inheritances and hand-me-downs, gift giving, freedom-to-carry, freedom to train and other factors combine to set us apart. We may rank below number one on the absolute scale of firearms freedom and availability, but all things considered, America is the place to be.

We know how bad gun laws can be, here and abroad, from a freedom perspective. Governments—far and away the greatest purveyors of death and destruction known—are armed to the teeth with everything imaginable and the approval of the UN, while so many of those being ruled stand in enforced naked defenselessness.

So how robust could freedom-oriented gun laws be? Is there a society that enjoys greater freedoms than America does? What's on the horizon that perhaps this nation could look towards to advance the freedom its citizens enjoy with respect to the much honored Second Amendment right to keep and bear?

This book sheds light on these important questions. Author Larry Grupp has toured the world more extensively than anyone I know and probably anyone you know, as part of his career's work. He has worked in some 90 countries, for between three-and-a-half weeks and three-and-a-half years—not just casually passing through. He used that opportunity to investigate first-hand the gun rights and policies of 64 nations and groups—a feat never before attempted or accomplished. For all its bragging about world order, the UN has not even touched the subject, except for partially cataloging the militarization of the planet. That is antithetical to what we have here—the civilian balance of power to the vastly superior forces aligned against the people—their own governments.

It's estimated that in the last century alone, 180 million human beings were victims of *democide*, murder by government. With that awful reality staring us down the barrel, it's a wonder more people don't cry out to arm the public for balance.

By now it's well known that the greatest murderers of human beings are their own governments. It's estimated that in the last century alone, 180 million human beings were victims of *democide*, murder by government. With that awful reality staring us down the barrel, it's a wonder more people don't cry out to arm the public as a balance against that very real, very insidious, imminent and evil threat.

Government's sole legitimate purpose is to protect your life, liberty and pursuit of happiness, and by direct implication your private property, according to the U.S. Declaration of Independence. What a cruel joke to find that just the opposite is true the world over.

When troops in some back-water African pesthole decide to wipe out a community, the members of the community are found helpless, unarmed, and overlooked by the world. Sneak guns in to help them save themselves and you are an international gun-running criminal. You'll be sanctimoniously proclaimed an enemy of that state, and one of the worst criminals in the eyes of the peace-loving UN. You're guaranteed to be portrayed that way by the "news" media. Turn your back, cluck your tongue, and deny the victims arms, and you are toeing the line and doing the right thing. Except you're not.

With any luck at all, this book will do something to alert the world to the problem of armed governments and disarmed populaces.

Some final notes: Prices strewn throughout the book provide a comparative sense of costs for guns and ammo, but are by no means meant as a pricing guide. The decade it took to compile all the information, and wild fluctuations in exchange rates make a true cost comparison impossible.

• One phrase in particular is nettlesome, in terms of precision. An *assault weapon* has a technical meaning in the U.S. military as a select-fire rifle, meaning it can be switched from single shot, to burst or full-auto operation (a machine gun). This book doesn't use it that way.

Bill Clinton used the phrase as a term of art, in an onerous federal law to describe a lengthy list of fearsome-looking one-shot guns, often called *black guns*, along with accessories based on their springs, cosmetic styles, grips and other peripheral features. That supposedly anti-crime law, which experience proved worthless, has since expired. Clinton succeeded however in spreading confusion, and vilifying modern *sport-utility rifles,* which are often black, and the "news" media continues to use the term to paint all sorts of decent and reliable firearms as bad. Grupp uses the term a lot, to reflect a general sense in the parts of the world he visited, but do not attempt to read into this a level of precision, because it is not there.

• *Assault,* you should keep in mind, is a form of behavior, not a type of hardware. It shows you how insidious the constant drubbing from politicians and the media is, when day in and day out they feed you preposterous nonsense that cannot withstand the simple light of common sense. We then adopt the words in our thinking, without thinking. They know this, and use the tendency to our disadvantage.

• *Machine pistol,* a term borrowed from the British, we in the U.S. may more commonly call a submachine gun, because it fires pistol ammo instead of a rifle cartridge. A *dewat* is a deactivated war trophy.

• With all the world's impediments to gun ownership gathered here in one place, an unintended consequence of this volume may be to aid those who seek to deny this fundamental right to humanity—they have a compendium of ideas to draw upon.

On the other hand, however, the world can now see unequivocally that the right to arms is a global phenomenon, and the vicious anti-rights lie that only America has a gun culture and gun rights is put to death, where it belongs.

The anti-rights masses and leaders will no doubt mindlessly continue to work to disarm the (civilian) world. In that sense the right to keep and bear arms represents a struggle in the true sense of the word. It is not a battle you win, or even lose, it is a fight in which you must perpetually engage. Eternal vigilance, as we well know, is a price of freedom. It's a good price.

• You might also wonder why the book isn't arranged differently. At first glance it seems haphazard—it's not alphabetical, geographical or hierarchical in terms of relative freedom. If you read from front to back, however, you'll see the line of thinking and continuity the author has built in. This is a personal work as well as a reference book, and retains a delightful sense of his adventures through the nations he describes. You get a comparative sense and a world tour with his arrangement. The index allows easy access for a regimented review of countries, if you're built that way, devoid of the tasty flavor the otherwise seemingly random text preserves.

My wish for the free peoples of the world—
May you forever remain armed and free.
For the not-so-free peoples of the world—
May your lot in life only improve.
And to the unfree peoples of the world—
Mao said power comes from the barrel of a gun;
Reagan said power comes from the barrel of a pen;
May the tyrants, dictators, monarchs, oligarchs, fascists,
socialists, communists, marxists, apparatchiks, kleptocrats,
bureaucrats, autocrats, theocrats, czars and other power-mad
suppressors of the human condition who rule you by armed might,
get the appropriate barrels.

Alan Korwin, February, 2011

Chapter Zero

Gun Laws of Planet Earth

On Jan. 4, 2005 *The Wall Street Journal* in cooperation with the Heritage Foundation published a ranking of all countries in the world by the economic freedom they extend to their citizens. Other than some surprising individual results, little was new about the process itself—this being the 11th report on these issues.

Their index scored 155 countries by the amount of fiscal burden their government imposes, government regulation, monetary and trade policy, as well as property rights, inflation, police and access to courts and competitive banking.

Shocking to note, the U.S. was no longer in the top ten, but little, newly formed Estonia was, at 4. Compilers suggested that this anomaly was the result of the U.S. standing still on the "highway to economic liberty," while the world made great—often dramatic—advances. They also pointed out that personal incomes were more than twice as high in "free" countries as they were in "mostly free" ones, and more than four times higher than countries seen as "mostly un-free."

Even more shocking for American gun owners who may know little about competitive banking, foreign-trade policy and courts, England ranked seven ahead of the U.S. (number 12). Could those doing the ranking have missed something?

England is that country where more than 50% of a person's income is forcibly taken by the taxman, citizens cannot choose their own doctor, it takes months for authorities to sanction new businesses, it is virtually impossible to build a new home, and private ownership of handguns is completely forbidden. England's Olympic pistol team, for instance, has to travel to France to practice!

How can England be considered to be a freer country than the U.S., or even a free country at all, we validly ask.

It can be argued that a country that prevents its citizens from the God-given right to effectively protect their own persons and property cannot truly be considered free. A nation that does not vigorously enforce and protect private-property rights suffers a nearly fatal freedom flaw. Looking out over the modern world we clearly see there are few human rights where there are no property rights.

Our Founding Fathers recognized this truth when they gave us our Constitution, including the vital Second Amendment. It's not about duck hunting—it's about property rights, safety and power to the people, cornerstones of personal freedom and economic prosperity.

"But this is an ancient, archaic and outdated view of things," gun-control advocates claim. Unfortunately, a significant number of Americans, who have not given pensive thought to this issue, do indeed believe that our venerable, old, tried-and-true constitutional guarantees are out of date. These constitutional guarantees really should be interpreted and applied on the basis of "modern society," they would say. This is a philosophy that Supreme Court Justice Antonin Scalia says would lead to rules of society based on how judges feel when they get up that morning. Many modern American judges unfortunately seem to agree.

Too few people find this less-than-a-rule-of-law approach distasteful, distressful or even worse.

"It's a 'living Constitution' we should operate under," gun-control advocates say. "One tailored to the needs of modern America, that adjusts for our post-modern existence. Modern societies don't need citizens with guns," they loudly claim, adding that America stands alone in its attachment to gun rights. Are they right?

How ignorant the ignorant are

Tiny, brittle, cold little shards of snow drifted through cracks in the rough-sawn, flimsy, cheap-brown-lumber barracks buildings at Camp Birkenau in south-central Poland. A fitting day on which to recall the intense and horribly inhumane suffering to which inmates here were once subjected.

Birkenau is a major part of the infamous Auschwitz death-camp complex where well over a million mostly Jews were cruelly murdered, either immediately upon arrival in cavernous gas chambers, or slowly under exhausting slave-labor conditions.

We escaped for a moment from this monument to man's inhumanity and the penetrating cold into the heated reception area of this now Polish state museum. Over stark, bare, dramatically realistic rough wooden tables in the lunchroom we were met by a guide supplied by the memorial. The fellow's English was graduate university level.

Continuing my pursuit of a now six-year quest taking us to well over fifty different countries, we asked if he could explain laws related to private ownership of firearms in Poland.

"I am shocked and dismayed that you would ask such a question," he quickly responded. "This [private gun ownership] is simply not done in Poland."

More shocking and dismaying still was to hear this from a man dedicated to explaining atrocities perpetrated by a conquering power, at a major memorial decrying the acts. Facial contortions and body language confirmed that this was, indeed, a terribly difficult subject for this young man.

Later we discovered that under a strict gun-owner and individual-registration system, pistols, hunting rifles and shotguns *are* legally available to private citizens in Poland. But this fellow could think neither of anyone who owned a gun nor a valid reason for private ownership—despite the horrors against unarmed victims he routinely described.

I suggested some basics. "Well, for example, sporting use provides needed resource management in the wilds, and recreational use is popular and develops character, firearms provide deterrence to crime, and the use of private firearms can discourage and stall national aggression." Just some reasonable, common-sense measures any intelligent person should be able to grasp.

His response was right out of the George Soros anti-gun-rights playbook. Quickly discounting the arguments, our guide said he believed guns cause crime and, most importantly, what would poor Poland with only 39 million people do with private firearms if they were invaded. Hmmm, only 39 million with guns.

"Same thing the Finns did to the Russians during their brief Winter War in 1939 and 1940, or what the Greeks did to the mighty German Fallschrimjägern when they dropped on Crete during WW II, the American colonists did to the British during our revolution, the American Nez Perce Indians did to the U.S. cavalry in our early West, kibbutzniks at Yad Mordechai did to the Egyptians in 1947 and the Boers did to the British during the Boer War as well as the example of little insignificant Switzerland during WW II," I quickly responded.

I was on a roll. "You, of all people," I quietly pointed out, "a guide at notorious Auschwitz death camp should understand the lessons of the Warsaw Jewish ghetto, the little known outside Poland Warsaw Polish ghetto, as well as guerilla actions against the Germans and often each other on the part of Jewish, Polish and Russian resistance fighters in the Polish Nalibock wilderness."

"You make some excellent points," our guide finally conceded, "but you Americans and your guns! No one else in the world so easily owns guns and no place in the First World is the crime rate so high," he said. A shockingly inaccurate contention, precisely mirroring similar statements by members of American gun-control groups such as the Brady Campaign to Promote Gun Violence.

The degree to which the world is uninformed about our gun laws is perhaps saliently summed up by a Brit who asked me, quite seriously, "How long has it been since you saw a shootout on the streets?" There have indeed been several shootouts in Idaho, very reminiscent of old western gun fights, but I did not see them. These mostly occurred in our early days in Idaho, 40 years ago. They were among consenting adults, so we paid them little attention. The only street shooting I have ever personally observed was in Malaysia, apparently a thief being pursued by a property owner. Most Americans, as readers of this book can attest, have never witnessed an actual street shooting. Ever. Not even by the police. But why let reality interfere with a self-selected worldview.

So just what is the international picture?

Unfortunately, too many American gun owners wishing to join debate on the issue of worldwide gun rights sit stupidly in suffering silence.

**Our research clearly demonstrates that private citizens
are reasonably and easily able to privately own firearms
in virtually all First World countries.**

Although framed somewhat along cultural lines, our research clearly demonstrates that private citizens are reasonably and easily able to privately own firearms in virtually all First World countries including Sweden, Finland, Switzerland, New Zealand, Luxembourg, Argentina, Crete and San Marino as well as a great number of what *anti's* (the anti-gun-rights crowd) refer to as Third World countries. Authors such as John Lott have convincingly shown that *more* guns equals *less* crime—debunking the knee-jerk destructive myth this man parroted that guns cause crime.

Problem is that no information on foreign gun laws has been readily available. Not at the UN, not at our State Dept. and only in fractured bits and pieces even at the National Rifle Association. This is supposedly because laws relative to private gun ownership are changing too rapidly and because securing accurate information is devilishly difficult and expensive. That ends with this publication.

Yes, difficult it is. Only the New Zealand police and an overly arrogant gun-control officer in Luxembourg responded to my written requests for information concerning their specific gun laws. Authorities in Norway and Israel responded by saying "it is illegal for you to have this information." I'm not making this up! Out of ten inquiries sent to our embassies abroad by my own U.S. senator, only one responded.

World wide, gun owners and dealers fuss about changes in their laws. There are some exceptions, but generally changes are modest and generally slow, following established cultural lines. In Ecuador, for instance, despotic government officials have worried about revolutions so long that intensely valuable old antique wheel-lock rifles and pistols in museums have been destroyed by removal and loss of their intricate firing mechanisms.

The study of international gun laws also provides an excellent insight into the tremendous emerging movement of illegal guns. Hint—it isn't commercial guns being smuggled and it isn't by law-abiding citizens!

In Portugal, as an example, a country allowing legal private ownership of pistols, shotguns and a few rifles via cumbersome, time consuming, expensive systems of registering both gun owners and their guns, Russian RPG-7s (rocket-propelled grenades) are said to be available on the street to virtually anyone with perhaps $2,500 cash. In many areas drug cartels looking for yet another profit center are said to be facilitators of extensive movement of military munitions.

**Foreign laws range from the ridiculous
to some that American gun owners could easily live with.**

Foreign laws range from ridiculous to some that American gun owners could easily live with. It's tempting, at times, to suggest that the most restrictive of these relate to kleptocratic tendencies of those in government authority, but this isn't always true.

**Are there other post-modern, gun-friendly countries
out there somewhere on this Earth?**

Other than this overly broad approach, the basic question remains debateable. That being—are there other post-modern, gun-friendly countries out there somewhere on this Earth? Ones to which we may turn for examples or to which American gun owners might move as our rights to personal private property and its defense are slowly eroded in the U.S.?

On the other hand, a significant group of American gun owners sincerely believes that their laws relative to private firearms ownership are the best in the world. "There are no other countries to look to. This is as good as it gets," they claim.

Obviously neither group has put enough thought and research into the question of private gun ownership around the world. The hard data has simply been lacking. Just knowing if there really are kindred gun buffs in Argentina, Germany, Israel, Thailand or New Zealand might be informative and interesting, do you think?

The Swiss, Liechtensteiners, residents of San Marino, and New Zealanders implicitly trust their government. As a result they tolerate a modest amount of permitting and licensure, but basically own whatever guns they wish. It is tough for me to really understand a culture where the government is trusted and respected.

Citizens in Crete and Argentina don't really trust any government. As a result, they just go ahead and own most any gun they want without worrying about legalities. Same also true of Mexico. Finland is somewhere in between.

What about illegal guns in private hands? How do they move in international commerce? What do they contribute to crimes against persons and property—or not? How easy is it to find them in various countries around the world? The gathered information addresses this to some degree.

We cannot expect rules and regulations in other places to replicate those in the U.S. Even the languages force differences. Is it true national gun laws are very cultural, and if so, to what extent are they? An answer is sprinkled throughout the text.

This volume looks at many different countries, their gun laws, living conditions and treatment of legal and illegal ownership. Some of these countries have extremely tortured and convoluted gun laws. Some nations have gun laws that rival or perhaps even exceed our own.

Some nations have gun laws that rival or perhaps even exceed our own.

But, briefly summarizing at this early point, American gun owners can take great comfort in the fact that theirs is definitely not the only gun culture in the world as so many control advocates erroneously claim.

It is often terribly interesting to look behind various national gun laws, and enforcement of them, to discover exactly why guns are allowed, restricted or even tolerated and preferred.

For instance, places recently overrun by invading armies, such as Crete and Finland, often tolerate widespread private gun ownership, up to and including crew-served weapons. But read on. I'll tell you how we did it and then how the issue of private gun ownership is officially viewed throughout the world. It was, as I believe readers will agree, a very fascinating journey.

A few final thoughts with nowhere else to place them:

First, does any nation impose a death penalty for mere possession of firearms? Japan, communist China and Vietnam are extremely restrictive of gun rights, but even if a firearm is used in commission of a crime, the result is not immediate execution in these countries, or an eventual death penalty. The city-state of Singapore has applied a death penalty for illegal possession of a firearm.

Certainly in war zones those with guns would logically become targets, but I don't know of any other specific examples. In my extensive experience, no country imposes a death penalty for mere possession of a firearm. In at least one infamous example in a major U.S. city, however, a man was summarily executed for brandishing a wallet. The last I know of where gun ownership in a nation led to instant or an eventual death penalty was Jews and state enemies in Nazi Germany.

Are nations with strict civilian bans disarmed? Mexico has extremely restrictive gun ownership rules. However, all Mexicans view their laws as suggestions. Many Mexicans privately and illegally own personal firearms. The same was and still is true of Washington D.C., and in Chicago, New York and many other places where officials feel good about bans, and citizens routinely ignore them—including criminals who are well armed and shoot each other with relative impunity.

Let me mention that I hunted pheasants in South Korea on Cheju Island using Remington model 870 pump shotguns that the guides actually owned under a very restrictive permit system. But, because I could only gain very fragmentary information on South Korean gun rights, I did not include South Korea in the book. In one notable instance at the Taegu, South Korea army base, an empty magazine for an M-16 went missing. The base commander immediately shut the base down tight till the errant mag was located. Also I know American GIs can privately own guns in South Korea, but the guns must be locked away in base storage. All the owners have is "visitation rights."

About the rankings

This was a late-to-arrive idea, as it could only occur when the research and book took final form. But as such ideas often prove, good things tend to happen at the end. The chart evaluates the freedom and ease with which private citizens can own guns and ammunition in the countries at which we have looked.

These rankings say nothing about property and human rights of these various countries and cultures, nor the available amenities, degree of civilization and culture or any sense of the desirability of living in these areas. Only the firearms-freedom parameters are weighed.

Intelligent folks, politicians, courts and law-enforcement officials know
that laws are suggestions. In some parts of the world, suggestions are
flatly ignored and no one cares much. This plays into the rankings.

For instance, in the Khyber Pass semi-autonomous area of Pakistan,
which ranked first in the world for gun freedom, life would be grim
indeed. Life there is within a culture that treats all non-Muslims as
enemies, even though ownership of virtually any firearm is possible
(with places to enjoy firing the rocket-propelled grenades you can buy
at stores in town). Lack of consensus on the ranks seems inevitable.

Life in Crete, on the other hand, would be pleasant indeed, but private
gun ownership there is illegal. This illegality, however, is only "lightly"
enforced, giving it the number 3 position on the world chart. Mexico,
by comparison, not only outlaws ownership, enforcement is arbitrary
and capricious, especially for foreigners. I would not want to own guns
in Mexico under any foreseeable circumstances, and the nation earns
a 55 near the bottom of the pile. Crete would be a definite option.

Consider also, because so many guns, ammunition and explosives
were taken from military warehouses at the collapse of the communist
government, illegal gun ownership is virtually universal in Albania, in
spite of what UN data or its suggested laws may indicate.

Albanian guns and ammo up through 20mm guns and mortars have
been exported virtually around the world. A great many illegal heavy
military guns, including 20mm cannons and big, heavy machine guns
have ended up in Crete of all places. Anyone in Albania who wants a
gun of any kind can easily have it, hence their ranking at a spot higher
than others might tend to score them.

In other words, my ranking is based on ease of availability, not just
legality or illegality. This shows in all the rankings, to wit, Crete.

In retrospect, I may have been a bit too hard on England and Australia
regarding their gun laws. Gun owners there have done a masterful job
of creating something usable out of what at first was intended by the
politicians as chaos—i.e., they wanted to make it so difficult to own
guns that folks would just give up. In inimitable British style, however,
the gun owners just "carried on." Nevertheless, my original analysis
(that the laws in those places, and the innumerable bureaucratic hoops
owners must jump through) is still correct. The two nations came in
side-by-side at 21 and 22.

In the case of the RPG-7 in Portugal, I was actually offered a live one
of these for $2,500 cash. I had the cash, but no safe, reasonable place
to shoot it. And, since I couldn't bring it home, I declined the offer.

Our ranking starts with complete freedom for adults to privately obtain, have and use arms of any type an infantry person would possess, with little or no government involvement of any kind, going on down to places where gun ownership is completely forbidden (with gaping loopholes and black markets for the rich, well-connected and fearless, as I have repeatedly seen and documented).

These rankings are, of course, subjective and easily subject to debate. Bring it on. I have no doubt they will lead to great, often heated, discussions which are needed on the world stage. They are based on my analysis of how easy it is to secure and enjoy arms, how many guns can be owned and whether ownership includes pistols, rifles, shotguns, light artillery, machine guns and submachine guns, as well as the ease with which ammo can be purchased. Read the book, see if you agree, and don't keep your opinions to yourself.

Larry Grupp, February 2011

::::

How I Did It

Authorities in at least two countries, Israel and Norway, huffed that it was illegal for me, a foreigner, to have the information I sought—their enacted laws!

All I was asking for was national code sections and interpretations dealing with laws relative to private ownership of firearms among their citizens. Evidently, guns in the hands of common citizens is a hot topic around the world. But is this information sufficiently sensitive that people cannot know it? Something of a state secret?

As years and years of research, letter writing, international calling and travel dragged on, I began to wonder. Seemed to me that, in order to obey laws, people are going to have to know what these laws are. Third-world nations such as Dominican Republic or the Philippines may not want their folks to know rules that are often bent, depending on who you know or who you are. But countries like Norway and Israel? Aren't they first-world places, supposedly run by rule of law?

Their official response was certainly curious!

**In an attempt to get a handle on gun laws
in as many promising countries as possible,
I condensed my questions down to a series of ten.**

Brevity and efficiency seemed important. In an attempt to get a handle on gun laws in as many promising countries as possible, I condensed my questions down to a series of ten. Answering these ten usually took knowledgeable gun-owning citizens about fifteen minutes, unless I interviewed them personally rather than relying on written responses. Phone or face-to-face interviews took much longer. Mutual gun owners have much to talk about. In virtually every instance, written or personal, I only used information that two or more resident gun owners/gun-store clerks agreed upon. Whenever available, I used "official" information.

When presenting my summary questions, I tried to be representative. Some readers may have other questions they feel would be more important. But answers to these few gave me a good idea of what ordinary citizens who wanted to own guns were up against.

In writing, on the phone, or in person, these are the exact questions and format I used, on properly formatted letterhead.

Dear [Name]:

I am the author of 41 books and a great many magazine articles mostly related to hunting, fishing, gun collecting and military history.

Currently I am working on a compendium to be used as a standard reference regarding laws pertaining to private ownership of firearms in various countries around the world. Could you please be of assistance regarding firearms laws in _____?

I have reduced my questions to the following. Please answer in as much detail as you believe is appropriate for a reference manual of this sort.

Is there regular private ownership of firearms in _____? Is ownership mostly legal or illegal? If illegal, as a practical matter, how vigorously are the laws enforced?

If private ownership is allowed, does this include pistols, rifles, shotguns and perhaps machine guns and/or machine pistols?

Is there any limit on total numbers of firearms a person may own?

If permits are required, how difficult and costly are these to obtain? Must one hire an attorney to secure needed permits? How, exactly, does one initiate the process of securing gun-ownership permits?

Is there any restriction on make, model, caliber or design of permitted firearms?

Is purchase of ammunition for privately held firearms controlled? Are there firearm and ammunition stores where one can purchase firearms and ammunition? Names and addresses you supply would be very helpful.

Is hand reloading of ammunition permitted?

Can non-citizens of _____ residing in the country privately own firearms? Can they practice shooting on local ranges?

Is importation of firearms by immigrants permitted?

How difficult is it to get a permit to deal in firearms, and to do experimental work on new gun designs?

Having answers to all of these questions provided a fairly good working knowledge of private firearms ownership in a given specific country. It also provided a measure of the general level of freedom, levels of arbitrariness on the part of authorities and, to some extent, fears with which they viewed neighbors.

Finland's relatively free, open gun laws are a good example in this case. Russia's naked aggression against little Finland in 1939 is still fresh in citizens' minds. Perhaps this explains why many citizens can and do own real assault rifles. Some private Finns even own heavy weapons such as mortars and recoilless rifles!

It may be hard to tell from the write-ups for each nation just how long we spent gathering information. We found a great deal of camaraderie within the gun community that, at times, made our interviews run much longer than they perhaps should have gone. Discussing issues of common interest among aficionados in this field can run hot and long—as readers of this book are no doubt well aware.

Unauthorized guns in private hands

There is an important provision in the questionnaire to explain and clarify possible illegal firearms ownership in various countries. Places over which wars and revolutions swept could be places where "left behind" weapons were common, open and perhaps even notorious. No perfect example springs to mind, but I wanted to be sure. Germany is as good as it gets as an example. At this moment, for instance, a reported avalanche of illegal Soviet bloc weapons are supposedly available in Germany. More numerous than legal weapons, many gun buffs claim.

Warring armies have rolled over many places in the world in the last 100 years. Logically we can assume some especially alert, motivated citizens picked up abandoned and cast off military goods, holding them secretly till an hour of need. Tales abound regarding the speed with which small arms and ammunition disappear from battlefields.

Perhaps apocryphal, but a story is told of Ukrainians who faithfully sprinkled gun oil on their flower beds or Vietnamese who still farm amid rubber inner-tube-clad bundles secreted deep in watery, muddy rice paddies. Exposing these situations seemed reasonable if we were to know about real on-the-ground gun ownership in these various countries.

Only officials in New Zealand and—way down the road into the project—Luxembourg responded to questions. Others ignored my letters and calls or continually maintained that they never received anything from me. I turned to their embassies in Washington, D.C., and then to our own in-country embassies. Still, little to no luck. Some State Dept. types who were obviously past gun enthusiasts made a stab at it, but their information was sketchy, abbreviated, and lacked knowledgeable authority. Questions regarding the intelligence, political bias and motivation of our State Dept. people that surfaced as a result of this research are beyond the scope of this book.

My U.S. senator at the time (and NRA board member) Larry Craig cooperated in this quest and sent the set of questions to various embassies on my behalf.

A little more information came in, but the real gold came from individual exchange students, in-country citizen gun buffs whom I was able to contact by mail or phone, and immigrants to the U.S. I was able to locate. In so much as time and funds permitted, I personally visited as many of these countries as possible, and this is woven into the text. Conversations with gun-shop owners, private gun owners, hunters, hunting-club managers and anyone else capable and willing to comment proved to be the real treasure trove for this volume.

As a result, the book's information may not be as complete, up-to-date or as accurate as we may otherwise wish. There is, however, a cultural thread that runs through all national gun laws. When laws are changed it is usually along pre-established predictable precedents.

Nevertheless, data we now have provides us with a good starting place. One that also gives us an idea of the type and degree of suspicion governments view their citizens or subjects.

The selection of places

Personal arbitrariness as well as finances and ease of travel characterized my selection of targeted countries. Since the turn of the last century, for instance, the government of the United Kingdom has maintained a paranoid fear and loathing of guns in general. So much so they had little to nothing with which to defend the homeland after Dunkirk. A few rifles and double-barreled shotguns are all that are permitted, and these only if one can sustain a costly, convoluted, arbitrary permitting process. No firearms inventors, designers or tinkerers currently work in the U.K.

Australia is another example. Following the English lead, they have virtually outlawed private firearms ownership. Given difficulties in securing information, there seemed to be little sense trying to assemble detailed reports on a place that takes citizens' freedoms so lightly. England and several others were eventually covered in this volume— mostly to provide really bad examples. The English Olympic Pistol Team has to train in France, for instance, yet sounds of gunfire are common each night in larger cities as rival gangs duke it out with commonly-held illegal weapons.

Other places such as the Khyber Pass area of northern Pakistan allow free, relatively unencumbered, private ownership of most firearms, in a system authorities would call lawlessness. Same is true of much of Afghanistan. Question is—would any of us actually choose to voluntarily live in these dusty, dreary, amenity-challenged places? Many of us simply could not because of dramatic religious and cultural differences along with an abysmal lack of plumbing. Again, I acted arbitrarily, deciding to research these places because they are currently in the news and because friends were available to personally gather information.

In all cases a bit of socio-economic data are included that should assist readers in their own evaluation of each country.

Some countries, I was told, have lovely, remote, and fairly civilized isolated locales that might be attractive to American gun owners where they could live unobserved and unbothered by weak central governments. Problem is, I am not fully convinced this is really true, having never seen most of these nice places personally. Let's just say the jury is still out in these cases. And of course most Americans, despite grumblings over major or minor gun-law injustices, like it where they are, and moving for a marginal improvement in gun laws would not offset the other hardships and obstacles to relocating.

This is the process. It isn't particularly quick or efficient and it may have a few holes. But with that we jump into information on specific countries. Without this, as we have lived up to this point, people could claim whatever they wanted without fear of the truth being known. That now ends.

On the face of the Earth, the United States still claims the brass ring for gun rights and a positive, productive gun culture, with some of her 50 states leading the way and others a heavy ballast. Internationally, the Gold Standard for private gun ownership I believe should go to little old free, immeasurably profitable, fiercely independent Switzerland, so we start amidst the Alps in central Europe.

FIREARMS FREEDOM CHART

World Rank	Book Chapter	Location	Page	Firearm Freedom
1	28	Khyber Pass	177	98%
2	54	Albania	308	96%
3	36	Crete	217	95%
4	51	Luxembourg	298	90%
5	1	Switzerland	37	89%
6	57	San Marino	323	88%
7	10	Finland	87	87%
8	15	New Zealand	113	85%
9	—	USA	—	83%
10	50	Liechtenstein	293	80%
11	37	Argentina	226	79%
12	5	Belgium	61	77%
13	30	UAE	186	76%
14	31	Oman	190	75%
15	56	The Netherlands	317	75%
16	60	Falkland Islands	336	70%
17	63	Malta	350	69%
18	29	Iran	182	68%
19	47	Czech Republic	280	65%
20	48	Slovakia	285	65%
21	62	Australia	345	60%
22	24	England	157	59%
23	64	Russia	354	59%
24	49	Austria	288	55%
25	9	Sweden	82	51%
26	4	France	56	48%
27	3	Germany	50	48%
28	44	Estonia	263	47%
29	43	Latvia	259	45%
30	42	Lithuania	256	44%
31	59	Chile	332	43%
32	13	Canada	100	42%
33	18	Thailand	126	40%
34	14	South Africa	106	39%
35	52	Afghanistan	301	39%
36	58	Italy	327	38%
37	53	Iceland	304	37%
38	35	Egypt	209	36%
39	33	Panama	199	35%
40	8	Denmark	77	34%
41	11	Norway	91	33%
42	19	Israel	133	32%
43	7	Portugal	71	31%
44	6	Spain	67	30%
45	46	Turkey	275	29%
46	41	Poland	249	28%

47	45	Brazil	270	28%
48	38	El Salvador	232	25%
49	55	Cyprus	313	24%
50	32	Papua New Guinea	195	23%
51	21	Guatemala	141	22%
52	2	Dominican Republic	46	21%
53	22	Kenya	148	19%
54	39	Ivory Coast	236	18%
55	25	Mexico	164	15%
56	27	Honduras	174	14%
57	26	Tanzania	170	13%
58	23	Ireland	154	12%
59	40	Ecuador	241	11%
60	16	Colombia	120	8%
61	12	Japan	95	4%
62	61	China	340	2%
63	17	Vietnam	123	0%
—	20	Ships at Sea	137	—
—	34	American GIs	206	—

This chart covers 61 formal nations, the semi-autonomous Khyber Pass region of Pakistan, two unranked but important groups (ships at sea and American GIs) and a rank for the United States, 65 items in all. A very concerted effort was made to assign ranks consistently, and we do recognize the somewhat subjective nature of the task. Disagreements are possible and the ranks are likely to change over time, which will generate updated rankings in the future. Reader input is welcomed.

These are the parameters used for assigning ranks:

• To what extent is private ownership of firearms possible.

• To what extent can private citizens own sidearms, rifles, shotguns, machine guns, submachine guns and military ordnance.

• To what extent is this ownership controlled by government.

• Are there limits on the numbers and size of arms that can be owned, types of actions, magazine capacities and barrel lengths.

• Are there limits on purchase and possession of ammunition.

• Is handloading of ammunition possible, and does cost and availability of ammo impact the ability to practice and learn.

Since a significant degree of routine firearms ownership and use in many nations occurs without official government sanction, absolute availability is a determinant and the ratio between legal and sub rosa ownership is not a ranking factor. Also note that the desirability of living in any of these areas is not a factor in the rankings.

Battle at Kibbutz Yad Mordechai in Israel

On May 15, 1948, when British forces withdrew from Latrun on the road to Jerusalem, local Arab forces immediately occupied the hills dominating this crucial road, cutting off the city and starving its people. This could have denied the Israelis any part of Jerusalem—their holy city. Israel had no organized army ready, no alternate road and no way to remove Jordanian forces holding the only road. If the Egyptian army had been free to take Tel Aviv, the Israeli army might not have formed, and Israel might not have been born.

Four days later, using scrounged, surreptitiously purchased, home manufactured and illegally imported private weapons, about 100 members of Kibbutz Yad Mordechai held up thousands of invading Egyptians—including tanks, infantry, artillery and aircraft—for six precious days. This allowed an army to form, provided access for relief of Jerusalem, and literally enabled Israel to come to be. The outdoor memorial shown here, depicting the battle at the site of the kibbutz, commemorates their historically significant heroic action—a citizen militia stopping the advance of an invading army, while a nation's fate hung in the balance. Walking this terrain, as the author and his wife have done, sent chills down their spines. Unfortunately, today's Israeli establishment and many other world leaders have forgotten such vital lessons of history. Gun laws that are unnecessarily stringent, like those now found in Israel, prevent such heroism, needed to impede tyranny and preserve freedom.

Chapter One
Switzerland
World Rank: 5 • Firearm Freedom 89%

Sheets of slushy, rain-like, wind-driven snow crossed the valley below with a wave-like rhythm. Standing there on a solitary open ridge, two extremely intent men evaluated for military advantage.

Had it been mid-summer rather than late winter, it would have been a beautiful view out across a verdant Swiss mountain valley. As it was, they stood icily—almost, but not quite, confronting each other.

On the one hand, a medium-built, ruddy-to-almost-brown man of average height and build, wearing a thick dark blue woolen shirt and pants characteristic of the pre-WWI Swiss army. Unusually fit and trim, he looked as though storming up yet another slick, icy mountain slope would have been no problem, even at his advanced age.

Who this was, exactly, is permanently lost in history. All we certainly know is that he was one of extremely few full-time professional senior military officers, perhaps one of only six or eight. Switzerland has never had full-time military, except in the most limited sense.

However, the identity of the other soldier officer is known without any doubt. Already Prince Wilhelm Hohenzollern was well known, respected and feared for his war-like tendencies. History would prove that, like the greatest of his predecessors, Frederic the Great, Prince Wilhelm would have great disdain for lives of individual soldiers. Some 15 years later, Hohenzollern went on to become Germany's Kaiser, a position he held till he was deposed, ending WWI. Both the prince and the Swiss officer fully realized Hohenzollern headed the most powerful, numerous, best-equipped standing army in the world.

The German played to the maximum what he genuinely believed to be his station in life. "How many men have you under arms?" he contemptuously sneered at the smaller, trim Swiss soldier. Bracing ever so slightly, the Swiss soldier politely responded that his country had one million men under arms.

"So your country can field an army of one million," Germany's future Kaiser and arguably the most powerful soldier in the world shot back. "What would your little country do if five million of my best men suddenly swarmed across your frontier?"

Always the consummate gentlemen, the Swiss commander softly replied, "Well, sir, each of my men would fire five times and go home."

Let the record note that the world believed him. Neither the Kaiser, nor Hitler, nor Mussolini—no one—has invaded tiny Switzerland since 1798, in spite of the fact that great transcontinental wars have ebbed and flowed around them. The Swiss are so neutral they make a business of it.

It is well said, "Switzerland doesn't have an army, it is an army." Virtually to a man and woman, all Swiss take great pride in who they are and what they are. Change comes very slowly, if at all.

The U.S. used to be like that but of course is no longer. Concern about such is beyond the scope of this book, other than noting with vicarious pride that this level of patriotism has not passed from this Earth.

Switzerland is a relatively tiny land-locked nation a bit bigger than twice the size of New Jersey. It is shoehorned into midwestern Europe between Germany, France, Italy and Austria. None of which are known for their prior pacifist tendencies.

Per capita income is an extremely high $33,800, indicating again that an economy can flourish given sufficient freedom and government enforcement of contracts, even in a place with scant natural resources past a pile of granitic rocks. Bring fat credit cards and checkbook, however, if you plan to visit Switzerland. It is one of the most modern, clean and pricey places on Earth.

Living is free and easy, for the law abiding, self-reliant person in Switzerland. But hold onto both your wallet and credentials! They don't want you unless you are independently wealthy, possess great skill and creativity in a desired field or are willing to work at menial tasks (at relatively high wages) in jobs the Swiss don't wish to fill.

Information for this chapter came from personal visits to Switzerland, from information supplied by several gun-owning Swiss nationals, from the editor of a Swiss gun magazine, from the Swiss embassy in Washington, D.C., and from several publications on the subject of private ownership of guns in Switzerland.

Until January 1, 1999, when a federal gun law went into effect, the various Swiss states, or *cantons*, each enforced their own version of gun-ownership laws, somewhat like the U.S. in that regard. Current federalized gun laws in Switzerland are a bit easier to understand, but Swiss gun owners worry that this concentration of authority has materially reduced their freedom to own guns of all kinds.

The Swiss like their freedom to own guns. Pressures to change come mostly from outside the country as a result of the end of the Cold War and are generally resisted by the Swiss. This sort of disclaimer is needed since, for American gun owners accustomed to numerous, senseless, arbitrary restrictions and changes, what follows is almost too good to be true. World over, gun owners worry about noises made by anti-gunners. In that regard, Swiss gun owners are no different than the rest of us.

Please consider all of this information in the context of an extremely low crime rate and an extremely high social-control culture that many Americans would find strange and intrusive. This low crime rate, I was repeatedly lectured, "does not depend on whether there is a weapon in the house or not. It depends on the Swiss state of mind, or a morality contrary to criminality in our society."

Virtually all firearms from pistols through anti-aircraft guns and howitzers are legally owned by private civilians in Switzerland. But Swiss citizens are required to learn to use their guns through mandatory militia training of a nature that many Americans would find absolutely abhorrent. Then their culture provides social controls that further limit freedom to levels below those enjoyed by Americans. Movies and books, for instance, can be arbitrarily censored in Switzerland as being overly violent or deviant. Even publication of racist opinions or revisionist history is controlled under Swiss law.

Private ownership of virtually all firearms is permitted. Swiss citizens purchase rifles, shotguns, and semi-autos including assault rifles over the counter with little restriction or limitation other than a gun-owner's purchase certificate. Handguns are sold at retail but only to those who have obtained a purchase certificate. Get these certificates from your local canton authorities at a cost of about $16. Full-auto ownership is permitted but is a bit more difficult. A canton license, essentially registering the gun, is now mandatory.

Certificates are issued to virtually every adult citizen applicant who is not a criminal, mental case, obvious pissant or otherwise blatantly unfit to own and use a gun. An investigation taking about ten days is made before ownership certificates are issued to first-time applicants. After that, issuance may take only a day or two.

Currently no firearms-purchase certificates are required for sales between private citizens if these sales are for handguns, rifles (including assault rifles) and shotguns. Transacting parties must sign copies of a bill of sale, which must be kept a minimum of ten years. No private, unrecorded sales of machine guns or machine pistols are allowed. All of these must be registered with one's local canton authorities. Oddly, lever-action rifles are lumped together with assault rifles by Swiss authorities, all of which require purchase certification.

Reportedly private sales of basic handguns, rifles and shotguns have spiked up a bit in Switzerland, apparently similar to the U.S. where concerned gun owners have attempted to stockpile pre-1968 guns having no paper trail.

Virtually every Swiss citizen who wants a canton firearms-purchase permit gets one. Unlike the U.S., canton police do not jerk their citizens around. After securing the permit, Swiss citizens can purchase up to a maximum of three guns at the same shop. These guns are now registered. Those who want more than three must secure additional purchase permits from canton authorities. Under their 1999 laws, records are kept by the canton police department. It's registration, but not of a national variety! Swiss citizens can and do own a great many types of military-style guns and they seem to trust their government more than many Americans. There's no limit on the number, kind or size of firearms Swiss citizens may own.

For several hundred years, each Swiss canton was responsible for enforcing gun laws. The variations this naturally led to in enforcement disappeared in January 1999. Basically, whether city or rural, everything is now similar throughout the country. Rather than state laws, all gun laws in Switzerland are now nationalized. It's somewhat like Canada in that regard. Looking on the bright side, this may be an advantage for gun owners in big cities where anti-gun sentiments often seem to originate.

Universal male conscription is alive and well in Switzerland. At age 20, virtually every Swiss man must go through 75 days of basic military training. This training is organized by the national government but has a definite local Swiss flavor and application. Depending on rank and specialty, additional training is required at the rate of no less than two to three weeks every second year.

Once trained, these people remain part of the active militia to age 42. They are required to keep their assault rifles, fifty rounds of ammunition, gas masks, packs and other military gear with them at home in a state of readiness. All is kept in their private residences under their own private control. Swiss military people are issued fully automatic assault rifles at state expense.

The few full-time officers and militia officers are provided with pistols also at state expense. With the end of the Cold War, keeping a two weeks' supply of emergency food and water is no longer mandatory for Swiss families, but remains highly recommended.

Swiss countryside

Even what passes for rolling hills in mountainous
Switzerland comprise a nearly impenetrable fortress, but
defenders of that terrain still must know how to handle it.
Universal conscription, along with firearms training and a
high level of personal firearms ownership have deterred
aggression against this low-crime, high quality-of-life state
for centuries, despite major wars that have swirled around
it. The Swiss train regularly nationwide with iron sights at
targets out past 300 yards, real feats of marksmanship.

Swiss gun-store window

Swiss gun laws have been tightened significantly since 1999, but it is still fairly easy for Swiss citizens to purchase fully automatic submachine guns at retail. Semiautomatic firearms like these items on display in a Swiss gun-shop window can be purchased with much less difficulty. Swiss citizenship is very difficult to obtain, which contributes to a cultural mindset that may have more to do with their safety than the particular types of hardware you can find in a store. The demographics of criminal-gang activity that burden others nations is not as much of a problem here.

Do note that, while some Americans might find compulsory military service to be objectionable, it does lead to a society of gun owning, trained, gun-appreciating citizens. It explains why Switzerland has a gun culture equal to or greater than the U.S.

Should a national emergency arise, this body of 20- to 42-year-old conscripts becomes the front line fighting force. In part because fears of a national emergency are fading, additional provision is increasingly made for both handicapped and conscientious objectors. Such people pay an additional special tax in lieu of military service. Unlike the U.S., alternate service for conscientious objectors is not more rigorous and difficult, but significantly longer than regular military service itself. Swiss women may voluntarily enlist for military service if they wish.

At age forty-two, Swiss men and the few women volunteer enlistees begin service in their equivalent of our National Guard, called "Civil Protectors." These folks handle natural disasters such as floods, avalanches or severe forest fires.

After basic, Swiss army conscripts are quickly placed in "specialist" training programs. Many of these occur at inconvenient times, according to some young Swiss businessmen in the process of building their companies. In that regard, I inquired about a 7.5mm Model 25 Furrer light machine gun. It and another one like it were on the rack of a gun store in Zurich.

All Swiss military weapons are their own design. They are beautifully made, "much like a fine Swiss watch," one gun collector observed. Few current designs are exported. Denmark adopted SIG's P-210 and Chile adopted SIG's 510-4 assault rifle, but that's about all. In the U.S. we see some commercial SIG pistols and surplus 7.5mm Schmidt Rubin rifles and carbines.

"That," the gun-store proprietor told me, "is the personal weapon of a prominent Swiss banking official." Seems the fellow just returned from his obligatory two-week mountain training program where he took it along to practice. "You don't expect a bank president to clean his own machine gun, do you?" the clerk asked in a somewhat puzzled tone.

"Well—no," I thought, "probably the dumbest idea since suggesting neutral Switzerland join the UN."

One thing that is required of all men in Switzerland is good marksmanship. You fail to make an acceptable score with your service rifle and it's off to a special two-day marksmanship refresher course! No excuses and no questions. You have to wonder how many big international deals fell through because a key member of the Swiss contingent was off getting more rounds into the ten ring.

Ammunition factories controlled by the Swiss army produce and sell low-cost military-practice ammunition for use by citizens. Well over eighty million rounds of service ammo are fired each year on the thousands of military and civilian ranges spotted around the country. This works out to be slightly more than eight rounds apiece for every man, woman and child in Switzerland.

Most Swiss ranges are open to bona fide long-term residents. Full-auto fire on these ranges is usually not allowed, but it is not uncommon to hear the controlled, calculated cackle of machine gun fire emanating from private property drifting across the valley. Residents pay this noise little to no attention.

U.S. gun grabbers who generally abhor Swiss openness on this issue make a great fuss about the fact that Swiss ammunition must be recorded if bought at private gun stores. But military ammo purchased at low subsidized prices at military ranges need not be recorded, an anomaly that the anti-rights community fails to mention.

Technically all ammo bought at the range must be used at that range. But this rule is either ignored (strange for hyper-law-abiding Swiss) or unknown. Most Swiss take their military ammo home or to other ranges where they happily blast away. Ammunition more powerful than .22 LR is recorded at purchase in the store's ammo-record book. Like our own BATF Form 4473, this information remains in the gun shop unless proper authorities ask for it. Nothing additional is ever done with this record. It is not meant to be used as a restriction.

Hand loading is also common and unrestricted in Switzerland. Supplies of powder, primers and bullets are easily purchased at any of many neighborhood gun stores. Components are recorded in the shop ammo book, but again this is not a restrictive registration or hindrance.

Switzerland frowns on concealed-carry permits. A few are issued to guards and private security personnel, but only after proper training and a thorough background examination. One does see literally scores of trainees carrying their rifles (light machine guns) down the streets or on public busses and trains.

Use of a firearm of any sort for self-defense is always assumed, but as a practical matter not encouraged. Switzerland is not Sweden or Finland where personal defense using a gun is practically and socially impossible. In general it is much better not to get into a gun battle or shootout with anyone in Switzerland. Not only is everyone armed, the other guy is statistically more likely to be a better shot. Onus for explaining and justifying even a crime-deterring shooting situation is always on the shooter, not the shootee.

After discharge from their final phase of service, old soldiers are given their weapons to take home. Many were full-auto rifles, now permanently modified to semi-auto only. As a result, the military is continually upgrading and improving its stock of weapons as the old are moved out into private hands and new models and types come on the scene.

Gun design, research and development are encouraged in Switzerland within their somewhat unique constraints. Society and custom are different, but proven American firearms-design people could go to Switzerland to work provided they realize Swiss gun designs are unique and that export sales will be very limited.

The army will sell anti-tank weapons, howitzers, anti-aircraft guns, cannons and sniper rifles to well-heeled interested purchasers. Usually sales are made to former military men. All sales of this class of weapon are registered. No doubt as a result of this registration, there is absolutely no howitzer crime in Switzerland.

Full-auto machine guns are also commonly sold to civilians through easily obtained canton licenses. These guns are registered. Current estimates indicate that there are about 600,000 fully automatic assault rifles, machine guns and machine pistols in private hands, including citizen soldiers, among a population of slightly more than seven million. Authorities also estimate half a million pistols in private Swiss hands. Ironically some Swiss gun owners currently complain that the cost of a machine gun license has become prohibitively high. Everything is high priced in Switzerland! Exact costs vary by canton.

There are only 1,500 full time soldiers in all of Switzerland. These include drill sergeants, tech sergeants, pilots and others. Nevertheless, they can mobilize about 400,000 men on twenty-four hours' notice. Because they fight on their home turf, literally for their homes, this is indeed a formidable force.

Military doctrine calls for intelligent, reasoned manning of Fortress Switzerland. They intend to operate in small autonomous units that slowly retreat from their borders while simultaneously extracting as many casualties among invaders as possible. Given their passion for marksmanship, this extraction would probably be even more severe than that accomplished by the Finns during their Winter War. Nobody, but nobody, has wanted to test this defense strategy. It's the old adage made real: "The toughest kid on the block seldom has to fight."

It is tough not to overly effuse over Swiss laws and culture. They definitely believe that if the government cannot trust the people with guns, then the people cannot trust the government. Whether Americans could successfully implement a similar system is a good question. Could we endure censorship of violent and perverted

American movies, community sanction of lawbreakers rather than prison, and be entirely on the honor system regarding bus fares?

Swiss gun owners are concerned about gradual degradation of their right to own guns, but on a worldwide scale the independent, free and unique Swiss gun culture is a breath of fresh air in a world where personal responsibility is becoming a lost attribute.

Chapter Two
Dominican Republic
World Rank: 52 • Firearm Freedom 21%

In contrast to free and easy Switzerland, where everything including gun ownership is easily and consistently defined, we move to a depressingly familiar third-world example.

The Dominican Republic shares the Caribbean island of Hispaniola one-third/two-thirds with Haiti. Hispaniola lies to the east of Cuba, perhaps 350 miles south east of Miami, slightly below the 20-degree latitude line. Physically the place can easily be characterized as a tropical paradise. Abundant, beautiful beaches, picturesque mountains, warm climate and reasonably fertile soil. A delightful place to vacation or live when the primary requirement is an inexpensive tropical paradise.

Land area roughly equals the American states of New Hampshire and Vermont combined. Their government is fairly characterized as being corrupt to very corrupt, severely limiting foreign investment and economic development in general. Dom Rep enjoys the dubious distinction of being tied for 121st place among national freedom rankings. Yet there is some limited sense of rule of law and of property rights. Outside investors who purchase property in Dom Rep find their greatest single problem to be illegal squatters who, by reason of their squatting, may acquire some sort of legally defensible property right to property for which payment has been made and a deed extended.

Per capita income is about $6,300. Unemployment runs about 17 percent. Average real growth is about 1.7 percent annually. Dominican Republic is economically about where the Cubans were in 1959 when Castro took over.

Because of its relatively sparse population, easy living style and low cost, Americans living on U.S. dollar incomes are likely to find life in Dom Rep attractive to very attractive. Spanish is the official language, but English is widely spoken, providing an added bonus.

Because this is definitely a third-world location, not characterized by a strong rule of law or set of property rights, and because the Caribbean in general is often characterized by an English system of "permitsitis" hostile to private firearms ownership, I was slow to pick up on Dom Rep as a place some gun owners might find interesting.

All that quickly changed when my son found several hundred acres of remote beachfront property for sale at about $3,000 per acre. At that time I happened to notice that several posh tourist resorts offered extensive shooting sports as one of their main attractions. Perhaps this was a gun-tolerant place deserving more study!

Finding someone who knew anything at all about gun laws in Dominican Republic was not easy. Letters to attorneys, realtors, and their tourist officers went unanswered. Perhaps they were never delivered. Mail service there is notoriously bad. But gun laws were probably not something the good folks in Dom Rep were anxious to talk about.

At the time I was perplexed and surprised, but this stonewalling soon became a universal pattern. As is true with much of the information contained herein, fortune soon smiled. I was able to proceed through the good efforts of a friend's daughter who married a citizen of the Dominican Republic.

Initially, gathering information seemed easy to this gentleman. All he had to do was return to his parents' home and ask a few questions. Then he came to believe he could not say or write anything about guns in Dom Rep before emigrating permanently to the U.S.—in spite of the fact that this man's father was a retired army officer who "owned several guns." Most of the answers to my questions were prefaced by his disclaimer that, "it isn't easy to get information on gun laws in Dom Rep."

In general, he says, gun ownership is fairly widespread in the Dominican Republic. Culturally it is not considered kosher to display weapons either at home or in the field, so few people know that other people have guns. There is even some slight cultural stigma relative to talking about guns.

Many of the guns owned by Dom Rep citizens are technically illegal but there is absolutely no means of estimating what percentage. "Perhaps ten percent of the illegal firearms come into the country from Haiti," he says. Because of this fact, the fellow senses that gun laws are becoming somewhat more restrictive, although he can cite no recently passed, more restrictive rules and regulations.

Legal guns are purchased from one of four gun stores in the country (he knows about) or from the military that also has a commercial outlet. He also recalls seeing a number of itinerant gun and ammunition dealers who operated from car trunks or the backs of pickups parked along the streets and roads.

One central agency handles distribution of all of the legal official weapons used by the police and military. The Imperial Police Headquarters handles all legal permits for gun owners. Both guns and their owners are registered. Cost for a firearm-owner's permit, which does not require an attorney's help, is about $150. Although the process is costly (in Dom Rep terms), and characterized by lots of forms, approvals and paperwork, most citizens who want them eventually get their permits, he says. For shop owners, he says, the process is routine.

Initially potential permit seekers must check in at local police headquarters for a mostly perfunctory approval to proceed. No known felon can receive a permit. Apparently non-citizen residents can also secure an approval to proceed. From there, one goes to the Imperial Police Headquarters in Santo Domingo.

There are no limits on the number of guns that can be owned under one permit. However, all must be registered. Shotguns, pistols and rifles with telescopic sights are all approved for private ownership. Those willing to pay a bribe can even take possession of an illegal submachine gun. He doesn't believe there are any full machine guns in private hands in the Dom Rep—legal or illegal. There are no restrictions of caliber, action type, or magazine capacity he knows of. This, however, may be subject to local interpretation.

Two kinds of permission are granted. One to have a gun or guns in your house is quite easy and common, the fellow claims. Another to carry for personal protection is more difficult, but far from impossible.

Although pig poaching is common, there are no seasons or hunting permits or even places to hunt in Dom Rep. Target shooting and plinking are possible on your own property, he says.

Most shooting is done on indoor ranges which are not terribly common but which are found at a few places throughout Dom Rep. The fellow was unclear how one would legally carry the weapon to the range for practice. Apparently out of sight, discreetly in a vehicle.

Apparently non-resident immigrants can bring their guns to Dom Rep. I would not test this statement without going down there to inquire of immigration and real-estate people personally, but the fellow believes this to be true.

Ammunition is available from gun stores or is frequently available from the military. He had no idea about cost, other than for citizens of Dom Rep making about $1.25 per hour it is "awfully high priced." He believes that gun-store officials must see a copy of one's gun permit before concluding an ammunition sale, but does not know if military sales to civilians are legal or under the counter. All ammo sales are recorded in a bound volume. Reloading, other than a very few shotgun shells, is not common, the fellow believes. He didn't know if reloading components were available, but was reasonably certain he had never observed gunpowder or primers of any kind for sale in Dom Rep.

A considerable traffic in homemade firearms existed, he said. These could be of fairly high quality, he told me. Most were manufactured in the city of La Romana, which is a sort of center for the home-built firearms industry. These are mostly shotguns that, because of their origin and type, tended to achieve a sort of quasi-legal status. He believed the authorities mostly ignored them.

Although this information is a bit sketchy and inconclusive, it does reflect reality, or at least reality as one retired army officer and one long time citizen and former resident of Santo Domingo sees it. Bottom line is that the legal route to firearms ownership in Dom Rep is ill-defined because rules and laws are ill-defined and even more poorly enforced. Most are subject to local interpretation which interpretation could be bent to suit individual situations completely dependent on one's ability to extend gratuities.

This is a nice place to live where gun enthusiasts are not immediately considered to be perverted criminals and where rules and regulations and enforcement are subject to local whim and interpretation. Some Americans could live with that, some could not. Apparently a few Yanqui gun owners currently live in Dom Rep. Extensive gun-sport enterprises at resorts are managed at least tacitly by the military for their (the Dom Rep military's) benefit.

Most people in Dom Rep can—and many apparently do—own guns. Before deciding anything certain about Dom Rep, including property ownership, guns, investments or whatever, spend time with local police officials to be somewhat certain how they would view your own specific case. It's an easy, inexpensive plane trip from our east coast to Dom Rep.

Chapter Three
Germany
World Rank: 27 • Firearm Freedom 48%

From the Dominican Republic where firearms rules and laws—when there are such—are mostly subject to local, individual interpretation, application and gratuities, we jump to Germany where everything is over-regulated. This is the same historic Germany that gave birth to the first successful bolt-action rifle and first successful semi-auto handgun, and where a vibrant gun culture still exists.

Germany is sometimes characterized as a place where "If it isn't specifically forbidden, it is obligatory." Everything in German society is very rigid, set down by central authorities in absolutely voluminous code sections. Germans are the benchmark autocratic society. German citizens draw great comfort and enjoyment having a government that basically acts as God for them. Their firearms rules and regulations reflect this philosophy, yet strange, hard-to-figure anomalies lurk within their culture.

Adolph Hitler developed, promulgated and oversaw implementation of their first firearms regulations in 1932. These were the infamous rules that brought forward the test of "sporting purpose for all private gun ownership," i.e. guns in private hands are okay so long as they are used only to target shoot or for some very restrictive, stylized pageant-like hunting activities. All of these gun "applications" are still heavily regulated, licensed and taxed.

Originally these laws were put forward to disarm the Jewish population lest they start to resist Nazi pogroms directed against them. Jews tended then not to hunt or to shoot at targets for sport, which is still true today. As evidenced by their sporting goods catalogs and gun magazines, Germans have a gun culture. But, to a great extent this same old autocratic—perhaps anti-Semitic-like—philosophy still permeates German gun laws.

Germany lies in central Europe, but with some seaports in the north providing limited access to the Baltic Sea. On the east, Germany is bordered by Poland, the Czech Republic and Austria (more to the south), with a climate more temperate than Americans might initially suppose.

Germany's rigid laws extend dramatically, to their disadvantage, into economics. It is, for instance, exceedingly difficult for German entrepreneurs to get permission to start new businesses. It is often even more difficult to close down and liquidate a failed, old, obsolete one. As a result, Germany has a tremendously—almost unbelievably— vibrant underground economy, both to avoid business licensing bureaucrats and the taxman's oppression.

Officially about 9.6 percent of Germans are unemployed. Many of these draw their government dole checks and then go to work for themselves in the underground economy. Real annual growth of the official economy is well under two percent. Total official *per capita* income is about $28,700. Other than all of their picky-picky rules and regulations governing everything from dumping trash into collection bins, to owning pet cats, to which exact stores can sell what at what hours, Germany is an extremely nice place to live. Clean, neat, with bright green vistas, little snow in the winter or heat in the summer and many of the folks speak some English.

My source of information for this chapter was a forty-something German ex-bureaucrat who worked in the local city hall as a clerk for the past twenty years till he quit to open a computer-related business. Fortunately he is a strong, vibrant gun enthusiast who looked out at more liberal gun laws in the U.S., Belgium and Switzerland with great longing. "Oh, how I wish I could afford a home in Belgium so I could buy guns there," he wrote.

The fellow is also a charter member of the recently formed German equivalent of the NRA. As a result, his explanations were some of the most detailed and accurate I received. If only I could get him to stop using fantastically long, multi-compounded German nouns that no one but a native gun buff understands, everything would have been fine. Good thing. German gun laws are amazingly convoluted and complex.

Germany does have both an extensive regular legal firearms system as well as a much larger illegal system. Their underground gun-ownership system developed because their legal system is so terribly complex and slow, I was told. Perhaps so, but we may also see it as the logical outcome of an area awash in left-behind military weapons.

Local German gun owners must secure a gun license called a Waffenbesitskarte (WBK). Cardholders are lumped together as Waffenbesitskarteninhaber. This apparently is their word for gun buff. Start this process at the local police headquarters and/or city hall. This document includes a processing fee of about $150, a background check, some fairly intrusive questioning and a long waiting period. No legal help is required, but success of these applications is heavily dependent on how and what you ask for. No permits are issued just for the fun of shooting or plinking. It's not what you ask for, but how you ask— perhaps arguing for professional help with licensing procedures.

This being Germany, it is reasonably cheap and easy to get a
Waffenbesitskarte. An estimated three million Germans have one.
Legally there are about ten million licensed guns in Germany.

Unofficially it is thought there are at least thirty million unlicensed
illegal firearms in Germany. Many of these flooded west with the
collapse of the Soviet Union and East Germany. Scandalously low-
paid Russian and East German soldiers, unable to purchase food and
clothing, sold their weapons and ammunition to make ends meet.
Movement of all these guns into the black market may also have been
directed by the Russian mafia, but no one knows for sure. It's only a
rumor.

This license is only to own guns. As an essential part of the process, an
applicant will be required to acquire a separate and very expensive
license to be a member of a target shooting or hunting club. My
German helper informant had, at the time of his writing, been in
hunting club classes for seven months. They met twice a week in
evenings and on Saturdays for practice. By his estimate, he would
finally have the coveted hunting-club license in another three to four
months.

There is also a higher-order permission called a Waffenschein, which
is roughly equivalent to our own permits to carry discreetly. Unless
you are a judge, police officer or employee of a licensed security firm,
it is impossible to get one. There is also a permit known as a
Bundeswaffen-gesetz, or a §37 BWaffG. This is the permit for
otherwise completely forbidden weapons such as large, full-auto
machine guns, bombs, grenades, recoilless rifles and such. Needless to
say, this is an industrial class permit, there being only three or four
issued in all of Germany.

As mentioned, no permits for guns are issued in Germany just for the
fun of owning or shooting. There must be an officially acceptable good
reason for ownership. Plinking and fooling around with various loads
is not one of these. Three different "good, acceptable" reasons to own
a gun in Germany are out there. One can be a serious, dedicated (and
most often moneyed) hunter, a licensed target shooter, or a serious
historic collector/student of firearms. Collectors must prove that they
intend to assemble a particularly cultural and historically significant
collection of guns before they are allowed to proceed.

The German authorities issue three colors, or grades, of Waffenbesit-
skarten. Yellow means you are permitted to own and use one single-
shot rifle or shotgun. Some single-shot .22 caliber free pistols (Olympic
style) are sold in Germany, but not to yellow cardholders. This class is
for single-shot shotguns and rifles only.

Crete airfield

This now idyllic airfield at Maleme, Crete, is where German invaders in WWII lost 5,500 of their best men to angry, determined, privately armed Cretan guards (fighting along with Allied forces), a classic example of a citizen militia and the ultimate legal and moral justification for the right to keep and bear arms. See the schoolchild's drawing in the chapter on Crete to gain a sense of the cultural attachment to freedom these brave people exhibited. To this day, with that desperate struggle still in memory, citizens of Crete remain some of the most heavily armed people on Earth.

Green card holders are allowed to own a wide variety of rifles, shotguns and pistols. Unless seldom-guaranteed special permission is secured for additional handguns, two each of these is the absolute maximum, but there is no limit on numbers of shotguns and rifles. These can be pump action and automatic shotguns as well as some semi-auto rifles. Ruger camp rifles, Mini-14s, and some H&Ks fall in this approved category of so-called "assault rifles."

There is no size restriction on rifles, shotguns or pistols. Shops and catalogs commonly offer three-inch 12-gauge mag shotguns, .458 Win mag rifles and .454 Casull pistols, for instance.

However, while large-capacity magazines are sold in gun shops, only special two-shot magazines are permitted for hunting. Germans can hunt with their semi-auto rifles but only with two-shot magazines.

German sporting-goods catalogs list a large number of different shotguns and rifles from a wide range of makers including many American companies. Prices in Germany are a bit tough to evaluate because European makes tend to be higher quality with engraving and other decorative features. Imported American models tend to be more nearly the top of the line. In general, expect to pay about twice as much for the same weapon in Germany as compared to the U.S.

Restrictions on total number of guns permitted leads, it seems, to some strange anomalies. One frequently sees sub-caliber devices allowing rifle rounds in shotguns or pistol rounds in rifles. There are also a number of often very expensive sets wherein several different rifle and shotgun barrels are fitted to common frames classed as a single firearm.

Western or "cowboy-type" guns are especially popular in Germany.

Ruger Mini-14s and a few models of H&K semi-autos are as close as common German gun enthusiasts can get to owning assault rifles. As mentioned, additional pistols on a green card are possible but not probable. All firearms are registered in the name of the WBK cardholder.

Red WBK cards are the most difficult for Germans to acquire. Supposedly red WBK cards allow unlimited pistols, some additional models of assault rifles and some submachine guns. This is generally a closely controlled collectors' permit. Applicants for a red WBK must demonstrate an almost burning interest and knowledge of historical firearms.

Collectors are allowed to acquire only on the basis of a common but narrow theme. This might be Mauser type actions, WWII weapons made by Walther, WWII Russian small arms, etc.

Even though penalties are severe and unforgiving, illegal ownership of everything from Mauser Schnellfeuer M712s to Russian AK-47s is thought to be common in Germany. First-time offenders, if caught, are subject to huge fines. Second-time offenders go to jail for a term up to one year. American M-16s, FN FALs, AK-47s, H&K MP-5s, and Steyr AUGs are all readily available on the street for about $500 apiece we are assured.

That large numbers of military small arms are available in Germany's underground is not surprising given the frequency with which serious wars rolled over the region. Yet it is surprising that there are forty million guns out there amongst a population of about 82 million in a country about the size of Montana (thirty million illegal and about ten million legal firearms.) Personal ownership intensity ranks right up with the U.S. Let it not be said that Americans are the only gun buffs in the world!

Handloading through all of Europe is not particularly popular, which is surprising since factory-new ammo is often ruinously expensive. Loaded .243 rounds, for example, cost about 76 cents each. Winchester .270 rounds are about 87 cents each, depending a bit on manufacturer and loading. Others include .308 Winchester rounds at 62 cents each, 7mm. Remington Magnum at $1.13, and .458 Winchester Magnum rounds at $2.47 each.

Boxes or single rounds of ammunition are sold only on display of a valid WBK card. All sales are recorded in a bound volume that is kept for official inspection. As a practical matter, quantities purchased may be limited, but there is currently no statutory provision limiting amounts of ammunition purchased other than price.

Another separate license test and application are required for hand loading. Courses leading to a hand loader's license are offered by larger gun shops.

Based on large numbers of kinds and amounts of hand-loading equipment shown in German shooters' catalogs however, there must be a great number of Germans with hand-loading licenses. Primers cost about $16 per carton of 1,000. Alliant Unique powder sells for $27.50 per one-pound can. Local Rottweil reloaders' powder is comparably priced.

German law does not allow shipment of reloader's powder by common carrier. All must be picked up in person at the selling gun shop.

Becoming a firearms dealer, gunsmith or inventor-tinkerer is difficult in Germany. The bureaucracy requires a strong show of dedication, which often translates into dozens of years working as an assistant or apprentice, along with numerous time-consuming, detailed and difficult applications. Many include mandatory training sessions.

Indoor shooting ranges are common in Germany. Often gun stores will have them, or there are those built and maintained by shooting clubs. It is difficult to find a place to shoot outdoors. No public land is available on which to shoot.

Silencers are legally available to German hunters only in .22 LR. Their only permitted use is on rats and rabbits. Ownership of a silencer also requires a separate special permit.

Can Americans going to Germany bring along their own guns? The only answer I can offer is that, at this time, no one I've been in contact with is certain. No one has tried it recently and laws pertaining to importing guns into Germany—probably in response to the flood from Russia—have been strengthened.

Americans living in Germany for a year and who have acquired shooting and hunting licenses and joined appropriate clubs can secure WBK cards.

Bottom line? It isn't quick or particularly easy, but there is a definite procedure whereby people with a few bucks, patience and determination can probably own quite a few different legal rifles, shotguns and even pistols in Germany. Germany is something of a gun buff's culture, but one with a strong bureaucratic inclination. Those who want to take the risk will find Germany's current Gun Underground to be an absolute collectors' paradise.

Chapter Four
France
World Rank: 26 • Firearm Freedom 48%

Gun laws in France stand in sharp contrast to those in Belgium and even Germany. One might expect such in a socialistic society where a ruling bureaucratic elite makes all life's decisions for the nation's lesser folk.

France's situation first entered my scope when, like Germany, a French correspondent wrote that he wished he could afford an address in Belgium so that he could legally acquire more of the firearms he enjoyed. So, there are gun buffs in France. Where do they get their guns and how do they flourish?

We take up France next, not because very many American gun owners would wish to live there, but because it is a natural progression through the continent of Europe, and because there are actually a great number of French gun owners. These people have successfully bonded together. Their tremendous political clout in adversity provides lessons America's gun owners would likely find interesting.

France is central western Europe. Germany and Switzerland border France on the east. Belgium on the north and Spain to the south. Both the mid Atlantic and Mediterranean Sea border France, tempering its climate and providing great topographical beauty. Given the great number of times France has been overrun by hostile armies we would validly suppose they would try to maintain a well-armed, well-trained, highly motivated citizen militia. Especially given Switzerland's close example (which has never been overrun in modern times).

France is large, about 80 percent the size of Texas. Lots of quaint rural settings characterize areas outside of the large cities. Contrary to popular dogma, English is widely spoken and the French people outside large cities are neither rude nor particularly arrogant.

Cost of living is high to very high. So high, visitors often question how common French citizens make it. There is a fairly strong rule of law, along with a highly established system of property rights. Unfortunately this rule of law and property right is often subject to severe, sometimes arbitrary, interpretation on the part of their vast bureaucracy, creating a classical fascist circumstance (over which the French are in continuous denial!) If not denial, they claim to enjoy fascism.

Per capita income is about $28,700, indicating that, for Americans charmed by French culture and countryside but who are also willing to give up many of their guns, living on U.S. dollars in France would be easy. Unemployment is stuck at a permanent 10 percent rate.

Gun ownership is legal in France, but owners must endure some fairly onerous additional turnings of the regulatory screws.

My informant, in this case, was an absolutely delightful French gun buff/adventurer whose nickname was Scorpio! I personally have spent time in France looking at their laws and economic philosophies. Like many other countries, gun laws in France are continually changing. Unrestrained bureaucrats seem unable to keep from continually tweaking, tinkering and adjusting. Yet their changes did not seem extensive or particularly onerous, given their myriad of already existing laws regulating just about everything.

Based on this fellow's analysis, we have a reasonably good snapshot of what gun owners in France face. Under their system of law, everything is supposedly written down in absolutely voluminous, but in difficult-to-research-and-understand detail. This complexity adds to the difficulty of accurately predicting what is actually happening out on the ground when either hostile or—giving them the benefit of the doubt—sympathetic bureaucrats do the interpreting.

Bottom line—some gun ownership is possible for private citizens in France. Potential owners must secure both gun-owner's permits and/or memberships in shooting clubs and hunting licenses. It can be either a shooting-club membership or a hunting license, but one of these is always paired with a gun-owner's permit.

Start at the local police office when requesting a gun-owner's permit. Gun-owner's permits are reasonably straightforward. No professional help is usually required and they are not particularly expensive. Gun permits must be renewed every three years. Renewal for an additional three years is somewhat perfunctory if you are still a member of a shooting club, have a hunting license and have not acquired a felony record. Local officials have been known to be arbitrary but generally no onerous restrictions regarding lawful use as they see it are in place.

Past wars and disintegration of gun-laden societies to the east of France are thought to have had an influence on numbers of illegal guns in France. There may be more left behind and smuggled machine guns and assault rifles out there than anyone wants to talk about. But no one really seems to know or will speculate about illegal guns in France. Penalties for illegal ownership runs up to three years in jail, maximum.

Membership in hunting and shooting clubs is apparently easy. No one mentions waiting lists, lengthy training sessions or ruinously high prices. Some clubs are pricey but other less expensive ones simply give members the right to tromp over blocks of rural private property carrying their guns. Sometimes they even get a shot at a pheasant.

French citizens with gun permits can legally own bolt-action .22-caliber rifles without hunting or shooting club memberships. It is illegal to hunt with a .22 rifle in France. Owning a shotgun always requires a gun permit and membership in the French Claybird Federation, or a hunting license.

Oddly enough, French gun owners with correct pieces of paper are allowed most civilian type side-by-side, over-under and semi-auto shotguns. But pump shotguns are complete forbidden!

Owning a hunting rifle or rifles requires a gun permit and a hunting license. Apparently acquiring a hunting license entails minimal amounts of paperwork. Not like Germany where a year of twice-weekly lessons is de rigueur, or Spain where the weight of the paper must equal the weight of the game.

Hunting rifles are defined as those having a civilian caliber. Essentially this requirement makes private ownership of assault rifles difficult but not impossible. Machine guns are never allowed to private citizens. Submachine guns are ruled out in another section of French law relative to pistols and revolvers. Only bolt actions, single shot and double rifles are commonly owned by people in France.

Some private shooting clubs offer specialized target shooting with semi-auto assault rifles. In most cases these assault rifles are owned by the club. Rules requiring use of civilian calibers are circumvented by calling a 7.62 NATO round a .308 or a 5.56 mm round a .223. Tough restrictions on assault rifles in England have created tourist shooting opportunities for French clubs specializing in semi-auto assault rifles. English shooters cross the channel to France for an opportunity to shoot semi-auto rifles and, in many cases, pistols as well.

Handguns, both in .22 caliber and larger military type configurations, are permitted. Any one person can own a maximum of seven .22-caliber handguns and five handguns of other larger calibers. There is no limit on the number of shotguns, .22 rifles and high-power hunting rifles one may own.

No fully auto or burst capacity handguns are permitted. Either revolvers or semi-auto handguns are kosher under the five/seven permission scheme. Collectors' antiques are covered in a separate section of French law. All rifles and pistols made before 1873 can be legally owned in any quantities by those with current gun permits. There is no limit on numbers and no club/hunting license provisions apply.

France has some, but not many, sporting-goods stores where citizens can purchase firearms. After receipt of their gun-owner's permit, buyers go to their friendly firearms retailer to purchase their rifles, shotguns and pistols. The retailer fills out a firearms acquisition certificate listing all of the gun's numbers and physical characteristics. They will also record personal information from the new owner's gun permit. After purchase, gun and buyer must go to the local cop shop where the gun or guns are registered in the owner's name.

Handguns and semi-auto .22 rifles are a bit different—more convoluted and time consuming. First, buyers must be members of a shooting club and the French Shooting Federation for at least six months prior to purchase of a handgun or semi-auto .22 rifle. These are not overly difficult memberships with onerous training and testing requirements. Then the local police make an investigation into the buyer's background, mental state, physical condition and criminal record. Usually this is a three-month long procedure. If your record is free from tax evasion, spousal abuse, felonious conduct and for being the community grinch, among other things, approval is given. Then you have three months to complete the purchase of your pistol and/or a .22 semi-auto rifle.

Ranges, both indoor and outdoor, are available in France. Both citizens and residents can use these ranges provided they pay required fees and memberships. Firearms ownership rules in general apply evenly to both citizens and residents of France.

Why aren't we surprised that purchase of ammunition is controlled in some strange and wonderful ways in France. Anyone with a gun permit and shooting club membership or hunting license can purchase unlimited .22 and shotgun ammo. Purchases are recorded in the gun-shop's books but that's all. The authorities can—but seldom do—peek at these records.

Heavy buckshot shotgun loads and hollow-point .22s are completely forbidden. Only qualified members of a target-shooting club can purchase .22 LR hollow-point ammo.

Purchase of rifle ammo is unrestricted for those with two pieces of paper and sufficient folding money. Rifle ammo is very expensive in France. Handgun shooters also face high costs and are limited to 1,000 rounds of center-fire pistol ammo per handgun per year.

Hand loading is permitted without additional licenses or authorizations. However, pistol components are placed in the same restrictive category as whole loaded ammo. Only 1,000 bullets per year are permitted. Primers and powder are license free. Within reason, no quantity restrictions apply.

French pheasant hunters, of which there are an estimated 15 million, produce crude shot shell reloads. This is mostly due to the astonishingly high price of store-bought shot-shell ammo. French pheasant hunters tend to be peasant farmers with limited financial resources—lots of cheap red wine, cheese and free medical care, but no money.

Pheasant hunting in rural France is something of a passion. Recent proposed changes to seasons and of some gun laws brought such an immediate howl of protest that officials quickly backed down. (French governmental rule often involves howls and protestations.) This protest was a united, concerted effort. Perhaps we can take some encouragement from this fact that somewhere, some how, some hunter/gun owners successfully acted together producing good result.

Perhaps France does not have a gun culture as we know it, but they do have a great many very vocal gun owners willing to bond together on a moment's notice. This may be the single greatest lesson to be learned from France and from the French gun situation.

French armament corporations still undertake modern small arms development and design. France gave us smokeless powder and the first production smokeless cartridges. Without a viable domestic market, things have slowed for small arms R&D people in France. By conventional standards, some of what they are coming up with is down right weird. Permits for military development and design are available to serious players. However they are so infrequently given, common French gun buffs have no idea how to obtain them. For all practical purposes this class of license is not available in France. An American gun designer machinist who wants to go to France to legally continue his research is certainly out of luck.

Firearms dealers' licenses are available to resident non-citizens. Like destructive devices and military weapons research, design and manufacturing licenses, these are applied for so infrequently that common citizens don't know how to apply.

Americans moving to France or coming there to hunt can bring some of their firearms with them, so long as they meet standards for those allowed French gun permit holders. In these instances a great many, often unpredictable, restrictions apply. Likely it would take years to get everything worked out with French customs. But, I am assured that, to an extent, importation is possible.

It helps—when bringing guns to France, I am told, if you are an internationally recognized competitor or designer, but otherwise it is a long, difficult and tiring process.

Chapter Five
Belgium
World Rank: 12 • Firearm Freedom 77%

Common wisdom throughout Europe suggests that only Swiss citizens enjoy free and relatively unencumbered private ownership of small arms—a legend that is often promulgated by the Swiss themselves. Official Swiss literature on the subject makes the claim that "while other European countries rigidly regulate private gun ownership, Swiss people are free to own whatever firearms they wish."

It's not an entirely true statement, regarding either Europe or Switzerland. The Swiss do have a few rules and regulations and, in Belgium for instance, gun ownership is surprisingly free and easy. In a few regards Belgian laws are more favorably inclined towards private gun owners than our own. Some 1.5 million Belgians currently own private firearms.

Gun-store owners, gunsmiths and citizen gun owners in Belgium are presently in a sour and dour mood over their current loss of gun-owning rights. "Our laws change monthly," one gun-shop owner scowled darkly. Perhaps anger over loss of gun rights shouldn't be a surprise. Belgium—Liége specifically—has, for centuries, been a center of firearms design, experiment, manufacturing and sales. It's a loss of a major profit center.

It was to Fabrique Nationale that John Browning fled when his contracts with Winchester soured in the early 1900s. Officials at Fabrique Nationale took an immediate interest in Browning's new commercial designs in part, it is said, so they could also access his many military models. At one point not too long ago (roughly the 1950s to 1970s), more of the world's armies used FN small arms than all others combined. Traditional old-world metalworking and gunsmithing are still practiced in Belgium. But will they ever again be on the forefront of modern design? Most citizen gun owners think not. Too much bias against modern innovation while maintaining expensive, historical hand-made traditions!

Historically Belgium has been the transshipment point for large quantities of modern small arms and ammunition moving through into the hands of the world's armies. These have been either established or revolutionary armies. Belgium was the place to look for supplies for the world's warriors. Sales were limited only by the buyer's ability to pay cash.

Although they still compete handily on workmanship, high labor rates in Belgium have driven a large portion of their small-arms business to communist China. Liége is now mostly a place of distribution rather than one of designers and manufacturers. Few to no rules apply to exporting guns from Belgium. Rumor has it that private yacht owners often take advantage, stocking up on on-board small arms while in Antwerp.

No matter what the enterprise, pocket-sized Belgium must rely on high tech manufacturing and technological innovation and trade for its existence. Antwerp, Belgium's major port, is often the world's busiest. Huge amounts of goods move through. As a result, Belgium can easily be characterized as a nation of traders and merchandisers. They have a solid rule of law and a strong sense of property rights. Modern intrusion into private economic affairs of its citizens ranges from minimal to severe depending on which enterprise one has in view.

Population in relatively tiny Belgium is only about 10.5 million. Pretty close packing for a place no larger than our state of Maryland. *Per capita* income is about $30,600. They govern with a figurehead king and a parliament. But something must really be wrong. Real economic growth rates are considerably less than three percent annually (2.6%.)

My interest in Belgium was intensified by comments from both a German and French correspondent who fantasized about affording a home or apartment in Belgium. An address in Belgium would lead to a temporary citizenship/residential situation, they both claimed, which would allow relatively easy purchase of many, many interesting guns. I personally spent a great deal of time in Belgium gathering information and dodging the dog poop that profusely litters their city streets.

Information that follows is from observations of French and German gun enthusiasts, from my own experiences traveling in Belgium, from a most interesting gun and adventure magazine (much like a French Soldier of Fortune) published in French in Belgium and from some of their sporting goods catalogs. What follows reflects general thinking about guns in that country. Fortunately I was also able to locate a large gun manufacturer who responded to direct inquiries with up-to-the-minute information.

Belgium is accurately characterized as being a place with a relatively vibrant open civilian market for all types of firearms. Firearms purchasers are split into two groups. Most common commercial non-military rifles and shotguns are available over-the-counter to any resident over the age of 18. Hunting, target and clay sports rifles and shotguns are classed as those that can fire no more than two shots. You sign in the book on purchases, and walk out the door with the guns. Storeowners are now obligated to notify your local police of the purchase, but that's all.

Private ownership of simple sporting guns is currently unencumbered, but talk persists of the need to secure permits from the central government in the near future, or to limit numbers of guns one can purchase per month. No one knows how difficult this will be because it hasn't been done yet. Like the world over, Belgian gun enthusiasts expect the worst.

Pistols, assault rifles, submachine guns, squad automatic weapons, machine guns and some military type shotguns are only available under a special gun-owner's authorization permit.

Purchase of this latter class of firearms is controlled by what they refer to as a "defence autorisation," a permit for pistols and military weapons. Currently if one lives in a smaller city and is known to the police, this permit takes from two to three days. In larger cities where extensive investigations may be undertaken, it has taken up to a year in one or two notorious but isolated cases.

Citizen gun owners believe it will become increasingly difficult to secure defence autorisation permits. In some cases, police permitting authorities are unilaterally insisting that new applicants take "appropriate" training courses. Some of these last twelve months and are relatively expensive. Increasingly, pistol ownership is being limited in Belgium. New applicants must have six months of range experience, but once a permit for purchase is issued, they may keep their pistols in their homes rather than at a club or range.

Cost of a defence autorisation is about $50. No consultant need be hired to be certain wording is proper and acceptable. Most Belgian authorities seem ready and able to accept the fact that their citizens might want this permit in order to own guns for their intrinsic historical and aesthetic value. Shooting for the plain, simple fun of it is acceptable in Belgium. At one time, Belgian gun enthusiasts owned as many guns as they wished, hundreds in some cases. Currently the limit is 20 to 40, depending on who you are and where you live. Those who wish to own more guns than this can secure a "gunsmith agreement." A very quick and easy additional authorization, according to Belgian gun owners.

Because all pistols in Belgium are sold under a *defence autorisation*, owners are registered both as permit holders and as holders of specific guns they purchase—the guns are registered in their names. Registration and pre-qualification include all military-type weapons including light machine guns, submachine guns and similar. Belgians have a wider range of pistols available to them than Americans, judging by offerings in sporting goods shops and catalogs. An advertisement for a CZ 75 in full-auto configuration with extended magazine and fore grip, featured in a Belgian outdoor magazine, is especially noteworthy and interesting.

Machine guns and submachine guns are sold in both live and dewat configurations. Dewats move over the counter without a gun permit. Live machine guns are, however, registered to the new owner. Most dewats are more expensive than the same weapon live, perhaps because they are easier to own. Because one can legally own either a dewat or live machine gun, official dewatting procedures are not as obviously destructive as those in the U.S. No one knew or would say how commonly these guns were rewatted. Probably not often.

Some guns appear to cost less in Belgium than in the U.S. A fully functional .30 caliber Browning Automatic Rifle (yes, a BAR) costs about $750. U.S. M-1 .30 cal. carbines currently sell for about $240 and a genuine old WW II German MP-40 (9mm submachine gun) on a permit is currently offered at about $600. A U.S. M-14 full-auto rifle sells for about $650, but in all these cases I can't say about condition. All the above are sold only on a defence autorisation permit. Prices of pistols in Belgium seem about the same or marginally higher than in the U.S.

Perhaps because they shoot often, in a densely packed, highly populated land, silencers were once popular in Belgium. They had them for virtually every kind and type of gun. Nice commercial models were available for everything from .22 LR to .458 Win Mags! Cost of some of the high-tech commercial models produced by Beretta, H&K or Norinco seem incredibly high. By our standards they were probably very high, up to $600 each in some cases. Until 1993, silencers were sold separately, but only to holders of a defence autorisation. No one knows for certain, but rumor has it that most commercial silencers made for large-bore pistols used by U.S. mafia hit men had their origin in Belgium. All this is changed now, confounding both gun-shop owners and citizen gun owners. Silencers are now illegal under all circumstances.

Illegal weapons available in war-overrun Belgium are said to be more numerous than legal weapons. Several gun-store owners said that 90 percent of the guns in Belgium were illegal. "We know this because in 1990 the rules changed," they said. "At that time there were 700,000 guns in Belgium. Only 70,000 were ever legally registered," I was told. Fifty percent were said to be left over from WW II, thirty percent from WW I! And now it's a flood of guns from the old Soviet Union. Illegal Soviet bloc weapons and ammunition are continuing to move west into Belgium in huge quantities.

Like most of Europe, hand loading is not terribly popular in Belgium, but perhaps there is a reason. Maybe it just isn't worth the time and hassle. Millions of inexpensive surplus rounds are available fresh from the world's battlefields and from national manufacturing plants. Much of this is advertised at relatively low cost to Belgians. I was quoted a rate of $130 per thousand for first quality, modern 9mm ammo.

Citizens seem to enjoy shooting their full-auto weapons. As a result, sales of relatively huge quantities of ammo are not viewed with suspicion.

Hand-loading components other than powder are sold over the counter without additional permits. Sales of powder are recorded in a permanent record and are made over the counter, after simple paperwork is completed. Powder sales are limited to one kilo per day. Prices are about as high as those in Germany. Total quantities of powder one may have on hand at one time are limited, but our various experts couldn't agree on how much that is. "Ask at your local gun shop or police station before it becomes an issue," they said.

Sales of ammo are lightly controlled in Belgium. Non-military, non-pistol ammo sales are recorded in a shop book which is held by that shop. These records are made available to the local police if they want them. No quantity or possession limits apply.

Purchasers of pistol and military-type ammo such as 8 mm and 7.62x39 must show their defence autorisation documents for that specific gun in that caliber. Like ammo for sporting firearms, there is no quantity limit, but purchasers must again sign in the record book.

Finding a place to shoot in tiny Belgium is a problem, especially for noisy full-autos. Making a lot of noise shooting carries great social stigma. As a result, there are a number of indoor noise-attenuated shooting ranges available to the public. Unlike Germany, no expensive membership is required. Walk-ins are encouraged.

Charges at some posh indoor public ranges seem high. Others simply require that users purchase all their ammo from the range. Anyone, resident or non-resident, can use these public ranges. Some even have exotic rental guns available so shooters can blast away with guns they would never seriously consider owning. Like my German correspondent said, "this is a sporting purpose I wish my country allowed."

Immigrants to Belgium can bring their guns with them. Strict registration and qualification rules are in effect.

Large numbers of firearms and ammunition are imported into Belgium virtually daily. Arms traffic in and out is still heavy, leading those with whom I correspond to conclude gun collections can probably be brought into Belgium by individual owners. At the least, gun buffs who own real estate in Belgium could bring guns into a bonded customs warehouse where they would be held safely till everything was sorted out.

Securing a dealer, inventor, or firearms developer's permit is not particularly onerous in Belgium if sufficient time and money are available. These approvals apparently take a great deal of money for store location, secure storage facilities, and tools, and for a soundproof indoor range. One fellow thought it best to try to work out a cooperative deal with one of the large gun manufacturers in Liége rather than trying to go it alone, setting up a store or experiment-and-development facility. As in the U.S., gun shops come and go. Most cities have several. I saw four in Liége and two in Brussels. Only one store in Brussels sells pistols. They had a very nice selection of modern, antique and military models.

Cost of living in Belgium is very high, quickly reflected by their prices for scarce land, buildings and groceries. Most food is imported.

Gun ownership rules and regulations in Belgium come as a surprise to most Americans. Many rare and desirable guns are on offer in the many gun shops located throughout the country. It really is a gun enthusiast's paradise. English is so widely spoken that somebody to interpret is almost always on hand. French speakers probably have the best opportunity of assimilating.

In some regards their gun commerce isn't much different than it is in the U.S. In many ways their system is simpler and easier, especially compared to places such as New York City, Washington, D.C. and Chicago under Mayor Daley!

Chapter Six
Spain
World Rank: 44 • Firearm Freedom 30%

Spain at one time supported a healthy, vibrant national gun industry. Many of their designs were cheap knockoffs, but they also produced some novel and futuristic designs as well as some truly quality, highly finished firearms traded internationally at reasonable prices.

It was to Spain, for instance, that surviving members of the Mauser factory moved after WW II in an attempt to keep their company alive. Reasonably priced high-quality double rifles and shotguns poured into our American market from Spain. Old timers recall that during the late 1950s and 1960s, Stoeger Arms carried high-grade Spanish Sarasqueta double rifles that competed handily with English doubles.

Oh, but how times change. Nowadays, Spanish citizens can privately own some firearms but it isn't easy. A ruinous civil war that saw the deaths of three-out-of-five adult males, a lengthy period of unrest that included massive numbers of political assassinations and extensive terrorist activity in the provinces have "put paid" (settled the matter) to the Spanish gun industry as well as individual gun rights. Currently, individual gun rights in Spain are at an all time low.

Economically and demographically Spain is no longer Europe's poor, underdeveloped backwater. *Per capita* income has risen to about $23,300. Real growth in recent years has been mixed at best. Due to rampant inflation, it has sometimes fallen into negative territory.

Spain's land area is about 195,000 square miles, making it a very large country by European standards. Oceans border Spain on two sides, the

Mediterranean on the south and the Atlantic on the north. To the northeast Spain shares a border with France.

Since the demise of General Franco and his classical fascist regime on Nov. 20, 1975, Spain has been a parliamentary monarchy with a strong man, center left, prime minister. Bringing back their king seven days after Franco's death turned out to be a stroke of genius. Most Spaniards trace their country's ascension from the economic pits to the basically hands-off management style of this uncommonly wise man.

Property rights and rule of law in their own Spanish cultural context are reasonably and evenly enforced in Spain. Some of the bloom is fading, but Spain has been a popular tourist/retirement destination for Americans. Changes occur rapidly, but currently Spain is inexpensive for Americans living on fixed-dollar incomes.

Sources of information for this chapter come as a result of travel in Spain and, more particularly as the result of the efforts of the wife of an American missionary living there. After living in Spain a total of 20-plus years, her Castilian Spanish is excellent and she knows a great many people whom she kindly contacted for us for this chapter.

Initially she called people at a Spanish gun-and-ammunition manufacturing company and then a sporting-goods store in Madrid. She also inquired at the offices of the Guardia Civil, the Spanish bureaucracy charged with enforcing Spanish gun laws.

She should have been able to secure good, accurate, current data but culture intervened. All of these folks thought it strange that a woman would ask such questions. Various people and agencies provided wildly conflicting information. As a result, she drafted a male member from another missionary family to inquire. This fellow was a hunter and gun owner used to dealing with Spanish gun-control bureaucrats.

Other than realizing that this information was heavily filtered through people with a much-deserved reputation as consummate bad-asses, this fellow's results were amazingly good. Only in the matter of illegal guns in Spain is it necessary to read between the lines.

From this we can conclude that private ownership of firearms by private citizens is presently possible in Spain. But hold onto your pen, wallet and chair, not necessarily in that order. There is lots of paperwork as well as numerous restrictions.

Gun-owners' permits are secured from the Guardia Civil Intervention of Armas office nearest you. Before and as an integral, simultaneous part of securing a private gun-owner's permit, you must secure membership in a private target-shooting association and/or a current hunting license.

Spanish hunting licenses are unique, perhaps throughout the world. They are issued by the Ministry of Justice after you have proven yourself to be a worthy qualified individual. This qualification must include the following:

• Proof that there is no outstanding criminal record.

• Results of a medical examination that demonstrates the applicant can hear and see, and has good adequate reflexes. Tests are actually prescribed to test an applicant's reflexes. Any current medications and past surgical procedures are noted relative to their possible influence on the applicant's ability to handle a firearm.

• Proof that the applicant has hunter-liability insurance as required by law. Minimum cost of this insurance is about $15 per year. A better plan for richer folks with more assets to protect will run about $25 annually.

• There is also the requirement that an $11 bank deposit be placed in an arms-permission account. This amount may eventually be refunded, but at this small dollar amount who really cares? Application requires proof of this deposit.

• Two photocopies of your passport, birth certificate or, for foreigners, their legal-residency permit. Usually it is only one of the above.

• All of this paper goes to Madrid to the Ministry of Justice for processing. Cost of the permit application is about $50, not including all of the expenses incurred in assembling the other stuff.

Count on a full month for processing unless your attorney takes it in personally. With personal service, approval can be given in as little as one working day. Attorneys are frequently required for the first gun-owner's permit, since it often isn't what you say, but how it is said on the permit application that matters. At the end there is a valid, current gun-owner's permit as well as a hunting license. Gun permits must always stay with the person carrying or owning the guns.

Gun owners now may legally own as many as six .22 target rifles (but, significantly, no .22s are allowed for hunting in Spain). A total of six shotguns, five rifles for big-game hunting, and ten pistols are also permitted. All pistols must be suitable for target shooting. All Spanish pistol owners must also be registered at a target-shooting club. Hunting with a pistol is not permitted. Hunting- and/or target-shooting-club memberships are relatively easy and can be relatively inexpensive or ruinously expensive, depending on whom you want to associate with.

Machine guns and pistols are absolutely forbidden, as well as any rifle or shotgun "that would be classified as military." This restriction effectively closes the door on semi-automatic hunting rifles, shotguns and assault rifles for private gun-license holders in Spain.

Shotguns must be physically taken every five years to your friendly neighborhood Guardia Civil office for an on-site inspection. Hunting rifles and target pistols must see the national police every three years.

Designation of weapons as to their "hunting purpose" can be arbitrary. After saying that no military-type guns are permitted, the authorities claim that virtually any make, model, caliber or design would be permitted if it is a hunting gun. Could this conceivably stretch into a G-3 H&K or an FN assault rifle? I don't know, but this is exactly what the man with the boots told us.

There are still a few gun shops scattered about Spain. Rather than supporting its own indigenous citizen hunters, Spain mainly attracts mega-rich Italians and Germans who throw thousands per day at shooting multiple quail, doves and rabbits. Spain is still a rural agricultural country. About 20 percent still live on the farm. Many of these folks hunt, both for sport and for food. Poaching is common. Land owners—many of them absentees—own all the game. Hunters who shoot game on the land of another must give it to them, in theory. Landowners often sell game back to the hunters who harvested it.

Some of these farmers may use illegal guns. Spanish officials won't comment on illegal guns other than to say that their laws are rigorously enforced. Yet, after all of their civil wars and commotion, it seems illogical to assume there are few or no illegal guns out there.

Border checks can be superficial in Europe. Russian firearms could easily move down out of former East Germany into Spain. We just don't know, and perhaps Spanish bureaucrats don't know either.

Ammunition is sold in sporting-goods stores, but only to people with gun-owners' permits. Corte Ingles, a large chain of department stores, handles ammunition for Spanish hunters. Shot shells are sold without restriction other than presentation of a valid gun-owner's permit.

Ammunition for pistols is very tightly controlled. How much is purchased and how much is fired at the range are both recorded in a permanent registry. Rifle ammo is also controlled. Within reason, given high prices in Spain, there does not seem to be a limit on quantity. But all rifle ammo purchased is registered to the exact rifle for which it is purchased.

Few Spaniards hand load. What few do find that all components are registered, same as for loaded rounds. All component purchases are reported to the Guardia Civil. Spanish bureaucrats at the Guardia Civil urge that I include a statement in my report that Spain has lots of paperwork and is known for its control of firearms.

Non-citizen residents of Spain can legally own firearms. They must go through all of the permitting process same as citizens. They can also bring acceptable shotguns, rifles and pistols into the country if they are willing to get all of the permits lined up after they are there.

One last comment about Spanish gun laws seems especially poignant. This also from a bureaucrat at Guardia Civil. "Spain is a beautiful place to hunt," he lectured. "Be ready for tight restrictions, but it can all be worked out with time and lots of money."

Members of Guardia Civil are notorious, my informant said, in this previously corrupt society, for not taking bribes. Perhaps he referred to subjective interpretations of their gun laws, or payment of additional fees. We just don't know.

Spain would not seem to be a favorable place for gun inventors, tinkerers and developers. Direct inquiry would have to be made at the Ministry of Justice on how to proceed on these types of licenses.

On the scarier side, it seems possible to detect some of the more onerous proposals made by American anti-gunners in Spanish licensing procedures. Their requirement for liability insurance, which in the U.S. would be very expensive, is a good example. From time to time this issue is floated by American anti-gunners, as a deterrent to gun ownership.

Chapter Seven
Portugal
World Rank: 43 • Firearm Freedom 31%

Reasons for covering firearms laws in Portugal say quite a bit about the philosophy, necessary procedure and background of preparing a book of this nature.

Rumor had it that officials in Portugal were mellow to very mellow—even lenient—about granting interested, financially responsible citizens the ability to own, tinker with, and do research on firearms of all types including military small arms. It's a small country where everyone knew and trusted everyone else and all that.

All it took, the urban legend read, was a modest amount of money to purchase a special permit. Just about anyone except known felons and obvious pissants could own and fire machine guns in Portugal as well as engage in design and development work on all sorts of guns.

Origin of this rumor is lost in history. Perhaps it's from the time I lived and worked there 30 years ago.

There is some logic here. Portugal is a rough and ready little place, known for export of hairy-chested adventurers to its many far-flung, rough-and-tumble colonies. I knew first hand there were lots of firearms of all kinds in their colonies and supposed that Portuguese citizens had to learn to use them someplace. There is also the matter of a tiny country not wanting to be overrun and of also wanting exportable technological development. As a single category, international trade in guns and ammunition is larger than trade in any other class of goods. Israel and China are good examples of countries that use the arms business to help balance their international trade. Perhaps the Portuguese were interested in profiting from international trade in guns and ammo. I found it important that we check first hand whether any of this is actually true.

Portugal is a tiny band-aid on the backside of Spain, stretching along the Atlantic coast about 350 miles. Ten million Portuguese inhabit this little Indiana-sized country on the west side of the Iberian Peninsula. Much of it is hilly and sparse, characterized by southern-California-type vegetation and soils with wine-grape covered sandy hills.

Until late 1985, Portugal was a hard-core socialist enclave. Lately there is some evidence that an open, free-market economy is being allowed to develop. But the government still takes more than half of everything produced in the country for its own desire and pleasure. *Per capita* income at most is about $17,900. Until the last few years this amount was increasing in a most laudatory fashion.

Here we find a pleasant, almost quaint place characterized by good roads and inexpensive living including many nice beaches and resorts. Theirs is a not quite mature system of rule of law and property rights. Currently many retired Americans, Brits and former citizens own retirement villas along beautiful beaches in Portugal. This because of their much lower labor rates—especially in the informal (read "black") economy—and because of easy access in this era to rapid jet travel. Nice second homes on a bit of Portuguese land are comparatively inexpensive. Historically, money sent by Portuguese abroad back to their home country has injected life into an otherwise dull economy. In summary, Portugal can easily be characterized as a clean, neat, orderly place far removed from its Third World origins but one still beset by an often heavy-handed government creating a stodgy, unremarkable economy.

Uncovering information on Portugal's gun laws was both difficult and then illuminating. I learned not to rely on rumor or hearsay or on information from others prone to engage in wishful thinking.

In a method somewhat reminiscent of Spain, my initial yet sketchy
source of information was an American missionary living in Portugal.
At the time he had lived there more than 22 years. He is also an ardent
gun owner/hunter. Additionally, we eventually managed to assemble
the following data from personal conversations with local gun-shop
owners, local police officers and local gun owners. All seems to be
completely logical, and at this moment authoritative. With exception
of rules regarding hand loading, there is no indication gun laws are
changing dramatically in Portugal. Most of these gun laws have been
on the books a great number of years.

Depending a bit on firearms type, private gun ownership is legal in
Portugal. We talked to several gun owners who currently owned
multiple weapons, leading to the conclusion that legal ownership is
even fairly common. Illegal ownership is thought to be endemic.
Sporting-type shotguns, a few pistols, and hunting rifles are among
those frequently seen in private legal gun racks.

Those who can convince the authorities that they have a legitimate
hunting or target shooting need for them can even own modern assault
rifles. We saw several current model H&Ks for sale in a gun store in
Lisbon, with a requirement that they use ammo not currently used by
the military. Under this definition, one rifle fired .308 Winchester—not
7.62 NATO, the other was for .45 ACP, also currently not a military
caliber—at least not in the eyes of the Portuguese bureaucracy.

As an aside, it seems Portuguese gun owners favor rifles firing pistol
cartridges, allowing them to more easily purchase ammo for an
illegally held sidearm. They also favor legal Ruger camp rifles using
7.63x39 rounds. This we were told is because so many illegal AK-47s
flooded in from the colonies and Eastern Europe. AK owners were
looking for a legal and convenient source of ammo, gun-store clerks
explained.

Machine guns, submachine guns or machine pistols were not legal
under any circumstances. Not even bank guards or security personnel
can legally hold them.

Portuguese citizens can legally own a total of two pistols, neither of
which can be in what the government defines as military or police
calibers, a requirement that rules out 9mm, .38 special, or .357 pistols.
As a result, .22, .25 ACP, .32 S&W, .32 Long Colt, 7.62 x .25, or .45
ACP pistols are popular. Citizens contemplating purchasing a pistol
must convince the authorities they need the weapon for self defense or
for target practice. Accomplished, proven target-pistol shooters can
qualify for an advanced ownership approval that includes .38, .357 or
9mm pistols. This last advanced authorization is uncommon.

Portuguese gun store

A nice gun shop in Lisbon, Portugal, with its "Abierto" (Open) sign prominently displayed, along with its phone number for easy contact. While here, I was informed that a Russian RPG-7 rocket-propelled grenade could be had on their black market for $2,500. I had the funds, but there was no place to try firing the thing, and since I couldn't bring it back to the states, I passed on the opportunity.

Pistols in these three calibers are purchased from local gun shops but ammo must be bought and paid for at central police stores by those with an advanced, proven target-shooting authorization.

No hunting with pistols is permitted in Portugal. Joining a pistol-shooting club is evidence that one needs a target pistol. Portuguese commonly join hunting or target-shooting clubs, but never show up at the club for meetings or to practice. On average, club membership runs about $125 per year. "Just a part of a gun owner's overhead," gun owners said.

Pistol-ownership permits, either for target shooting or for defense, also convey an immediate right to carry concealed. "We would be amazed and perhaps shocked to realize how many Portuguese currently carry concealed," we were told, but there's little violent crime in little Portugal. Significant numbers of the pistols on offer in local gun stores were smaller, easily concealed North American Arms derringer-type revolvers. Incidence of illegal carry is also said to be high.

Portugal is not characterized by the three-locks-on-every-door paranoia common to Spain. Perhaps because so many folks carry and because shooting an intruder is legal so long as the homeowner can maintain he thought the intruder had "fire in his hand." Portugal is no different than the rest of the world where fear of instant retribution is a significant deterrent to criminals.

Permits for shotguns and .22 or .17 rimfire rifles are relatively easy. More citizens have these permits than for large-bore rifles and pistols combined. Permit holders can legally own pump, double-barrel, single-barrel and semi-auto shotguns as well as rimfire rifles of virtually any style. Many gun stores have some of each. Supposedly no limit on numbers of these one can legally own. Military or police models are allegedly permitted, but we did not see them for sale in gun shops.

Start the process of gun ownership by going first to the Office of Public Safety at the local police department. There, after paying the $150 fee, you receive a stack of forms to fill out, with different forms for each class of weapon. Applicants must demonstrate fiscal responsibility, soundness of mind and no criminal record. Approval usually takes about two months. Although one-year licenses are available, most gun owners elect three-year ones. Renewal is said to be reasonably easy.

Local police use the forms to do a background check. After the check, you must submit to a personal interview with a bureaucrat from the Office of Public Safety. Although securing a shotgun permit is the simplest, all of these procedures are a bit tricky. Local gun dealers often supply neophytes with politically correct answers.

Theoretically no limit exists to the number of shotguns and rifles an individual private citizen can own in Portugal. Although large-scale collectors are out there, local bureaucrats have arbitrary powers over decisions regarding how many guns a person really "needs." Permits are issued for each and every gun. Officials demand a good reason for approving any and all guns. As a practical "on the ground" matter, severe restrictions on total numbers are frequently enforced.

As mentioned, rifles travel through a much more difficult permission process. Owners must prove they will always use their rifles for lawful hunting or target shooting. Membership in either a hunting or target-shooting club may be construed as proof of actual legal intent.

Oddly, absolutely no rifle that has been altered or modified in any way from its original factory commercial configuration is permitted. This probably rules out most inexpensive military surplus guns and "sporterization" of such.

Once a gun-owner's permit is authorized and issued by the police, the recipient takes this authorization to a local gun shop. This authorizes purchase of a pistol, large-bore rifle, shotgun or rimfire rifle. As mentioned, authorization of a shotgun or rimfire rifle is much easier than for a large-bore rifle or pistol of any kind.

Having made a selection, the gun owner trots back to the police to have the weapons or weapon listed down on the permit. Only then can the new owner take actual physical possession.

There are some stores that sell firearms in Portugal, but not many. Few outside big cities try to stock rifle and pistol ammo. Perhaps because more citizens own shotguns and rimfires, shot shells and rimfire ammo are more commonly available. Ammo sales are tightly controlled. Show your gun permit and record in the book, please. Only 100 rounds per day per firearm listed on your permit are allowed. Prices for both guns and ammo are about the same, in Euros as in Dollars in the U.S., which means guns and ammo cost about 25% more in Portugal.

There is no limit on amounts of rimfire or shotgun ammo one may purchase in total, and all sales are recorded to the license.

Hand loading ammunition is currently permitted in Portugal. Sales of powder, primers and bullets currently occur without restriction or registration. Price of a kilo of either smokeless or black powder is under $50, a bit more than in the U.S. ($16-$18 per pound.) Both Portuguese gun bureaucrats and gun owners envision this current lack of control on hand loading as cautionary. They expect more severe controls soon. No restrictions currently apply on sales, ownership or use of muzzle-loading rifles, pistols or shotguns.

Tens of thousands of illegal guns of all types and kinds—even including Russian RPG-7 rocket propelled grenades—are easily available, we were told. Reportedly their origin is former Yugoslavia, Portuguese colonies or Eastern Europe. Portuguese claim to track illegal ownership by numbers of incidents that occur with them.

Silencers are illegal but at lest one private gun owner we talked with had a permanently mounted homemade model on a Walther .22 semi-auto rifle. Oddly, it was out in plain sight. Seemed to be very well made. The owner said it functioned very well.

Bringing some guns into Portugal by those moving there is possible if they are of the correct type and you does your homework prior to showing up at the border with them.

Portugal last experienced a military revolution in 1974. But, this was a quick and mainly bloodless affair confined to the military and to adult participating politicians. Guns were involved, but not in the hands of many citizens.

Portuguese soldiers fought in WW I, but their government kept neutral in WW II till it was obvious in 1943 that Hitler would not prevail. After that they leased some ports and airfields to the Allies for use in the war effort. As a result, left-behind guns and ammunition are probably pretty tough to find.

Portuguese government officials have absolutely no desire to form a world-class small-arms industry or interest in experimental weapons. They have some military manufacturing of guns and ammunition, sometimes seen on world surplus markets. These are actually military owned and run concerns. Often they sell for less than the cost of production, judging by the low prices they put on their stuff.

Although a very nice, clean, neat, orderly society with many modern goods and services, this is not a place gun owners would ever consider living. Legal gun ownership is possible for many makes and models, but certainly not easy.

Chapter Eight
Denmark
World Rank: 40 • Firearm Freedom 34%

Scandinavian countries have a bit of a reputation both for fairly easy gun ownership and for indigenous gun cultures. Something to do with their Nordic warrior heritage and being overrun from time to time by each other and their other near neighbors.

Denmark is a tea-cup-sized nation, about half the size of Maine, on a peninsula and some islands directly north of Germany. Copenhagen, the capital, is actually on an island. It isn't even a very big island. English is widely spoken in Denmark, especially in gun stores.

Denmark is the southernmost of the Scandinavian countries, but its climate is still a tinge rigorous. It lies on the same latitude as central Canada, and would be as cold as central Manitoba and Saskatchewan were it not for surrounding oceans and their warming currents.

Something slightly less than five-and-a-half-million souls call Denmark home, dramatically increasing their difficulties accommodating hunting and a gun culture. This is in part because—like their German neighbors—Danes insist on a sporting purpose for all civilian-owned firearms. They just don't have the luxury of much land for sport shooting and hunting.

Old money constitutes much of Denmark's wealth. *Per capita* income has been relatively high for a great number of years now. Currently it is about $32,200, indicating that Denmark would be an expensive place in which to live. While doing research for this chapter in Denmark, we set a new world record—$51.86 for two pots (four cups) of coffee, two very small pieces of chocolate cake and one medium chunk of Black Forest torte in the tiny rural village of Schackenborg. Not to worry. We got off easy. The same would have been $81.86 in expensive Copenhagen.

Most changes occur gradually in Denmark. They have been a constitutional monarchy since 1849. Although their society has veered sharply off into socialism, rules of law and property rights have remained well established.

Denmark was suddenly and capriciously invaded by Germany in 1940. King Christian X reluctantly cautioned his countrymen to quietly accept the situation in which they found themselves. Germany, in turn, attempted to rule their near cousins "with a velvet glove," but there was still widespread insurrection and resistance. Denmark was finally liberated by British soldiers in May of 1945.

Danish citizens quietly acknowledged some limited role of left-behind guns in their country as well as the fact that black-market military guns from the east easily cross into their essentially borderless nation.

Information for this chapter came via a Danish gun collectors' association, numerous visits on the part of the author to the country, and a delightful interview with a lady exchange student attending one of our universities. Coincidentally she was an accomplished hunter and gun buff of the first order. Her practical knowledge in these areas was superb and much admired.

In spite of these many sources, it seemed that my gun-law information on Denmark was a bit filtered and biased, and at times purposely left incomplete. It's as if each correspondent attempted to protect some private secret regarding parts of this issue. Perhaps there is more illegal gun and ammunition ownership in Denmark than they let on, and they were part of it. We just do not know.

Denmark's gun situation is characterized by several anomalies unique in all of the world. They are a society that, till very recently (15 years ago), enjoyed some of the freest gun laws on Earth. Then they quickly moved to a restrictive situation with several overlapping licenses required. At the same time, it became trendy in Denmark to be a gun owner/shooter. It is sort of a mark of an aristocrat who had arrived at a just station in life with sufficient funds to support the sport.

Relatively large numbers of Danes voluntarily subject themselves to the considerable hassle of getting all the permits necessary to own guns, in part so they can impress their friends. Private ownership of rifles, pistols and shotguns and—to some restricted extent—machine guns and pistols, is allowed in tiny, real estate-challenged Denmark.

Ownership is allowed, but each and every gun must be separately approved and separately licensed. This approval requires multiple, overlapping, complementary licenses and permits, some of which are difficult to obtain. Expect the process to span about four months.

Simultaneous with going to their local police headquarters for a gun-owner's permit application, potential gun owners must establish membership with a shooting club and/or begin the process of securing a hunting license. Shooting-club membership can be expensive, but does not require schooling, testing and qualifications other than those regulations imposed by the shooting club itself. Those who wish to take out a membership can usually do so by just signing on the dotted line and forking over enough Kroner. Private target-pistol clubs charge about 260 Kroner/year ($44) for a basic membership.

After two years of active membership it is possible to successfully apply at the local police for a permit to purchase a pistol, with no limit on numbers of pistols, so long as there is a valid (in the eyes of controlling bureaucrats) reason for each. Target shooting is the only valid reason for pistol ownership in Denmark. Popular permitted ones include .22, .38, .357, .45 and 9mm. This seems to be about all of the pistol calibers except .32 and .30, which may be construed as police calibers and arbitrarily forbidden.

In so far as applying for permits to own rifles and shotguns, application for a gun permit and membership in a hunting/shooting club can be simultaneous. Yet, it still takes about four months for firearms paperwork to wend its way through the system in Denmark.

Hunting licenses are something else again. Great obstacles are thrown up, ensuring that not many citizens can get them. Applicants are extensively tested for their knowledge of guns, ammunition and game characteristics and habits. About one third fail the first time they take the test. Between classroom study, practical field-craft practice and testing most applicants take a year to get their hunting licenses.

Once granted, a general hunting license is valid as long as the 370 Kroner annual fee is paid ($67.20).

No public lands exist in Denmark on which hunting by the general public is permitted. Private landowners, including farmers, have a somewhat easier time securing a license for a rifle or shotgun than others who have no specific place in which to hunt.

The answer, for non-farmers and those with no land holdings, is private clubs that have leased tracts of land for members to use. Memberships range in price from little to a whole lot, depending on how much game and how well tended that game. Pistols are not allowed for hunting.

Rifle permits, including rifles with telescopic sights, are issued only for hunting or target guns, with no restriction on model or caliber so long as it is not a military rifle. Assault rifles under this scheme of things are completely prohibited. Only bolt actions, single shots, double-barreled rifles and drillings are acceptable as hunting rifles.

Having recently been overrun by militant neighbors, one would expect Denmark to be accepting of a standing citizen militia. They are, to some extent. Called the "Home Guard," these people have military assault rifles, and machine guns and pistols under their own care and protection at home. These people are all members of the regular Danish Army.

Non-citizens of Denmark cannot secure permits to own guns, nor can they be members of the "Home Guard." This also precludes non-citizens moving to Denmark from bringing any of their personal guns.

Recall again that multiple pistol, rifle and shotgun permits are allowed, but that a separate permit from the local police is required for each and every gun. These permits are never issued unless there is a valid reason for that specific gun. Apparently research and development collecting is not a valid reason. Are reasons subjective and obscure? Danish bureaucrats say "no," and that each individual should fill out their own application rather than having an attorney do it.

All firearms permits must be renewed annually. Oddly enough, shotgun permits are not appreciably easier to acquire in Denmark than rifle permits. In this, the Danes are unique throughout the world.

Shotgun applicants must be members of a hunting club, have a hunting license, or be members of a trap-and-skeet club. Heavy restrictions exist on makes and models of shotguns. No pumps, semi-autos, and no shotgun pistols are allowed. Denmark is one of the few places to specifically mention shotgun pistols.

Hand loading is permitted if you have their special permit for such. All reloading components are registered, similar to loaded ammunition. Still, hand loading is said to be common and popular in Denmark.

Other than the fact that ammunition is ruinously expensive, there are no restrictions on amounts that can be purchased. Sales are restricted to those with specific gun permits and are all recorded to that specific permit and weapon.

Rules regarding gun and ammunition storage are also severe. All guns must be stored in special gunrooms of a prescribed (and expensive) soundness and construction. In all cases double locks are required. Ammo must be locked away separately from the guns. Ammo can never be legally transported with guns when traveling to the shooting club or target range.

Even given its pocket size, there are several reasonably large gun stores spotted about Denmark. Quite a large selection of guns as well as extensive inventories of ammunition are available to qualified buyers. Entrance into locked and guarded retail gunrooms at these stores is only possible on display of one's current gun-owner's permit.

Danish citizens seem genuinely surprised by reports of illegal guns among them. They recall that several years ago members of a local Hells Angels motorcycle club were caught with illegal machine guns. The news scandalized the country. Nevertheless, most acknowledge that left-behinds from wars and guns illegally smuggled into Denmark from the eastern nations could be around. Illegal gun ownership in Denmark is considered to be a very serious crime.

Denmark has no indigenous gun industry and appears not to want one. There are no licenses or permits for collectors, tinkerers or developers. Dealers' licenses are difficult for citizens and impossible for non-citizens.

Due to climate, expensive living and very restrictive rules and regulations, it is doubtful if any American gun owners would wish to take up residence in Denmark.

Chapter Nine
Sweden
World Rank: 25 • Firearm Freedom 51%

Sweden is a pretty decent place for gun owners. Many aspects of their rules and regulations bring Switzerland to mind. In some regards their system is superior to the U.S. Yet there is something about the country to discomfit almost everyone.

Liberals dislike Sweden's generous, open, trusting gun laws and low crime rate. Conservatives take great exception to Sweden's socialistic government, terribly high tax rates and Swedish tolerance of pornography. Some conservative American gun owners are inherently suspicious of the actual manner in which Swedish society extends its liberal gun rights.

Researching and analyzing Swedish gun laws proved to be difficult and, at times, uncertain. This uncertainty because they are so culturally different than the U.S.

Modern Sweden occupies roughly the eastern half of the Scandinavian Peninsula. Norway lies to the west and Finland and the Baltic Sea to the eastern south. Swedish territory stretches way up north into some extremely inhospitable country. One hundred and seventy miles of Sweden lie north of the Arctic Circle. Not many people, cities or even reindeer roam in these barren parts.

By European standards, Sweden is huge, rough-hewn and somewhat uncivilized. Sweden is fully a tenth larger than California. *Per capita* income is roughly $28,400. Their real growth rate, after inflation, has been stuck in the mud for a number of years. Cost of living for Swedes is high. Part of this is attributable to their need for warmer, better-built houses and factories, and part to the fact that the government forcibly takes more than half their income.

Economists attribute Sweden's less-than-enthusiastic economic expansion to the fact that twice as many citizens are on the government payroll as in the private sector, and to the fact that there is little incentive to work hard because of sky-high, confiscatory tax rates.

Neutral Sweden sat out both world wars. As a result, their cities, factories and roads survived intact. Reasons the Nazis did not attack Sweden are roughly similar to why they left Switzerland alone. Similar philosophies apply. Losses at the hands of irregular citizen defenders would have been unacceptably high.

Both Sweden and Switzerland are countries of rough, rugged terrain, easily defended by determined citizen soldiers who know how to man the fortress. Both countries have very high percentages of citizen gun owners who already know how to shoot well, and who could be counted on to resolutely defend the homeland.

Surrounding oceans temper Sweden's climate a bit, but generally theirs is a land of ice and snow, even in the south. It isn't for nothing that many Swedish immigrants to the U.S. choose to settle in northern Michigan or Minnesota. English is widely spoken. It is the second language in Swedish schools and has so infiltrated their firearms nomenclature that speaking with Swedes in gun shops was easy.

Information on Swedish gun laws was so startling I rechecked several different sources. It might have been easy to get caught up with the optimism of some Swedish gun buffs with whom I first checked. As a result, I checked with other sources to be certain what I was hearing was substantially correct. A gun-owner friend in the city of Unca, Sweden, got the ball rolling. Then I checked with some gun stores and a gun collectors' association. Eventually I visited there myself.

What follows suggests that American gun owners may be justified in worrying that a conquering aggressor might use gun registrations to roll up internal resistance. All of the many guns Swedish citizens own are registered with their authorities.

Private ownership of pistols, rifles, shotguns, submachine guns and machine guns is legal and possible in Sweden. There are multiple rules and regulations, but these are generally not overly difficult. As a general rule, the rules are administered by folks who are at least somewhat sympathetic to the gun-culture citizens they serve.

As a quick example, hunting licenses are required as a demonstration of a need for some rifles and shotguns. Applicants must correctly answer 80 questions as well as demonstrate proficiency with a shotgun and rifle. Proficiency, in this case, involves six shots for a shotgun and a three- or four-round series from a rifle at standing and running moose targets. "An easy test to make," to quote my Swedish hunter friends.

Although virtually any gun is theoretically permitted, absolutely every gun must be covered by a permit issued by the local police. For each and every one of these permits, there must be an acceptable reason to own that specific gun. Hunting with rifle and shotgun is almost always a good, acceptable reason. Collecting, studying and doing design work is a good reason. Being a member of a club that target shoots with assault rifles, machine guns or pistols is also generally considered to be a good reason.

Plinking in the back yard of your summer home is not an acceptable reason. An immediate desire to own a pistol is not a good reason, but six months' membership in a recognized pistol club is a good reason.

Because some reasons can initially seem a little arbitrary, Swedish gun owners often conspire with shop owners or other private gun owners to come up with acceptable reasons. They may even ask their local bureaucrat what reason would be acceptable. Sweden is a society of strong property rights and rule of law. It is seldom, if ever, a matter of an under the table payment for a favorable opinion. It is a matter of asking correctly and of being a reputable person.

Each firearm must be registered and approved by the local police. Registration costs about $20 per firearm, but is for the life of the gun or the owner, whichever expires first.

As a practical matter, there is official stigma to owning too many guns. Swedish rules suggest that one can have a total of only six rifles, unless you are a professional hunter or target shooter. But what is that? Rules, in this case, seem flexible. High-powered pistols are easily permitted for target shooting, for those who have already been members of a pistol-shooting club six months. No pistol hunting is allowed here. For the next two or three pistols, reasons must be increasingly clever and original.

Purchase and possession of three .22 LR pistols is far easier than purchase of three .44 mag revolvers. Even in the case of multiple .44 mag revolvers, if you can make a good case for the fact that you are a serious target shooter, collector or design expert, permission will likely be given.

Some restrictions on use of semi-autos for hunting apply. Nevertheless, Swedish gun stores carry Browning semi-auto hunting rifles (BARs) (cost is about $370) and some Finnish Valmets ($520).

Assault rifles are permitted if the purchaser can show a need to use these weapons for competitive target shooting. Fortunately there are many target-shooting clubs from which to choose in Sweden, including some for machine guns, assault rifles and submachine guns.

All types and models of shotguns are permitted. Like all other weapons, shotgun owners must demonstrate a need by having a hunting license or a skeet or trap-club affiliation. Current gun catalogs show Browning pumps ($790), Beretta semi-automatics ($550), and Merkel double barrels ($600).

Although we might take exception with how they reach their final conclusion, Swedish gun laws are generally calculated to keep pissants, ne'er-do-wells, and convicted felons from owning guns. Local officials in small rural areas take great pride in knowing exactly whom they are dealing with, and for not issuing permits to bad actors.

Virtually every town and village in Sweden has a gun shop. Mostly they carry utilitarian type sporting rifles, shotguns and pistols. Some larger specialty shops have or can order machine guns and pistols.

Sweden has a great number of private and a few public shooting ranges. They are scattered about the country. Anyone who pays their fees can use these ranges. Fees are not particularly high. Foreigners can use these ranges but may be asked to demonstrate that they legally own the guns with which they wish to hunt or target shoot—i.e. you may be asked to show your gun permit.

Foreign residents living in Sweden cannot generally secure a gun permit. Therefore it is impossible for foreigners to go to Sweden to purchase firearms. Residents of other Scandinavian countries can legally bring their guns with them when they come to Sweden. As a practical matter, these are the only outsiders who can easily shoot on Swedish ranges, especially if they use legally owned guns borrowed from a friend.

Gun owners with a valid permit for a weapon can purchase as much ammunition as they wish for that specific weapon. While quantities are not restricted, there is again the necessity of demonstrating a need for ammunition for a specific firearm that is legally held by the owner. Gun-store clerks keep a record of ammo purchases which is generally not checked by the authorities, unless there is a problem.

Ammunition is not particularly pricey in Sweden. They have their own manufactured at the Norma Projektilfabrik at Amotfors. American gun owners probably recognize the name Norma, or perhaps Dynamit Nobel-RWS. Surplus ammo is available, but even that is considered to be high priced by Swedish gun owners who shoot quite a lot.

Hand loading is common in Sweden, especially for frequent-blaster Swedish gun owners who want to shoot more on a limited budget. Powder, primers and bullets are easily purchased across the counter. There's no necessity to show a gun permit or any other authorization and no limits on quantities.

Swedish gun owners are tightly constrained however by rules requiring their guns to be stored in an approved, locked, welded steel safe.

Firearms research and development is possible for Swedish citizens living in Sweden. Should an actual, workable weapon spring from this work, a permit must be secured well before that gun is finished and functional. Again, a need to have it must be demonstrated before permits are issued.

Dealers' permits are reasonably easy to secure. Swedish rules require sales of at least 20 guns annually or the license is lost. Securing a zoning permit to build a store, or to locate to an existing building, seems to be more challenging than securing a license to deal firearms.

Illegal firearms do not seem to be a problem in Sweden. Authorities do take a dim view of illegal, unlicensed ownership, but even this seems a bit relaxed. Definitely enforcement is subjective. "If you are an old man caught with a WW II Mauser rifle, it is much different than being a young kid with a stolen submachine gun," I was told.

No modern wars have rolled over Sweden with their left-behind guns. Like most of Europe, Sweden has no patrolled borders. Just drive across one place to the next. Lucky travelers might receive a smart salute from the guard in a little wooden house and that is all.

Illegal AK-47s could easily arrive from former East Germany, Russia or Lithuania. Maybe they do, but the Swedes seem largely unaware or perhaps they don't wish to talk to me about the situation.

Registering most guns in the country would seem dangerous, perhaps overly trusting of the bureaucracy, to most Americans. Especially for a country that prides itself on its neutrality among many war-like neighbors. Not much prevents an aggressor from seizing the country and then lists of gun owners who might resist.

Oddly, the Swedes also license the more powerful air guns, stun guns, muzzleloaders made after 1890, silencers and even crossbows. Permits to carry in self defense are very seldom granted. Shooting a person, even caught in the act of a heinous crime, is not legally acceptable.

As mentioned at the start, their rules and regulations are different. Gun buffs, of which there are many in Sweden, find them workable and acceptable, especially when they look out at places such as Portugal, Spain, France, or even the U.S. where full-autos are difficult.

American gun owners, who couldn't, under Swedish law, bring their guns to Sweden or purchase some when they are there, would probably not choose to live in Sweden. Still, their situation is extremely interesting, especially when we hear comments from American anti-gun people, "that there is no other civilized country on Earth that allows as many guns as in the U.S." Sweden proves "it just ain't so" and that their society probably accommodates more different guns than ours—and without unusually high crime rates.

Chapter Ten
Finland
World Rank: 7 • Firearm Freedom 87%

It doesn't really matter that Finland has only two seasons. Cold and damp, followed by cool and damp. Or that Finns do weird things like running naked in the cold snow from sauna to sauna, beating themselves with birch branches. The people, their laws and their personal resolve and responsibility are truly exemplary.

No doubt my perception of all of this is colored by the fact that we delighted in the year-long company of a Finnish exchange student and that time spent in Finland watching barley, potatoes and birch logs grow was some of the best.

Misguided travel editors with a limited concept of what is really important often gloss over little, remote Finland. Getting there is air-travel easy and, once there, visitors must dig deep to understand its delight. Most Finns speak English. Years ago they realized that, in a world economy, few people would ever lean difficult and archaic Finnish. Now their common second language, which all Finns learn well, is the *lingua franca* of the entire world.

From the moment one lands in Finland, there is the overpowering, ever-present breath of freedom. Not to be confused with their fierce sense of independence and can-do self-confidence, this general philosophic atmosphere prevails throughout. Only Switzerland compares. It is something very difficult to put in words. It must be experienced.

Plucky Finns tore their country from despotic Russian hands in 1917 at a time when the Russians were busy fighting each other. Finland is the eastern most of the Scandinavian countries, sandwiched between Russia on the east and Sweden on the west. Ohio is about one third the size of Finland. At least 20 percent of the country lies north of the Arctic Circle. High mountains in Finland's north create a cold, barren, wind-swept, rock strewn, desolate landscape.

Helsinki, Finland's capital, lies sufficiently north that it has, on average, only four hours of daylight daily during the long winter.

For a pile of rocks and endless birch groves, Finland is a surprisingly rich country. There are only about 5.5 million Finns. They earn about $29,000 annually, each. It's remarkable when one looks east over the same type of country and sees the abject poverty that still characterizes

Russia. Logically one would suppose envious Russians would copy the Finnish success rather than attempting to pillage and occupy.

Mistrust of anything Russian still runs extremely deep in Finland. Memories of the Russian invasion linger, and the citizenry maintains a high sense of awareness that it could happen again. They have privately retained heavy-duty arms to forestall such a possibility.

We should never allow American anti-gunners to tell us that we are the only people in the world who have a free, unencumbered firearms ownership system. Finland also puts the lie to those who claim that a citizen militia is of no value against a modern, well-trained, organized army. Not only do we have the example of the Spanish Civil War, the Warsaw ghetto, and partition of Israel—we also have the example of the Finnish Winter War.

The following is not apocryphal. Citizen Vickström proudly and confidently sits next to the Raate-Suomussami Highway in a small dacha with his private, legally owed Raikka 81mm recoilless rifle waiting for Russian T72 tanks. Too young to have participated in 1939 and early 1940, Vickström recalls with great pride how a mere handful of citizen border guards and teen-age reservists stopped two whole attacking Russian armies with full complement of tanks and artillery absolutely cold in their tracks. There were no anti-tank weapons other than Molotovs. Using little more than small arms and their ubiquitous cross-country skis, they broke up the invaders into small clumps and then systematically annihilated them virtually to the last man. Little Finland with its then four million beat the Russian bear with its 186 million. Few, if any, attackers made it home again.

Finland is a country of citizen soldiers. Russia has already bullied and bruised them twice in the last century. Today their firm commitment is that they will never, never do it again. This explains why Citizen Vickström holds himself in constant readiness and why he goes to the considerable private expense of owning his own recoilless rifle and ammunition on a retirement stipend. Finns exhibit an unusually high sense of personal responsibility.

Information for this chapter comes from a personal visit to Finland, and some of their gun stores, from official government literature, and from extensive conversations with our former exchange student who became a commissioned officer in the Finnish navy. To a limited extent, this information may be biased by the fact that our friendly Finn is now in the military where firearms ownership is easier, and that Finland must spend disproportionately on defense. That they share Scandinavian tendencies toward socialism might also bias this report in the opposite direction.

Private citizens in Finland can easily own shotguns, revolvers, pistols and rifles including semi-automatic assault rifles. Their laws are somewhat similar to Sweden's with the continuing test of need, but the needs test seems much easier to satisfy in Finland. Valmet of Finland produces some very high-quality assault rifles, ownership of which is not only permitted but, in many cases, seems to be encouraged. Gun shops in Helsinki, the capital, display a great number of rifles, shotguns and handguns.

I looked for some bargains amongst the many Sako rifles on display. But, alas, their exchange rate at the time worked against me. There were some Russian .22-caliber pistols at excellent prices, but I didn't recognize make and model and didn't want to fight my way back through to our starting gate in Germany with a pistol in our baggage.

There is no limit on the number, kind, make and model of guns that can be owned, including pistols. When a citizen wishes to purchase a shotgun or rifle, make application for a permit at the local police. You provide your name, address, social security number, profession and the gun model, serial number, caliber and other possible specifications. Permits are relatively inexpensive, about $20 each, and they are not difficult to obtain.

Perhaps because they do a more thorough background check, pistol purchasers must apply to the provincial or state police for that permit to purchase. Virtually anyone except those with obvious mental and physical impairments or criminal records will receive a pistol-purchase permit. This does not include the right to carry concealed or for use in one's defense. Like Sweden, Finland takes an extremely dim view of anyone who shoots another, even to prevent what we might regard as an extremely heinous crime.

Purchasers must have a reason for owning each and every gun. In Finland this is not a particularly high or onerous bar. Hunting and target shooting are commonly accepted reasons. Membership in a hunting or shooting club is helpful but not a requirement. Hunting and shooting club memberships are relatively cheap in a country where things tend to be fairly pricey, about $20 per month on average.

There appears to be little mystery to filling out a gun application. It is more important to be up front, than to phrase it correctly, Finnish gun owners claim. Given their past history, no doubt exists that these records will ever fall into an occupying enemy's hands.

Permits are also available to tinkerers and researchers who want to be licensed gun collectors. Cost is a one-time fee of slightly less than $100. Gun collectors are allowed machine guns and pistols, full-auto assault rifles, recoilless rifles, mortars and other such similar heavy military hardware. These permits come from provincial or state police offices nearest them. Given time, a reasonable demeanor, a demonstrable interest, ability and aptitude in these types of weapons plus a safe place to use them as well as a safe, secure place to store same, and a collector's permit is not particularly difficult to acquire.

The red carpet is out in Finland for any proven firearms-design engineers who wish to set up shop. Finland has an active military-hardware design, construction and export industry. Invitations to work in this business are extended on an individual basis, depending entirely on reputation and proven ability.

Finnish weapons collectors have several military supply centers where heavy weapons and ammo can be purchased. They also have dozens and dozens of little, medium and big gun stores strung out across the country. No Finnish citizen is ever far from a source of guns and ammunition. Retailing firearms in Finland reminds Americans of how it was forty years ago in the U.S.

Sales of ammunition are controlled, but not restricted. Buy just about as much as you want, need and can afford. Ammo sellers want to see a copy of your gun permit and some identification. Ammo in Finland is inexpensive to cheap. Lots of surplus ammo is available as well as their regular, home-manufactured varieties.

Hand loading is not common, but it is done by some Finnish shooters. All components are available at most gun stores. There are no restrictions on buying reloading components—no licenses, no recordings, no nothing.

As in Sweden and Demark, Finnish authorities are cranky about firearms storage. They require something safe and secure that can be locked up tight, especially for those in big cities or those who are accumulating several guns. Collectors are required to keep their heavy weapons and automatics out of sight in heavy steel lock-up cabinets.

In the instance of foreigners entering Finland with their guns, the laws and their application seem a bit unclear, and some change or shifting is in progress. Official documents suggest that visitors and/or legal immigrants can bring their guns, but Finnish gun owners claim the procedure is increasingly difficult. Apparently, foreigners legally living in Finland can own firearms, although no one there can cite a recent example of such. I could, for example, have purchased a rifle or pistol over the counter from a gun store in Helsinki several years ago when I was there, and walked out the door with it.

State-of-the-art silencers are currently available in Finland. These include some extremely effective models fitted to high-power rifles. The author has used Finnish silencers on .308 and .243 caliber rifles while deer hunting in the U.K.

There are quite a number of WW II guns and rounds of ammunition lying around remote areas of Finland. Russian soldiers in their mad dash to escape Finnish ski-soldiers ended up frozen solid in some very weird and unusual places and positions. Now Finnish teenagers make a game on weekends out of hunting up old, left behind military equipment and, in some cases, skeletons. As a result, illegal ownership is said to be very common but not much of a real problem.

But not to worry. Finnish authorities do not take an extreme view of what is obviously a common and unavoidable situation, other than concern over dud Russian heavy ordnance that still also turns up from time to time. Military disposal units are there to safely defuse and remove these. Other than this, no one seems to have an opinion on illegal smuggled eastern bloc guns. Any illegal gun can be turned in at any time without penalty or repercussions.

Finding a place to shoot in Finland can be a problem, especially for a recoilless rifle or heavy machine gun, or with regular small arms if one lives in the city. Almost all land in Finland is closely held by private people. Purchase of land is possible, but even small tracts are very expensive. Some clubs allow machine guns and pistols. Rule of law and private property ownership are well established in Finland.

Finland lost 24,923 men killed or missing in the course of repulsing Stalin's three-month military adventure in 1939-40. Russia eventually massed a total of forty-five divisions of men against the plucky Finns. Of these, it is conservatively estimated 200,000 died at the hands of Finnish sharpshooters and Finland's desperately cold winter. Many Russians died alone and unknown in some remote pile of snow.

Although they had little to no AA and anti-tank weapons, the Finns killed over 1,600 Russian tanks and well over 900 of their aircraft, a record that will probably go down in all of history.

As long as they have grandfathers to tell the tale, and history books to explain matters, the Finns will remain free and armed. Collectively and individually they say, "Never again." And so it will certainly be.

Chapter Eleven
Norway
World Rank: 41 • Firearm Freedom 33%

"I am always happy to help fellow members of the gun fraternity," read the e-mail message from someplace deep within Norway. After years of often discouraging effort including numerous phone calls to their mysterious and elusive ministry of justice, as well as scores of letters, I finally had private gun-law information on Norway in hand. Norway is unusual—it's one of the few places where I was told by government officials that "it is illegal for me to have this [gun law] information."

Probably because they have so often been brutally overrun, Scandinavians tend to be pretty good about private guns. For this reason alone, Norway needed to be in the book. My dear friend, the crazy Finn, even suggested that I simply say that their laws are pretty much like ours. True enough. As it worked out, the Finn pretty much knew what he was talking about.

There are, however, some important differences, likely due to the fact that Norwegians don't see themselves as the front line against enemy armor, and they aren't active in the international arms trade. Nothing in Norway is remotely like Finland's Sako or Valmet, nor do the Norwegians share a 650-mile border with the growly, grouchy Bear.

Spitsbergen, Norway, lies closest of any settled community in the world to the North Pole. Much farther north than our own Point Barrow, it reflects the fact that Norwegians have grown accustomed to living a cold, darkened, damp life at least half the year when days tend to last four hours or less. Yet most, if not virtually all, of the 4.5 million Norwegians manage to maintain a very good humor and positive outlook on life. As evidence of this, we learn that an estimated 600,000 Norwegians are legal gun owners. There are perhaps 1.2 million registered handguns, rifles and shotguns in Norwegian hands.

Norway stretches up over 1,100 miles from just north of Denmark on the western edge of the Scandinavian Peninsula. For eight or nine hundred miles Norway is bordered by the Norwegian Sea and then, at the top of the world, it's the Arctic Ocean. Taken in its entirety, Norway is just a bit larger than our state of New Mexico. By our standards, nearly 70 percent of Norway is uninhabitable, covered by harsh Arctic mountains, frigid glaciers, moors and rivers. There are thousands of deep isolated fjords that create a 12,000-mile coastland.

But rugged Norwegians live there anyway. They make their living in the world's riskiest occupations, including lumberjacks, professional hunters, deep-water fishermen and offshore oil-field roughnecks. On average they pull down about $40,000 annually, making them one of the highest paid, most wealthy peoples in the world. Rules of law and property rights are historic and currently prevail. About the worst that can be said is that their tax rates are ruinously high, running over 70 percent of wages in many cases. Were it not for general income from North Sea oil, Norway's economy would be in the pits.

"Norwegian gun laws are really no secret," I was told. They are on the web. But since I am weak to completely ignorant of Norwegian, I had to get this information from English-speaking gun buffs in Norway and from a spokesman from the Norwegian Weapons Owners Association. This latter fellow's English was interesting to a challenge, but far, far better than my Norwegian. I have also spent time working in Norway.

As mentioned, gun ownership is legal and widespread in Norway. But, like many other countries around the world, it has its very own peculiar cultural twists.

Private citizens over the age of 18 (21 for pistols) can own just about any semi-automatic rifle, pistol or shotgun they wish. Under most current circumstances they are limited to perhaps 15 to 20 different guns of all types, styles and calibers. Each of these guns must have a sporting purpose, unless one can secure an obscure sanction as a collector, inventor or developer.

Here is how it is done. Join a pistol, military, rifle, target rifle, shotgun or hunting club of your choice. It may be that you join more than one club to represent all of your shooting interests. In all cases the club should offer shooting and guns of the type you prefer, for example, target shooting with military-style rifles. Now it's time to stay active with the club, using members' or club guns with which to practice.

Clubs dot the country. By our standards they are a bit pricey. But, as mentioned, at least 1.2 million Norwegian gun owners pony up.

After six months of active membership, the club issues a letter of recommend, which is taken to the local police, along with your club-membership certificate. Your friendly local police will run a check to be sure there is no criminal record, habitual drunkenness or incidents of wife beating. Cost of the application is about $35. Conserve your Kroner by applying for several guns on each application.

Approval takes from a week, to about a month in busy metropolitan districts. After approval, take the paperwork to one of Norway's many, many gun shops to pick up your gun. This is a bit convoluted because new owners must pick out the gun they want in the shop, put a deposit on it and then apply for police sanction on that specific weapon. Perhaps because Norwegians have little else to do during their long, dark nights, they have mostly accommodated this process. The entire operation is said "not to be complicated, difficult or recriminous."

In an anomaly peculiar to Norway, police approval of specific designs (with a sporting purpose)—including caliber and function—is determined and sanctioned not by the authorities but by the country's numerous sport-shooting and sport-hunting federations. Initially this sounds ominous, but in practice "almost everything is allowed from

.22 short up to .44 magnums and .454 Casull handguns." The federations make sporting determinations for various makes, models and calibers and the police enforce this list of permitted guns.

If you can convince the local cop you are a credible collector or designer, machine guns and machine pistols can be yours. This is not a common permit. Norwegian cops are not bribable, but will actively listen to credible, reasonable people on this issue. Having a good knowledge of military weapons and great, detailed knowledge of those you wish to collect counts for an immediate ten points.

Ammunition is commonly available in whatever quantities in many local stores. Gun owners with proper permits are entitled to purchase all the ammo they wish and can afford for their legally owned guns. It is unknown if cheap, surplus blasting ammo is available. Plinking is not usually a justifiable reason to own a gun in Norway. Phrasing it as "informal target shooting" works a lot better.

Most ammo on offer seems to be extremely high priced, perhaps because of high taxes that are ubiquitous in Norway. As a practical matter, everything in Norway is high priced—even herring that they catch by the boatload in the Norwegian Sea.

Reloading is permitted and perhaps encouraged. Registered, papered shooters purchase all of the powder and primers they wish over the counter. Projectiles are purchased without paper or formality.

Immigrants to Norway can bring their guns. Shooting on local ranges is allowed but follows the same ownership-permitting process required of regular citizens.

Currently the complaint is made that Norwegian authorities are overly lenient regarding issuance of permits, both to do experimental weapons design and/or to become a firearms dealer. Guns laws in Norway have been stable for at least a decade. Only in these last two areas is there any propensity to make changes.

Permits to carry, either openly or concealed, are uncommon in Norway. They have their own private security police, but these are relatively few in number. Like other Scandinavian countries, the Norwegian custom is to take a dim view of shooting someone, even in the very act of committing a heinous crime.

As in the U.S., the subject of illegal gun use and ownership really gets Norwegian gun buffs going. It isn't chronic or severe as yet. "Not as bad as England or Germany," they say, but incidents of armed gangs fighting it out in poorer sections of Oslo are beginning to be reported.

An estimated 300,000 illegal firearms out of 1.2 million legal ones remain from WW II and from before 1991 when shotguns didn't have to be registered. Fines for illegal ownership range from $250 to $600, including up to four years in the slammer. Norwegian gun owners don't appreciate even modest increase in illegal gun activities. They press for maximum penalties.

As in many other parts of Europe, some illegal machine guns are arriving from old Soviet empire sources. No one knows for sure how many. Norway is a bit more isolated from Europe than just about any country, including England.

Again, it isn't the U.S. in terms of ease and freedom. But Norwegian gun owners can engage in their sport and own modest to sufficient numbers of most guns without undue intrusion on the part of the state. They seemingly have a better, non-confrontative relationship with their police than we do. This helps average gun owners immensely.

Americans find it takes far more money to live here than in the States. But for the rugged, determined individual gun owners, Norway is not all that bad. Property and many human rights are guaranteed by strong laws and by tradition reaching back centuries in some cases.

Chapter Twelve
Japan
World Rank: 61 • Firearm Freedom 4%

Japanese gun laws are included in this volume not because any thinking, alert, freedom-loving individual would ever want to emulate their laws and culture or voluntarily place themselves under them, but because anti-rights activists often throw the Japanese situation up as an example of how the U.S. could be, if we copied their example. Even irreligious people who care little about guns but cherish general personal freedom should pray that never happens.

Japanese people are the most regulated, controlled, nameless, faceless, hapless, hopeless humans on the face of the Earth. Moving someplace else is about all individual Japanese could do to control their own lives. This fact is frequently obscured by their also being a large democracy. At best, Japan illustrates that American's who worship on the false altars of democracy can actually be on the road to hell. If not hell, certainly serfdom.

That the Japanese voluntarily elect to spend their entire lives as colorless, opinionless workerbees in their appointed cells should be of no great concern to freedom loving gun owners, so long as we also realize few Americans—gun owners or not—could endure such oppressive regimentation and restriction. Be thankful, many say, that these flesh-and-blood robots are willing to sit years on end turning out modern electronic marvels. If it were not for these folks and their single-minded, insect-like, production-line dedication, this world would have missed out on some of those electronic doodads. The jobs this may have cost us may not be a very valid cause for alarm.

Most Americans already know Japan is a four-island nation far west out in the Asian Pacific. Montana and Japan have roughly similar total land areas, not including the many smaller islands that also make up the country of Japan. All similarity ends there.

Since WW II, the Japanese and their cultural system have often been seen as an exemplary economic powerhouse. Claims on the part of some Americans, who never observed Japan close up and dirty, "that we should emulate their model," have been muted in recent years. Twenty full years of bone crinkling, destructive recession leaves little about the nation's economy or culture on which to brag.

Per capita income in Japan has fallen dramatically but is still a respectable $29,400. But of all places in the world, this is an illusory figure. Because of extensive rules and regulations leading to gross inefficiencies related to distribution, sales and marketing, costs of even the most common items are ruinously high. Expect to pay $55 each for a plain cheese pizza, $8 for a Big Mac, $5 for a cheap Styrofoam cup of coffee, $400 for a common hotel room and $120 for a bottle of Scotch whiskey!

Superficially Japan is a crime-free society, where a strong sense of shame rather than rules of law prevail. We are led to believe that contracts are fairly and rigorously enforced. By their standards, this may be true. Yet, when westerners get to digging around in Japanese crime statistics and situations, they find many crimes of violence (rape, for instance) are not counted using common international standards. Even holdups and muggings often go unreported because of some sort of sense of shame on the part of the victim.

Forbes magazine recently carried an article pointing out that investigation and prosecution of crimes involving bank and securities fraud and even suspected murder were often "waved off" by high government officials. Japanese police, prosecutors and judges have great latitude regarding pursuit of criminals as well as their actual prosecution. Apparently torture and coercion are common, to the great dismay of Americans used to a standard system of investigation.

Civil rights as we commonly understand them are non-existent in Japan. Police have the power and incentive to come into your home at any time for any reason without warrants, to search your person, to keep personal files or do whatever they personally consider to be wise without any recourse on the part of citizens. They keep track of what they believe to be deviant and aggressive attitudes. They closely monitor membership in any political or activist organizations. They have great, broad powers of search and seizure. Japanese courts routinely allow use of even blatantly illegally seized evidence.

America's anti-gunners who routinely advocate Japanese methods of crime control and prevention don't really understand what they are talking about. Even if a few anti-gunners could endure the harsh regimentation and loss of basic rights, most average Americans could not and would not. Start to enforce this sort of thing and we would have a civil war on our hands.

Information for this chapter comes from experience with two Japanese exchange students, numerous (in excess of twenty) personal visits to Japan, multiple contacts with Japanese citizens interested in guns and shooting, and with some of the very few gun dealers in Tokyo. I also consulted several printed sources of information including government volumes, material from American anti-gunners and from American pro-gun-rights people. It is a stretch to characterize some of the Japanese people with whom I discussed their laws as gun buffs, but there is a tiny genuine gun culture in Japan.

Generally these gun-loving Japanese content themselves with collecting extremely detailed, accurately reproduced, non-working replicas of guns and with traveling to Thailand, the U.S., and the Philippines for shooting holidays. Shooting at floating bottles with .22 caliber or 9mm pistols in the Gulf of Siam is wildly popular with these folks. Big bucks involved here.

I also encountered some extremely well-heeled Japanese businessmen hunting pheasants on Cheju Island off South Korea. Incidentally they were such lousy shots it was comical. In one instance they couldn't even hit a pheasant sitting on a rock a short distance in front of them.

Contrary to popular belief, Japanese citizens can legally own some guns. Unconnected non-military, non-police-type Japanese can legally own shotguns privately, but never rifles or pistols. There are a very few small-bore rifle owners grandfathered into their system dating from a time in the early 1970s when some few rifles were legal. These people still have some of these rifles. As they die or lose interest in the onerous process of re-licensing, their rifles are summarily confiscated by the police. In effect, this moves their society back to one in which there are no private rifles.

Japanese police carry a Nambu .38 revolver of their own design but very similar to a Smith & Wesson. Use of these sidearms, even by the police, is severely restricted as well as discouraged. No Japanese police carry off duty. Shooting at a fleeing felon is unlawful under any circumstances. According to police spokesmen, the entire Tokyo police force may fire half-a-dozen rounds in an entire year, and there are literally tens of thousands of police in Tokyo.

A great many rifles and shotguns are manufactured in Japanese factories for sale in world markets. If anything, Japanese are consummate exporters. Presently these exports are mostly Browning replicas. Some few pistols are also produced for police use in small as-needed batches on what seems like an every three- or four-year basis. Production rotates from factory to factory, not so much for security purposes but to spread political favors. Current pistol production is done in the Omori Factory Division of Minebea Co., Ltd (Tokyo).

Citizens who want to own and use a shotgun to practice trap and skeet or to engage in the limited hunting available in Japan are subjected to a typically daunting, convoluted, stylized licensing procedure.

Aware of the traders and salesmen they are, I inquired about purchasing a Miroku Charles Daly double shotgun to take back to the States. "It is forbidden to even touch a gun without proper licensing," I was quickly informed. They would, however, arrange delivery, sight unseen, to the airport where I could carry the shotgun on to the U.S. Currently no Miroku rests in my gun rack.

For your gun-owner's permit, apply at the local police station. Many, many police boxes and small station houses are scattered about all of Japan. This is never a very long walk.

Purely at the discretion of local officers, citizens may be allowed to enter into licensing procedures. This procedure has four different and difficult steps specifically calculated to discourage applicants.

First, applicants must attend weekly classes allegedly necessary to teach safe, responsible handling of shotguns. Classes last about a year, are expensive and are scheduled at inconvenient times and places. This alone precludes attendance for most salary men who must labor in the hive. A tough written test follows the classes. Second, an applicant must attend shooting-range classes followed by another rigorous shooting test. Third, applicants are required to take a "mental test" at a local hospital. This is to be certain they are not suffering from delusions, dementia or any other psychiatric disorders. Disillusionment with their system would certainly be classed as dementia.

Next individual, intrusive, detailed police investigations are made into the applicant's background and family to be sure there is no criminal history. Unreasonable interest in aggressive political groups or a history of activism constitutes grounds for immediate disqualification. Local police already have extensive files on every citizen residing in their districts. These files even include observations regarding sexual misconduct, roaming about the community till midnight and allegedly unsound companionship.

If and when a shotgun permit is finally issued, it will be for only one or at most two shotguns. There are competitive-type pistol and rifle shooters in Japan. These are always members of the police or military.

Possession of a firearms certificate allows holders to purchase "several thousand rounds of shotgun ammo" per year. All ammunition purchases are recorded, bringing ammo possession under tight control.

Reloading in Japan is completely unheard of. Absolutely no components are available for purchase under any circumstances.

Shotgun owners must store their guns in an approved steel safe. Ammo is locked away safely elsewhere. Apartment floor plans showing locations of safes and ammunition must, by law, be provided to local police. They can and do inspect at any time without warrant or prior notice. At least once a year certificate holders must endure a day long scheduled inspection. At the conclusion of the three-year life of the certificate, there is another all day safety and gun-handling refresher lecture and personal examination at police headquarters.

As a result of all of this, as American antis love to point out, licensed guns in Japan are almost never stolen and used in commission of a crime. Reported crime rates in general are low to extremely low. This does not mean there are no crimes with guns in Japan.

At this writing, Japanese law enforcement authorities are extremely agitated over illegal guns flowing into the country. Mostly these come from the Philippines, Thailand, and the U.S. Often these guns are brought in by members of an organized crime syndicate. It is reasonably possible to purchase a black-market handgun (but not a rifle) and a few rounds of ammo in Tokyo. But hold onto your seats— prices are stratospheric, and penalties for those caught can be severe. Maximum is ten years in prison and a million Yen fine ($1,000), unless you are somehow politically or socially shielded. Often shop owners do not report holdups or pilferage because of social stigma or fear of retaliation by members of a local organized crime syndicate.

Japanese police are the most powerful, overreaching government agents in the world. Partly because they lack legal constraints and partly because of their great social authority within Japanese society, they are feared and revered by average citizens. Amnesty International labels Japanese police interrogation customs and polices as being "flagrant violations of UN human rights precepts."

Some firearms remaining from WW II occasionally appear on the black market or are confiscated by the police in the normal course of events. It was over sixty years ago when returning soldiers might have brought in a few souvenirs. Mostly, these weapons are no longer a factor, they have been swept up and out of circulation. We must also confront the truth that Japanese total homeland resistance at the end of WW II was a myth. They had no small arms and could have distributed nothing with which to resist. News photos of young girls flailing sharpened sticks portray the extent of their possible resistance.

Western gun owners would not wish to live and work in Japan. A democracy, yes, but Japanese freedom is an oxymoron. Occasionally we hear from antis who have never observed Japanese handling of basic God-given human rights, who want to emulate their laws and customs. Some misguided folks also thought the Japanese had something worth copying with regard to their fascist economy. But now after twenty years of horrible economic contraction, these folks are mostly silent.

Americans commit approximately seventy times as much violent, non-gun crime as reported in Japan. Take away all our guns and all our human rights and we could still have more crime than the docile Japanese. Perhaps even more crime than we have now, judging by John Lott's benchmark analysis in "Less Guns More Crime."

Japanese citizens cannot even own large knives. Weapons in their culture were always accepted as the mark of rulers, not of the ruled. As unfortunate as this seems, their culture has grown to enjoy and accept this level of central control. They do it to themselves voluntarily, hopefully something few thinking and informed Americans would ever sanction.

Chapter Thirteen
Canada
World Rank: 32 • Firearm Freedom 42%

Even the more geographically challenged among us already know Canada is our immediate neighbor to the north. Several additional facts about our near neighbor are not as widely known or understood.

How many among us, for instance, realize that Canada is larger in land area than the U.S. or that the country is actually richer in natural resources than the U.S.? Yet Canada has a much lower *per capita* income than the U.S. About $31,500.

Canadians display a rich love for government in general and their own government in particular, a phenomenon scholar Dave Kopel labels *cratophilia* in his seminal text, *The Samurai, the Mountie and the*

Cowboy (Prometheus Press, 1992). That book, by the way, may be the only detailed treatment of gun laws in other parts of the world prior to this book you are holding. In large measure, cratophilia is the polar opposite of what most Americans hold dear. Several interesting anomalies come into play as a result of this cultural heritage.

Canadians are much more likely than Americans to ask for, and be granted, special government favor which, in the long run, is little more than officially sanctioned robbing of Peter to pay Paul. "My business can't compete unless I receive a special government subsidy forcibly taken from other taxpayers," or "it is the government's duty to provide health care," are two quick, and perhaps dirty, examples.

I've always wondered if Canadians have really wanted to enslave doctors and nurses by coercing them into providing "free" health care—a question far beyond the scope of this book.

While I have been extremely critical of some governments and their treatment of subjects relative to their gun laws, it is genuinely not my intent to be critical of Canadians or their government. But without understanding that Canadians are descendants of North American Tories who left the colonies in disgust when King George was no longer their head and that Canadian civilization is glued together by an in-depth and abiding dislike and distrust of Americans, we will never be able to understand their culture and motives, much less their own peculiar rules and regulations.

Somewhat similar to New Zealanders, Canadians genuinely appreciate, love and trust their government. They have little to none of the adversarial suspicion and mistrust of their police, abundantly evident below in the lower forty-eight states. As a result, they trust their government to provide their human rights without written documentation and judicial history. Not only are Canadian human rights less well defined, they are—in fact—much fewer in number. We need to keep in mind that Canadians are not Americans who happen to be living north of an imaginary line in a more frozen wilderness-like portion of the globe.

Within their own cultural context, Canadians do have fairly strong rules of law and of property rights. However, Canadian legal authorities can and do confiscate property without due process. Rights to a trial by jury exist only in cases that could bring a jail term of at least five years. You are acquitted by this jury? Under the Canadian system, prosecutors have the right of appeal!

Information for this chapter came from several Canadian gun owners, a Canadian gun dealer, an American book on Canadian gun laws, official Canadian government rules and regulations, a brother who moved to Canada to avoid Vietnam and a hunter friend who recently retired to Canada. For a variety of reasons I have traveled through Canada on a number of occasions.

Many Canadian gun owners firmly believe their private firearms laws are far superior to those in the U.S. They proudly point to the fact that their laws are national in scope—not a confusing, inconsistent mixture of state laws, as one Canadian gun dealer told me. Because Canadian gun laws are uniform countrywide and because they are enforced by a national authority, many of the big city restrictions common in New York City, Washington D.C. or Chicago are avoided.

On the other hand, there is the tendency to formulate gun laws in Canada to please more restrictive, big-city jurisdictions. As a result, gun owners in rural, open Saskatchewan, for instance, must comply with gun laws that satisfy people in densely populated Ottawa. Although Canadian gun laws are a bit more restrictive in general than the U.S., Canadians like to point out they are not as restrictive as those in Massachusetts and New York. They certainly have a point!

Some Canadian nationalists firmly believe American television, which many Canadians can easily receive along our long, relatively open and common border, is subversive to Canadian culture. This in part because "it leads Canadian young people into believing that they have some sort of constitutional rights." Otherwise, Canadians generally believe that they do not have a right to carry a gun for personal protection but they also firmly believe they have a right to own a rifle or shotgun for sporting purposes if they wish to.

As a result, private gun ownership in some areas of Canada is often as high or higher than in the U.S. Approximately half of American homes contain a gun. On average, in Canada it's about 20% except in remote rural areas where gun owners reach virtually 100%! Of their 30 million citizens, minimally six million are estimated to be gun owners. Perhaps 21 million private firearms are said to be in Canadian hands.

Canadians can easily own most guns that are commonly used for hunting or other sporting purposes, such as target shooting and for trap or skeet. On the other hand, their bureaucracy prohibits or limits ownership of certain predetermined assault rifles, short-barreled rifles, folding-stock semi-autos, machine guns and machine pistols, and pistols with barrels less than 4.14 inches.

Some small amount of fully automatic ownership is grandfathered in from 1977 when the laws were dramatically changed. This grandfathering allows owners from that time to keep and use their machine guns, but not to pass them on—even at the owner's death. In times past, some Canadians could own some restricted weapons that were also registered to the owner. All pistols fell in this category. New rules and regulations still allow legal ownership of some pistols and assault rifles, but these are becoming more stringent and difficult.

New Canadian gun owners start by applying for a Firearms Acquisition and Possession Certificate (FAPC) at your local RCMP headquarters. Applications are then immediately forwarded to the Canadian Firearms Center in New Brunswick. Simultaneously, new young gun owners must sign up for an exam, which they must successfully pass, before any certificate is issued. Some Canadians purchase a self-study book to brief themselves up for the test. Rules and regulations as well as safe handling of firearms are stressed in the test, which I'm told isn't perfunctory. If not a self-study book, new applicants may take classes, which are seldom offered at convenient times and places. Initially fees were set at $30 Canadian, but have been increased to $50 Canadian for both the test and the FAPC.

It is easy to flunk, which requires taking it again in the future. Costs of the test and for the certificate are thought by citizens to be "nominal." Currently it takes four to five weeks to receive a new firearms certificate after passing the test and submitting an application.

If the purpose of the new gun owner is to own and shoot a pistol, the person will likely join a shooting club where they can practice at that range with other club members' guns. Handgun hunting is not permitted in Canada, and use of a handgun for self-defense is both culturally and legally sensitive. Even the national police, who do carry pistols, seldom use their guns to prevent a crime. After a trial period, shooting clubs are expected to issue certificates of membership and letters of recommendation for new members for use before local police when acquiring a pistol.

After selecting and paying for a handgun at a local gun store, applicants take their FAPC, bill of sale, club-membership certificate and recommend letter to the local police. The police run a background check on that individual, which may include a visit to the home and chats with neighbors. They may even wish to interview a spouse if there is such. Canadian citizens currently express concern over the massive amounts of police time that compliance with new gun laws is requiring. "Gives criminals a real advantage," several people told me.

By the year 2003, all guns—shotguns, rifles, and of course pistols—were supposed to be registered to someone with a firearms certificate in Canada. Non-compliance with this registration requirement in passive, government-worshipping Canada was massive. At that time, the procedure was to be the same for all guns. Private sales among individuals were to be possible so long as they are handled between certificated individuals through the police.

Recently Canadians elected a new, more conservative government.
There is talk about throwing out the gun-owner's certificate
requirement and the gun-registration requirement. This as a result of
massive non-compliance and dramatic cost overruns coupled to the
observation that the only measurable result is a greater mistrust of their
government on the part of Canadian citizens.

Supposedly computers in New Brunswick were to take care of most of
this purchase and transfer business. Authorities promised issuance and
transfer approvals were to be speedy. Canadian gun owners enjoy
pointing out that their Canadian Police Information Computers (CPIC)
are similar but much faster than our own FBI run National Instant
Crime System (NICS). Speed of issuance of an initial Firearms
Acquisition & Possession Certificate may not be an issue. By Canadian
law, at least 28 days must elapse between application and issuance.

Theoretically there is no limit on the number of hunting- and sporting-
type rifles, shotguns and pistols a holder of a FAPC can possess. Also
bear in mind that many, many types and kinds of guns sometimes have
no sporting purpose in the eyes of Canadian bureaucrats. These
include some assault rifles, extending down to WW II M-1 carbines
and police-type shotguns! Pistols with barrels less than four inches are
also never authorized. Sometimes, to their anguish and consternation,
legal gun owners find the bureaucracy has arbitrarily changed the
definition of their legally registered "restricted weapons."

Hunting with semi-auto rifles is permitted. Target shooting with assault
rifles is generally permitted, but may depend on local interpretations of
sporting purpose.

Since every gun—not only pistols—must now be authorized and
registered, this new approval speed may apply only to issuance of
permission under an existing FAPC for additional firearms, not to new
applications for firearms possession and acquisition certificates.

Canadian authorities insist on safe storage procedures, which generally
require a steel gun safe, locked storage room, trigger locks and
separate locked storage for ammunition.

Canadian FAPC holders can currently purchase as much ammunition
and loading components—including pistol ammo—as they wish, so
long as they present their FAPC. All ammunition sales are recorded to
the purchaser's FAPC. Sales of reloading components, even for pistols,
are common in Canada. All component sales are also recorded to the
purchaser. Depending on the region these purchase records may
seldom be reviewed by the authorities. There seems to be little cheap
surplus blasting ammo available.

Illegal guns are really not seen as a particularly great problem so long as they are not involved in the commission of a crime. Violent crime is less common in Canada because of Canadians' deeply held values of orderliness, trust in government and nonviolence. Gun turn-in days are often very successful, at least compared to those in the U.S. where gun turn-ins work only with cash incentives, and then not really well.

Pools of illegal firearms that could theoretically arrive by illegal importation from the U.S. are viewed as "not much of a problem"— except when brought forth by big-city American-bashing politicians. American anti-gunners laud Canadian gun-certification programs and lack of crime without understanding cultural differences that allow and even cause these differences. They also fail to note the fact that gun-owner and gun-ownership licensing failed miserably in Canada. Even police chiefs in large Canadian cities now point out that the vast sums of money spent on gun registration schemes could have been more wisely and productively invested in actual law enforcement.

No such thing as collectors' or research and developers' permits exist in Canada. Some special provision may possibly be made for people with proven talent, but in general Canada does not wish to be part of the international arms industry.

Dealers' permits are available to citizens. There are about 20 to 30 items on a checklist with which compliance must be proved before issuance of a dealer permit. Most of these are not particularly difficult or onerous, things like burglar alarms, lock-up rooms and the like. An approximately $200 annual fee is assessed that includes a yearly on-site inspection of your store by the national police.

Because Canadian gun laws are changing dramatically, it is not entirely clear at this writing how an immigrant would bring guns into Canada. Likely they would be held in official storage till an FAPC could be acquired and/or inspections be made to determine if they were permitted models with requisite "hunting/sporting" purpose.

American hunters traveling to Canada must register their rifles or shotguns as well as show proof of a valid current Canadian hunting license. There is a $50 Canadian registration fee and all data collected are forwarded to the American BATFE. As a practical matter, non-resident hunting licenses are only issued in conjunction with booking and paying for expensive Canadian guide services.

Of all countries on this Earth, people of the U.S. and Canada are the most similar. I am continually reminded of this fact during my many visits to Canada. Yet there are important differences. Many Canadians see no valid reason to own pistols and assault rifles, and many currently have little concern about registration systems. Most are pleased and content with their own peculiar rules, a fact that might elude Americans who irrationally assume we are all one big, homogenous cultural family.

As mentioned, Canada's new gun laws have potential to change their entire society, as Canadians become increasingly crabby about what their bureaucracy has done to them. In part this may explain the resurgence of Canada's Conservative party.

Chapter Fourteen
South Africa
World Rank: 34 • Firearm Freedom 39%

Reading through the fairly new sixty-page Firearms Control Bill now promulgated for the country by South African legislators leads to several conclusions. First, you might be inclined to suspect that this bill was drawn up by unpracticed, lightly educated, inexperienced lawmakers. Next, you might sense a strong belief that any social wrong can be made right by application of the proper government edict, which permeates the code. This is a confusing, contradictory, grossly overly-detailed piece of work, at best.

Secondly, a strong philosophical undercurrent suggests that drafting lawmakers were heavily influenced by clever gun-owning lobbyists who managed to insert great, long sections and wording that essentially nullifies many of the bill's toughest sections.

As a result this is a very contradictory, open-ended piece of legislation that will no doubt be subject to great government abuse and widely varied interpretation. Official duties of regulating authorities are most often framed in terms of "may." Very few "shalls" are included. Throughout, authorities "may" enforce various sections of what already is a convoluted, often foolishly detailed code section.

If we accept editorials in South African gun magazines, some South African gun owners believe they may have snookered the government into a contradictory, unenforceable gun law. On the other hand, many others believe this is only the first step to total prohibition. Only time will tell who is correct.

No doubt, for some, bribery leading to subversion of the act will run rampant. In that respect, the law is doomed to failure. Using other countries and other cultures as an example, we can accurately predict it will not accomplish its stated goal of cutting crime. Historically we now know fewer guns in the hands of common citizens lead to more crime, not less. Currently, thousands of illegal guns are available to anyone who wants them anywhere in Africa. This is especially true of countries bordering those with severe internal problems such as Somalia, Mozambique, Liberia and Chad. South Africa is no different.

By some folks' reckoning, South Africa has the highest crime and incarceration rate in the world and perhaps in recorded history. Their horrendous crime rate is a great problem, touching the personal lives of all South Africans—black and white. As a result, when legislators realize their gun laws are not working, they will change them again, perhaps instituting dramatic additional restrictions. The following analysis of gun laws in South Africa can only be viewed as transitory.

To an extent, South African gun laws are modeled after English law where "permitsitis" reigns and where ownership of guns is reserved for the elite, not the common man. Pity, because at one time South Africa had some of the most enlightened, permissive gun laws in the world— if you were white-skinned of European descent. A gun culture among this class almost rivaled the one in the U.S. White South African gun owners had their own gun magazines, shooting clubs and active collectors as well as some really fine experimenters, designers and manufacturers. The flip side of this situation involves the fact that indigenous Africans, for the most part, failed to learn proper, responsible, safe gun-ownership patterns.

As a result, the more numerous black South Africans came to view all firearms as a tool of repression wickedly deployed against them by the white minority. Now in power, it's no surprise the native Africans wish to remove these hated symbols of white domination while also reducing their epidemic crime rates. It is a miracle that black South Africans listened to any concerns from white South African gun owners, or will even grudgingly sanction some private gun ownership.

In summary we have gun laws written by well-meaning neophytes heavily influenced by members of the South African gun culture, aimed at extensive criminal activities that are very real, but which will not be controlled in the least by this complex, expensive and overreaching measure. All we can do is report "what is" at this moment in this very unhappy land. Laws and information about them will change. But this is how it is now.

Information for this chapter comes from contacts with about ten younger professional citizens of South Africa, the editor of a South African gun and shooters magazine, reading South African gun magazines, from an actual reading of the South African "Firearms Control Bill" and from personally having lived in South Africa. This entire chapter was thoroughly vetted by three African citizens. As an aside, absolutely every young professional South African citizen I have recently talked with is currently working on a plan to move elsewhere.

It's extremely unfortunate, since these people are vitally needed if South Africa is ever to rebuild its economy and grow economically.

South Africa is on the far southern tip of the continent. Waters off Cape Town, South Africa's southernmost port, are rough and tumultuous as a result of collision of the cold south Atlantic and warm Indian oceans. Land area of South Africa is roughly three times that of California.

Dutch settlers first landed at the future site of Cape Town in 1652, not very much later than U.S. pilgrims first landed at the Massachusetts Bay colony. Unlike the U.S., early colonists in South Africa found the land devoid of native peoples.

The country before them was rich in natural resources. Like our own native North Americans, indigenous people had little clue how to use this natural bounty—as a result they stayed well away, in areas where they knew how to live off the land. As early settlers tamed and worked the land, native Africans from the north moved down to accept employment from these hardy Dutch settlers. Historians claim this early migration south to find employment established a pattern of racial discord that persists to this day.

Currently South Africans share a *per capita* income of about $11,100. While this seems low, many if not most countries to the north have *per capita* incomes of $200 or less! Yet because of the collapse of the rule of law, and of property rights, this amount is thought to be dramatically shrinking. Not in freefall as yet, but general reductions in living standards are evident to everyone in South Africa.

As currently envisioned, some limited private firearms ownership is permitted in South Africa. Numerous, often contradictory, layers of licenses, permits and authorizations are required. Exact requirements and conditions for issuance are uncertain at best and obscure at worst. Currently it takes the inept African bureaucracy up to 18 months to process a permit to sell or own any kind of firearm. Given that the law requires renewal every two years, this is certainly an intolerable situation. We don't really know if the South African gun bureaucracy is lazy, inept, or willfully dilettante.

Members of the white minority government, which collapsed in 1994, suggested that many Africans were not ready for the responsibility of private firearms ownership. Current events may vindicate this belief. Legislation promulgated by the majority government seems to recognize a kernel of truth here. Great emphasis is placed on teaching and establishing responsible gun ownership before required permits are issued. If government, perhaps through the local police in a system reminiscent of New Zealand, can teach proper private gun-ownership responsibility, this system may be salvaged. If not, illegal guns will continue to pour into the country where they will be misused.

Private South African gun owners are required to secure both a Firearms Competency Certificate and a gun-owner's license. According to their code, there are nine classes of gun-owner licenses. Every firearm must be registered to a license.

Apparently the government will establish criteria and procedures for competency certificates, but it is too early to determine what these will be or if these tests won't be arbitrarily changed to suit shifting political whims. Only South African citizens or legal residents can qualify for Firearms Competency Certificates. This requirement perhaps recognizes that illegal immigration into South Africa continues to be something of a problem.

There is also an obscure reference in their code to issuing a single document for multiple guns. Total numbers of guns permitted vary according to the type of license issued.

No fully automatic firearms, cannons, recoilless rifles, mortars or other military-style weapons are allowed. In theory, pistols are permitted, but they are limited to a maximum of one per permit holder. All firearms must be registered with the central authorities in a bureau recently established for this purpose. Estimated costs for all the new agencies run into millions of dollars. Perhaps the South African government simply cannot afford to adequately staff their recently mandated bureaucracy. We just don't know.

Applications for Firearms Competency Certificates for the various classes of licenses are to be made at the "Designated Firearms Officer responsible for the area in which the applicant ordinarily resides." No person under 21 may qualify for a FCC but the code itself contains numerous, often contradictory, age exclusions and exemptions.

"For those conducting a business, gainfully employed, a dedicated hunter or dedicated sports person, or finally a private collector," additional code sections read, thereby allowing for under 21 years of age gun ownership. In this instance and in all others it is important to note that the registrar of firearms is never required to issue licenses or certificates. Always, the law reads, "may issue."

In yet another modifying addendum to their code, it appears that licensed gun owners may legally allow youngsters under their direct control to use firearms for lawful purposes. Only time will tell if teenagers will be allowed to legally hunt and own guns here.

Among handguns, both revolvers and semi-automatics are permitted without regard to magazine capacity, caliber or type. Machine pistols are completely verboten. Sporting-type rifles and shotguns are permitted except that no semi-autos are allowed on what is referred to as a license to possess firearms for occasional hunting and sports shooting. Apparently a total of four different firearms may be legally possessed under this section. It is currently envisioned that this will be the most common and popular license.

The nine different categories of firearms licenses are: self defense—wherein one pistol is allowed, restricted self defense allowing for ownership of one assault rifle or semi-auto shotgun, occasional hunter and sports shooter—covered above, dedicated hunter and sports shooter who is a registered member of an accredited hunting or shooting club who can own virtually unlimited numbers of rifles, shotguns and a pistol including semi-autos, a private collector member of an accredited collectors' association who can also own unlimited numbers of guns (but only one pistol is ever allowed in any category).

There are also separate licenses for collectors of ammunition, both private and public, licenses for those conducting a hunting business and for those requiring firearms whose business does not involve hunting. Most licenses expire after ten years. Self-defense and restricted self-defense are for five and two years respectively. Hunting permits are only being issued for two years.

There is also a permit to transport guns and ammo, which is very nebulous and uncertain in its intent and meaning within the code. Only time will tell how this is interpreted and enforced.

No person in South Africa can trade firearms or ammunition without a license, although private sales or donations of private firearms appear legal with permission of the local "designated firearms officer." Mention was already made of the fact that this act will probably aid, encourage and abet bribery and subversion of the law. Non-issue of gun-store licenses has become an important consideration. At this writing, a reported 640 of 720 gun shops have closed as a result of tardy or non-renewal of their trade licenses.

Manufacturers and gunsmiths are also licensed under this act. Supposedly a gunsmith with some retail sales would require two separate licenses—one to work on guns and the other for over-the-counter sales. The law requires anyone who clerks in a gun store to possess a firearms competency certificate. There's nothing wrong with gun-store clerks knowing what they are talking about, providing the government can actually define that skill.

Manufacturing of ammunition is strictly forbidden under Part 2 Section 45 of the Act without a manufacturers' license. But Chapter 10 Section 93 says this section does not apply to holders of a license to possess a firearm, to hand load ammo for their own legally licensed firearms.

All sales of ammunition are recorded and made only to license holders through licensed dealers. Holders of firearms licenses may possess a maximum of 200 rounds of ammo for each gun unless they have special dispensation from the Registrar of Firearms to acquire more. Those who purchase their ammo and shoot it at an accredited shooting range can legally own more ammo while they are shooting. No restrictions exist at present on caliber, type and kinds of ammo. All of this notwithstanding, the days of cheap military surplus blasting ammo in South Africa are probably gone forever.

The Achilles' heel here is that the registrar of firearms either doesn't know how to make special dispensations or is unwilling to do so.

Hand loaders face a legal maximum possession limit of 2,400 primers. Bullets and powder do not seem to be controlled other than that all sales are recorded and are made only to certificate holders.

South African lawmakers seem to recognize that sport hunting contributes mightily to their economy. Provision is made for persons who wish to temporarily import firearms and ammunition into the country for purposes of participating in an organized guided hunt. No restrictions on make, model or amount of ammunition seem to apply. Some restrictions may apply on hunting licenses, however. No person in South Africa can legally transport a gun or ammunition across country without a permit if they are doing so for "reward." Secure these transport permits from the local police. It seems doubtful, under their new laws, that hunters coming to South Africa will be able to bring a pistol with them.

Concealed handgun carry permits are supposedly issued, but there are extensive detailed provisions requiring that the gun must always be under the owner/license holder's "effective control." There are also the exceedingly curious code sections that set aside some designated areas in the country as being "firearms free." How this might be enforced is anyone's guess, and make-believe "gun-free" zones are well known to support criminal activity.

Police in South Africa can make warrantless, arbitrary searches for illegal firearms, making all searches now warrantless and arbitrary. All the cops have to do is say "I was looking for an illegal gun." This is, no doubt, some of the apartheid pigeons coming home to roost. The whites did it to the blacks and now it is the other way around. Persons owning property on which illegal firearms are discovered arbitrarily lose that property without hearing or recourse.

There is, however, a provision for the right of appeal to an established Board for a license denial. Those who believe they have been wrongfully denied a competency certificate, license, permit or authorization can appeal to this board. Specific and quite stringent criteria for denial are included in the body of the law. This process seems either to not work, or to be intentionally overlooked.

As one would expect, members of the European community who have enjoyed reasonably open gun laws since the country was established grumble mightily about the new law and its incredible complexity.

Some realization seems to be out there that the vast African community who now control the government, who have had limited experience with firearms, must now be instructed in responsible gun ownership. This and the fact that the European community here is mostly made up of people of English extraction, who seem genetically inclined to accept a system of "permitsitis," seems to explain what to Swiss, Belgians, Finns, Americans and even Canadians must seem like an impossible horrible situation for private gun owners, especially given the country's high level of lawlessness.

As is generally true of societies devoid of ingrained personal responsibility, an attempt is made to address absolutely every contingency, outcome and eventuality, in the writing of their gun bill. One size never does fit all, but in the case of South Africa, they make a valiant effort to overcome this restraint.

Statistics seem to indicate that South African women are the greatest supporters of strict gun laws. As a class of civilians they are most likely to be shot in their homes, the victims of domestic violence.

Readers who cannot decipher the above summary should be welcomed to the club. South African citizens can't really figure all of this out either. There is something for everybody in their current gun laws. Enforcement will probably turn on the numerous "mays" contained in the bill.

Native Kenyans tell me there is no country in Africa where private ownership of firearms is permitted and there is no country without large numbers of illegal guns. In that regard alone, South Africans have something of which to boast. At least tacitly they have decided guns are just tools, not free agents capable of independently running around and killing people. Let's hope they get their crime situation resolved before all human rights are forever lost in this rich, beautiful and wonderful land.

Chapter Fifteen
New Zealand
World Rank: 8 • Firearm Freedom 85%

New Zealand is often characterized as a strange and wonderful land, "unique throughout the world." Keep this fact in mind, to fairly and honestly evaluate or even understand their rules, regulations and policies relative to private ownership of firearms. Traditional American gun people would find the NZ system strange and unacceptable, if they don't first know some ground rules.

The unique location and geography is an element of this, but it's their socio-economic situation and culture that stand out. New Zealand may be the only country in the world where citizens are not pitted against their own government and where these same citizens no longer attempt to legally use their government to plunder their fellows. New Zealand was one of the first countries to pursue "humanitarian socialism" and one of the first to give it up as a bad deal. Since 1996 any kind of governmental action in New Zealand is extremely difficult and convoluted to implement. New Zealand is frequently said to be the freest place on Earth. Re-establishing socialism is said to now be impossible—structurally, if not socially.

Police in New Zealand seldom, if ever, carry firearms. As a group they are respected and trusted in a manner unique on Earth. New Zealand cops are the average citizen's good friend and are treated as such. Teaching and encouraging responsible firearms use and safety among the country's young people has been one of their traditional roles and missions. They encourage, rather than discourage, responsible private gun ownership—how's that for a unique, freedom-centric approach.

From about 1920 to 1983, the country did have a form of firearms restriction, including registration. In 1983 the New Zealand police promulgated and approved a statement saying they found no correlation between crime and the numbers of guns in the hands of private citizens. The police themselves persuaded the government to recodify New Zealand's gun laws, doing away with all forms of registration. In part this helps explain their extremely low crime rates.

As mentioned, New Zealand is a strange and different animal. This level of trust and cooperation is not otherwise found among humans.

New Zealand distinguishes itself in many other regards. *Per capita* income is a very middle of the road, but respectable, $23,200. Based on these figures alone, we might be tempted to conclude this is a mostly middle-class society, in which virtually everyone struggles to make ends meet.

Not true. New Zealand is an incredibly rich country but there are few to no incredibly rich individuals among them. Taxes and cost of living are miniscule compared to other places. This in itself contributes to the extensive middle class we see there. While the very rich are few in number, the very poor are even more uncommon. New Zealand's overall cost of living is very modest.

It is extremely easy to eat meat and fresh vegetables in nice restaurants and to stay in perfectly adequate motels for $50 per day! Life is very easy for New Zealanders content to live within and on their own economy.

Although they have few codified civil and human rights, most citizens quickly admit these are always in the background. Police may legally engage in warrantless searches of private homes in pursuit of illegal firearms (and drugs) but, as a practical matter, New Zealanders know and respect their police. They don't seem to object to what we might consider a gaping hole in their civil rights. Citizens are inclined to just let their police come on in, and perhaps stay for tea and cakes as long as they are there already. Moral and social constraints in favor of basic civil rights seem adequate in the face of an obvious lack of codified ones guaranteed by a written constitution or other such document.

New Zealand is a hugely rich country. So rich citizens engage in some very unusual social customs. A few commentators refer to this as a Brahmin mentality, i.e., life is not sufficiently difficult as we now find it, and so we add artificial impediments and barriers in an attempt to make things more suitably difficult.

For instance, during the mid-1980s when I first worked there, New Zealand was in the throes of a very real, in depth anti-nuclear hysteria. This tiny two-island nation the size of Colorado that must import all of its energy at great cost, turned its back on a modern, cost-efficient system already proven and in use by its neighbors. During that same time, for instance, Japan cut their energy bill significantly by generating eleven percent of their electrical energy via nuclear.

Whipped on by red-hot journalistic rhetoric, corporate New Zealand even went so far as barring nuclear-powered vessels from visiting their ports, a move that put severe strains on regional defense pacts.

New Zealand had changed when I was back again in the late 1990s. Anti-nuclear fever had abated a bit. Now it was genetic engineering. Individual New Zealanders privately confided that reports of dangerous problems related to this remarkable technology were greatly overblown, but corporately they remained extremely agitated. As a country mostly reliant on agricultural production and export, they seemed to be turning their backs on the future.

I enjoyed asking people in the ag industry how they expected to maintain technological parity with the rest of the world if they maintained this philosophy. Or how it would be possible to feed starving peoples in neighboring Indonesia, Bangladesh or North Korea. At that time, New Zealand deployed a number of their young soldiers into East Timor, partly over concerns that the turmoil there might eventually reach New Zealand. "Starvation might cause these folks to look with covetous eyes at New Zealand," I was frequently told.

This Brahmin mentality continually manifests itself in their daily lives. "Just throw it down and let's get going," my guide hollered. We were out hunting possum, rabbits and hares. Their huge rabbits and hares would have been excellent eating and skins from the many plump possums we took were valuable. But we left them to rot. "Beef and lamb are much better eating," I was instructed, "and besides we don't have time to fool with them." Lush, deliciously fat meat pies containing at least a pound of beef or lamb cost about 30 U.S. cents in New Zealand supermarkets.

As a group, New Zealanders are extremely close knit and they are more intrinsically law abiding than any other society on Earth. I never locked my car or motel room door. Neighbors thirty miles distant often drew accurate, detailed maps directing me to remote farms.

Yet crime is on peoples' minds. In times past, berry and produce vendors displayed their wares in roadside stands. No attendant in these booths, just produce for sale. Simply place required funds, as marked on the produce, in a convenient basket. I usually left an American penny, in addition to the marked price, to let them know we could also operate that way. Alas, at least on the North Island, those days now seem gone forever.

Folks in Dannevirke complained that a car was stolen last year by joyriding kids. Hooliganism, they said, is dramatically increased in this small agricultural village! It was, after all, a 100% increase in car theft.

"How long has it been since you personally have seen someone shot during a holdup or been the victim of some crime in the U.S.?" I was frequently asked. I have seen people shot during a holdup, but not in the U.S., but they didn't want to hear it. "We don't want New Zealand to get like the U.S.," they lectured. I don't either, but their perspective is somewhat unique.

Americans generally know New Zealand is "down there someplace, near Australia." As a matter of record, New Zealand is 1,250 miles southeast of Australia. Sufficient differences exist so that most knowledgeable travelers say "do one or the other, but don't try both." They aren't close and they are not similar in any regard. Either it's the former prison colony or the former farm colony.

Besides, their well-placed trust and partnership with their police and government, their inherent richness and prosperity, small, collegial structures and their desire to atone for their obvious easy and good life by adopting a Brahmin way of life, there is one additional, typically New Zealand, trait we should know about. It relates to their laws concerning private ownership of firearms.

Similar to Finland, New Zealand citizens are seldom to never legally and socially justified using a handgun to prevent a crime. Even the police seldom, if ever, carry or use pistols. Rifles and shotguns are infrequently used, but never handguns.

If used at all, handguns are exclusively for target shooting. New Zealand offers extensive hunting for a large variety of animals, great and small, but not with pistols. Pistols within this society are just not seen as important, desirable firearms even by members of their own gun-owning society. Outside the gun savvy, New Zealand citizens are often really surprised to learn that legal pistol-owner sportsmen exist in their country. Nobody talks about or uses pistols to any extent.

Information for this chapter came from two extensive personal working residences in New Zealand, interviews with dozens of gun owners including several pistol owners, interviews with New Zealand police and from a book on New Zealand gun laws. As something of an aside, the New Zealand police were one of the very few governmental bodies worldwide to respond to my questions about their gun laws.

Of the almost half-a-million gun owners licensed in New Zealand, less than 5,000 hold Class B or Class C types, wherein pistols, and some machine guns and assault rifles are permitted. Many license holders who own and use pistols admit to the fact only reluctantly. They just don't think about pistols.

Private gun ownership is permitted and, in fact, even encouraged in New Zealand. About one in four citizens legally owns a rifle, shotgun or, in a minor sense, a pistol.

Some assault rifles and some machine guns and pistols are permitted. Ownership of any type of machine gun in New Zealand is a bit uncertain. Owners tell me they have them and that they fire their machine guns at targets and out into the ocean. Local police tell me that this is okay. But spokesmen at the National Police Headquarters say a vital part of the gun must be removed or that these guns must be altered so that no live ammunition can be fired in them.

New Zealand gun owners must first apply for and receive a current "Firearms Owners License." This license, valid for ten years, is issued by passing a relatively easy written exam after taking a firearms safety course, taught by the local police. You take the course, pass the written, are 16 years of age and are of good moral character with an unblemished record, and the owner's license is yours. Unlike in some countries, New Zealand police don't try to stonewall on this one. Citizens are encouraged to get their "FOLS."

Firearms-license holders can purchase as many sporting rifles and shotguns as they wish. All calibers and types are permitted. A surprising range of makes and models, including semi-auto hunting rifles and shotguns are available. Prices in the very numerous gun shops are only slightly higher than in the U.S. Local gun shops may legally sell guns to anyone with a firearms-owner's license with a Class A endorsement. Records are kept in the shop—not at a central governmental agency—for five years. Then they can be destroyed.

Holders of Class A firearms-owners Licenses can seek a Class B endorsement that allows possession and use of any type of pistol or revolver. As many pistols and revolvers as one wishes may be purchased and used under a Class B endorsement. But there are differences and some restrictions.

First, keep in mind that very, very few New Zealanders want a pistol, much less a number of them. Pistol owners and shooters must be members in good standing of a bona fide, incorporated, police approved pistol-shooting club. After six months' membership, these clubs issue the written recommendations needed for a Class B license. For this and Class C endorsements, the police do a background check including friends, relatives and neighbors. The first person they interview if there is such is the spouse. If the spouse doesn't want it, you don't get a pistol endorsement.

It takes about one month. Then owners can legally keep their pistol around the house as well as legally transport it to and from their pistol club/range for use by the owner. This carrying virtually never includes personal protection. Pistols cannot be carried anyplace but around the home or to and from the range. Pistols are registered with local police.

Gun-storage requirements are very stringent and exacting in New Zealand. Your friendly local police will tell you exactly how it should be done. Some owners comment on the cost and complexity of constructing secure rooms for their guns and ammo. In all cases, ammunition must be locked away from pistols.

Class C, or collectors, permits allow for machine guns, machine pistols, rifles, pistols, and shotguns and include some assault rifles. New Zealand police have a list of exactly which assault rifles are permitted. There aren't a great many, because New Zealand hunters and collectors see little practical value to these type firearms. Ownership of assault rifles is controlled by issuing few import permissions for them.

Lock-up storage requirements for C-level endorsements are even more stringent, involving double locks, steel bars and doors and more. All storage lockups are subject to police inspection. As a practical matter, far more inspections are made under Class B and C permits than for Class A ones. As a practical matter, New Zealand farmers carry rifles or shotguns as a more-or-less permanent fixture on their all-terrain vehicles or trucks, rather than locked away in some secure storage.

Ammunition in any quantity is freely sold to anyone with a firearms-owners license. Inexpensive surplus ammo is available in most gun shops, with no restrictions on ammo caliber, type or size. American and Australian commercial ammo is also on offer. One also sees pistol ammo on offer in most gun shops. Sales records are kept in house. These are not forwarded to any central authority.

Reloading is permitted and encouraged. Bullets, primers and powder are all available. Just show the friendly clerk your firearms-owners license and away you go.

Non-citizens legally living in New Zealand can shoot on the ranges or secure temporary membership in some of the clubs. Importation of private firearms is problematic. If they are all sporting-type weapons and if you are willing to wait for necessary owners' licenses and proper classes of endorsements, many types of assault rifles can be imported. Minor changes are frequently made. For example, there are current restrictions on double-barreled shotguns with exposed hammers, shotguns with barrels less than 20 inches, pistols with barrels less than four inches, bullpup type firearms or bullpup stocks. Ask and you will be helped by government people whose first reaction is not antagonism but understanding of your own personal desire to own these particular guns.

Dealers' licenses are available to citizens who want to go into the business. Tinkerers and designers find at least initial acceptance of their work in New Zealand. Given their tendency to Luddite excesses, successful modern designers may find they eventually incur the wrath of the citizenry.

Record keeping requirements and lock-up facilities for dealers are stringent, but many, many variety and general stores carry some guns and ammo so they must be reasonable. Dealers tell me there is a great "to do list" but it is not an overly onerous one.

Private sales are allowed. Law abiding New Zealanders make it a practice to only sell privately to legal license holders. Private sales of pistols must be cleared through local police. Property and contract laws are rigorously enforced and guaranteed in New Zealand.

New Zealand is, of course, a remote and distant island. Nothing much is near down there in the South Pacific. For this reason, it is a shock to learn that there is something of a problem with illegal pools of guns in their society. However, like all crime reporting in New Zealand, this may be relative! Their crime rate is very, very low. Guns are used in commission of only about one fourth of these very few crimes.

Given their national propensity to fuss over rising crime rates, this pool of illegal guns is certainly of concern. Police claim illegal guns come to the country as war trophies, are stolen guns, and might be guns taken from armories and, in a very few instances, from the police. Sounds like a classic example of grasping at straws. I did see an occasional article in the local newspapers regarding discovery of illegal guns, mostly in relation to searches for illegal drugs.

At this writing, stringent new private-gun-ownership regulations are being proposed by the Labor government, not the police. Not to worry. New Zealand is one big pretty happy family used to talking things over together, so that the best possible solution for everyone concerned comes forward. They will accommodate the one fourth of their number who currently own guns.

As mentioned, in 1996 a new form of government was approved and implemented in New Zealand. Their constitution was changed, effectively precluding anything much from happening very quickly and, in many cases, from happening at all.

Their gun laws may be a model of simplicity, but acceptance of something similar in the U.S. would be iffy. New Zealanders have very different ways of looking at things, and they do have shared common concerns. One million of their four million are gun owners. Their police are their friends. It may not be on the Swiss or American pattern, but private gun ownerships will persist in New Zealand. And God bless them all.

Chapter Sixteen
Colombia
World Rank: 60 • Firearm Freedom 8%

There is a lesson here! It's not because most gun buffs would voluntarily choose to live in a land riven with open warfare between contending rival government factions, drug armies and common gangsters that we explore private gun ownership in Colombia.

Peaceful, freedom-loving American gun owners need to look carefully at the example of the South American country of Colombia. Here we find the future, if we are not careful, diligent and hard-working. Many other lessons apply to Colombian gun laws, some which are not immediately obvious, but basic to conduct of our society. As is so often true, ignore this at your peril.

No one answered the phone at the Colombian Dept. of Control of Small Arms, Munitions and Explosives, for four days. We decided to take the 30-minute taxi ride across Bogota in an attempt to score an interview with someone who knew about "private" gun ownership.

Since we had no appointment, we were politely asked to write out our questions regarding firearms ownership and then wait for the colonel in charge to call back with a time to come back and talk. Seems the Head Man was in an extremely important UN conference, wherein vital issues of "private gun ownership" were being urgently discussed.

Gun "ownership" in Colombia, we soon discovered, is a completely notional, erroneous concept. You only *rent* you guns from the quasi-military/police control organization that controls all legal firearms. Legal possession is possible only under the strictest of rules. All guns legally held are subject to instantaneous confiscation without any reasons or prior warning given. Absolutely no written rules and regulations set out terms and conditions for summary confiscation.

Several "kind of" sporting good shops were scattered up and down the road across from the Army Dept. of Arms Control in western Bogota.

They handled knives, web gear, holsters, gun-cleaning supplies, binoculars, scopes, sights, and pistol and rifle magazines but, other than a few very wimpy, cheap air rifles, no real guns or ammunition. Air rifles, we later learned, are not controlled in Colombia. Supposedly these shops also offered gunsmithing services including repair. But it was not obvious to what extent or level these services extended.

A very busy clerk in one of these shops agreed to fill us in on Colombian rules and regulations relative to private gun ownership.

Immediately, almost reflexively, this fellow confirmed the fact that—other than illegal gun ownership which was quite common in Colombia because securing a legal gun was so awfully time consuming, expensive, humiliating and difficult—citizens really only rented their guns from the military.

These could be rifles, shotguns and/or pistols. No one person could legally own more than five guns. Two of these could be pistols, which theoretically could be legally carried. But at that very moment, other bureaucrats in Bogota—Columbia's capitol city—were proposing a two-week-per-month limit on legal carry. I am not making this up!

Were there limitations on size and type of action of these five guns? Yes, tremendous limits, enforced by the fact that the army imports any and all legal guns and ammo into the country, other than a few manufactured in Colombia under strict military oversight and control. In other words, only makes, models and calibers the military bureaucrats think appropriate are legally allowed into the country.

Additionally, no sanction for any gun is given without a good, valid and sound reason for ownership—in the eyes of military bureaucrats.

Supposedly bolt-action, lever-action and single-shot rifles are sanctioned. No semi-auto rifles, but three-shot semi-auto shotguns in all common gauges are OK.

All semi-auto pistols must include permanently altered magazines that hold only nine rounds. Our friendly clerk knew of one police/military officer who was "caught" with a ten-round magazine for his service pistol. In penalty, he was immediately stripped of his sidearm. "How was he to protect and enforce in an ugly situation?" the clerk mused.

Magazine capacity for .22 LR and .32 ACP pistols is not limited to nine rounds, but full capacity .32 ACP pistols certainly are not common. Special permits, costing about $2,700 U.S., are issued for full-capacity pistols, but these have to be renewed and paid for *annually*.

Because all ammo is (or is not) imported or made by the military, some perfectly legal gun owners keep guns for which no ammunition is available. We were told later, in the ministry, that special-order guns and ammo for Alaskan or African hunters was sometimes imported, but it was such a pain they were very reluctant to do so.

Prices for imported and domestically made guns and ammo are set arbitrarily by the military. As a result, prices are five to ten times higher than in the U.S. Few Colombians can afford to purchase and pay for permits and taxes for the five guns individually sanctioned.

Purchasing ammunition is even more convoluted and expensive. Legal pistol owners are allowed to purchase 100 rounds every six months,

only for guns on their permits. Similarly, shotgun and rifle owners can
purchase every six months, but the total is a grand 300 rounds, unless
you belong to a shooting or hunting club wherein allotments of ammo
are slightly more generous. All ammo in Colombia is frightfully
expensive—about $1 per round for 9mm.

Only two places in Bogota and one or two in outlying areas sell
ammo. You take a signed, notarized letter to the military store along
with a notarized copy of your gun-owner's permit necessary to
consummate the transaction.

Travel in Colombia on their treacherous, narrow mountain roads is not
easy. Much of the country, including Bogota, is severely mountainous
characterized by severe terrain. Numerous wild rivers rage down out
of the mountains, necessitating a great many often one-way bridges,
again creating long delays while awaiting a turn to cross. Colombia
lies on the north edge of South America, bordering both the Caribbean
and the Pacific. Land area is about 75% the size of Alaska.

Colombia had, and still has, a bad reputation as being a lawless, drug-
sotted place, where living is dangerous and uncertain. True up until
about six years ago. Back then, murders and kidnappings were world-
class epidemic. No one really believed they were safe in Colombia.

While this is no longer true, be prepared—some gun-control fanatics
may falsely claim that Colombia's draconian gun laws helped turn the
tide. This is simply not true, because part of the pacification program
included some relaxation, not hardening, of Colombian gun laws.

According to the U.S. Embassy nine years ago, the legal limit was just
one pistol. No rifles or shotguns. It wasn't their gun-controlling laws
that reduced crime. It was a series of enlightened policies that
extended amnesty to the guerillas along with very rigorous, brilliantly
organized military action that turned the tide. Today, Colombians live
in relative peace and freedom. Their *per capita* income has spiked up
to about $9,400.

But I digress. The next day, the chief minister of the Dept. of Arms
Control surprised us, calling to set an interview. I thought of this as we
lay trapped often for two or more hours in monstrous traffic jams. Very
difficult to set an appointment and be there on time.

Colombian police are a curious mixture of police and soldier. They do
not know how to effectively take charge of a traffic incident. A small
reminder of the fact that we should not expect our military to properly
handle police problems either (and they are banned from acting as
police, under the famous *posse comitatus* law).

Colombians, used to sitting up to days at a time in traffic jams, are a
patient lot. I thought of this fact as we walked through a waiting area

containing dozens (perhaps hundreds) of folks waiting for their number to be called so that they could submit their applications (or renewal applications) for gun ownership cards.

The colonel in charge was friendly enough. He informed us that it cost between $2,200 and $2,700 for *each* gun permit, not including gun purchase and taxes. Applicants must be 25 years old or more. They can wear eyeglasses but not hearing aids. An expensive medical, economic, psychiatric and criminal exam is part of the process. Takes from three to four months for one's application to be processed. Permits are mostly good for three years, but can be renewed after that at slightly reduced rates. Permits to carry nine shooters are another $130 every three years.

In conclusion, the colonel informed us that they have successfully confiscated and destroyed more than 242,000 illegal guns since 1992. He would not venture a guess about the origin of these guns. He was intensely proud of the fact that Colombia met the UN world standard for private small arms control—he claimed he knew the exact model, type and location of every legal gun in Colombia! So, there we have it, the absolute gold standard for private gun ownership on the part of an ignorant, fearful bunch of bed wetting, anti-Semitic, overpaid, under-accomplished UN bureaucrats. And that stops crime, how, exactly?

Chapter Seventeen
Vietnam
World Rank: 63 (last place) • Firearm Freedom 0%

April 30, 1975. North Vietnamese tanks penetrate South Vietnam's dispirited, feeble defenses around their capital. Saigon falls! After more than 20 years of open warfare, the communists finally have their wish. Vietnam is unified under a single autocratic government. The victors begin setting their agendas, including draconian rules and regulations for private property, contract law and civilian ownership of firearms.

Many of us recall these times, some lived and fought in Vietnam. Now ageing veterans tell me they can still smell the country, 30 years later. Reportedly, the average Vietnamese is in their mid-20s. More than in the U.S., Vietnamese recall of these incidents is mostly from textbooks and historical photos, mostly driven by official propaganda.

A merchant-seaman friend was in and out of the port of Saigon during the wild and crazy days of the 1960s and 1970s, delivering war materiel. The U.S. spent over $141 billion on war in South Vietnam.

Each time he called in Saigon, he purchased a new Chinese AK-47 and a case of ammo. It was good fun, he said, blasting away on open sea as they charged over the bounding Pacific waves in pursuit of the next cargo. By the time they reached Portland or Seattle, their ammo was expended and they simply tossed the AK overboard. Simpler and cheaper to get a new one next time they were in Saigon.

Vietnam, at one time, was a haven of individual gun ownership. There were all kinds, types and calibers. Everything from small .22 short auto pistols to heavy machine guns. North Vietnamese brought guns and ammo down by the ton, and we shipped entire depots of WWII European surplus to the country. South Vietnam issued firearms to soldiers and civilians alike.

Civilians got them as part of a hamlet defense program. To be sure, lines of legality were often blurred. But we do know lots of folks in South Vietnam had large numbers of guns.

Even back when Vietnam was making history, Americans had trouble keeping track of where exactly the country was physically located. Now, as then, it occupies the eastern and southern portions of the Indochina peninsula. Vietnam and its immediate neighbors to the west—Laos and Cambodia—are Southeast Asia. The South China Sea borders Vietnam's entire eastern coast. Arizona is one half the size of both North and South Vietnam—divisions that the communists never did recognize.

Their economy since the takeover has really been stuck in the mud, one of the worst on Earth, by just about anyone's measure. Only the political elite have any semblance of modern life. *Per capita* income is only about $2,700—if you believe official data. Vietnamese principally have the opportunity to export their labor at a rate of a few cents per day, earned in horrible sweatshops.

Some 1.3 million Vietnamese died for a better life. Their goal of a better life has completely and absolutely eluded them. This is not the people's republic promised. There are absolutely no property rights, no rule of law, and absolutely no human rights. Older, lower echelon Viet Cong wonder what they personally fought for. Whatever it was, they didn't get it.

Information for this chapter comes from two books on Vietnam, and from conversations with ex-GIs who have recently returned to visit their historic battlegrounds. Best information came from an American married to a Vietnamese lady who heavily researched this topic for us. He closely questioned the issue of private individual gun ownership in Vietnam among elders in a Vietnamese community in the southern U.S. Their conclusion follows. It is based on current, actual, on-the-ground experience in their native land.

At the conclusion of the war in 1975 the victorious Viet Cong government hastily issued strict orders that all persons holding any arms and ammunition must immediately turn them over to the police or to military cadres. Private ownership of any firearms by anyone but police and military personnel was, from now on, strictly forbidden.

Newly self-installed government leaders required that all citizens report existence and location of any guns they knew of including all in civilian hands. New laws stipulated that citizens who even talked about guns to the wrong people could be held in jail for up to one month without being charged or provided opportunity for bail. Reportedly these extremely severe measures were often deployed.

In a land awash with small arms up through heavy mortars, where many peasant soldiers kept their guns and ammunition cached in sealed inner tube containers under rice paddies, such measures were seen as necessary by the political bosses. It was the only way to disarm a well-armed population, thus forestalling a counter-revolution including political assassinations. Police were given a free hand to interrogate any citizens they suspected of not turning in their guns. Amnesty International characterizes this interrogation as raw torture.

Hunting is completely forbidden in Vietnam. What little wild game remains is taken by rural people with clever traps and snares. Vietnamese elders say the economy is so bad rural folks could not even afford firearms or ammunition of any kind under any circumstances, even if legal.

Reloading is not legal. No components are available for sale. Reloading as an emergency measure may be undertaken illegally by some very few rural people or by members of some of the many illegal gangs, but not as a legitimate pursuit by honest, private gun owners.

The Vietnamese government has sold tremendous numbers of guns and ammunition they've collected, on the international market. Despite these extensive exports, there are still a great many illegal guns in the country. Reportedly about anything up through 20mm cannons can be purchased through contacts on the street. Vietnamese are so poor they do virtually anything for cash. Meanwhile no such thing as a legal gun shop or hand loading among citizens exists in the country.

To this day the government is extremely paranoid about private gun ownership. They saw first hand what happens and validly concluded that armed citizens who already know how to organize and fight successful revolutions are a real danger to their autocratic regime.

For this reason their gun laws are unlikely to change. Many other countries around the world have displayed similar philosophies. In Vietnam the fear of an armed populace is more open and notorious.

In the meantime, crime throughout Vietnam is endemic. Much of it is perpetrated by government personnel with tacit government sanction. But no matter what type of crime is visited on Vietnamese, they have little means of defense. Knives, pointed sticks and machetes are all.

Vietnam is undoubtedly one of the worst examples of politicians promising one thing while doing the absolute opposite. Freedom's promises were never delivered. Lessons learned there, including the moral hazards of following an idealistic, impractical, pie-in-the-sky social scheme, should not be lost on American gun owners.

Chapter Eighteen
Thailand
World Rank: 33 • Firearm Freedom 40%

Thailand is, for all practical matters, the only oriental country in which citizens can legally own private firearms under any circumstances. Only three guns per person including a pistol, shotgun and small-caliber rifle, but it is something—especially when compared to other Asian countries.

Numerous private armies and insurgent groups operate in surrounding Burma, Laos and Cambodia, but the many weapons they possess are completely illegal. So illegal in fact that central government forces spend huge amounts of time and money chasing around trying to take these weapons away. Get caught with an illegal gun and it could lead to life in prison in Thailand.

Here is another regional example. Private gun ownership in the highly fascist, oriental city-state of Singapore, for instance, can be a capital offense. Contemporary Straits Times newspaper articles confirm that a resident discovered with a pistol buried in his back yard for more than 20 years, who probably didn't even know it was there, was recently given an arbitrary 30-year prison sentence! Singaporeans have been sentenced to death for illegal gun ownership in a city-state where legal ownership is impossible.

But back in good old fun-loving Thailand, conditions are dramatically different. Business people brag that they can own a gun if they wish. As a kind of back-handed confirmation, Japanese businessmen and police complain bitterly that most of the illegal guns they find in Japan have their origin in Thailand. In competition with sex tourism, Japanese and Chinese tourists come to Thailand to charter boats that run them out into the Gulf of Thailand to blaze away at floating bottles. Big bucks and great fun, these visitors claim.

But in this case especially, it isn't that simple. Understanding Thai gun ownership requires that readers know a bit about Thai culture, customs and—of course—the law. Information for this chapter came from my 3-1/2 years spent in and around Thailand working in every district from north to south, a DEA agent who lived and worked in Thailand, a U.S. government employee married to a Thai, and a U.S. State Department employee. I also talked to a great many gun-shop owners and proprietors, many Thai businessmen and some Thai students.

In the case of the employee married to the Thai lady, we are left to ponder which agency and what duties he has for the U.S. government. We don't know and he isn't volunteering any information. We do know that this fellow was an avid big-game hunter/sportsman who probably shot the last man-eating tiger in the country while living in rural Thailand.

Thailand, Indonesia and Mexico are notorious world over for political corruption and bribery. Perhaps only Nigeria is worse. Requests for payoffs are more pervasive in Indonesia and Mexico, but it goes on in Thailand with a distinctive Thai flavor. Mexican officials are poorly paid as compared to Thai officials. For this and cultural reasons, police in Mexico will leave their assigned post and duties to specifically shake down a gringo for $5 on some foolish, trumped up charge. We see it often; Mexican police lose all sense of duty, decorum and personal integrity in an immediate attempt to extort enough money for a new dress for their mistress.

On the other hand, Thai police and government bureaucrats seem never to lose sight of their agreed-upon duty and decorum. They are softly accepting of the competency needed to enforce existing rules and regulations, to provide for their citizen charges and to make a few bucks under the table without being overbearing about it—i.e. that police do not desert their posts as traffic cops to collect bribes.

At the same time, it is often said that virtually everything is illegal in Thailand! Prostitution is very illegal in Thailand—a huge surprise to tourists who have seen its vast sex industry up close and dirty. Thai citizens, especially those in business, survive because they pay little to no attention to the vast bureaucracy and all its rules and regulations, while spreading a few dollars where they do the most good.

Those who have experienced mellow, accepting Thais first hand are usually shocked to understand that perhaps no culture on Earth ignores more of its own rules and regulations than do the Thais. If they didn't, life could not go on. But as a direct result of these permissive attitudes, gun laws since 2003 are much changed here. Bureaucrats in the Thai Department of Interior now control gun-owners' permits.

While rules and regulations are frequently ignored, this does not lead to anarchy. Cultural tradition and social pressure preserve order in Thailand (about the size of France.) A great pool of reverence for the king and his authority is also out there. Also, Thais firmly believe that little or nothing should be done by force. Voluntary exchange—cash for this or that good, favor or service—is not viewed as force. Such is virtually a religious conviction.

As a result, almost anything is possible. Change often comes very slowly. New laws seldom alter Thai behavior very much. Rules and regulations regarding private gun ownership accomplish the impossible by being both flexible and unchanging.

One other anomaly of Thai culture must be understood. It may be far, far in the background but, ultimately, the military has the final say in virtually all affairs. Thai army officers are often involved in major businesses and industries. Gun-shop owners complain that the Thai military now imports its own personal small arms rather than going through dealers. There is little they can do about this loss of business. At times, military people sell firearms at cut-rate prices, further infuriating legitimate dealers.

Most Americans find Thailand to be a very nice place to live. Thais have very old, well-established cultural rules of property including strong rights of private ownership. Their country's climate—especially in the north—is moderate and benign. *Per capita* yearly income is about $8,100. Those on American salaries or pensions find their money goes a very, very long way indeed. Virtually anything available in the U.S. can be purchased just as cheaply in Thailand or, in many cases, much cheaper.

As both a practical and legal matter, limited private ownership of firearms is legal and possible in Thailand. Pistols, rifles, shotguns and even some semi-auto .22-caliber rifles are permitted. Rifles are limited to .22 rimfire or .223s. Larger caliber rifles may be permitted but are not sanctioned for import, creating a permit of no value. Semi-auto shotguns and lever action and semi-auto .22s are approved. Full-auto machine guns, assault rifles and machine pistols as well as silencers are verboten.

Each separate legal weapon must be approved by the local district officer who administers through the Department of Interior. These authorities decide both if the applicant is worthy of that weapon ownership, and if the person really needs the gun applied for. As alluded to earlier, this authorization may not be based entirely on current code sections, and it may not even be based on an outright bribe. Officials may look at the social status, business position and/or the threat under which the applicant operates. Jewelry stores in

Bangkok and even remote Chaing Mai, for instance, routinely inventory three to five million dollars worth of stones and gold! Government officials generally don't want the sole responsibility of being sure these shopkeepers are not held up. Pistol permits for these folks are routinely extended.

No restrictions exist relative to a pistol's caliber or magazine capacity. Both revolvers and semi-autos are sanctioned. In times past, privately held assault rifles were possible, but under current law, not.

Strangely, it is generally thought to be quicker and easier to secure a legal permit for a pistol or shotgun than for a rifle in Thailand. Little hunting except for birds remains in Thai jungles. Such as they are, hunting licenses are issued by the Thai Department of Agriculture.

Wars and insurgencies on their borders and sometimes within the country have decimated Thailand's big-game populations. Small game animals and birds are still hunted to some extent. Catching sight of hunters with rifles slung over their backs riding out into the country on their motorcycles is still fairly common. These folks may have permits as well as current hunting licenses, required by law, but it is doubtful. Perhaps half the guns I saw appeared to have been home made.

Officials seem to reason that if a shopkeeper wishes to own a pistol, life and property are probably at risk, so best to allow the application.

Each government bureaucracy desperately wants to operate with as much autonomy as possible. This is an advantage when a gun-owning citizen makes application at the local Interior Department office. Local bureaucrats tend to be jealous of their prerogatives. As a result, an effort is made to handle everything themselves without outside consultation or interference. Yet Department of Interior people—we are told—still cooperate closely with local police.

Entertaining the local police captain, military commander or Interior bureaucrat with dinner and drinks occasionally before application is thought to be "helpful." Not only when securing a gun permit, but for all of life in Thailand. "It is a good way to indicate you are a substantial person actually in need of a personal gun," we are told.

Firearms applications cover several pages but are not judged by Thai gun owners to be particularly onerous. Cost of the application itself is only a couple of dollars. Applications include fingerprints taken by the police. Your record provided by the police, and a strong letter of recommendation provided by a disinterested third party are attached to the application. Applicants must have full-time employment and may be required to demonstrate financial capabilities.

Guns and ammunition are available at stores in Bangkok. Many gun stores are scattered throughout the nation, about 250 total, we are told, all run by Chinese. A good selection of pistols, shotguns and .22 rifles are available at these stores. We counted at least 19 gun shops in one small area of Bangkok alone. As in other countries, purchasers take their bill of sale—including all identifying characteristics of the gun—to the local district officer where permission is sought for that specific weapon. A temporary permit is issued. Using this, new owner and gun-store personnel must appear together at Interior with that specific gun for final inspection and registration. This assumes one's firearm-owner's permit is approved.

Gun stores also sell ammunition. A separate permit is required to purchase and keep ammo, but only for guns on one's permit. Prices by our standards for everything—guns and ammo—are usurious. By Thai standards, prices are prohibitive. No doubt this places great restraint on average Thais who make only about one-fifth what Americans make per year. Other than severe price constraint, holders of valid firearms permits can purchase as much ammunition for their guns as they wish, including pistol, rifle and shotgun ammo. Pistol ammo is frequently available at reduced prices from gun clubs. Ownership of other gauges is permitted, but only 12-gauge ammo is imported—thus only 12-gauge shotguns are on offer at Bangkok gun shops.

Reloading is not done. No stores have powder and primers for sale. This issue is neatly sidestepped because no reloading components are legally imported. No hunter, citizen or businessman with whom I talked in Thailand has any knowledge of hand loading.

A very cost-effective, modern, competent, custom metal machine parts industry operates in Thailand, including manufacture of some fairly sophisticated, but yet homemade, guns.

Gun shops in Thailand seem to make most of their income from things such as spare parts, holsters, belts, binoculars and to some extent knives, magazines, carrying pouches and such. Officials deny it, claiming the only major area where one can find illegal guns is on the Burmese border, but one might conclude there are great numbers of guns, legal and illegal, floating about the country—requiring accessories and small repair parts. How else to explain shops able to keep their doors open with sales of only a few guns but lots of custom small stuff and parts?

Clerks in Thai gun stores are as knowledgeable as any American gun-store clerk about modern gun operation, disassembly, and idiosyncrasies. A friend, for instance, had replacement trigger sears custom made for FN FAL rifles as well as number of holsters for Beretta Model 92 pistols. Everything was made by hand one at a time. Fit and function were perfect. He didn't bring parts or the pistol to the shop for examination and comparison. The clerk—a woman—understood perfectly what was wanted and produced it either from memory or by copying stock items already in the shop. We don't know which, but suspect the shop had examples to copy.

Numbers of guns owned and permitted are controlled by both economics and arbitrary decisions of local bureaucrats. Three guns total would be the most any local bureaucrat would sanction—unless there were other significant extenuating circumstances. If you are a collector, designer, live in an especially dangerous place, or are a close friend of the captain, and exceptions might be extended.

Permits—when local authorities really wish to issue them—take a day or less to process. Otherwise expect several weeks to a month. Pistol permits allow you to store in your home and carry back and forth to a gun club. Permits to carry concealed are separate matter, leading to the reality that a gun owner in Thailand may require three separate permits. A gun-owner's permit leading to registration, an ammunition purchase and storage permit, and a concealed-carry permit.

A few shooting ranges supervised by the military are spotted about the nation. Citizens and permanent residents can—depending on the whim of the local captain—use these ranges, as well as purchase some less expensive military-grade ammo. A charge of from $20 to $60 is frequently assessed. You are, after all, a moneyed *farong*. Spreading it around a bit is laudatory. Finding and using a range is not essential. Thailand has lots of open countryside where practice shooting can be done. Shooting clubs featuring trap or pistol ranges are available. Club membership is seen by authorities as a valid reason for gun ownership.

Storage rules are not enforced, but let a gun registered to you get out of your control and it's big problems.

Thais are not big on trap and skeet, but some small amount of this is undertaken in the country or at gun clubs. Shotguns for trap or skeet are permitted. It's harder, probably, to find unbroken clay pigeons in Thailand than to secure a shotgun permit.

Government-type foreigners living and working in Thailand seem to have little to no problem securing necessary permits for pistols or shotguns. Current thinking is that non-citizen businessmen and perhaps even women who have been in Thailand for a time would be quickly given permission to possess a pistol, single-shot rifle or shotgun. No one can think of a recent example, so no one is sure. Yet it is necessary to be a resident of Thailand for at least six months and be over 21 years old to secure a gun-owner's permit under normal circumstances. Oddly, no students in Thailand can legally own guns. This privilege is generally limited to moneyed business people and, of course, the military. Thai military people make their own rules.

Embassy people believe it would be possible to make arrangements to bring a limited number of non-military type guns and ammunition into Thailand. They caution, however, that permits issued by a remote district officer may not be recognized by customs officers at the airport in Bangkok. Perhaps other means of persuasion would be required.

During the Vietnam conflict and currently with the American war on some drugs in full cry, illegal guns are flooding into Thailand. Drug lords, who maintain private armies, have small arms in abundance. Mostly Chinese, these range up through heavy mortars and rocket-propelled grenades. Military actions in the northern Golden Triangle are frequently characterized by a surprising amount of small-arms fire.

Drug-related bad-asses are common in Thailand. One armed with an M-16 chased me out of a poppy field north and west of Chaing Mai. I think I kept him out of range by pretending to use my large telephoto and camera mounted on an old wooden gun stock as a weapon. He probably thought I had a Garand. Good thing. He certainly could have run twice as fast as I through those heavy oriental hills.

Where does this flood of illegal, military-type weapons originate? Best guess is from Laos, Cambodia, or Vietnam, where tons and tons of left behind military hardware are still in storage. Some of the people who supplied information for this chapter suggest that at least some of the ammunition as well as many of the new AK-47s and Makarov pistols one can buy on the street come directly from Chinese arms merchants. Some seem to operate with government approval. Thai generals may, in some cases, be middlemen for some of these deals.

Securing a new license to sell guns and ammunition is now impossible. All gun shops are currently grandfathered in, from many years back. No new licenses are being issued. Interior Department weenies closely audit all business activity of Thai gun shops.

Unlike many other Asian societies, Thais do not appear to irrationally fear and suspect guns. During Vietnam, some Thai military people suggested selling guns and ammunition at reduced prices to village peasants, in an attempt to keep insurgents out of town. It was a genuine suggestion providing a workable solution to the problem of local terrorism and control. Principal opposition to this device came from American do-gooders who could not fathom the utility of personal responsibility for one's protection involving private gun ownership. Thai officials readily adopted the bad suggestion.

Chapter Nineteen
Israel
World Rank: 42 • Firearm Freedom 32%

Strike Israel off your list of countries where private citizens can reasonably and easily own firearms.

Changes in Israeli gun laws since the Rabin assassination in 1995 can only be characterized as draconian. Net results, on the ground, have been equally dramatic, none of them good.

Officials in countries such as Israel, surrounded by extremely hostile neighbors publicly intent on occupying and destroying every man, woman and child, usually allow and encourage citizens to own and become proficient with firearms. This, of course, encourages citizens' participation defending home and hearth. Disasters as a result of foolish, misguided national actions usually do not strike as quickly as they have in Israel.

In its brief but calamitous war in Lebanon in 2006, Israel paid dearly with the blood of its young men. Israeli infantry were being sent into mortal combat never having become proficient with their rifles. Most had not fired twenty rounds practicing during the prior three years. Marksmanship was worse than abysmal. Personal maintenance and operation of their otherwise excellent Galil assault rifles were completely inadequate.

As a result, Israeli Defense Forces lost confidence in their basic tool as well as in themselves. In many cases, Israeli grunts were simply unable to stand up to more experienced and practiced Hezbollah fighters.

Until the Rabin assassination, private gun ownership was herky-jerky unique but, in the final analysis, okay in Israel. A European philosophy on the part of recent arrivals, suggesting that guns in private hands was basically bad, was kept in perspective by their recent national history. Anguished, detailed records from the time of partition in 1948 graphically documented the tragedy of young citizen volunteers who paid dearly for their lack of knowledge of firearms. Frequently these desperate young men and women charged enemy machine guns with empty rifles because these European city kids didn't know how to place a loaded stripper clip in their Mauser or Enfield bolt-action rifles. Even when loaded and fireable, marksmanship on the part of these non-hunters was abysmal.

And don't count on a cadre of experienced hunters to do the work. Jews don't usually hunt, since they cannot religiously eat what they kill. Not Kosher!

Yad Mordechai provides another reasonably recent and now overlooked example of the vital importance of private gun ownership in Israel. In 1948 at the time of statehood the Egyptians invaded. Some 110 members of Kibbutz Yad Mordechai, using only private firearms which the British tried mightily to confiscate from them, held up the entire Egyptian army six vital days.

Kibbutz Yad Mordechai still exists. It lies today as it did then, slightly above the Palestinian area called Gaza. It straddles the main road from Cairo to Tel Aviv and Jerusalem.

Using tanks, artillery and huge numbers of infantry, the Egyptian army tried to break through, but they couldn't. By holding out six days, the Israelis in Tel Aviv were able to form and supply a viable defense.

One would suppose that Israeli gun laws would reflect a "never again" mentality. One that said we will never again be treated like rats in a barrel to be summarily executed at the whim of some insane dictator. Sadly this is not the current mentality.

Information for this chapter comes from three in-depth personal visits to Israel, numerous conversations with gun owners and soldiers on active duty, information from an Israeli author-writer and, ironically, the proprietor of the country's oldest retail gun shop. They started business in 1949 while the smoke of the war for independence still drifted about. Israel's gun laws have changed dramatically since then.

As an interesting aside, I also participated in a fifth-grade school field trip—to the site of the David v. Goliath rumble. Of the parents along on the outing, at least five were packing heat. Although now extremely restrictive, there is still a curious mix of tight private restrictions along with some grudging recognition that they do live in a very dangerous, hostile environment.

Reloading, for instance, is mightily discouraged in Israel. Licenses to buy powder and primers for reloading are rarely given. Generally only factory-like facilities turn out machine-perfect rounds.

This may be due to fear of allowing explosive components out into the general population. More likely this prohibition recognizes that Jewish guns and ammo are seldom used for sporting purposes. Deadly purpose, for which they are deployed, recognizes that everything must be as nearly perfect and reliable as humans can make them.

Some Israeli officials with whom I spoke complained bitterly regarding hot tempered, passionate gun-owning citizens who caused mayhem with their private firearms. Pointing out that confusing police and cultural matters with national defense could be deadly, in their case, was a non-starter.

Less-than-Massachusetts-sized Israel lies along the far eastern edge of the Mediterranean Sea. Egypt borders to the southwest, Jordan to the east and southeast, and Lebanon and Syria to the north and northeast. Currently Jordan and Egypt are mostly okay with Israel. The others are hostile to extremely and openly hostile.

Per capita income in Israel is about $20,800. Israeli taxes are high to confiscatory. Living expenses can also be ruinous. Pistols we saw in stores start at a low of $400 for a used Hungarian Browning Hi-Power to about $1,000 for a new, top of the line Glock. Nevertheless Israeli gun buffs can generally afford at least some of the guns they covet.

Only Jews who live in areas officially recognized to be "hostile" can own a single pistol! Rifles of any kind are never permitted. A single exception sometimes occurs in the case of a very few remaining gun clubs that feature target shooting with .22 rifles and air guns. Only members of these clubs can shoot rimfire rifles which, in all cases, remain the property of the club, stored at the club.

A few sniper-type long distance shooting clubs were once active. They used larger centerfire rifles with scopes sometimes supplied by the government. Ironically club members could be called out in times of national emergency to do a bit of real-life target practice. Tragically, during the last seven years, all these gun clubs have been forced to atrophy and shrivel and, in many cases die—ending what little large-bore rifle ownership that once existed.

Shotgun ownership is permitted if one is a member of a skeet or trap club and/or has a valid hunting license. A maximum of one shotgun per activity will be sanctioned. Ironically no new hunting licenses have been issued for seven long years. Most pump, sporting semi-autos, doubles and single-barreled guns are okay. Most are 12-gauge, but 16, 20 and .410s are also okay.

The real clincher is that a two year's "experience" membership in a sporting-clay club is required before personal ownership permission will be given for a shotgun. Since no hunting licenses are being issued, it's a single sporting-clay shotgun per person situation in Israel.

There are no restrictions on make, model, magazine capacity, caliber or barrel length for those sanctioned their single pistol, living in dangerous areas.

Time was when kibbutzim in dangerous areas could get and store military small arms and ammunition in their arms rooms. These guns and ammo supplied by the government could include submachine guns, light and medium machine guns and even mortars in some cases. Kibbutzniks didn't really own these guns, but the price was right. And, members could enjoy practicing with them if they wished.

Generally this government support has also been phased out, much to the consternation of many kibbutzniks. This stand down was probably because of the potential for armed dissent on the part of Israelis in contested areas when they were forcibly evicted from their homes. Yet the greater need for continued strong national defense again comes into view in this instance.

Club memberships cost about $100 per year. In times past, clubs were formed around major political parties or religious organizations. People joined clubs reflecting their political sentiments. Today they just join, no politics involved. Clubs in Israel can be anything from sports to car to debating-society-type organizations, including guns and shooting. There are likely about 100 shooting clubs currently in Israel among the thousands of clubs formed for other purposes.

Application for a gun-owner's permit starts with a four-page form filled out and delivered to the Ministry of Interior. It is said that everything in Israel starts with one's government identity card. This card can give evidence of past training and experience—in the military, for instance. Evidence of club membership and participation is also necessary. A doctor's statement regarding eyesight, any debilitating medical conditions such as Parkinson's, medications and one's mental state must also be submitted with the application. One's papers go to the police where records searches are made looking for any legal issues or problems. Even very minor infractions can be used for denial. Every owner must have what is judged to be a "good reason" to own a gun.

A gun-owner's permit costs about $40, good for three years. Reissue is pretty much automatic if you pays the man and don't rock the boat politically or legally. Usually takes four to six weeks for a new issue.

Ammunition sales are a bit strange in Israel, somewhat like Switzerland in part. Pistol owners are allowed 50 rounds every three years, and only for the pistol on their permit, except owners may purchase and use unlimited amounts of ammo at reduced prices at their clubs. Supposedly all this ammo must be used at the club. None is supposed to be taken out. All ammo sales, even at the club, are recorded to the gun-owner's permit.

Fifty rounds of 9mm pistol ammo costs about $25 at the local gun shop we visited. There are some but not many gun shops sprinkled about Israel.

Pistol and rifle silencers are said to be "common as goat poop" among the police and military but are very illegal for common folk.

Shotgun owners with proper papers are allowed 600 rounds per year, and of course, recorded to their license. At the club they can purchase as much shotgun ammo as they can afford. Skeet ammo, 25 to the box, costs about $10 in Israeli gun shops.

Judging by the great success amnesty turn-in drives still generate, there is said to be a huge number of all kinds of illegal weapons in Israel. As one might suppose, these are left-behinds from the many, many wars fought over that land. Penalties, especially when discovered illegally in non-Jewish hands, are severe.

Many weapons are still turned in, probably because in tightly packed Israel there are few places to safely enjoy them. On the other hand, sounds of gunfire and heavy munitions, especially along the West Bank and Gaza, are extremely common.

And that's the way it currently is in Israel. Doesn't take a Phi Beta Kappa in philosophy, given the hostile nature of the region, to conclude that Israel is courting disaster with its restrictive gun policies.

In the advent of an emergency leading to a general call-up, quickly distributing sufficient weapons will be next to impossible. The current level of weapons expertise and knowledge among average Israelis is demonstrably and abominably inadequate, even among active-duty soldiers.

Chapter Twenty
Ships at Sea
Not Rated

Here is a suggestion for bypassing at least some of the innumerable laws and restrictions that infringe upon private gun ownership. It's not applicable to everyone, perhaps, but it might affect you. It was made to me by some of the hundreds of people worldwide, with whom I have spoken about problems of free, unencumbered gun ownership.

Either by hiring someone qualified, or by taking necessary schooling and tests, become the licensed captain and/or owner of your own vessel operating on the high seas—out of reach of any government! Vessels operating on the oceans, twelve or more miles off shore, can carry and deploy all of the guns and munitions the captain or owner wishes—or can afford.

Other than the obvious constraint that any vessel must occasionally touch what may be a hostile shore, this is not an entirely dumb idea. Especially in this age of great affluence. Romantic notions of sailing a vessel 'round the world, in and out of exotic ports of call, quickly come to mind. Could dedicated, well-to-do gun enthusiasts purchase their own vessel, which they sail about the world, accomplishing the goals of personal freedom and unencumbered gun ownership while still occasionally sailing into exotic, interesting ports? Could they pick up all the unique and different firearms they wish? Thoughts of private ownership of a 20mm gun, RPG-7 grenades, heavy machine guns and other such come to mind.

"Medium cargo ships and even smaller, high-seas yachts have lockable arms cabinets," I was instructed. You sail into a restrictive port in a totalitarian country and the captain simply secures the arms locker. That's all there is to it, according to several old salts.

Some also thought arrangements could be made in many ports around the world to purchase a variety of weapons up through some fairly heavy hardware. Even in countries with terribly restrictive laws, guns can supposedly be legally delivered to vessels where they are locked up pending quick return to the high seas. Once past the twelve-mile limit, all guns could be unlimbered for unlimited enjoyment of those on the vessel. Sounded too good to be true, in spite of the high cost of yacht ownership, qualifying for captain's papers and problems securing the firearms in distant, often hostile, ports.

Would this scheme work on large, ocean-going yachts as opposed to cargo vessels? Initially the answer was a cautious "yes" from the many we queried on this issue. Vessel registrations along with rules and regulations regarding on-board firearms differ from country to country. Obviously some additional research on this general concept was in order. Some of us who have never lusted for a private yacht might change our minds!

In the process of checking with as many different "old salts" as possible, it quickly became apparent it wasn't that simple. Several licensed captains, engineers, sailors, deck hands, private boat owners and similar such persons of knowledge contributed to this chapter. Often their information was contradictory and included many cautions, but one never knows until they investigate.

Increased piracy on the high seas was a common theme. All agreed that this was now a pervasive, serious problem. Principally in the alley formed between the Philippine islands of Palawan and Mindanao, down to Jakarta. They also reported severe problems with robbery and banditry in general in the Gulf of Siam and in the Caribbean.

One captain who crossed the Atlantic solo several times in his private 42-foot sailing vessel and had continued on as far as Athens gave the following account. Readers must judge its truth and relevance for themselves.

"I would carry a heavy machine gun and a bazooka if I could," he said. "But this is impossible. In many countries, including the United Kingdom and all of the Caribbean, port authorities search private yachts thoroughly for drugs and guns. They are totally paranoid about firearms. No such thing as sealing the gun cabinet while it is in port, at least on small vessels," he told me.

Nevertheless, this captain always carried several pistols and rifles as well as large quantities of ammunition. Owner/captains who know their own larger vessels apparently have little trouble successfully hiding their guns and ammo from the authorities, according to this fellow. Good thing.

One night our friendly Atlantic-crossing captain was sleeping alone peacefully on his little vessel anchored out in the bay near the capital city of what must remain an unnamed Caribbean island country. He wakened to a soft splash and then a heavy, rubbery thump. Browning hi-power in hand, he investigated. According to this fellow's telling it, he caught an intruder sliding over the side of his sailboat. "I jammed the pistol in his mouth and pulled the trigger." After kicking the carcass overboard, he pulled anchor and quietly slipped away. By daylight he was fifty miles gone. Could have happened—this is one crusty old fart.

Nothing official came of the incident but, as mentioned, the fellow is a strong advocate of carrying as much heavy armament as possible on any vessel operating anyplace in the world. Libertarians who thirst for government-free lawless living should keep this framework in mind.

For a time, piracy mostly disappeared from the oceans. Way back in history it was a full complement of deck guns, then some rifles, needed to protect the crew and cargo. After continually drifting down to just a couple of old .38 S&W pistols, numbers and weight of weapons carried by large cargo freighters for protection has again increased exponentially. "In the old days we had a carbine at most," one engineer said. "Now it's at least six modern assault rifles and dozens of loaded magazines. This because of the worldwide increase in piracy," he pointed out.

Whether small arms can be legally carried on board a vessel depends partly on its country of registration and partly on how vigorously those regulations are enforced by that country. None of the seafarers I spoke with had any ideas as to how to determine what rules applied. In many cases nothing is said. It is just assumed that a licensed captain will be responsible for his vessel and his crew's safety.

Can owner/captains of small or large private yachts keep virtually unlimited unlicensed guns on board their vessels? Both a U.S. customs agent and a Coast Guard official told me that basically they enforce the laws of the state where the vessel is anchored. They claimed not to be as specifically worried about guns as are officials in the U.K. or the Caribbean countries. "We often see them," the customs guy said.

No one could, as a practical matter, tell me how rigorous these state laws were enforced. Some private captains and engineers claimed there was little to no problem in U.S. ports so long as the captain has his papers in order, guns were locked away and it wasn't something overt or obvious. "Like a 20mm gun. That would be questionable when discovered, raising all kinds of red flags," one guy said.

But what about a simple Model 1919 A4 Browning air-cooled machine gun? Nobody knew for sure!

There appears to be a dramatically different standard for large, several-hundred-foot-long, obviously commercial vessels and smaller personal yachts, even yachts in the fifty-foot-plus category costing ten to twenty million dollars.

We do know that levels of armament on these larger personal vessels is increasing dramatically and that at least some authorities, even in intensely gun-paranoid places such as the U.K. and Portugal, sometimes overlook this armament when the master has a good story. An engineer recently in and out of ports in these two places confirms this, but only for very large private vessels operated by a full-time professional captain and crew.

But who is going to risk their multi-million-dollar yacht checking out levels of enforcement? I tried by asking the captain of a very large and obviously luxurious personal vessel tied up in harbor at Cabo San Lucas, Mexico. He wasn't very talkative. In reality the private yacht theory seems to be a non-starter, at least for private yachts of a size most boating enthusiasts are likely to own.

Many details of this issue are uncertain. We do know large, obviously commercial vessels can and do carry some fairly heavy firepower. Small private yachts are checked for guns in some ports. Many captains successfully hide their guns in the bowels of their vessels. Guns on very large private yachts are a question with no answer.

This leaves one last issue. Can licensed masters of even smallish private vessels purchase interesting guns and ammunition in foreign ports around the world? Here is the latest from the "been there done that" folks, subject—of course—to ever shifting situations.

No chance of purchasing any guns, legal or black market, in any port in Scotland, Wales or the U.K. International gun sales are supposedly permitted, but don't hold your breath waiting for required permits.

Purchase of a great many interesting and different guns can successfully be done in the Belgian port of Antwerp. Take a taxi to one

of the gun shops in the city and ask the clerk. It will take a day or two
and the prices will be high (yet not ruinous), but success can be yours.

Purchasing firearms in U.S. ports is a matter of state law. New England
states are stringent. Southern and Gulf states are a bit more relaxed. All
U.S. dealers require evidence of citizenship and residency so that they
can do a federal instant NICS background check.

Back in Europe, ports in Spain, Portugal and France are out of the
question. Yet reliable people claim just about anything a person might
wish is available in Hamburg under the counter. Start by asking a few
bartenders in local taverns. Selection and price are reportedly good.

Other places in the world where active, almost uncontrolled black
markets operate are Crete, Vietnam, the Philippines, and Somalia. The
port of Muscat in Oman is also reported to be a good place for those
interested in this type business. Great care must be exercised,
especially in Somalia and Oman. These good folks sincerely believe
they can and should reinstitute the slave trade (they were some of
Africa's most active slave middlemen.) White eunuchs were, in the
Somali scheme of things, the best and most valuable. Black market
dealings are extremely dangerous the world over.

Two other situations are observed. Some newer vessels are being
specially constructed that make it difficult for boarders to climb onto
the vessel or gain access to the bridge once on the vessel. Otherwise,
captains and crews on older vessels arm to the teeth while muscling
through dangerous places and Pirate Alleys at full speed.

The general philosophical concept of unencumbered ownership of
guns at sea kept in one's private floating castle has great charm.
However, vessels must come to shore where they are subject to
arbitrary, capricious and despotic, yet frequently inept governments.
Some of us may ponder pros and cons of guns on the high seas, but
this concept seems to have limited application at this time.

Chapter Twenty-One
Guatemala
World Rank: 51 • Firearm Freedom 22%

Americans who think about Central America can be forgiven for
conjuring up visions of wars, mayhem, insurrections, terrorism and
kidnappings along with breathlessly rapid changes of government. It's
an accurate characterization of the region for decades. Thankfully

Guatemalan gun store

Gun shops in Guatemala cater to a large extent to the expansive private-security trade. This store is in a major shopping center in Guatemala City, the nation's capital. It will sell to private individuals with the correct government papers in hand. Note the "burglar barrier" double-entry doors that entrap a person before they can enter, so they can be observed by the staff before being buzzed inside. The signs say, "The best in arms for your security," and "Guns, Ammo (Munitions) and Accessories." Credit card emblems include Amex, Visa, MasterCard and Diners Club.

most of these activities are in the past for Guatemala, a country that seems able to learn lessons from history.

Perhaps as memories of these "unsettled times" fade into the distant past, Central America will come to be known for its wonderful climate and scenery, friendly and outgoing people and its rich cultural history. Given their historic baggage, it is perhaps remarkable that we have anything at all to review on the subject of private firearms ownership in the region. Most of us probably assumed these basic rights also faded into the past for most Guatemalans and other Central Americans as a result of generations of internal warfare. Not so.

Currently theirs is not a system or pattern most citizens of the U.S. would find comfortable. But ask virtually any Guatemalan if private gun ownership is allowed, and you will receive a quick and resounding "yes." Even from women and old folks who otherwise know or care little about firearms.

Guatemala is the little Tennessee-sized country lying immediately below Mexico on the thin neck of land between North and South America. Belize lies to the east. Honduras and El Salvador are south and west. Guatemala is the first of the so-called Central American banana republics as you drive south through Mexico.

Per capita income is about $4,200, but rising with gratifying speed. This a much-appreciated response to a more stable, honest government. The country's economy is booming. As a result, some American investors, tourists and retirees are turning their interests from Costa Rica to Guatemala. Retirees and immigrants tend to find Guatemala's cool central highlands an absolute delight. U.S. dollars go a long, long way. Some even find visiting the jungly hot Pacific and Atlantic coastal areas interesting. Bird and animal watching, as well as biodiversity is robust!

Perhaps because Guatemalans are direct descendents of ancient Mayans, we are not surprised to learn that they have their own unique culture and set of laws, including laws pertaining to private ownership of firearms. Even their Spanish is somewhat different. Only the uninformed would lump all of these folks in Latin America together as one happy, homogenous family.

Guatemalans have a reasonably strong sense of private property, rule of law (or at least they know immediately when such has lapsed or is lacking), personal pride and a sense of the value of private contract.

Information for this chapter comes courtesy of two exchange students who lived with us for well over a year and who now have children about to become exchange students themselves. These folks are not in the Guatemalan gun culture, but graciously sought out those in the country who were, and who could provide in depth information. They also unselfishly and unabashedly provided follow up, personal interpreter services for the several in depth interviews undertaken with gun-store clerks and owners in Guatemala City.

Private, legal gun ownership is fairly easy and straightforward in Guatemala, but is overshadowed by the tremendous number of illegal guns left from their fairly recent wars and mayhems. Illegal ownership is common, including everything from M-16s and AK-47s to medium mortars. Punishment for illegal firearms possession is still jail time and fines, but Guatemalans admit there are a tremendous number of "unpapered" guns floating about the country. Enforcement of illegal gun ownership can be subjective.

Officials tend to look at the circumstances behind that ownership, how it came to the attention of the authorities and who is involved. In other words, an old man caught with an ancient unpapered Winchester lever action in his house won't be treated identically to a young man found with an AK in a stolen car transporting a load of illegal drugs. The sheer volume of illegal guns forces Guatemalan authorities to take a more pragmatic approach, which is probably a good thing in their circumstances. So-called rule-of-law often features such latitudes.

An office with the acronym of DECAM (Firearms and Ammunition Control Department, in English) is staffed and operated by officers in the Guatemalan army. They handle all the paperwork necessary for legal, private ownership of firearms throughout Guatemala.

Citizens can own just about any kind of sporting rifle, shotgun or pistol they wish, with no restriction on total numbers of guns other than a prosaic nine-gun-per-day purchase limit. Only full-auto machine guns, machine pistols, submachine guns, pure assault rifles and guns using NATO calibers such as 7.62mm are forbidden. Sporting type semi-auto shotguns are perfectly legal. Bolt action, lever action and pump rifles of any caliber are permitted.

Guatemalans can legally purchase a great variety of commercial and military surplus pistols. One sees S&W, Glock, Bersa, Sig Sauer, Beretta, Colt and many other lesser brands in gun stores scattered about the country. No restrictions on caliber or magazine capacity exist for this class of guns. Most sporting goods and gun shops are located in one district in Guatemala City, but other stores are located throughout the country. Guatemalan gun shops tend to be located in toney, expensive, new shopping centers. Many of these shops are owned and operated by ex-military people, mostly retirees.

Securing a license to open a retail gun store is said to be fairly simple. Fulfill a few basic requirements and a dealer's license is yours, I was told. It is unclear if this simplicity relates only to known ex-military people or to citizens in general. Perhaps the former.

We do know with certainty that gunsmiths are heavily restricted in Guatemala. No production of new guns or major parts, or major alterations, is officially permitted. The authorities are especially wary of anyone who might take civilian guns and put military modifications on them. As a result, most Guatemalans requiring gunsmith work take their weapons to local machine shops. Some extremely skilled and able artisans work in these places we are told.

No guns, ammunition or reloading components are manufactured in Guatemala. Everything is imported.

No one knows how a tinkerer-inventor who wanted to do gun design work would be treated in Guatemala. Some believe the military hierarchy would warm to this sort of "economic activity" but we really don't know.

Securing a gun-ownership permit is relatively quick, simple and straightforward. The down side, from the perspective of someone living in the States, is that all legal guns are papered. Go first to a local attorney to attest to the authenticity of a copy of your national-identification card. This precludes use of fake ID.

From the Supreme Court or local police, secure a copy of your records authenticating that no criminal record exists. This forces known criminals to secure firearms outside routine retail channels. Cost is about $4 and it takes about ten minutes. But this is Guatemala time. Applicants figure on spending an hour. Ten minutes is seldom more than a figure of speech in Guatemala.

Lastly the DECAM folks require a letter or other certificate from one's employer or bank documenting their income. This, they claim, precludes pissants from securing firearms but really it just assures Guatemalan authorities that the applicant is paying taxes. Perhaps forty percent of Guatemalans work in the black, off-the-books, economy. Some become quite wealthy at it.

Take these documents to your favorite gun shop. Hard core protracted bargaining over price is common in Guatemala. Make the best deal possible. Note there is no testing, club membership or other qualifications. Membership in shooting and/or hunting clubs is common in Guatemala, but not necessary to secure a gun-purchase authorization. Annual gun club memberships are about $350. There are some, but not a great many, gun clubs where members can practice shooting throughout the country. Guatemala has extended uninhabited areas. Local gun owners often set up temporary ranges in these open spaces. There are no hunting licenses in Guatemala. There also appear to be no seasons, and very little game as a result.

At the gun shop they charge an application fee of about $10 plus 50 percent of the price of the gun you have selected in order to proceed. The store will forward all three documents plus a tentative bill of sale to DECAM. After DECAM reviews all documents they send a release/sell authorization to the store. Upon receipt of an official okay, the store will call you, approving pickup of the gun, permit, invoice and a copy of DECAM's purchase authorization.

Minimum age for gun ownership in Guatemala is 25. Normally the bureaucracy takes about three weeks to complete its paperwork unless, in rare instances when DECAM has recently processed an owner's buy application for the same purchaser. This gun-owner's permit allows possession of that gun in the home, transport to and from a gun club and to and from a place of hunting. Other than the fact that Guatemalans are a "lock the front wall gate with two locks and the front door with three locks" society, there are no official gun storage requirements.

Permits to carry discreetly are probably easier here than in the U.S. Concealed-carry permits are issued on a national basis, again by DECAM. Their process is amazingly fast and simple. The assumption seems to be that a gun owner who wants a pistol and is willing to pay relatively high prices will also want to carry discreetly.

With a copy of the sales invoice and copy of DECAM's sell authorization, go back in person to the local DECAM office. Fill out an official document listing make, model, serial number and caliber. Pay a tax of about $15 plus a license fee of from $27 to $81. Carry permits cost about $27 per year and are issued for up to three years at a time (at a cost of $81). As many as three separate pistols may be placed on each individual carry permit. Including taking a current picture and laminating everything in plastic, most concealed-carry permits take at most thirty to forty minutes to complete.

Hand loading is permitted, but not encouraged. A special hand-loading registration is usually given to gun clubs rather than to individuals. Gun clubs are a source of cheap, reloaded ammo in Guatemala. Reloading supplies are sometimes available but very scarce in Guatemala, and so must be special ordered. In times past, a reloading registration was required before reloading supplies could be purchased. Because reloading supplies are so scarce, the authorities have dropped their insistence on a "reloading registration."

Ammunition is available at gun shops. Daily limits are 500 rounds/gun/day. In Guatemala, pricey ammo is a real deterrent for those making $4,200/year or less. Twenty-five round boxes of 12-

gauge ammo cost between $8.50 and $10.50. 9mm ammo, 50 to the box, costs between $12.50 and $16. Rimfire .22 LR ammo is something of a bargain at about $2.25 per box of 50.

Ammo sales are only allowed to DECAM gun-permit holders for that specific weapon in the caliber shown on the owner's buy permit. Purchase records are maintained by sporting-goods stores, but not forwarded to the authorities unless the storeowner becomes suspicious about quantities purchased.

Private sales of properly papered guns are fairly easily undertaken. Consenting parties simply to go DECAM to have the gun taken off the seller's record and placed on the buyer's gun-owner's certificate. A quick, simple undertaking, I am assured.

People legally visiting Guatemala can bring their firearms if they wish. There is, as a legal matter, no restriction on total numbers. Before landing with guns, a visitor or immigrant must secure a temporary importation permit from DECAM. These temporary permits often lead to a permanent permit. A photocopy of your passport, evidence documenting absence of a felony record, and salary/income information are also required. These documents must be taken personally to a Guatemalan consulate or embassy for validation before leaving home.

As a complete aside, it is always curious to speculate where America's anti-gun-rights people get their ideas. Any gun legally imported into Guatemala, for instance, must be tested by DECAM. This means every legal gun in Guatemala must go directly from customs to DECAM to be fired at least twice. Cases and bullets recovered from this testing are held for the record for future identification purposes. It is doubtful if this expensive and time consuming exercise ever aids in the identification and apprehension of a criminal. But it is the rule in Guatemala. At the urging of anti-rights advocates, similar measures have been proposed in several states in the U.S.—is there a nexus? Guatemala is apparently one of the few countries to require this expensive, convoluted and often uncertain procedure.

Legal gun owners in Guatemala wring their hands a bit over the widespread incidence of illegal ownership. Prices are said to have recently increased dramatically as supplies dwindle, but a nice, clean AK-47, M-16 or FN FAL can still be had for $600 or under! Left-behind UZIs, they say, are even cheaper. Police and military agencies conduct frequent and extensive campaigns to collect illegal firearms. They ask for volunteer turn-ins during amnesty periods and have even tried buy-backs. These efforts have not met with much success, we are told.

There have also been some civil campaigns in favor of more restrictive gun laws. Perhaps because common citizens wish to individually resist terrorism still fresh in many people's minds, these campaigns have not been successful. Guatemalan gun owners believe their current laws are not in flux and will remain constant for the foreseeable future and that gun banners will not be successful.

Guatemala has something of a national gun culture, somewhat similar to our own. The sight of guns in the hands of police, military or average citizens does not immediately excite people. Armed guards, mostly toting Remington Model 870s, or 18-inch 12-gauges with pistol grips, are out in the thousands in Guatemala. Visitors will also see a great many guards with Ruger .223 mini-14s and Valmet .223s.

Gun accessories, including sights of all types, laser devices, holsters, bullet traps, full-capacity magazines, grips, cleaning equipment, etc., are all imported free of duties and restrictions. Some Guatemalans even shop on line for gun accessories!

Chapter Twenty-Two
Kenya
World Rank: 53 • Firearm Freedom 19%

Numerous pervasive cultural and historic factors argue against expecting any sort of private gun ownership in this East African nation.

Prior to being granted self-rule by the colonizing British on December 12, 1963, firearms ownership in Kenya was strictly limited to persons with white skin. Other than a few African police and colonial soldiers, average native Kenyans looked on guns as dangerous, evil instruments owned by an elite few that had no place in their lives. Africans who owned guns were thought of as dangerous rebels with whom the controlling colonizers needed to deal severely.

A Kenyan exchange student in America was initially extremely fearful and agitated at me personally because of the guns we owned, right out in plain sight, on display. "Under our tradition you must be a lawbreaker and criminal," the fellow later admitted.

When the fellow's 58-year-old dad came to visit, he touched, handled and then fired a gun for the first time in his life. His emotional baggage was severe. "We don't even allow toy guns in Kenya," he said, perhaps explaining where American antis get some of their antagonism toward completely inert objects.

The elderly gentleman didn't then know if he had irrevocably sullied himself after firing a gun, nor if he would ever again be accepted in regular, law-abiding Kenyan society. Obviously, psychology against guns runs deep in Kenya.

Sports and control hunting and shooting were, at one time, a major factor in Kenya. But only for the white elite! Stores that sold guns and ammo as well as wide selections of gun accessories were common. Even after ten years of self-rule, I was able to observe several stores scattered about the country, mostly in larger cities.

Then the dead hand of politics began to play a major role in Kenya's private gun-ownership pattern. Like most, if not all, of the newly independent African nations, leaders who assumed command quickly learned to like their jobs and all the attendant perks. All too soon it became these people's principal purpose in life to remain in control. Not a terribly difficult task when you have all of the guns, and most citizens under your control neither know about guns nor believe that having them would fill a utilitarian purpose.

We shouldn't be surprised that Daniel Arap Moi, Kenya's president since 1978, gradually tightened the screws on private gun ownership to the point where even white farmers were required to store their double barreled "12 bores" at local police headquarters. A somewhat unworkable situation when marauding lions were eating the prize bull out on the ranch!

Not only did the pillars of English elitism, control and disdain for common "natives" come home to roost in these farmers' lofts, they also left behind a kind of philosophy that still argues against private guns. English folk like armies, but not ones made up of private citizens with guns.

But realistically and honestly, we can report private gun ownership is coming back in Kenya. That, and how this is happening, makes informative and fascinating reading. A valuable lesson lies at the heart of an analysis of Kenya's gun laws.

Kenya is the twice Nevada-sized country lying on the east coast of Africa. Look where the equator line runs into the continent. Tanzania is south, Somalia north and Uganda west. Kenya's geographic location, in close proximity to these nations that have all undergone recent severe upheavals, is significant.

Kenya's *per capita* income is about $1,100 and rising very slowly, if at all, against an extremely high birth rate. AIDS is a factor, but not to the extent of some other African nations. Kenya has a diverse climate along with some extremely deep, rich soils. Knowledgeable agricultural people claim the country is so rich agriculturally that all of Europe's food could easily be raised there, if only Kenyan farmers had access to modern seed, chemicals, technology, markets and property law. Kenya's farmers still tend to raise and collect cattle as a sign of wealth, without any actual thought of selling them to provide income. Rather than going to the butcher for human food, they die of old age going for hyena food.

Compared to other African nations, the rule of law prevails in Kenya. There is violent crime and bribery. But Kenyans know this is wrong— no matter who perpetrates it on whom. Life is relatively easy in Kenya but, for Americans with light skins, it would be tough—especially on a day-to-day basis.

Information for this chapter came courtesy of three Kenyan exchange students, one of whom lived with us for well over a year, those people's parents, and a pioneer missionary who grew up in Kenya. Now living back in America, this last fellow was born in and grew up in Kenya. He was there as a young man during Mau Mau and is now easily characterized as a member of the American gun culture. I also lived, worked and hunted in Kenya for almost three months. However, this was many, many years ago.

After reaching a depressing low, legal private gun ownership is returning to Kenya. Not in a form Americans would want or accept, but it is coming back. More importantly, laws are changing for the correct reasons. In this regard alone, it is instructive to learn what is going on.

Three immediate realities color Kenya's legal gun-ownership rules and regulations. First, illegal gun ownership of everything from AK-47s to light machine guns and submachine guns and pistols is rampant in the country. Most have their origin in the military forces of countries surrounding Kenya, putting the lie to a UN pronouncement that most illegal guns around the world have a commercial origin. "Do away with private commercial guns and you do away with insurrections," these UN antis claim. Definitely not true in Kenya, or in any other place in the world we could discover.

Kenyans who will settle for illegal guns can easily acquire them. Cost for a gun and 100 rounds of ammo is one cow! To an extent, cattle are still units of currency and a medium of exchange in Kenya. Common cattle fetch about 1,500 Kenya shillings each, when sold. Exchange rates are currently about 75 shillings per U.S. dollar.

Secondly, wars, massacres, insurrections and coups have swept over virtually all adjoining countries. All of us are familiar with the horrible experience in Rwanda and the extensive tribal fighting in Somalia. Collapse of civilian authority has placed a great many military weapons in East African underground commerce. Starving soldiers frequently peddled appropriated guns and ammo to black market civilian arms dealers. Results are a kind of perverse good news/bad news situation.

As insurrections threatened otherwise staid and steady Kenya, government officials seemed honestly concerned. They feared that the class or tribal warfare mentality, possibly on the scale of Rwanda, would spread to Kenya. They also feared the tens of thousands of illegal guns in private untrained hands. As mentioned, average Africans have little or no cultural background in proper gun management, use or restraint.

Third, organized crime, often bordering on paramilitary-type actions, is scaring Kenyan government officials. Raiders from Somalia and Ethiopia have made it a kind of blood sport, raiding into northern Kenya around Lake Turkana for cattle and women.

Perhaps unique in African history and throughout the world, government officials seem genuinely concerned about the potential and actual slaughter of their own citizens. Strange, since by all reasonable estimates, President Moi was not elected in a fair, honest contest. More like the U.S. experience in Chicago, my Kenyan friends say. This makes it all the more curious that President Moi relaxed rules regarding ownership of private weapons, and that this trend continues. Also, in some very high-profile incidents, some high-level officials and their families have been kept from grievous injury by deployment of private firearms. These lessons are not lost in today's Kenya.

Government officials and well-connected, wealthy individuals have always been able to secure gun-ownership permits in Kenya. Some even legally own pistols for self-defense. But times are changing. Currently common citizens willing to pay necessary permit fees (about 1,000 shillings – $15) and go through an often-convoluted political process can own some rifles, military shotguns, assault rifles and commercial shotguns.

Kenya is a small nation wherein everyone can at least know everyone else's family, allowing for a kind of individual screening.

Pistol ownership is sometimes allowed, but an anti-English attitude continues to prevail regarding pistols. Regrettably, permits—especially in crime-ridden places such as urban Nairobi—are still very tough to secure. Yet, legal pistol ownership is dramatically easier than it was even ten years ago. Though the system is more relaxed, the best, easiest procedure is to convince authorities to make you a special deputy police officer and acquire a pistol from police themselves.

As a result of this relaxation of laws prohibiting private ownership, a precious few gun shops are opening again in Kenya. Mostly they sell shotguns to farmers as well as 7.62 NATO, .22 LR and 12-gauge ammo to those with a valid gun-owner's permit.

Hunting of any sort has been completely banned in Kenya for about 25 years. As a result, much or even most of its once-abundant game has been poached into oblivion. Now Kenyans would like to bring back paid hunting, similar to the Zimbabwe model. This where most of the considerable license fees revert back to local people who come to see wild game as a potential benefit, not something that destroys their gardens along with the potential for their next meal.

Kenyans believe they might start this process by opening the country to legal bird hunting. Not an easy task given pressures from some environmental groups who view all hunting as unacceptable. Often these groups are the source of rich grants in aid made to key individual Kenyans. Not much difference between them and a common bribe, but this, again, is an issue beyond the scope of this volume.

As a result, opinions and instructions from these folks carry disproportionate weight. Many don't want private guns and hunting. Like everywhere else, Kenyan officials listen to the money.

As mentioned, average people living outside major cities can get gun-ownership permits. Start the process of securing a legal G-3 H&K, FN assault rifle, or M-16 by going to the local district commissioner. DCs in Kenya are a kind of appointed governor over a small state. On being comfortable and confident of the applicant, a DC will refer you to the local police captain. On instruction from the DC, this local police captain will issue one full-automatic assault rifle of his choice—such as an FN, H&K or Armalite—into the care of the applicant.

Theoretically you don't own it. Yet, on the positive side, there is no charge for these guns. On the down side, you lose the gun to hostile action or theft and it's off to the grey stone hotel for an indeterminate term. As a practical matter, illegal gun ownership is often not dealt with to such a severe extent. Outright bribes, under-the-counter purchase of some item from the arresting officer, after-the-fact permits at super-high prices and other such subterfuges often allow illegal owners a free ride, depending a great deal on who they are and how the matter came to official notice.

Shotgun ownership is somewhat similar. Go to the local police—either through political contacts or as the result of long-term lobbying—convince them you are a reasonable citizen with a reasonable need who won't embarrass or threaten the government, and a permit to buy and store a personal shotgun at police headquarters will be granted.

All of this sounds convoluted and impossible, yet I am assured by numbers of Kenyans that numerous permits—along with free government assault rifles in many cases—are currently being issued. Finding good, responsible people who already know how to own, hold and use guns seems to be the current governmental challenge. Strange in a world where civilian gun owners are virtual pariahs. Kenya is close friends with Israel. Perhaps their gun-owners' philosophy is imported from that country!

No one is sure how to get a permit to open a gun store. Perhaps the very few coming onto the scene are all run by the military, I was told. Kenya is not interested in weapons development and research. Requests for permits for such would not be understood.

After years of atrophy, Kenya's small-arms bureau is expanding again. Once political contacts are made, issuance of a gun or permit can be speedy. Issuance of a second permit is not an issue, since citizens are currently allowed only one gun each.

No guns can legally be brought into Kenya. Travelers' guns are held by customs till they depart.

As mentioned, small amounts of ammo can be purchased in a few gun shops. If not there, both the district commissioner and the police will often legally sell or even give ammo to legal gun owners for practice and to defend against bad guys.

Reloading is not done in Kenya. No stores sell components. There are some vague reports of travelers importing reloading tools and components, but there must be very few of these. Officially the Kenya government doesn't know anything about reloading.

On the flip side of this issue, manufacture of homemade guns is ancient history in Kenya. Today nobody bothers. Too many illegal guns and cases of ammunition floating about the country, we are told.

Folks who assisted with this chapter stress that currently it is still easiest for politicians, the well connected and the rich to secure private firearms permits. However this situation is changing so fast they cannot keep up with it. Totally unlike other of the world's nations who have not learned their lesson regarding protecting citizens, reducing crime and assuring tranquility via private gun ownership.

Many Kenyans believe that, in a few years, private gun possession in their country will be fairly widespread and common, enough so the average citizens can afford guns and can learn to use them safely.

Given the average Kenyan's fear and ignorance of guns and their efficient, proper use, this is something to be seen before belief. Certainly it will be interesting for American gun owners to watch developments in that corner of the world.

Chapter Twenty-Three
Ireland
World Rank: 58 • Firearm Freedom 12%

What kind of gun laws could we expect in a tiny island nation—half the size of Arkansas—that, for centuries on end, was arbitrarily and often capriciously occupied and dominated by its strong near neighbor? Especially an occupier whose own citizens came to fear and loathe firearms? Guns, in the eyes of the occupying British, were the exclusive domain of the privileged ruling class. A philosophy bound to spread, we might suppose, to those they dominated.

That the Irish used illegal guns for centuries during their extensive revolts and resistance does not help matters.

As a result, we have a situation in Ireland that is predictable but not particularly encouraging to freedom-loving Americans. Yet it certainly is of interest. Perhaps we should be encouraged over the tiny scrap of remaining freedom some Ghillies still have.

Ireland is comprised of everything except six small northern counties of a bowl-like Island situated in the Atlantic Ocean. At its greatest width, approximately 100 miles of ocean separate Ireland from England, Wales and Scotland.

To the intense embarrassment of the U.K. and Europe, Ireland's economy has boomed in recent years. Some say because Ireland has fewer rules and regulations regarding going into business. *Per capita* income is an extremely high $31,900. This resolute economic growth is also attributed to the fact that the Irish have a strong rule of law securing contracts and property rights. They also have a very strong work ethic and, as American businessmen continually remind us, virtually all Irish speak English. Literacy is right at 100 percent.

Numerous American companies use international computer links to employ huge banks of Irish workers to do mundane tasks such as data entry. Chances are that at least some of our credit-card and medical-records-data entries were made by Irish clerks.

Other than their often foolish, incomprehensible gun laws, Ireland would be an interesting and comfortable place for Americans on a fixed retirement income to live. Their major airports are convenient to all parts of Europe as well as many places in the Near East and Africa.

Irish citizens can own up to a total of three sporting rifles and shotguns. Those judged to be sporting are closely controlled by ruling authorities. In many instances, what constitutes sporting is a surprise to

American gun owners. Since hunting opportunities in Ireland are limited, few people import guns, even temporarily. No one knew with certainty what rules applied to importation of guns. It was generally assumed that importation of any foreign gun would be impossible.

Among shotguns, only double- and single-barrel models are considered sporting. Mostly these are 12 gauge or .410s. As is also true in the U.K., Irish authorities have a fear and loathing of pump and semi-auto shotguns and it isn't because they are more subject to breakage during times of hard use! Double-barreled firepower is sporting and acceptable. Anything beyond that is not.

Only .22 Hornet single- and bolt-action rifles are permitted. In a wide departure from most countries where .22 rimfires are viewed as mostly inefficient and benign, absolutely no .22 rimfire guns are allowed in Ireland. "Twenty-two Hornets and that's it," was the direct quote from a hunter/fisherman guide living in rural Killarney who contributed to this chapter.

I also received information from an American sportsman who visited Ireland with a stock list of gun-ownership questions in hand. At times this fellow's information was fragmented or uncertain, but a phone call to rural Killarney cleared things up. Irish gun laws are relatively simple. In most cases. "it is forbidden."

Absolutely no pistols are permitted in private hands in Ireland. Other than those occasionally packed by police or soldiers, most Irish have never actually seen a real live handgun in person. A gunsmith there claimed that in 35 years of business he never touched a pistol! He said he had no idea how to work on or repair one!

Ghillies start their journey toward a gun-ownership permit by joining a gun/hunting club. There are a number of convenient competing clubs throughout Ireland. Entry, for reasonable people, is quick and easy. "Other than the £80 to £120 Irish ($72 - $108) annual fees, it's the easiest part," the Irish hunter told me. Signing up at a gun club is said to be simple and straightforward.

After that, new gun owners must secure written permission from an Irish landowner-farmer to hunt on his property. This property and the attending hunting activity must be at least one mile from a public road. Seems like a high standard in that Ireland is a well-developed country with a great many roads.

Securing written permission to hunt is not seen as being particularly onerous or difficult by Irish citizens. Farmers are anxious to get rid of hares, rabbits and crows that are viewed in that society as vermin, I was instructed. Yet people in large cities might find locating, befriending and then securing cooperation of a farmer to be a daunting task. But our Irish gun-owner friend did not think it to be particularly difficult. Perhaps the Irish are even more friendly and gregarious than we might have first supposed. I personally have trouble envisioning a complete stranger driving up to a strange farmer to ask if he can hunt vermin on his property.

You now have successfully acquired a club membership and written authorization from a friendly farmer to shoot critters infesting his farm. Next it's off to the friendly gun shop. This may be a sixty- or eighty-mile drive. There are only six or eight gun shops in the entire country, most of which are in larger cities.

Pick out the gun you wish to purchase from among the admittedly limited selection. Pay a deposit, secure a receipt and head off to what may not be a too friendly local police commissioner. At the cop shop, pay 20 ($25) and fill out the considerable forms they have for you.

After receipt of the written application, the police will run a very thorough check of the applicant's past record. Successful applicants absolutely must be completely transparent to the law. Otherwise it's no gun permit. Even minor infractions made years ago in one's youth (called misdemeanors in the U.S.) will disqualify an applicant.

At this point, assuming no blemishes, the police commissioner will place your paperwork into the giant bureaucratic paper mill. Apparently Ireland's paper mill is unique. The authorities do not automatically notify applicants if their permits are denied. You didn't hear anything and three months have elapsed? Stop by the police commissioner's office to find out why the permit was rejected, my Ghillie informant said.

But time spent waiting is not wasted. Local police officers will visit the applicant's home to determine that the applicant has an appropriate, suitable, sanctioned, steel gun safe. All guns and ammo in Ireland must be securely locked away. It's a new regulation.

Additional police visits will occur every year around gun-permit-renewal time. This to be sure all guns are suitably locked away. Irish gun owners believe this is little more than a not-so-subtle device, allowing police entry and inspection of one's private residence. Perhaps they are really looking for illegal booze and drugs among other things.

Gun-owner permits give owners the right to purchase ammunition at the six or eight outlets around the country. No limit on amounts a proper permit holder can purchase but, of course, the small number and kinds of guns allowed argue against large ammo inventories.

"Please explain what is hand loading," was the response to questions about legality in Ireland. Ghillies not only don't know what that is, they can't purchase components. If they could, assembling them would probably be illegal.

Unlike silencers or sound modifiers in the U.K., where these devices often sell over the counter without restriction, silencers are very verboten in Ireland. You lose your gun license permanently if caught with one of these, an Irish gun owner says.

Illegal guns are uncommon in Ireland. Apparently all that ocean is a good barrier against the flood of illicit arms and ammo from Russia that is impacting other portions of continental Europe. Penalties for illegal gun possession are extremely severe in Ireland. That plus difficulties importing seem to strongly argue against very many illegal guns on the Emerald Isle.

Sales of guns are permitted between private individuals provided both have gun ownership permits and the new owner is approved by the local police.

It seemed counterproductive to inquire about licenses to sell at retail or to do experimental work on firearms in Ireland. Obviously the authorities would not like this sort of economic activity. Certainly costs in terms of time, actual money and killed trees for piles of paperwork would be excessive. Almost certainly the effort would be without tangible result.

And this is how it is the Emerald Isle. A beautiful place with lots of nice sheep and very little in commendable gun laws.

Chapter Twenty-Four
England
World Rank: 22 • Firearm Freedom 59%

Because their gun laws are so convoluted, fast changing, intrusive and restrictive, it was my original plan not to include England in this study. Especially given the fact that any reasonable observer could quickly see that each new layer of restrictions added to England's crime problem rather than resolving it.

As a result of increased crime in general and crime involving guns in particular, English bureaucrats and politicians keep tinkering with their regulations in the wild hope that they will find something that actually works to reduce crime. So far, none of this tinkering has produced the desired result, which may be the lesson and principal reason for any change of plan and for this chapter. It was a personal matter from which I eventually relented.

Information for this chapter comes from eight or ten personal visits to the U.K. in as many years, from hunting deer, pheasants and rabbits there, from personally exploring a great many English gun shops, from the experience of an American gun-owner friend living in the U.K. and from the generous and open help of the game keeper at the castle estate where we stay when we visit. Ownership of firearms for this last fellow is remarkably easy compared to average English citizens. Please keep this in mind when evaluating the following information. Those having game to manage on thousands of acres of land have an easier time of it in the U.K. Although I have spent a great deal of time in the U.K., accurately summarizing their gun laws is elusively difficult.

Not unlike other countries throughout the world, England has anomalies that should be identified before looking into their gun laws. First, the English generally have very little use for pistols. Some English gun buffs, such as our friendly estate forester/gamekeeper, have extensive experience with them, but this is unusual to rare.

Ask an average, even rural, Englishman if he can legally own a pistol and invariably the first response will be a question. "Why would anyone want to own a pistol?" There are, of course, a number of excellent reasons but average Brits absolutely don't see them.

Additionally, gun ownership in England is virtually always seen as a perk of the privileged ruling class. It is never a citizen's right. Gunsmiths and gun-shop owners agonize over this philosophy. "Our gun owners won't even push local authorities over gun ownership they badly want, even in the face of what is sometimes very arbitrary enforcement of unclear laws," some of these gun-store owners tell me.

The U.K., or England as it is often also called, is the great large island—about twice the size of New York State—lying off the west coast of Europe. Although one may occasionally call the title into question, it is called United because England, Wales, Scotland and Northern Ireland make up the U.K. As a rule this is a fairly densely populated place—about 622 people per square mile on average. Shooters sometimes have problems not impinging on this large density of folks, many of whom are wholly antagonistic towards all guns.

Surrounding oceans warm the country. Their climate is more temperate than one would suppose for a place that far north—about 51 degrees north on the same latitude as frosty Winnipeg, Canada.

Per capita income is about $29,600. Taxes and fuel prices, inflated by high taxes, are extremely high. Yet, living is easier than one might suppose. Extensive economic development came very early to England. Most of the infrastructure of economic development—roads, sewer systems, water treatment plants and such—have been in place for centuries. For example, a vineyard a couple miles down the road from the castle where I stay was planted by the Romans about the time of Christ. This investment, made over 2000 years ago, is yielding financial returns even today. As a result, many English may be living on current depreciation of extensive past investments!

They do have an extensive rule of law, but property rights are not as fully evolved as one might think or hope. Fox hunters, for instance, can and do tally ho across private rural property with impunity. Hikers and bird watchers following centuries-old paths arbitrarily hike across private property any time they wish. Barring them off the land is very illegal! Police and other civil authorities can enter and search a home without warrant or prior notice. Trial by jury is not a fundamental English right. English citizens cannot choose their own doctor, etc. When people point to other lands as examples for Americans to follow, they rarely if ever look at the whole picture, because if they did, our nation, the linchpin of freedom on Earth, would shine in a very bright light indeed.

Some Americans find living in the U.K. to be delightful. Like any place, it is certainly better to go and look around first before moving there. English bureaucrats as well as regular citizens tend to become involved in the convoluted. Difficult governmental procedures and permit systems govern a frightening amount of their daily lives. Some people find great comfort in the certainty of such a system. Others definitely do not, and many are anathema to The American Way.

As mentioned, changeability and obscurity characterize current English gun laws. However, we can safely say—at this writing—that under some conditions most English citizens can personally own some shotguns and rifles. That's as long as the local police firearms officer considers the specific guns to be of a sporting nature, suitable for your specific purpose, and you are a reasonable, stable, competent person and that you have a bona-fide need for these firearms. Often these criteria are arbitrarily and subjectively enforced.

No assault rifles, machine guns, submachine guns or pistols are permitted in private hands under any circumstances.

Some black-powder replicas and single shot .32 caliber pistols used in abattoirs (slaughterhouses) are permitted, but this is the extent of legal pistol ownership in modern U.K. Black-powder rifles and pistols are permitted only with a specific firearm-owner's certificate, with a black-powder endorsement or permission. All modern replica black-powder guns are registered with the authorities.

Potential new gun owners go first to the firearms officer at their local police headquarters. This person provides the applicant with two copies of a gun-owner's certificate application. Take one of these to a responsible, upstanding local resident who has known you personally for at least two years. This person should be a member of the clergy, a lawyer, a well-known local businessman, banker, local police official, local governmental employee or some other reliable person. Give this form plus one of four pictures of yourself to this reliable, upstanding citizen who also agrees to complete the form attesting to your good character, sign the picture and forward all directly to the local firearms officer. Applicants never see the completed package submitted by their reliable attesting co-sponsor.

Applicants complete one of the forms and personally bring it and three pictures—one of which is also signed—to the police.

At the police station, pay a fee of about $75. Also sign a medical-release form giving permission for the authorities to go into your medical records if they wish. Current applicants believe these records are not explored unless there is some sort of problem or the firearms officer wants to arbitrarily reject an application.

Now it's time to wait for the bureaucratic paper mill to churn. In most cases, expect to wait from one to two months. But—as in other restrictive countries—this time is not wasted by the authorities. Soon the local firearms officer will pay a visit to the applicant's home. A trained, skilled interrogator, he will conduct a warm yet intense interview designed to uncover your personal life, finances, politics, means of employment, world view, religion, family situation and knowledge of firearms. This person will also want you to show him exactly where you will hunt and/or shoot, your intended game and if there is a written permission from the landowner when it is not on your own property. If it's deer, it can't be a five-acre wooded spot surrounded on three sides by a housing estate! Membership in a hunting/shooting club or paid-up status in a pheasant-hunting scheme might also qualify.

Once a gun-owner's certificate is issued, a separate permission for each and every gun must be secured from the firearms officer. Good, valid reasons must be given for each and every gun. Plinking is a weak reason, self-defense is a completely unacceptable reason and serious target shooting is a good reason. Records of each gun owned are entered individually on each person's firearm-owner's certificate.

Part of current English policy toward guns is to sharply reduce the numbers in private hands. In many cases, owners' certificates or later permission for a special gun are denied if the bureaucracy can think of a good reason for doing so. Private transfer of guns is only legally possible if noted down on both of the firearm-owner's certificates and if the police firearms office approves.

Four or perhaps five classes of permissions are noted, depending on how one counts. Applicants can own a .22 LR rimfire rifle for small-pest control, if you can prove you have small pests to control. Again, written permission from landowners may be a requirement. The only classes of weapons in semi-auto configuration are .22 LR. Nothing like assault rifles are in private hands in the U.K.

A second class of permissions includes .22-caliber centerfires such as .22 Hornet, .223, .22-250, and similar. This class is for controlling or hunting foxes. Theoretically applicants can go up to a .243 but this size rifle is often resisted by the firearms officer deciding if you have a need for a gun that big.

Third are the "big guns" used for deer. Thirty-ought-six rifles are the largest allowed in this category, and applicants must actually show the nice officer the deer they intend to shoot. Deer hunters in the U.K. also like .308 Winchester, .270s and even .303 British cartridges.

Ownership of large, double rifles and heavy African-type guns is permitted to a limited number of people, decided on a case-by-case basis. Applicants must prove they travel to Sweden, Africa, Alaska or the Baltics to hunt regularly in order to qualify. In some cases, citizens take out memberships in large-bore rifle clubs. Such a membership may be enough to convince local firearms officers that you have a valid need for big-bore double rifles. Then again, your request for ownership permission may be summarily rejected.

Shotguns are the last category of approved guns. It is generally easier to show a valid place to hunt or shoot or a sporting purpose for a shotgun. Contrary to rumors, some firearms officers will give permission for a pump or semi-auto shotgun if and only if the gun is permanently modified to accept only three rounds. This is seen as something of a departure from the past. English hunters and shooters far prefer double guns. Firearms officers may be sufficiently prejudiced against pumps and semi-autos that they will never give permission for such even though the law itself is on the side of the applicant.

There is no limit on the number of guns one can own, provided the applicant can make a good case for each and every one to the authorities. Up to nine guns can—and must—be stored in a steel cabinet. More than nine must be in an expensive vault complete with electronic alarm. Your friendly, helpful firearms officer will make it a point to closely inspect all gun-storage facilities. Ammo must also be locked away. Our cooperating estate gamekeeper has 16 guns, placing him in a rarified class in the U.K.

Rifle ammunition can only be purchased on one's ownership certificate, fifty rounds at a time maximum, for a specific gun or guns listed on the certificate. All purchases are recorded on the certificate. Certificate holders are not supposed to hold more than 200 to 300 rounds of ammo for any one gun at any one time. One is tempted to suggest it might be difficult for officials to know how many rounds a person holds, making the rule difficult to enforce, but that's true only in theory, because British gun owners have no protection from unwarranted search and seizure.

Firearms officers in the U.K. have the ability and power to inspect certificate holders' gun lock-up and home anytime, unannounced. Variation from this strict standard could easily result in loss of one's firearms certificate and forfeiture of all guns. One wonders if this is a model American anti-rights advocates would support as a common-sense crime-fighting measure—erasing the Fourth Amendment.

New guns are purchased from local gun shops by certificate holders who make a selection, put down a small deposit and then attempt to convince their firearms officer that they need that specific gun. Mail-order shipments of guns and gun-related items are now completely forbidden. Parts, accessories and brass are very expensive as a result. English gun owners view this limitation on mailing as pure harassment. All gun-related items must move by expensive special-delivery carrier. Americans have to wonder if United Parcel Service got their restrictive, expensive pistol-shipping regulations from the U.K.

There are no restrictions on quantities of shotgun ammo a shotgun certificate holder may purchase and hold. Amounts are noted on your owner's certificate.

Over-the-counter silencers sales are still permitted for .22 air rifles. Ones for larger guns including .410 shotguns are recorded on your ownership certificate. Silencer ownership is said to be becoming a bit easier in the U.K. Perhaps it's an occupational-safety measure—it prevents deafness! And avoids upsetting the neighbors.

Reloading in England is common enough that most gun shops carry at least some of the more popular supplies. By visiting several area gun shops, reloaders can usually eventually find the powder, bullets and primers they require. Prices are about 50 percent more in dollars than for the same items at retail in the U.S. Other than a gun-owner's certificate listing all your guns, there is no separate license for hand loaders in the U.K.

Purchase of up to 300 bullets (projectiles) daily is permitted. No more than 350 are supposed to be held at any one time by any one person. All purchases are recorded on the owner's certificate. Presently there is no recording on powder or primers. Black powder for muzzleloaders is considered to be a particularly dangerous explosive. Sales are tightly controlled. All purchases are noted down for inspection and possible approval by the authorities.

It is not considered to be particularly more difficult to go into the retail gun business in the U.K. than to go into just about any other business, but opening just about any business in the U.K. is arduous. Before a local council will issue a permit for any business, a professionally drawn business plan must be submitted. This plan must list what will be done, where the business will be located, what exactly is the business, where wholesale supplies will come from, who will make purchases and what are the qualifications of the new proprietor. Sometimes this is an easy task; sometimes there is local antagonism to the venture. Once local permission is secured and the local police firearms officer gives approval, the shop can open. As in the U.S., some small gun dealers manage to ply their trade out of their homes.

Permanent importation of guns into the U.K. is just about impossible. All Americans I know who own guns in the U.K. have purchased them there. They go through procedures similar to regular citizens.

Perhaps all of this sounds a bit reasonable? It is, for an applicant who lives in a rural area, and deals with rural firearms officials. As a practical matter, potential gun owners in the big cities have a much more difficult time. Again, finding a reason to own a specific gun can be difficult. Personal defense is absolutely never a good reason. Crime—petty to serious, including murder—has increased dramatically since their gun laws were "strengthened."

Illegal guns are currently an issue in the U.K. Like the U.S., some borders in Europe are lightly controlled. Few bags are opened and inspected. As a result, it is very easy and quite safe to import an illegal pistol and ammunition from Germany or one of the Scandinavian countries. These guns, as well as some left over souvenirs from England's many wars, are continually turning up. It seems maddening that the English politicians blame and punish honest gun owners for this breach, but that is what is happening.

England is characterized by what is known as "hot burglaries." This is when burglars break into homes known to be currently occupied by their owners. Since owners cannot legally resist (yes, that's correct!) and cannot own a gun for doing so, criminals take precedence. Usually a homeowner's only recourse is to sit quietly while the burglars take whatever they wish, while hoping they depart without doing any physical harm. This seldom happens in the U.S. because American second story men don't really know if an owner has a gun that they will use to resist.

London newspapers periodically wail and howl about the fact that, "in America, it is not only a right but a duty to shoot criminals to prevent a crime. We should implement this system here to stop our epidemic crime situation," they editorialize. Politicians, protected by heavily armed guards, ignore the pleas. Anyone who thinks America should follow the British example needs to take that into account.

On American I know personally owned several rifles he brought in quietly from the U.S. One day some men in blue from Scotland Yard showed up. They arbitrarily searched his home and, on finding the guns, hauled his weary ass off to the gaol. By week's end a magistrate sentenced him to 180 days, which he served immediately. Very little sense of humor among these folks on this issue.

English politicians in search of a solution to their exploding crime situation are frantically tinkering with their gun laws. Obviously none of this has any impact on crime.

Our lesson here is obvious. As the National Rifle Association says, don't ever compromise with the gun grabbers. When their programs don't work, they won't be honest enough to admit it. Instead, they will engage in endless, foolish tinkering with the laws rather than repealing the one that didn't work.

Chapter Twenty-Five
Mexico
World Rank: 55 • Firearm Freedom 15%

Apparently Mexico is the only other nation in the world besides the U.S. where citizens have a constitutional right to own firearms. "For self protection or legitimate self-defense," their document reads, "excepting those firearms specifically forbidden by law, or which are exclusively reserved for use of the military." What initially seemed a constitutional right really isn't.

Add it all up and I personally have spent years in Mexico, mostly working in rural areas. During this time, spanning some 35 years, I have seen thousands of guns of all kinds in Mexico. These ranged from tiny .22 cal. full-auto palm pistols to wonderfully made M-16 Colt knock offs. Before 1968, when gun ownership was widespread and legal, I paid little attention. Lately I seem to see a great many more guns, all of which their Mexican owners tell me are very, very illegal. For instance, there is the scope-equipped Ruger Mini-14 kept in a huge produce distribution warehouse in Los Mochis, a Ruger Standard Auto pistol kept in a secret compartment in a taxi dashboard in Guadalajara, and an AK-47 in the super-posh home of a Mexican millionaire living in the Saltillo area. All illicit if one believes the owners.

I asked how they got there. "Either they are smuggled in from Guatemala, Nicaragua or the U.S. in produce trucks or the family has owned them forever," I was informed. It was obvious to me that there are a lot of guns in Mexico. So many that I began to suspect that legal gun ownership in Mexico, if not impossible, was seldom attempted because it was too much hassle.

A recent hunting expedition in Mexico reinforced this conclusion. At present it takes a Mexican accountant a total of about three working days and $250 in wages to complete the volumes and volumes of paper necessary to temporarily import a shotgun into Mexico. "Officials don't want more guns in Mexico," I was told, "so they make the process as difficult, costly and time consuming as possible."

For source information, two brothers, owner-operators of their own hunting/guiding/resort services in the Obregón area, came to the rescue. They also recruited an extremely knowledgeable, articulate gun-owning hunting Mexican national. This fellow was willing to answer all kinds of questions in English! In his Mexican eyes, some of the questions had to be positively silly.

But he persevered and—adding in my experience plus input from the hunting camp pair—we now have a good, accurate picture of how things *really* work south of the border.

Mexico, as hopefully all Americans know, is our immediate neighbor to the south. Many Americans may not realize that Mexico once included much of Texas, California, Arizona and New Mexico. All this territory was ripped away from them by force—the same method every nation uses when it establishes itself.

As a result, many Mexican army people still regard an open, overt U.S. military invasion of their country as their greatest potential threat. American conduct during our war on drugs doesn't help. Recent personal conversations with Mexican military officers confirm that this surprising philosophy is still on their minds.

Another amazing but little known fact about Mexico: theirs is a relatively large country, probably comprising the single richest land area in the world. Mexican tycoons confirm that Mexico has tremendous deep rich soils capable of feeding all of North America, tremendous gold, silver and copper reserves, a super abundance of natural gas, timber, oil and a wonderfully rich commercial fishery. Yet *per capita* income is only $9,600—held captive, my Mexican friends tell me, by an often foolish, corrupt, inefficient and criminally self-serving, crony-capitalism-type government.

Private ownership of many types of rifles, pistols, and shotguns is legal in Mexico. Ownership of any full-auto weapons, submachine guns, some military pistols and assault rifles is very illegal. Under current Mexican law, whenever these latter weapons are observed in private hands, they are contraband. No facility or device exists to make them legal unless the owner has, by some means or another, secured an individual concession from the military or some other high-ranking government official. Probably the M-16 I saw in the young fellow's truck near Sinaloa really belonged to the military. It was a Colt patent, made in Mexico!

Worldwide, it always seems that whenever a country's military takes over regulation and enforcement of their nation's private gun laws, there is oppression, violence and a loss of basic human rights. Be alert for abuses—arbitrary uneven enforcement of unclear rules and regs.

All legal private guns in Mexico absolutely must be registered with the Secretaria de la Defensa Nacionál, or the Secretary of National Defense. Registration costs a one-time fee of $4.50 per weapon. Start at your local army headquarters.

Unlike virtually any other country, Mexican gun clubs act as the conduit go-between for necessary permits for Mexican gun owners. It is also interesting that these mostly private, yet quasi-governmental agencies survey local gun situations and make recommendations to the government. Based on this information, local gun clubs set game seasons and bag limits. They also regulate and coordinate competitive target shooting including trap and skeet.

Before bothering your local army commandante with a gun registration issue, purchase a local gun-club membership. Depending on the club, memberships cost from $250 to $350 per year plus a one-time joining fee of from $300 to $550. Obviously most Mexican nationals can't and won't afford a start-up fee of $550 to $900 total plus an annual fee of $300 to $550. There are, however, quite a large number of these clubs located in virtually all larger Mexican cities. Perhaps there is more interest in legal gun ownership than we might have first supposed.

After that, applicants must give evidence of successfully passing a urine test proving there is no drug addiction or habitual use. Numerous letters of attestation as to one's status and character are also required. These include one from your local police affirming there is no criminal record, one from an MD certifying good mental and physical health, another from the local mayor citing you are a good neighbor and lastly a letter from your employer certifying income and the fact that you make an honest living.

All of this paperwork is collated and vetted by your friendly local gun club. After being satisfied with its completeness and correctness, they submit it to the Mexican authorities that handle gun-owner permits. Expect a response to take anywhere from two days to two months depending on your circumstances. Circumstances in Mexico vary by individual and may, in my opinion, depend on how one holds their mouth and perhaps a happy-peso handshake.

Registration of one's guns only allows owners to keep their guns at home. Hunting licenses and registrations do not provide permission to transport to the field or range. This permission comes later with separate paper and, of course, more fees.

Along with sporting type rifles and shotguns, pistols are legally owned in Mexico. There are some peculiar and sometimes difficult to comprehend restrictions. Most of these are settled on a case-by-case basis. For example and speaking only generally, only pistols that are .380 auto or smaller are allowed. Obviously larger than .380s, .38 Specials are legally permitted. But 9mm pistols are all reserved exclusively for police and military use—even though this is a smaller cartridge than a .38 Special. Generally this smaller than .380 auto designation includes .32 ACPs, .25 autos, and .22 LR rim-fire pistols.

Magazine capacities or types of actions are not restricted. Five-shot semi-auto shotguns are frequently carried by hunters. It's okay as long as they don't look like ugly military guns. Shotguns must have barrels greater than .25 inches and 12 gauge is the largest. No 10-gauge shotguns are permitted.

Rifles, including telescopic sights, are legal in all calibers. Military people exercising their constitutional prerogative may except out private assault-rifle designs, but they don't care about military calibers such as 7.62 mm NATO, 5.54 mm M-16 rounds so long as they consider the rifle to be of sporting design.

Is there a limit on total numbers of firearms a person can own? I got what appears to be a "definite maybe" on that question. You decide!

Mexican gun owners can apply through their gun clubs to the military and police for a special collector's permit. Collectors' permits are said to be somewhat difficult and arbitrary to secure, but do allow for private, registered ownership of a great many guns. But other restrictions on numbers apply.

A separate permit to carry for self-defense and to transport to and from a range or to one's hunting territory is required. Again, the local gun club handles these additional documents, suggesting that their membership fees are not nearly so onerous as first supposed.

Permits to carry/transport cost $4 for each gun per six-month period. A maximum of ten guns is allowed on these permits. Every six months a new round of fees and paper is required. Permits to transport are limited to a maximum of five different states in Mexico at any one given time.

As an aside, Mexico is organized into 31 states. Generally each state government is given a great deal of autonomy.

Ammunition purchases are limited to 1,000 rounds of shot shells and 1,000 .22 rimfire rounds per month. There are some—but not many—sporting goods stores across Mexico that sell 12 and 20 gauge shot shells as well as .22 ammo. Legal gun owners must produce their gun registration papers at the time ammunition is purchased. All purchases are recorded in the name and certificate number of the purchaser.

Legally purchasing center-fire pistol and rifle ammo in Mexico is something else again. Absolutely all legal sales are handled by a single military gun and ammo store in Mexico City. Amounts available, prices and various sizes are arbitrarily controlled by this military store. One can definitely say that, while purchase of several hundred rounds of centerfire ammo may be permitted, if they don't have it available in the only store in the country, then permissions are meaningless.

Purchasing reloading components illustrates this concept nicely. Technically reloading is probably not allowed in Mexico. Nobody knows for sure. Only the military store far away in Mexico City sells components and, as a general rule, everything is always out of stock. No powder, shot, bullets or primers from the only store.

Only the minister of defense can give permission to legally import guns and ammunition. Some few American hunters who travel to Mexico with their own guns bring their own shot shells. Apparently this is handled by some sort of special dispensation arranged by Mexican guides on a case-by-case basis.

Recall again that our in-country informant said there was no limit on the number of guns one can own, so long as they are registered with the military. But all new sporting arms are supposed to be sold through the military gun store in Mexico City. They will only sell up to a maximum of three separate sporting guns per individual and that's all.

This limit works an incredible hardship on Mexican hunting-guide outfitters who frequently keep loaner shotguns in their lodges for use by foreign hunters who don't wish to endure the rigmarole, uncertainty and expense of bringing in their own guns. Guest hunters often put from 800 to 1,000 rounds through these guns day in and day out. As these guns wear, it is practically impossible, under the Mexican system, to replace or repair them.

Guns purchased through Mexico's military store are 45 to 60 percent higher priced than in the U.S. But—price notwithstanding—their three-gun-sales limit is throttling an otherwise lucrative business.

Registered private sales must be handled through the gun club and military. Non-citizens living in Mexico can go through similar procedures as Mexican citizens to legally own guns. In other words, join a gun club, get your many letters together and register with the military. Immigrants cannot, however, bring any legal private guns with them into Mexico unless they first join an American gun club, then a Mexican one and then play the bureaucracy game for months and months.

There's no such thing as a firearms-dealer permit in Mexico, and they definitely do not want people doing experimental design work on firearms. Pity. Mexico, at one time 30 years ago, had a vibrant, active gun design and manufacturing industry. They turned out some very nice, solid single-shot shotguns, bolt-action rifles, semi-automatic pistols and some nice knock offs of Winchester and Springfield rifles. The world's first reasonably successful semi-auto infantry rifle was invented in Mexico in 1908 by a fellow named Mondragon. During the 1950s and 1960s, an arms wizard named Rafael Mendoza turned out some really nice, futuristic designs all his own.

All that is history now in Mexico as government officials labor mightily to hold their positions against extensive, well-armed, well-organized, insurgency groups, drug armies and Mafia cartels. As previously mentioned, illegal gun ownership has a pervasive presence in Mexico.

Tourists and travelers often run into police road blocks, military stations and other official outposts supposedly guarding against illegal guns and drugs along the nation's highways. It's best for visitors to take these in stride without notice or concern. Some English citizens with whom I traveled were terrified at worst, and very concerned at best, when it happened recently. Although it is rapidly coming to their own nation, the sight of pistol-packing police is still unsettling for them.

Officially, illegal guns are acknowledged and are sternly dealt with in Mexico. Residents say that, "it is like any other place in the world. There are a lot of illegal guns in the hands of criminals, drug dealers, kidnappers, assailants and robbers. How many and to what extent, I have no idea. But they do exist in Mexico."

Like everyplace else on Earth, Mexico is unique. Their gun laws and enforcement reflect their culture. But beyond all this, keep one quote from an extremely rich Mexican don in mind: "In Mexico, anything is possible! We don't have rules and regulations. Only official suggestions subject to arbitrary interpretation and enforcement."

Chapter Twenty-Six
Tanzania
World Rank: 57 • Firearm Freedom 13%

Given their three-guns-per-person private-ownership maximum, gun laws in this pint-sized grass-shack-poor East African nation are not particularly exciting or instructive. At least not unless one is willing to look back in history and study its relationship to how Tanzanians ended up as we now see them.

Tanzania came on the world scene December 9, 1961 when the land reverted from a British custodial relationship to full independence. Some still incorrectly reference Tanganyika, its old name. It was the spoils of WWI at its worst—a whole country wrenched from German losers and given to victorious England.

Germany was and is a nation of gun buffs, to a far greater extent than England. Perhaps this explains why a hard-core socialistic country with few freedoms, such as Tanzania, allowed some private firearms ownership. Kenya, their immediate neighbor to the north and a virtual twin sister, is only now slowly coming 'round to a posture of allowing some private gun ownership.

I personally lived and worked in Tanzania in the very late 1960s. At that time, President Julius Nyerere (the Great Teacher) was still trying, among many other things, to fulfill his promise to provide a free bicycle to every citizen. If he was anything, Nyerere was certainly the most charismatic and—as amply proven later in history—the most honest of the newly emerging African leaders.

From day one when he assumed the presidency in 1961, Nyerere was committed to taking his country's economy the "African Way." Translated, that meant communal everything. Little to no private property was permitted. All capital was to be held and investment made by the central government. Goods and services vital to an emerging nation's economy—including trucks, cars, hotels, fuel, repair garages, cement and construction materials, goods shops and what few light welding/fabrication factories existed—were forcibly wrenched from their owners by a central government that firmly believed they could run them smarter and better.

Of course this system did not produce the goods. Kenya, where a more capitalist friendly and free-market approach was implemented, grew slowly to a *per capita* personal income of about $1,100. Tanzania, with almost identical population and resources lying immediately south, struggled mightily to only recently achieve roughly half that figure. *Per capita* income in Tanzania is thought to be only about $650, or only $54 per month. Thankfully, their economy is finally growing again after almost three decades of stagnation and decline. Fifty-four dollars per month barely compares to the amount many Americans spend on their pets!

Under most circumstances, citizens of virtually identical lands who look out to see neighbors prospering while they languish take to the barricades. Overthrow is usually imminent for socialists who fail to confiscate the guns. As a result, they cannot allow citizens to own even a few guns. Socialistic government officials seem to intuitively know that they will soon be hanging from the lamppost by their heels, Mussolini-style, if they don't severely limit private gun ownership.

Assisted mightily by one of the most charismatic and loveable leaders of the 20th century, Tanzania may be the only exception. If he was anything, Nyerere was also honest and smart. Suddenly, in 1985, he announced that his leadership of Tanzania proved that there was no such thing as "an African Way." If there was, it did not produce a workable economy. Socialism in any form doesn't deliver goods, services and well-being to the extent that free-market capitalism demonstrably does, Nyerere boldly announced. Although still loved and honored to the point of virtual deification by his people, Julius Nyerere turned the reins of government of his beloved Tanzania over to others with a different vision. Since that time, more than twenty years ago, freedom and private property have again started to reestablish themselves in Tanzania.

Any reestablishment has not been even or certain. Government control is still pervasive in many areas of the economy. As a result, people in the gun-sport-related businesses that provided some information for this chapter do not want—even tangentially—to be identified. They provided some good information but it was veiled and incomplete at times. I also relied on my own experiences in Tanzania and on the advice and counsel of some Kenyan nationals. A man who recently completed a hunting safari in Tanzania also helped with information. Even so, the gun law information that follows is fragmented and to an extent untested.

That we have only a basic outline of their rules and regulations should not matter. No American would likely go to Tanzania to enjoy their gun laws. Property rights and rules of law there are still primitively defined. Those traveling to Tanzania to hunt will rely on the advice of their paid hunter/guides. Information on bringing hunting guns to Tanzania is a one-off affair, good only for that single event as arranged by those securing your hunting license and game concession.

As mentioned, Tanzanian private gun-ownership laws are certainly not complex. Basically private citizens or residents can legally own a limit of three guns, so long as potential owners can convince local police charged with enforcing gun laws that they really need those guns and are competent to use them. Permitted guns could theoretically include one rifle, one pistol and one shotgun. Many African nations are attempting to move away from any use of .22 guns because of the role these play in surreptitious poaching. Currently Tanzanian law does not permit legal private ownership of a .22 rimfire.

No other guns are legal, especially machine and submachine guns and assault rifles. This even though Tanzania is awash with these type weapons. Full scale warfare with Uganda in the late 1970s as well as current unrest in Burundi, Somalia, and Ethiopia, has pumped tens of thousands of military weapons and millions of rounds of ammunition into Tanzania. Penalties for illegal ownership vary dramatically depending on the individual and the circumstances. White- or brown-skinned folks expect to spend either lots of money or lots of time in a pretty cruddy slammer if caught with illegal guns. Infractions on the part of black Africans may be overlooked. It depends on circumstance.

Local police handle requests for legal sporting rifles and shotguns. Applications are lengthy, fairly expensive, and require multiple signatures on multiple copies. Expect to wait at least three to four months for approvals unless "extra application money" is also given.

Permission for a pistol, assuming one can make a case for a self-defense need, are said to be easier for those who already have a rifle or shotgun permit. Pistol permits are issued for the whole thing—including permission to carry and to carry concealed if necessary.

Rifle and shotgun designs judged to be non-sporting military types are completely forbidden. No legal assault rifles or military shotguns are allowed in Tanzania. Other than this, there is no limitation on caliber or gauge, except .22 rimfire rifles and probably pistols are currently never sanctioned. Pistol permit applications go to police headquarters in Dar es Salaam for approval. Don't expect speedy service.

Tanzania is about three times the size of New Mexico. Theoretically gun owners could drive to one of the two officially sanctioned gun and ammo stores. These are run by the police and military. Using their newly police-issued gun-authorization permits, new owners can purchase a gun. In theory ammo is also available at these stores.

Heavy duties and taxes dramatically whoop up prices of guns and ammo at these "semi-governmental outlets." Quantities of ammo purchased and amounts that may be legally held are severely restricted. Perhaps even Tanzanian bureaucrats don't even consistently and accurately define this restriction. Resident gun owners don't seem to know exactly how many rounds a person could legally purchase. Based on my experience in Tanzania, I would guess it is something like fifty rounds legally allowed for purchase, but the only store in the country might have little for sale. Authorized purchase amounts, under these terms and conditions, would be meaningless. Twenty-two ammo is never legally available. Cynicism on my part may be setting in, but surely this approximation based on personal experience is not unreasonable.

Hand loading is completely unknown in Tanzania. In part this is understandable. Illicit military ammo is often available at prices that compete with purchased components alone. Old fashioned large bore English cartridges loaded with cordite and primed with Berdan primers do not lend themselves to reloading. Not only is reloading illegal, and impossible because no components are available for sale, it is unknown because it has not been practical.

Tanzanian authorities have probably never thought of attracting and keeping a firearms designing engineer here since such work is not authorized. Officially there are no gunsmiths other than military armorers. Unofficially a few skilled artisans called *fundis* are around to repair guns. Some of these are extremely skilled. Mostly they work as welders, village fabricators, and machinists. Only general skills are advertised, never gunsmithing.

Private gun and sporting goods shops are not even dreamed of in Tanzania. Tanzanian law does not provide for such. The military and police don't want the competition. A single public shooting range may be coming to Tanzania. Talk of such presently circulates.

That even a modest three-gun limit is available in Tanzania is a surprise. Few other African nations allow private gun ownership. Significantly most, if not all, of these countries are hard-core, desperate, mean dictatorships. Living is tough in Tanzania, but it is because they picked a bogus economic system, not because they have bloodthirsty rulers.

Perhaps we can conclude that, while Tanzania's private gun-ownership pattern is not attractive to most Americans, it is interesting. Especially given the country's history and examples of near neighbors.

Chapter Twenty-Seven
Honduras
World Rank: 56 • Firearm Freedom 14%

During the 1980s our own Central Intelligence Agency pumped thousands of guns and tens of thousands of rounds of ammunition into tiny Honduras (slightly larger than our state of Tennessee). The U.S. ran training camps, recruitment centers and staging areas from which a mixture of Honduran, Nicaraguan and even Salvadoran mercenaries sallied forth against the dreaded Nicaraguan Sandanista communists.

Did all of this firearms activity create a national gun culture in Honduras? We sent assault rifles, military shotguns, pistols, light machine guns, submachine guns and even mortars and grenade launchers by the truckload. Today no one knows for sure exactly what and how much. But we do know that a significant number of Hondurans ended up trained and proficient with firearms. Significantly the Russians also sent uncounted tons and tons of small arms and ammo, mostly through efforts of their client states. Lots of this stuff is still around. Hondurans today claim that gangsters, kidnappers and bank robbers prefer and use AK-47s while simple law-abiding citizens might own modern weapons of U.S. origin such as M-16s. In other words, good guys use American guns while baddies prefer Russian! Interesting how national perceptions sometimes run.

Yet, back to Honduran gun ownership in general. Knowledgeable, credible people postulate that WW II contributed mightily to an American interest in guns. "All those interesting makes and models," the gun culture says. Veterans apparently came home with both an interest in and knowledge of military firearms.

Today Honduran gun laws are a strange anomaly among those of various countries around the world. They combine some aspects of registration and limitation with practical, on-the-ground realization that there are already too many guns and rounds of ammunition floating around the country for any central government to control. Honduran gun laws are in a state of both accommodation and dramatic transition. They are unevenly enforced and there is definitely a regional component to their enforcement, i.e. what is allowed in one region is often forbidden in others. Strange and perhaps unworkable for so tiny a country.

Information we were able to assemble on Honduran gun laws is admittedly fragmented. Partly because their laws are in transition and partly because both the informant and the airline employee who rustled up that informant in Honduras were pretty ignorant about firearms in general. "Cero," she says (zero in Spanish) but she was not antagonistic toward, or afraid of, guns.

There were also translation problems. Rather than referring to submachine guns, machine guns, assault rifles or semi-auto assault rifles as such, they used the term "machines." As a result, some sort of sorting out and assumptions had to be made. What we do have here, we have with thanks. There are lessons for American gun owners.

As far as we know, their "General Police Department Circular D.6.PNP No. 19-2000" is unique throughout the world. This directive orders the police not to confiscate certain guns found in private hands where there is no permit! If you are an otherwise normal, employed Honduran citizen without a police record found with an unregistered .22, .32, .38, .40, or .45 caliber pistol or revolver, all that is required is that you temporarily register the gun with the local police. It will not be confiscated. Significantly, no 9mm gun is permitted. Apparently this prohibition applies to pistols and submachine guns. We don't know if 9mm rifles are also prohibited. Since 9mm rifles are rare, this is probably an unimportant question.

"Machines" (full-autos) of any kind are never permitted and are not registerable. Anyone found with one of these will have it confiscated. We don't know if these folks will also be prosecuted. Common, standard bolt-action rifles and shotguns of all makes, models and calibers are all permitted but—under new laws currently envisioned— might be subject to registration. No other restrictions on these so long as they are not military in appearance.

There is, however, talk of a limitation on the total number of guns a citizen may legally own as a result of newly contemplated legislation. Either the new law will specify three total handguns or three guns total including rifles and shotguns. No one we found is currently sure how the new rules will come down. Even a three-gun limit may not be nearly as onerous as we might first suppose given limited economic resources of average Hondurans.

Forbes, the American business magazine, ran an article some three to four years back about Hondurans and Central Americans and their rapidly expanding economies. It was their contention, at that time, that the sudden and dramatic sweep of conservative, charismatic evangelical Protestantism running through the region would quickly have a dramatic effect on the region's social structure and economy. We really don't know if the Honduran real growth rate of about 4% per year is the result, and if a healthy, vibrant and expanding economy has contributed to a more relaxed attitude toward private firearms ownership. We do know Hondurans now enjoy a *per capita* income of about $2,800, placing them far, far ahead of many strictly Third World lands where incomes are $200 per year or less. At least nine nations of the world are in this latter poorest-of-the-poor category.

At the time of U.S. meddling in the 1980s, Honduras was among the poorest of the poor. Although they lag Guatemala's current $4,200 and Costa Rica's $9,600 *per capita* incomes, the economy of Honduras—at least till the recent world turndown—has expanded dramatically.

Honduras is bordered to the south by Nicaragua, on the west by Salvador and on the north by Guatemala. While some American tourists and retirees visit Costa Rica (the other side of Nicaragua to the south) and Guatemala to retire and play, few Americans find Honduras' climate, topography or economy to be attractive. Either as a result of their gun laws or their general living conditions, this is not a place to which most of us would elect to move or to go for a vacation. Their economy is based on borderline, subsistence agriculture, large banana and coffee plantations, mining and some limited light manufacturing, principally textiles.

Honduran gun ownership in the areas around San Pedro Sula, Ceiba and Olancho is reportedly very common. These are places up on the north coast facing out into the Gulf of Mexico. Mexico's Yucatan Peninsula lies to the east.

The Honduran military controls registration of guns as well as new and used private sales of guns and ammunition. Those wishing to purchase guns must go to their local police office where they will find a military representative or be directed to a nearby office that has one of these bureaucrats. Places to handle firearms matters are said to be numerous, spread in great number throughout the country. Apparently Hondurans register specific guns to owners. Unlike other countries, no general gun-owner's license is required.

At this writing, registrations are easy to acquire. The government isn't requiring them and is, therefore, not writing new ones. This may all change with some new laws, but no one who is talking is prepared to say for sure. Securing a specific registration for a gun may be much more difficult in the future. Will registrations be required only for pistols and revolvers, and not rifles and shotguns? Current prohibitions seem to be on military "assault" rifles and shotguns, and pistols—not on sporting rifles and shotguns.

Called La Ermeria, there is only one company authorized to import and sell guns and ammunition, as well as reload brass. This is a state-owned, military-run enterprise. They have stores in most principal cities as well as many of the smaller interior ones, suggesting an active gun trade in Honduras. Specifically, gun stores are located in San Pedro Sula, Tegucigalpa, and Cieba. Their phone numbers are 504-

225-0401, 504-225-0420 and 504-225-0416, call for more current information. But you gotta speak Honduran Spanish!

These military gun stores reload ammunition. They are the only place in Honduras where this is legal. As a result, powder, bullets and primers are not available to citizens. No other gun or ammo dealers are permitted. Legally and officially, private gun sales must start in the office of the appropriate military authorities. All ammo sales are handled by La Ermeria. Currently there is no limit on amounts one may own or purchase, but this may change. Ammo is sold only for specific, legally owned guns.

Peace and order are said to currently be somewhat tenuous in Honduras. A great number of illegal guns and ammunition are said to be "out there," but these are subjective evaluations offered without substantiating statistics by citizens who may have recently been impacted by crime.

Perhaps there is a grain of truth here. We could reasonably cut the government a bit of slack and suggest that because crime is so bad and because there are so many guns out there anyway, they are allowing private citizens to defend themselves, at least until the situation stabilizes sufficiently that they could do a credible job of identifying firearms within the country.

Private importation of guns under any circumstances is said to be impossible. Design and development work, on the other hand, may be possible under some limited circumstances. Our informants say the politicians are anxious for any economic development. "Ask, in the correct places," they say, "and you may be surprised."

About six million people call Honduras home, quite a few for such a small place. There are no open ranges for civilians but informal shooting does sometimes take place in the countryside according to our informants.

Chapter Twenty-Eight
Khyber Pass Region of Pakistan
World Rank: 1 • Firearm Freedom 98%

Several excellent reasons are out there for not including this place in any reporting of foreign gun laws. This, in spite of the fact that *per capita* gun ownership is probably higher in the area than in many other parts of the world. Locals liken their situation to Americans with cameras—"You have your cameras and we have our guns," as quoted by one reporter who wrote a book about traveling to Afghanistan and the Khyber Pass.

Officially Peshawar, the principal city in the Northwest Frontier Province of Pakistan (sometimes referred to as the semi-autonomous region of northern Pakistan), is subject to the same rules and regulations as the rest of Pakistan. According to an indigenous Muslim imam who agreed to help with this chapter, Pakistan has private gun-ownership laws very much like those in England. Very restrictive!

Not much of interest here for American gun owners. But that is only the official line. Illegal gun ownership in Pakistan is widespread. In the Khyber Pass area, it is open and notorious. "Anyone who wants a gun in Pakistan and can pay for it can probably have it," the imam claims. Expand this out to ground-mount heavy machine guns, recoilless rifles and grenade launchers in the Northwest Frontier and Peshawar.

Even Pakistani police, bureaucrats and politicians who could easily legally own a gun seldom do so. Much easier to avoid lengthy paperwork by buying illegally on the street, these folks claim.

As a result, the peace and order situation even in Karachi, the capital city, 700 miles south of the Northwest Frontier Province, is bad. So bad that the last time our friend, the imam, visited his southern Pakistan homeland, he called his friends and relatives from the airport. "Those who wish to see me must come out to meet at the airport," he told them.

"Complete and uncontrolled anarchy, unfettered by any milk of human compassion," is the way one of the Soldier-of-Fortune-type adventurers who provided information for this chapter put it. No government writ has run here in the Northwest for at least the last 300 years.

British occupiers, for example, who came in the mid-1800s left these fierce, independent Pathans to their own devices. No one, before or since, has enjoyed any greater success taming this wild region.

The Khyber Pass is not a country. It does not really operate with any sort of written rules and regulations. To compare this region, on any basis, to any other country in the world is disjointed.

Tribal custom and morés prevail. These are usually incomprehensible and unfathomable to otherwise reasonable people. The imam suggests that the only way he or I or any other westerner could ever safely visit the region would be under the personal protection and guarantee of a powerful local warlord!

Machine-gun fire interrupted conversation of the Soldier-of-Fortune guys while gathering information for this chapter. Perhaps it was only some shop owners test firing a newly manufactured gun, or perhaps it really was a violent, deadly renewal of tribal rivalries common to the region. For whatever reason, we are again come 'round to the question, "who would be interested in information about a place no one would or could ever visit or live in, no matter to what level they were interested in guns?"

Perhaps by reporting on the law-and-order private firearms situation in this lawless little land tucked up between the northwest of Pakistan and the southeast of Afghanistan, we play into the hands of the antis. Obviously the Northwest Frontier Province is not a civilized area. Will our nation also degenerate into some sort of armed anarchist camp if we also sanction free and unencumbered gun ownership? Do Khyber Pass guns cause a lack of civility, or is there another answer?

Probably it is cultural. Historic reports from the time of bows and arrows, broadswords, knives and spears suggest things were not much improved during these times in this unhappy land. At the very least, American gun owners should be aware of the area, its idiosyncrasies and the fact that they may well hear about it from the antis.

Economic reference material says nothing about the Northwest Frontier Province as a stand-alone from Pakistan. Probably because no one in the Pakistani department of economic statistics has a clue. And they sure won't try sending someone from Karachi upcountry to ask!

Pakistan itself has finally managed an estimated *per capita* income of about $2,200. Both the Pakistani imam and the SoF types who have recently been there reckon Khyber Pass residents to be materially poorer than the rest of Pakistan. Perhaps not an accurate estimate!

Pakistani, U.S., UN, Saudi and even Russian aid has poured into the region. Lots of folks in the region are refugees and there is a great appearance of abject poverty. But there is also a great deal of commerce "of sorts."

Peshawar is a gun-owners' Mecca, but Darra Adam Khel, a smallish village some 25 miles south of Peshawar on the road to Kohat is more than that. *They have well over 100 gun shops.* Were it not for the tremendous number of smelly, open-stall single proprietorships, often consisting of little more than one bag of flour or half a goat peddled by a single shopkeeper, gun shops would vastly outnumber everything else in this little town.

It is conservatively estimated that these tiny machine shops produce at least 20,000 new firearms per year. About 55 guns per day selling, our informants claim, for a conservative $100 each. That's a gross of at least $2 million annually. You'll find rockets, hand grenades, anti-aircraft guns with ammo, mortars, mortar bombs, grenade launchers, small-arms ammunition, recoilless rifles and ammo all turned out and offered for sale by the ton, by these super-industrious brigands.

All of this material is produced in tiny one-or-two-man shops, deploying hand tools such as files, bench grinders, Dremel tools, drill presses turned into milling machines, and small hand forges. Questions arise regarding the safety and reliability of all these "homemade" guns and ordnance, but otherwise the fact remains that all of this would be impossible if it were not purchased for cash and eventually used somewhere.

Certainly no one in the region has ever even heard of product liability or insurance. Instead, their culture allows offended family members to extract lethal vengeance called *badal* by the locals. Someone is buying and using this vast provision of arms and ammunition. If they didn't have money, or weren't satisfied, we have to conclude Darra Adam Khel's gun industry would quickly atrophy and die as its craftsmen were killed off by vengeful relatives of dissatisfied dead customers.

Virtually every male and a few of the women in the area own guns. Boys of eight, up to ancient men tottering along with both a submachine gun and a walking stick are there. They have favorite firearms including everything from old model bolt-action Enfields up through heavy machine guns and pistols and revolvers. All can be seen out on the streets. No workable laws can or will disarm residents in this wild and woolly region.

Obviously no gun-owners' certificates, registrations, make and model restrictions or other gun-ownership restrictions apply. You got the cash? You get the guns!

Some guns are obviously manufactured around salvaged barrels and other bits and pieces of older model guns. No such thing as the junk-gun parts here. In addition the claim is made that large numbers of old truck springs, rail iron, old and worn tank treads, steel drums and other such often find their way into local guns. Khyber Pass gun makers deny it. "We use new, tough, modern alloy steel imported from Belgium and Germany," they claim.

Modern guns with close-fitting gas pistons and intricate locking systems made of space-age alloys are currently beyond the expertise of Khyber Pass gunsmiths. These definitely include H&K G-3s, M-16s and probably M-1 Garands although they do produce a nice knock-off of our M-1 and M-2 Carbine. Some of these are really weird—in .32 ACP, for instance.

Yet in this gun-rich environment, one might also spot a G-3 (made in Pakistan under license) or an Israeli UZI (from the Iran/Iraq dustup). There are also some genuine American M-16s (purchased from gun merchants in Southeast Asia or delivered by the Americans when we supported the Mujahadeen.)

Local firearms prices range all over the bazaar. This in a gun-buyers' paradise among some of the best hagglers on Earth. Weird, hybrid, locally designed submachine guns fabricated using numerous miscellaneous bits and pieces start around $100. Names might be Special Rolex, Frontier Arms or Haji Farhad & Bros. Arms and Ammunition. I am not making this up!

Homemade copies of Russian Tokarev pistols, complete with magazines and holsters, run about $70. Originals, made in Russia, no doubt liberated from the Russians, sell for about $220.

Not all prices are even this logical. Worn but serviceable Russian AK-47s, a virtual commodity in the region, sell for about $200. New more desirable Chinese-made AK assault rifles cost about $1,000. Poor folks—unable to afford an original—can purchase very nice, allegedly serviceable, local knock-offs for about $375. They use Pakistani rupees printed in Russia.

Locally made rockets are about $900. Launchers are very inexpensive if you can convince the makers that you will need lots of rockets to go with the launchers. Khyber Pass grenades, at about $3, are said not to be especially reliable, which certainly hurts repeat sales at any price.

Local gun makers also produce and sell nice copies of American and Russian light and heavy machine guns. Mostly these are custom order deals. Expect to pay anywhere from $1,500 to $2,500 and more.

Hand loading is common in the region, with no restrictions anyone is aware of. For many of Khyber's gun shops, production of small arms ammo, rockets and heavy-ordnance ammo is a principal source of income. Skilled labor is cheap, and those who wish to do so can easily purchase bullets, primers and powder in quantity. Quality, especially of primers, is sometimes dubious.

Smokeless rifle powder is often homemade, reconstituted from powder salvaged from Russian artillery rounds and who knows what else. Burn rates, pressures and standards are very inconsistent, leading not only to numerous malfunctions but dangerous situations. As a result, while hand loading is permissible, it is not always practical or wise.

Other than economics, there is no limit on the number of guns, types, or models one may own. No age limits, no magazine restrictions, no government forms, no size, caliber or ammo type limits. HE rounds, for instance, are available over the counter for your recoilless rifle.

Anyone can be a gun dealer. Anyone can import guns into the Khyber Pass area so long as they don't run afoul of rules and regulations of neighboring countries or, for some unknown reason, upset the locals. Some, but not all, of these neighboring countries take a dim view of this gun trafficking. Pakistan does a bit to control it, while the ex-Soviet bloc countries to the north seem to enjoy the commerce such as it is. Khyber Pass gun running by another name is unbridled freedom.

As discussed going in, the Northwest Frontier Province of Pakistan is a complete anomaly. Their social mores and customs guarantee that. Neither those who are anti-rights on the gun issue nor those who support the right to keep and bear arms can validly use this place as an example. It isn't a country. There is absolutely no rule of law, and never has been in recorded history. Their culture of violent unforgiving personal vengeance and retribution does not fit or match anyplace else in the world. Anyone who seeks to belittle gun rights by singling out the U.S. as the number one spot needs to change their target to the real number one, the Northwest Frontier Province, the Khyber Pass.

Chapter Twenty-Nine
Iran
World Rank: 18 • Firearm Freedom 68%

With Iran we come to a series of countries having especially interesting private gun-ownership law. "Their situation is not valid," the antis claim. "These are rough Arab countries, not a modern, civilized place, and provide no lessons for American gun owners," we hear. Well, perhaps Iranians are not civilized—at least not in terms we commonly use. But again, all depends on whose analysis and standards apply.

At one time a few years ago, a beautifully assembled, raven-haired, articulate young Iranian woman adamantly and pointedly lectured me regarding the truth that her civilization was at least 3,000 years older than mine. "And what do I know about civility?" she pointedly asked. Wisely, perhaps, I kept my mouth shut.

"Notorious" probably best characterizes Iran for Americans who know anything at all about the country. Older citizens may recall Iran's vicious, dirty and bloody seven-year war with Iraq, ultimately ending in a stalemate in 1988. There also was the violent occupation of our embassy and the 444-day detention of our 52 State Dept. employees. A complete breach of civilized behavior, Americans concluded.

Iran does actually have something of a rule of law and system of property rights. Mostly these rules and rights are only understood in terms of Iranian tradition and culture rather than in code sections or through written laws. To be sure, foolish, arbitrary and counterproductive edicts continue to emanate from religious/political clerics and other government officials, further complicating the picture. But Iran continues to exist and function because citizens pretty much ignore these edicts—especially relative to minor day-to-day matters. Fortunately, the reach and power of the central authorities is weak and ineffective, especially in smaller, rural areas.

As a result, small, obscure start-up business ventures are possible. Growing these ventures into national job and wealth-producing entities would be thwarted by layers upon layers of religious bureaucracy and red tape. Iran is a society that follows Islam. But suggesting that Persians are Bedouins or Arabs invites a sharp response. They are not Arabs, as they will quickly explain.

Even rural Iran is not a place where most Americans could and would choose to live, work and raise a family. For most of us, their culture precludes such. Theirs isn't a land of opportunity, demonstrated by the great number of intelligent, hardworking, successful and able Iranian expatriates living in more opportunistic places around the world.

Our informants in this instance include Iranian nationals who operate hunting, fishing and general tourist-type sightseeing operations in Iran itself, as well as in the United Arab Emirates and Oman. One fellow, in particular, is an avid hunter, fisherman, and gun collector who won't admit it but probably served in the Iranian army during the time of its war with Iraq. Unfortunately, he permanently carries serious and grotesque scars from an upper arm and shoulder wound. A hunting accident, he says, caused by an errant 7.62x39 bullet. "God gave me another life," he says. Perhaps Iranians really do hunt with AK-47s. He has mostly healed from what is obviously a very serious incident.

I personally have been very close to Iran while never actually having been on the ground there. Americans are prohibited from legally entering, under most circumstances. Entering illegally would be okay if I were younger and still able to run a six-minute mile. Since I can no longer run, we must make do with info from in-country citizen expats.

Iran is that country located twelve time zones east of San Francisco on the sunny side (facing west) of the Persian Gulf. Until 1935 it was known by its historic name of Persia. Citizens continue taking great pride referring to themselves as Persians.

Iran is a relatively large country, about three times the size of Arizona. Russia lies to the north and east. Pakistan and Afghanistan frame the rest of its eastern border. Crabby, militant Iraq borders to the northwest above the Persian Gulf. Then it's Turkey and the Caspian Sea.

Officially Iran's *per capita* income is about $7,700. Certainly this figure fails to recognize a generally higher standard of living. Because of their extensive black markets and underground economy, any government figures are mostly illusory.

Fully one third of Iranians are still employed in direct agricultural pursuits or in agricultural service and delivery. No one really knows how much rice, wheat, barley, sugar beets, cotton and dates are produced. No doubt a great amount is personally consumed without making prior notification to the taxing authorities.

As many as three in ten Iranians may be unemployed, and inflation may be as high as 30 percent per annum. No one—least of all their bumbling, myopic government—really knows.

Two very separate and perhaps unique patterns characterize gun ownership in Iran. There are both legally owned as well as an extensive network of illegally owned guns. Because enforcement, especially in rural areas, is weak and bribery rampant, Iranian gun owners seem to seldom bother going the legal route, especially for more desirable pistols, submachine guns and assault rifles. Smuggling, battlefield pickups, and the stealing and selling of weapons and ammunition by officers all contribute to the large pool of guns and ammo easily available to Iranian citizens illegally.

Iran definitely has an active, vibrant gun culture. Sport hunting, for both big game and birds, is common. Resident hunting licenses cost about $10. Ownership of guns is common in Iran—at least at the family/clan level. Iranians prefer big, heavy Mauser or Enfield-type rifles. However they also frequently own and shoot pistols, assault rifles, light machine guns and submachine guns. Shotguns are tools. Concealed pistol carrying is common but it's the big, heavy public rifles that characterize their culture and which they still enjoy.

Iranians generically refer to commercial rifles and shotguns as "Winchesters." Numerous gun shops found in virtually every city throughout the land cater to this trade. These shops also handle bullets, powder, shot and primers as well as loaded ammunition and telescopic sights. It is uncommon for them to sell brass empties, but used shotshell hulls are frequently on offer. There are absolutely no restrictions on sales of reloading components, telescopic sights, mounts or most other accoutrements.

Silencers for most commercial and military guns are available to those who want them. Mostly these are homemade a few at a time by skillful artisans in local shops available only on the black market.

Probably because most of their ammo is comprised of surplus military Berdan-primed cases, reloading pistol and rifle ammo is said not to be nearly as common as reloading shot shells. Iranians are not wealthy. In spite of this, I was told, ammunition is very, very cheap in Iran. "We don't bother to reload because of the price," I was informed.

It isn't always open, overt or legal, but at least one gun broker/dealer operates in every souk (market) throughout the land. Locals know whom to see or to ask about purchasing a gun.

Legal ownership works basically as follows: Go to your local police headquarters. Pay a fee of about $20 and fill out their extensive forms. Approval, assuming a clean record, takes about three days.

Firearms-permit holders are then authorized to own a total of three hunting-type rifles or shotguns. No pistols, assault rifles or commercial semi-auto rifles are allowed under this first classification. Pump and semi-auto three-shot shotguns are allowed on this level of permit.

On securing a permit, holders hot-foot it down to their favorite legal gun store where they can purchase their three commercial shotguns or rifles. Forms listing guns legally purchased are sent to the local police. As a result, Iranians are both licensed to purchase and recorded as purchasers of specific guns.

Legal ammo purchases are tied back to one's original police-issue gun-owner's permit and to a specific registered gun. Ammo purchases are allowed only for specific, legally registered guns.

Ammo buyers are legally allowed up to 200 rounds of high-powered rifle ammo, 500 rounds of shotgun ammo and 1,000 rounds of .22 rimfire ammo per purchase. These are also the maximum numbers of rounds gun owners can legally have in their possession at one time.

Higher levels of licenses are available for those who wish to legally own pistols, assault rifles, light machine guns or more than three guns. There are tests and bribes as well as genuine fees that make these licenses difficult to secure. Our informants hold this process in complete contempt. No one they know bothers with this complicated, expensive and uncertain process, they said. While the first level of license for commercial guns is routine and easy, decisions on higher-level licenses are often capricious and arbitrary.

They also regard questions regarding legal importation and permits to do experimental working on gun designs with disbelieving disdain and humor. No one has ever or would ever do this in Iran, they said with great smiles, so why even bother to address that question.

No one could guess what was involved in getting a store-owner's permit to legally import and sell guns. As mentioned, reasonably well stocked gun stores are common, but knowledge regarding their legal standing and official approval was unknown to our informants.

On a final note, H&K G-3 assault rifles in .308 are apparently the preferred illegal weapon for Iranians concerned about increasing their firepower. There are probably tens of thousands of these floating around the country. Many, no doubt, are left over from the war with Iraq. Our gun-buff informant claimed they were both inexpensive and common on the Iranian black market. "Two hundred U.S. dollars buys both a nice new G-3 and a case of ammo," they said.

Curiously, Iran's enemy Iraq used only Soviet-bloc infantry rifles, according to "Jane's Infantry Weapons." These included AK-47s, SKSs, and SVDs, but not a G-3 in a car load. Iranian armed forces, on the other hand, extensively used H&K G-3s.

Apparently all of those many G-3s on Iran's black market were stolen from their own military and resold on the black market. Or, the Iranian government purposely released these guns and then turned a blind eye. As a means of arming for home defense? We don't know for sure.

Chapter Thirty
United Arab Emirates
World Rank: 13 • Firearm Freedom 76%

Private gun ownership in the U.A.E. is a strange, strange anomaly only possible in the never-never land of arbitrary nationalistic Muslim political intrigue. Their laws and ownership patterns are not difficult or complex. Explaining them in terms of western culture and rule of law is what is difficult.

The United Arab Emirates, or U.A.E., was formed in 1971 by a loose confederation of seven emirates or sheikdoms. The state-like federation allows joint policies for foreign relations, defense and infrastructure development, while allowing member sheikdom to keep its own local internal system of courts, civil law and administration. On the face of it, gun laws in each of the seven separate emirates could be quite different. As a practical matter, common social customs, history and political outlook create great similarity.

Each emirate has a cultural bias favoring big, heavy, showy rifles as a sort of symbol of independence and masculine macho authority. All of the emirates also have a hearty aversion to disorder, uncertainty and impropriety. All share similar bare, stark topography characterizing a land devoid of hunting, farming or other agricultural opportunities. Citizens are seldom hunters.

Official literature in my possession actually affirms that zero percent of their land is under cultivation. This material makes much of the fact that a total of 19.3 square miles in the entire U.A.E. are irrigated! This includes parks, parkways and a bit of greenery around the airport.

This is a nation almost exactly the size of our state of Maine. Saudi Arabia lies to the west and south. Until very recently this boundary was uncertain and unsettled. Much to the consternation of UN types, neither party cared. Nobody went there and few people gave a rip just where the line ran. "Somewhere out there" was good enough.

Toward the west the Emirates border Qatar. East and south they border the mystical kingdom of Oman. Visualizing this place is difficult without looking at a map. Look for the relatively small portion of the Arabian Peninsula that juts out, forming the Gulf of Oman and the Straits of Hormuz.

As a result of lying near other economically rich countries and because the U.A.E. originally formed as a pirate state, these folks have historically made their living as smugglers. In times past, I personally have seen mountains of crated VCRs, clothes, washing machines, TVs, Japanese kerosene heaters and microwaves piled on the docks waiting for dhow transport to Iran or some other equally nefarious destination.

Seems smuggling, at least on a grand scale, is a thing of the past. Modern U.A.E. owes its great wealth to the fact that, by some accident of geology, the country formed over a huge pool of relatively easily accessed crude oil. Government ownership of this liquid gold led to strange anomalies. Current average per person income for native Emiratis is well over $25,000. Basic average personal wealth at these levels is difficult to comprehend. Especially in a region where $50 per month or $600 per year is a king's ransom.

Perhaps the following observations will help put it all in context. Abu Dhabi, the Emirates' largest and most prosperous city, has a population of about one million. But carefully note that this total includes 850,000 guest expatriate workers and only about 150,000 native Emiratis. These natives are, as their literature says, indistinguishable from the sitting government. Native Emiratis are empowered to make policy and law on the fly as they go, as they wish. We must keep this important distinction in mind when we later look at their culture and gun laws.

It's a sure formula for internal strife and disorder, you may suggest. Yet, until this time, disorder has not been a problem in the Emirates. This is due to the fact that guest workers from dirt-poor countries have no chance for advancement or improvement in their native homelands. As a result they make great personal sacrifice to keep their coveted, relatively high-paying jobs in the U.A.E.

Most guest workers are not government employees. Some may work for government entities such as schools and airlines, but most work out on the economy as taxi drivers, restaurant operators, mechanics, cooks, construction workers and clerks working for Emirates' natives or other expatriates. Expats work for private firms, owned by natives, who contract with the government for that company's services. Street cleaning, maintenance, sewer, water and electric are other examples, complicated by the reality that the natives are the government. In essence, we have the government contracting with the government.

Information for this chapter comes from an American lady living and working in the U.A.E. She is an English teacher working at one of the principal women's universities in Abu Dhabi. Her leads, contacts and observations—while not definitive in themselves—were valuable. As an aside, she is a hunter and gun owner, and is not fearful of the subject of private ownership of firearms.

In addition we have the benefit of information from the Iranian gun buff/hunting-fishing guide living and working in the U.A.E. During the time I personally spent in the U.A.E. I talked to him for several hours about private gun ownership in various countries in the Near East. Having been there and done that, Hussein was probably the best person in the world to explain it all to me.

In times past I personally have traveled and worked extensively in the U.A.E. Absolutely nothing from the past prepared me for I saw during my recent fact-finding incursion as prep for this chapter. Everything, especially the buildings, roads, piers, channels and streets were replaced. It was totally different than I remembered from 20 years ago.

While there I encountered an Indian taxi driver whose account may put things in perspective. Originally from Madras, he had now spent 11 years in the U.A.E. driving a hack. To conserve funds he ate and slept in an 8x12 room with 11 other countrymen! By reason of his incredible industry and frugality he was able to send $50 per month home to a wife and children, enough for food, shelter, education and a brighter future for his family. Once every other year, for one month, he returned to Madras to meet his new child and to reimpregnate his wife.

Now lets try to make sense of gun ownership in this place. For starters, absolutely no expat in the U.A.E. may own a firearm under any circumstances. Doing so risks his whole life and his family's future.

Native Emiratis, on the other hand, may own any and all the firearms they wish without any restrictions whatsoever. As far as anyone can tell, no formal code sections exist defining this right. Unlike many other Arab countries, native Emiratis are not part of a gun culture. But unlike other near Arab cultures, they are not enamored with military heavy weapons such as anti-aircraft cannons, rocket-propelled grenades and heavy, ground mount .50 caliber machine guns. Their police do not carry. Only a very few firearms are seen out on the street, usually carried by military personnel.

Recall, natives are the government. Making up the rules as they go is *de rigueur*. Except for a few souks in the interior, there are no gun stores. With exception of the fact that family ownership of a big, heavy bolt-action Mauser or Enfield rifle, which is kept mostly for quasi-ceremonial activities, Emiratis don't think much about guns.

Few to no target or trap-shooting opportunities exist. They don't hand load. It's too time consuming and physically demeaning when abundant, cheap surplus ammo is easily available.

Apparently natives can and sometimes do legally own pistols, assault rifles and light machine guns. They are mostly brought in from Iran or Oman. Knowing which man in the souk is the gun dealer/importer is part of their culture. Although U.A.E. police don't carry, it seems a bit different than in the United Kingdom where there is always the impression that English Bobbies have immediate access to firearms when they need them.

Graphic local TV sometimes shows live arrest and detention of some violent lawbreakers. No guns are ever in sight. U.A.E. police merely overwhelm the offender, truss him up pig style and haul him away.

Crime, as we know it, is not a big deal in the Emirates. At this writing there are a total of 271 inmates in the Abu Dhabi jail. Fourteen are women! Great arguments spanning a great many large books could be made pro and con relative to their system.

At a minimum we can accurately point out that there are few to no lessons there for American gun owners. In contrast to even native Emiratis, Americans enjoy many, many rights. Not only are expats forbidden to own guns, they don't enjoy freedom of speech or assembly, or freedom to vote, and are subject to arbitrary arrest including search and seizure. Emirati natives don't really vote. Their press is lively but not really free. The only real freedom is to make piles and piles of tax-free money.

Crime is non-existent. Everything works and runs on time. Restaurants of all kinds abound. All is just as the ruling class—comprising 15 percent of the population—like it. As long as crude oil is in demand, all things will probably continue as they are.

Americans living there seem to do so temporarily for the money. No doubt an American with appropriate connections could secure permission to do experimental firearms design and testing. Significant subsidies might also be made available, courtesy of the wealthy central government, to the right person with the right connections.

While the orderliness, certainty and income would appeal to some modern Americans, there is no indigenous innovation, creativity or individual technological advancement here. No future for those who elect to stay there, built on one's own efforts. Expats can never become citizens. Their only future is to continue as relatively well-paid worker bees in the government hive. Analyzing the good and bad of it is a personal matter. Certainly beyond the scope of this volume.

Chapter Thirty-One
Oman
World Rank: 14 • Firearm Freedom 75%

Oman, in many people's eyes, is a fabled place of which legends are spun and ballads sung, especially from a gun lover's point of view.

European expats in the Persian Gulf area with sufficient funds scheme and plan for visits to this little, exotic, out of the way place. Having once visited, they are not disappointed, and they tell friends who also plan excursions, speaking volumes about the wonders of this little-known kingdom. Oman is about the size of Kansas. Their current government is seldom arbitrary—it is an absolute monarchy.

Omanis are Bedouin Arabs, ruled by a sultan, but with an incredible difference. Explaining this difference is a challenge. Let's try, without engaging in derogatory comments about other sheikdoms or other Arab countries.

Oman entered the modern world with a sudden jolt on July 29, 1970 when Said bin Taimur, the old sultan, was deposed by his son in a bloodless palace coup. Visitors to the newly opened kingdom found shocking medieval conditions, including great isolation, illiteracy and things like political prisoners chained to dungeon walls in the country's many brown-sandstone castles.

Simultaneously oil was discovered in the kingdom, creating huge, previously unimaginable wealth.

Oman's new, young, educated sultan Qabus bin Said proved to be world class. Although a staunch Muslim, he did not believe the infidels (Christians) had nothing to show the Arabs. The sultan's vision, compassion, intelligence, self-confidence and consistency were and are unique among the world's leaders.

Some of his first acts were to open the kingdom to investors and visitors, establish Oman as a Hong Kong-like free-trade zone and he set up an elected consultative assembly. Establishing a council of advisors is very Muslim, but in this case some of these elected officials have been women! Few Americans who have not also lived, traveled and worked in the region can understand the uniqueness and significance of this fact.

Omanis are not culturally burdened by deep-seated feelings of inferiority, which feelings eventually fester into intense resentment in other Muslim countries. Western visitors quickly note that they are treated as peers, even by poor rural farmers peddling cucumbers and eggplant fruits in the markets. In turn, westerners find it is easier to treat Omanis as peers. It fits better with our basic egalitarian nature. As a result, Omanis—including shopkeepers, government bureaucrats and day laborers—are not fearful and suspicious of western culture, technology or people.

Experts who have studied this philosophy postulate that Muslims who once dominated the world's science, medicine and mathematics fell hopelessly behind when they refused to accept that infidels had anything at all to teach them. This isn't true with Omanis in their headlong plunge to catch up technologically.

By contrast, the Omani leadership looked out to observe many horrible, foolish errors made by other Gulf countries as they attempted to modernize using their vast, newly acquired oil money. Omanis, under their new, confident, modern-educated sultan, resolved to do things differently. And they did.

The best and brightest among them were immediately sent to engineering, medical, agricultural and business schools in the U.S. and Europe. Omani students went to live and learn. Be a boozing playboy as long as your sponsor didn't find out about it through failing grades in tough subjects. Fail at this first most urgent task of education and you summarily lost your stipend, tuition, honor and any other support.

Abundant Omani oil money also went for roads, sewers, clean drinking water, hospitals and schools, vital national capital goods. And nothing for high-paying, worthless bean-counting make-work jobs for the sons of important princes.

Expat workers are deployed to some extent but native Omanis will readily take construction, maintenance, equipment operator and manufacturing work involving tough physical labor.

From ancient times various in-migrations have blurred lines between natives and expats. Swahili, for instance, is frequently spoken in the souks! Hearing this pleasant, simple language with its many characteristic short "a" word ending sounds, comes as a surprise to many first-time visitors. They expect the harsh, guttural sounds of Arabic rather than a lilting African trade language.

Obscure little Oman is tough to pinpoint without a map of the Gulf area. Look at the very bottom of the Persian Gulf on the east side of the Arabian peninsula. Muscat, a relatively short drive from Abu Dhabi, is the capital. Oman stretches boomerang-shape around the empty quarter of Saudi Arabia. As a result of its funny little crescent shape, Oman enjoys hundreds of miles of clean, delightful and mostly deserted beachfront on the Arabian Sea.

Some tourists do come to Oman for its luxurious yet relatively inexpensive resort hotels facing effectively private beaches. Others come for the beautiful medieval castles, forts, colorful cities and their bazaars. Old-fashioned Arab hospitality still comes into play in their colorful little rural villages. Although I visited the deepest inner sanctum of their largest, most disorganized market in the wee hours of the morning, I never felt threatened or even the slightest apprehension. Crime in Oman is virtually non-existent. The sultan won't have it, nor will citizens put up with it.

Assume everyone in Oman is armed. In a classical sense, assuming everyone can and will protect themselves leads to great civility. Unlike the Khyber Pass area where everyone carries both a gun and a chip on their shoulders, Omanis are self-confident and friendly. Like in the rural U.S. where common gun ownership leads to dramatically reduced crime, universal gun ownership in Oman obviously contributes to the pleasant state of affairs we now see.

In addition to my own on-the-ground research, we have information from a university-professor tourist who recently visited Oman, from a Bedouin gun buff and from an Omani university student currently living in the U.S.

Rules of law and property rights are well defined and very strong in Oman. Culturally, they recognize the great importance of private property. However, there are few to no constitutional guarantees of such. Freedom of speech is not assumed. Seriously criticize the sultan and you will find yourself in deep doo-doo. Because their guarantees come at the hand of one man, the situation could change drastically with the advent of a less gifted, less visionary, less self-assured sultan.

Omani farmers produce a significant portion of the food the country requires, mostly on recently developed irrigated farms. Including their considerable oil money, average *per capita* income is about $13,100! Given relatively primitive living conditions from which many Omanis have very recently sprung, this is a princely sum of money.

As mentioned at the beginning, private gun ownership in Oman is a delight. Unlike some other Muslim countries, Omanis do not attach great significance to heavy ceremonial bolt-action rifles. Also unlike the Yemenis to the south, Omanis do not favor heavy military weapons such as .50-caliber machine guns, 20mm cannons or rocket-propelled grenades. These are available from some gun dealers. Yet they are not commonly sought after or available. Those who want heavy weapons and who have the money can special order them.

A wide array of sporting rifles, shotguns—simple to expensive and ornate—submachine guns, pistols, assault rifles and light machine guns can be seen on display at the gun sellers' booths in most local souks (markets). You buy across the counter. No questions beyond "show me the money" apply.

However, two additional problem-like situations come into play for those making their weapons purchases in Oman. First is the bewildering array of guns on offer. Some few are immediately familiar. Some are vaguely familiar and some are weird as three-dollar bills!

The answer lies in the fact that, like Khyber Pass weapons makers, Omanis are experts at fabricating their own close copies as well as homegrown designs. Dealers also carry and sell a huge array of the world's factory-made commercial and military firearms.

Nobody could tell me where this commercial stuff came from. Gun dealers tend to speak English, but often poorly. Either they didn't know or didn't want to tell me. I doubt if Winchester, Beretta and Smith & Wesson have publicized wholesale distributors in Oman!

Obviously some of it is military left-behind or surplus, perhaps brought in from Iraq or Iran, or even purchased from Vietnam after we withdrew. Some of the many AKs obviously came directly from Russia and Eastern Europe. But what about the many telescopic sights, holsters, replacement stocks, boxes of bullets, primers, canisters of powder and such? Looked to me as though these merchants or their distributors in the background scrounged the world for all of this miscellaneous stuff.

The second problem is most of these guns appear to be breathtakingly expensive. More so for genuine commercial and military models than home manufactured ones. It's a good question if less expensive, locally designed-and-manufactured weapons would be sufficiently reliable.

Initially I attributed their sky-high prices to the fact that Omanis expect buyers to haggle fiercely for anything they want to take home from the souk. Perhaps they figured I was not a real buyer and perhaps they shot me a highball figure, being a rich American and all. At any rate, prices started very high and they didn't accept VISA or MasterCard. However, my ATM card worked at their banks.

Although canister powder, shot, bullets and primers were available I was told that, other than a few shot shells, Omanis mostly don't reload, since surplus and commercial ammo is so very cheap. And Berdan-primed surplus-military ammo is often a challenge to reload.

Apparently almost any commercial ammo is available to those who look hard enough and are sufficiently patient. Testing this proposition was impossible given the relatively brief time I was in Oman.

The only restriction on ownership I could uncover was a very recent order by sultan Said prohibiting the open carry of assault rifles, submachine guns and light machine guns in the larger cities. This probably an attempt to avoid scaring tourists, or to placate American politicians. In spite of the decree, there is every reason to believe concealed carry of all kinds of pistols, exists under the population's flowing robes. Some of these discreetly-carry weapons are very nice, perhaps original AR-15s and AK-47s modified to pistol configuration.

Women do not wear veils in Oman unless they wish to. Some may also carry but I don't know that for sure.

My questions regarding how one goes about securing official approval to deal in firearms was met by wide-eyed merriment and disbelief. I still don't know how this operates. Apparently people interested in dealing guns simply rent a stall in the souk and start in. It's about like dealing in pots and kettles, I guess.

Americans on a relatively high fixed income would find Oman to be a pleasant and interesting place to live. Lots of wide-open desert places in the interior exist, to shoot whatever gun took your fancy.

Genuine gun-design people would, no doubt, be welcomed with open arms by the sultan if they agreed to set up shop in Oman. They actually seek virtually any kind of international investment. Expats would have to law abiding, basically non-political and not inclined to maliciously impinge on Omani culture.

Lessons for gun owners from Oman? Include the fact that this is a place that is modernizing with amazing speed that does not feel the need to place any restrictions on gun ownership. In small countries, especially in the short run, a democracy is not always superior to a monarchy. Lawlessness is more cultural than causative, and does not necessarily follow universal ownership of firearms, even if many of these are military-class automatic weapons.

Chapter Thirty-Two
Papua New Guinea
World Rank: 50 • Firearm Freedom 23%

Overlooking Papua, New Guinea while undertaking this analysis would have been easy. Few Americans know of the country's existence, much less its location on an obscure island far out in the Pacific. Other than the country's strange gun situation and lessons we can draw from it, there is little to recommend or to identify this hot, jungly little out-of-the-way place.

No doubt gun-control fanatics will become infuriated by obvious lessons and conclusions we draw from this California-sized country. But this gets us way ahead of ourselves.

First we must understand a few things about PNG's culture, topography and location. Definitely in the case of PNG, reach for an up-to-date world atlas. Without an atlas it is impossible for most Americans to visualize or locate the country. Look at the eastern half of the Island of Guinea just north of Australia. PNG includes many of the outlying islands in that cluster including such "famous" names as Bougainville, Manus, New Britain, and New Ireland.

Don't believe official guidebooks claiming that all of PNG's super-rugged, mountainous, hot, muggy, jungly terrain has been explored, residents advise. What recent exploration has been undertaken has been superficial, mostly aerial reconnaissance, these folks say.

This is a cut off, remote island country with very few roads through its oppressive, wet, muddy, difficult, roadless interior. Most of it has never really been looked at by anybody you might encounter.

Super-abundant gold, copper and silver, harvestable tropical hardwoods and natural gas are there. Yet average *per capita* income is only slightly more than $2,200. This a direct result of their poorly designed and enforced property rights, contract law and rule of law. Without guarantees that they will not be ripped off by the government or powerful citizens, outsiders seldom invest. As a result the country cannot grow to be a modern economically viable member of the global village moving past its present third-world status.

Culturally, citizens of PNG seem simultaneously to be involved in low-grade blood feuds with villagers on the other side of the mountain, with the spirit world, and in a constant state of readiness lest they be robbed, burgled or ripped off. As a result, many, many citizens are armed. Best to assume they all are, expats claim.

Mostly residents own illegal guns. Perhaps half of these are homemade shotguns or crude single-shot pistols. More than anything else this reflects the poverty level at which average citizens live. Better is available, but they can't afford such.

Our informants in the case of PNG, are two missionaries who have lived and worked in PNG along with their wives and children. In both cases they were there a total of almost eight years. One man in particular was responsible for security for his entire mission organization. I personally have also frequently visited that part of the world, but not PNG specifically.

Sneak thievery and mysterious disappearance are a problem in that culture, especially in the larger cities, these missionaries claim.

Laws regarding legal ownership of private guns are rigorous and difficult in PNG. Most citizens, many of whom live in wild, remote areas, don't bother with niceties of complying with the central government's difficult, convoluted, uncertain licensing and registration procedures, especially when access to illegal guns is simple and easy.

One pool of illegal guns is said to be exhumed caches of hastily buried military supplies left behind at the conclusion of WW II. These are Australian, Japanese and some American in origin. Apparently large quantities of relatively good, clean, serviceable ammo is also available from this source.

High-grade marijuana is one of PNG's principal agricultural commodities. Most of this production is exported as a cash crop to Australia. More stringent and better law enforcement, and high labor costs, work against profitable local production in Australia. As a result, PNG farmers have access to excellent, highly profitable markets in Australia. On return, it is thought marijuana producers smuggle in about as many commercial pistols, rifles, shotguns and some submachine guns and assault rifles as the home market will bear.

Large quantities of ammunition of all kinds also are said to come in from Australia. Strange, since private, unencumbered, smugglable pools of guns and ammo are thought not to be available in Australia. Especially since the Aussies have severely clamped down on private gun ownership in the last few years. Could it be that not every Aussie turned in all of their guns and ammo?

Minimally 150 miles of open water separate PNG and Australia. It's sufficient distance, we might suppose, to make smuggling difficult and enforcement easy, but apparently not true in this instance. One has to wonder which is easier to control—illicit traffic in narcotics or guns?

American M-16 assault rifles are reasonably common in PNG. Perhaps Vietnam is the source of these. Our informants speculate that these are really left-behind Vietnam era guns, but no one is certain. There is some indication additional illegal weapons come across the mountains from Irian Jaya, lying to the west of PNG. Illegal sales of guns and ammunition on the part of ill-paid military and police are another source of illegal weapons.

Collectively, home manufacture, smuggling, military left-behinds, and surreptitious sales out of official stocks seem to provide enough guns for everybody who wants one. Okay—but guns last a long time while ammo is rapidly consumed. Is this a weak link?

Other than some few, crude field-expedient methods of loading shot shells, reloading is not a factor in PNG. Legal or illegal, there is no place to acquire shot, powder, bullets or primers. A couple of legally licensed and sanctioned gun stores sell loaded ammo in Port Moresby, the capital city, but no components. PNG gun laws don't even mention reloading.

Availability of ammo, even for assault rifles, does not seem to our informants to be a severely limiting factor. Apparently smuggling, left-behind military supplies, and theft from official stocks is sufficient to meet the country's ongoing black-market needs.

Legal ownership is theoretically possible. Well-connected, wealthy business people, expats, government officials and those operating the numerous security firms are most likely to receive official sanction. Mostly these gun-owner's permits are for pistols, although a few rifles and shotguns as well as a very small number of submachine guns are legally sanctioned. Because legal permits must pass through tortured levels of authorization, each requiring its own bribe, missionaries in PNG do not own firearms. Some have considered attempting the permit process and then returning from furlough in the States with a shotgun in their baggage, but so far this has never been done.

In theory, permit applications are available at the offices of one's local police. Given poor roads and the scattered thin, rural nature of the country, a local police station may not really be very close at hand.

Once completed and submitted, the police may arbitrarily hold the application. For them personally, little reason exists to take action on the application. Payment of a bribe may supply necessary motivation.

When the application does move, it is to the next level at provincial police headquarters. Without good reason not to, they may also "sit on" the application. Our informants are not certain, but believe gun-owner applications eventually end up in the National Office of

Attorney General for final authorization. There are three total levels of investigation and approval.

Legal gun owners in PNG are personally authorized, and their specific legal guns are all registered. With gun-owner's permit in hand, citizens proceed to one of two official gun shops in Port Moresby. Prices of legal guns and ammo at these shops is said to be breathtakingly high. It is so high many poorer citizens find it much cheaper to purchase on the black market. Occasionally, depending on the applicant's social and economic standing, some illegal guns are registered, thereby moving them over to legal status.

Tragically, licenses are good for only 12 months. In many cases legal owners immediately start the relicensing process on receiving their first license. From three to eight months are usually required to "cycle" a legal license.

Numbers of guns that can legally be owned by one person depend entirely on who you are and who you know. Some politicians are thought to have "dozens" of weapons. As a practical matter, more than three are probably impossible for average citizens, we are told.

Common citizens caught with illegal guns are likely to receive three and five years in the Grey Stone Hotel. Prosecutions are fairly common, but usually undertaken in conjunction with another more heinous crime. Rape, murder, theft, fighting or illegal-drug trafficking are examples. Falling out of political favor apparently counts too.

A few legal firing ranges are available in PNG. Users must have proper paper. Hunting, as we know it, including seasons and bag limits, is unheard of. Wild pigs, water buffalo and some game birds are the most commonly shot animals. Citizens seem to usually use snares or bow and arrow, rather than firearms, in pursuit of edible game.

The bottom line in Papua New Guinea is that, despite strict anti-gun-ownership laws and remote location featuring formidable borders, everyone who wants a gun has one—even including some extremely poor folks. The only restraint is the ability to pay.

While not on a level with Khyber Pass or Omani gunsmiths, PNG has craftsmen who turn out some fairly credible products. "You get what you pay for," our informants claim. Laws of economics apply, even in poor places such as PNG. On the other hand, a few reports circulate that some homemade guns, using field-expedient ammo, have come unhinged, creating casualties among users.

As mentioned, it is curious that a remote, difficult place such as PNG supports such a widespread, virtually universal gun culture and that guns are supplied despite huge obstacles. As a result we easily conclude that guns and ammunition will never disappear from any society that continues to want and need them. Supplies will continue to be provided by those who home manufacture, or from small machine shops. In our own country, for example, some machine-shop operators with computer-controlled lathes and milling machines have inventoried computer programs that allow completion of a finished gun almost automatically from simple steel bar stock.

When "official" forces are expanded sufficiently to effectively police the illegal gun business, those who really want guns and ammo will buy them from this expanded pool of gun-toting officials.

In many places, left-behind military arms make the situation even more impossible for antis. We might even conclude that removing all guns would be far more difficult than banishing illegal drugs. And we all know how successful that program is, in spite of billions spent on enforcement.

Chapter Thirty-Three
Panama
World Rank: 39 • Firearm Freedom 35%

One dramatic lesson alone makes an analysis of gun laws in this otherwise unremarkable (in so far as gun ownership is concerned) little country worthwhile.

At one time, a scant ten years back, Panama enjoyed a relatively open and unencumbered "gun situation." Estimates of the number of "semi legal" firearms remaining in the country from this era run into the hundreds of thousands or perhaps even millions. Like many Central American countries run by wary, fearful kleptocrats with poorly disguised fascist tendencies, Panamanian government officials have succeeded in adding layer upon layer of new and ever more onerous laws designed to harass legal private gun owners.

Nothing very remarkable about this! Yet, as mentioned going in, talking to Panamanian gun owners and gun-shop owner or managers provided a valuable, virtually dramatic insight, answering the question, "what happens when legal gun ownership is tough and crime is on the increase, in a place where citizens have traditionally enjoyed private firearms ownership?"

Information for this chapter came from a recent visit to Panama, interviews with four gun-shop owners there, talks with members of the Panamanian gun culture, and with expats now living in the U.S. There was also a small amount of published literature—but not very much.

Panamanian gun shop and shooting range

Even tiny Panama has gun stores, and this one features a full shooting range as well. It was in this gun shop that we finally learned how illicit guns move through private hands, and the extent to which organized crime syndicates have succeeded in making guns a viable profit center. The more restrictive a government is on gun rights, the greater the impetus and the more lucrative the opportunities for a black market to develop. Government bans on rights often do little more than serve as an unintended consequence— price supports for criminals and organized crime.

Visiting Panama is not much of a trick for Americans. It lies just three hours south of Miami. Everyone knows about Panama's strategic location on the hair-thin isthmus connecting North and South America—or do they?

Quick—when traveling through the world-famous canal from Pacific to Atlantic, which direction does the vessel track? Those who said "north" or, more accurately, "northeast," win the golden ring. Contrary to popular opinion, the canal does not run west to east.

Other strange anomalies abound. Residents in Panama City on the Pacific Coast watch the sun come up in the east over the Pacific Ocean! Those who thought they had to be in places out in the Pacific such as Japan, Okinawa or South Korea to experience this strange phenomenon forgot about the S-like twist in the isthmus.

Originally Panama was part of the north coast of Colombia. When president Theodore Roosevelt decided to complete a French trans-ocean ditch-building project back in 1903, Colombian government officials unwisely procrastinated on an offer of a treaty. Not a smart move! Teddy sent in the Atlantic squadron to support a tiny number of hand-picked revolutionaries. Newly ensconced leaders of the little South Carolina-sized county of Panama were much more agreeable to offers of a treaty.

Currently Panama's population is about three million, and expanding about 2.1% per year. Perhaps as a result, citizen *per capita* incomes appear to be steady, currently estimated at about $6,900.

As a fascinating aside, Panama is one of the growing number of countries that do not print or use their own currency. Everything is done in U.S. greenback dollars, except coins, which can be either special Panamanian or U.S. Size, shape and weight are identical.

Rule of law and enforcement of property rights is said to be better than in many other Central American countries, but still not on a standard that most North Americans would find comfortable. Panama is an interesting and exciting place, but not as a result of their gun laws or legal structure.

Three or four legal gun shops operate in Panama City, the capital. Colón, their other much more primitive, poorly developed big city, has none. Colón still has a free-trade zone. Other than those used by numerous security people inside the zone, no guns are allowed.

Currently Panamanians are paranoid about crime, both petty and major. As a result, private security is one of Panama's major growth industries. Security people, police and army personnel saturate their urban areas. Unlike the Philippines where a cop or two stands on every corner with little more than an empty holster, Panamanian police all carry.

Private Panamanian citizens purchasing their first legal gun from an established gun shop must fill out a form there. When completed, this goes with several supporting documents to local police. If approved, the application goes to the Panamanian FBI—called the PTJ. Private citizens can legally sell to each other, but both must be licensed. In this case, unlicensed buyers must secure a license before proceeding. For a fee, gun shops will assist new owners with their applications for a gun-owner's permit. Those who don't want to use a gun-shop's services can—at least in theory—go directly to their local police.

Several other documents must support the gun owner's registration and permit application. Gun shops have recognized psychoanalysts, to which they refer applicants for a necessary psychological evaluation. Cost for the shrink's report is about $20.

Gun purchasers must also verify and certify their current and past employment and monthly income, and provide some fairly detailed statements of financial condition. This is supposedly so no unemployed ne'er-do-well secures a legal firearm.

All of this, including the legal form requesting a gun-owner's permit, the psychological evaluation, employment record and financial data, goes to the local cop shop. They also want an $11-per-year fee, up front. Gun-owner's permits last up to five years. Most gun owners do either three years ($33) or five years ($55).

If you believe what is written in the law, anyone over 18 can secure a gun-owner's permit. In Panama, as a practical matter, no one under 23 years of age need apply. Applications of under-23 persons either won't be approved—or will take until they are 23 to be approved.

On receiving the packet of material, local police do a background investigation spanning back as much as 20 years for those sufficiently ancient to warrant such inquiry. All is okay? From the local cops it's off to the PTJ for another check on the basis of their more extensive records. Assuming everything still looks okay, they approve the application, sending it back to the local police. Local authorities then do yet another check of varying intensity. Gun owners complain bitterly that this is the third, mostly repetitive check. Got to keep all those thousands of police bureaucrats gainfully employed!

If all goes smoothly, expect to hear about your gun purchase in 60 to 90 days. Panama does have *mordito* (a Mexican word for "the bite"— or petty bribe.) Most gun owners and general citizens try to avoid it.

Panamanians are legally entitled to purchase and own virtually any kind or type of handgun including 9mm and .45 ACP. Theoretically they can even legally own semi-auto submachine guns such as look-alike UZIs or MAC-10s. In practice these pistols are not really available for new purchase, but more on this later.

They can also own just about any kind, type or size of shotgun including pumps and semi-autos. Any gauge or size is allowed, but because it's tough finding ammo they usually go for 12-guage models.

Sporting rifles of any non-military caliber are theoretically permitted. No semi-auto assault rifles or ones in .223 or 7.62 NATO are ever sanctioned. Older bolt-action 30-06 rifles are okay. No full-auto, submachine guns or machine guns under any circumstances, even for bank guards or security people in hard-core areas. Security people are usually limited to .38 special revolvers with 4-inch barrels and/or 12-gauge shotguns. Some of these shotguns are sawed-offs or have shorty pistol-grip stocks.

Pistol permits also entitle owners to carry concealed. Supposedly there is a lot of concealed carry in Panama among general citizens. That's the consensus of some tour and travel people there.

Scope sights are no problem, except virtually no one sells them. Hunting in Panama is not entirely forbidden, but it is socially unacceptable and, at present, infrequently undertaken.

Gun shops do not sell silencers. Yet their deployment in Panama is said to be common. Reportedly most silencers are homemade in some of the many high quality machine shops there. Although Panamanian law is silent on silencers, local gun owners say they would not want to be caught carrying both a pistol or rifle and a silencer.

But back to our friendly local gun store, and approval to be a gun owner. Previously licensed purchasers of additional guns list down exactly which type and model gun they wish to purchase. Gun-owner certificates are actually composed of two parts. First, citizens are authorized to possess firearms. Second, the exact firearms are recorded to that individual on the authorization. Then, when final approval is finally secured, in a very Panamanian twist, the police withdraw that specific make, model and serial number weapon from the gun-shop's inventory held at the police station. They list that gun and its serial number down on the license, and do a ballistic test on that specific gun to be held in perpetuity by the cops. Finally the gun is sent over to the gun shop for actual delivery to the weary customer.

Gun shops are legally allowed to keep only one example of each gun in the store's inventory. These single examples are a kind of showroom sample customers can actually fondle.

All legal importation of firearms is done by gun shops. But their inventory remains at the cops' storage area. Authorization to import both guns and ammo comes infrequently. Legal gun and ammo sellers must take immediate advantage of any importation window offered. Inventory costs are thereby inflated, adding greatly to the expense of doing business in Panama.

Panamanian gun-store owners comment with great bitterness regarding the fact that numbers of new guns and ammo allowed for legal importation and sales are often severely restricted, thus effectively reducing numbers they can offer customers. This import restriction causes prices of ammo in particular to cycle wildly.

Pistols and ammo are imported from the U.S., Brazil and Israel. Rifles and shotguns may come from the U.S., China, or even the Philippines. I spotted one ARMSCOR 12-gauge single barrel on one gun-shop rack. A compact Bersa .22 LR handgun was on offer for $450 plus their 5% tax. Another Bersa .380 pistol was priced at $695 plus tax. A plain Marlin .22 mag bolt rifle with an extra mag was $325 plus tax. Extra mags for the Bersa pistols were priced at an astounding $78 each!

Up to a total of nine different guns can be registered on a single gun-owner's permit. More are apparently and theoretically allowed, but this takes another separate collector's authorization. Other than some well-positioned politicians who have those authorizations, Panamanian gun owners couldn't tell me how or under what circumstances such permits would be issued. Apparently there is great pressure to dewat guns past the magical number of nine. For practical purposes, nine guns is the limit for one person.

In theory, women in Panama are allowed to own legal firearms. Infrequent but possible, I was told. In practice, many applications for gun permits from women are summarily denied.

Two legal ranges are available to firearms permit holders in Panama. Lots of informal shooting takes place in the remote hills and valleys.

As mentioned, prices of ammo spike up and down dramatically relative to amounts authorities sanction for import. A 25-round box of Winchester 12-gauge shot shells was available for $14. Fifty rounds of 9mm were available for $19. Single boxes of .22 LRs cost $4.20.

All ammo purchased is recorded to the gun-owner's permit on a special form held at the gun shop. No limit on quantity except price and general availability. But buy too much (more than a couple of boxes per month) and the police come around asking "for what purpose?" Those without a good answer may have their ammo confiscated. Records of all ammo purchases are turned over to the local police on 30-day intervals.

Panamanian law is silent on reloading. One gun-store proprietor claimed legal purchase of components was possible in Panama, but not at his store. Others said only range owners, police and the military could secure reloading components. No powder, shot, bullets or primers were seen in stores. Legal importation is apparently tightly controlled, and reloading is seldom if ever undertaken in Panama.

Becoming a gun dealer is very difficult. Essentially there are but four legal shops in the entire country. Because of import restrictions that tie up the shops' money for lengthy periods, profits were said to be slim. If they were prosperous, the four shops we visited hid it well.

The gun shops in Panama City employ a full-time, on-site gunsmith. They require a separate license with additional vetting and backgrounding, I was told. Apparently a great number of illegal gunsmiths operate in Panama, some of whom are capable of turning out complete functional guns.

Legal importation of gun parts and repairs is tightly controlled. As a result, a fairly large local sub-manufacturing gun-parts industry has grown in Panama.

Although legally owning a gun in Panama is tough, there are an absolutely huge number of illegal guns. Illegals are said to sell for about half of legal ones. Abundant ammo is also said to be readily available on the black market.

Depending on who is talking, illegal guns flood in from (1) Colombia, (2) Costa Rica, (3) Nicaragua, (4) all of the above. Illegal buyers can easily secure anything from AK-47s and M-16s on up to Browning ground mount .30 cal. machine guns. Russian pistols and HK submachine guns are also available for enough cash, I was told.

Private security guards are reportedly a large source of illegal guns. Gun owners and dealers universally claimed that lax oversight of the huge numbers of guards who illegally sold their sidearms was a major source of weapons in Panama. Either the guards simply report their guns stolen, or they rent them to criminals, legal gun owners claimed.

Now for the really dramatic revelation! Probably advice good 'round the world for those who absolutely must have a firearm. Where to best find these many illegal guns and whom to talk to for the best prices? "Go see any commercial fisherman who is operating his own small boat in pursuit of reef fish, shrimp or large game fish," I was told. "These men take their boats all over the place, easily visit other countries as well as fellow fishermen from other countries." As a result they always can supply good quality, illegal guns and ammo at good prices. If they don't have it, and the price is right, they can get it.

Apparently poor individual Panamanian fishermen find this trade profitable and easy. So much so, they are heavily involved with it. Probably true anyplace in the world where fishermen ply their trade.

At one time about ten years ago a Brazilian gun manufacturer set up shop in Panama. They found the economic and legal climates so hostile they quickly pulled out. Panamanian gun owners conclude that their authorities do not want this type of research and development.

Tourists cannot legally bring firearms into Panama. Expat business people willing to prove they aren't pissants by going through the legal processes, and who have a legitimate need, can purchase legal guns.

Like we said, Panama is no gun buffs' paradise unless you are willing to own illicit firearms, available in tremendous profusion. If that's okay, go see the local fisherman. This is the dramatic lesson of Panama! One that those with whom we talked were amazed I did not know.

Chapter Thirty-Four
American GIs
Not Rated

Do not act on any of the information in this chapter without making further inquiry. This is generally true for all of the contents in this volume as even a casual reader can easily see, but even more so for GIs taking guns overseas or especially for those who may be tempted to bring home a war trophy. American military rules and regulations can be arbitrary and in flux, and customs, culture and rules overseas can be—foreign.

Used to be, at a time when U.S. gun laws were reckoned by the score rather than by thousands in fat volumes, that military personnel on official duty could be characterized as "exempt." Ownership, carrying and perhaps even deployment with non-issued arms were understood as an official privilege and perhaps duty of the office.

The author, for example, sold hundreds if not thousands of personal sidearms, knives and other related items to GIs headed to Vietnam. Stretching back into history, we can easily recall specific instances of returning GIs legally toting along a sparkling new chest enclosing a complete Lewis gun plus accoutrements, a German 8mm Maxim machine gun, numerous different submachine guns, including German MP-40s, WW II assault rifles and even some live hand grenades in a few isolated instances.

Vietnam changed all that. Vietnam changed a great many things in our society, but one of the most obvious was the military's view of private gun ownership. For gun lovers, collectors, historians and shooters, the changes were especially dramatic.

Starting with Grenada, it became a serious violation for any GI— officer or enlisted—to bring any kind of firearm-type war trophy home! Rigid, inflexible warnings enforced with similarly rigid, inflexible inspections effectively scared military personnel from something that had always been seen as the right of victorious soldiers triumphantly returning to a free society. As recently as WW II, entire military units collected war trophies together for fair and even distribution to returning GIs. Carrying back enemy weapons was encouraged.

Reportedly, some softening of this position is currently occurring, and apparently some small differences exist between the various services, but GIs of any branch on deployment or active overseas duty had best inquire of their executive officer before attempting to bring any firearms home. This includes firearms shipped as part of household goods or as personal items carried along on planes or ships. Penalties, especially for those looking to the military as a career, are severe.

Taking personal guns overseas is similarly restricted. One officer retired from lifetime duty, which included command of several large bases in South Korea, described current private firearms ownership in South Korea as being a kind of "visitation rights" situation. All private weapons, including large knives, air rifles and guns of any kind had to be registered and stored in the base armory. Owners could occasionally come to the armory to look at their guns, but removing them for any purpose at all was completely impossible, including commercial hunting-type shotguns as well as pistols and rifles.

A Coast Guardsman stationed in Puerto Rico was similarly informed. Too many rules and regulations, he reckoned. Eventually he left his considerable personal gun, ammo and accessory stash safely stored back in his resident state.

As a result, few military personnel currently elect to go through the hassle of taking personal firearms with them to overseas duty stations, even if they are passionate hunters, historians or gun collectors. However, several situations may come into play that modify this.

Some pilots still carry along private sidearms, which are usually kept locked away in an official armory. At times of an actual mission, their pistols may be checked out and taken along. You are back from that specific mission? Immediately take your sidearm back to the MP's storage area. Private holdings in one's barracks are never permitted, especially for naval pilots serving on vessels.

There are other factors. America is an exceedingly rich country. To a great extent, our military personnel are currently seen as being so sufficiently well equipped that no extra "non-standard" weapons or equipment are needed or tolerated. All of those requiring a pistol are officially issued one. Same for a shotgun, back-up ankle guns, assault rifles and even a boot knife.

GIs on their way to Bosnia, for instance, had a complete list of everything they were both supposed to take and were allowed to take, with no deviation allowed. No private knives over three inches, much less a .22-caliber back-up pistol as was often true during Viet Nam. Rigid inspection procedures ensured complete compliance.

Although most GIs currently do not take along their personal guns when being transferred overseas, some elect to attempt to purchase private civilian-type guns when they get to their foreign duty stations. The general rule is that all private firearms ownership while at a U.S. base in a foreign country must mirror and comply with gun laws in that host country.

As a result, some GIs in Germany, for instance, join gun or hunting clubs. By so doing, they secure necessary in-country gun ownership and hunting permits. Often, official military hunting and shooting clubs affiliate with local indigenous clubs to facilitate necessary permits allowing purchase of guns and ammo. Then purchase of legally permitted guns and ammo are made, either out on the economy or in some cases from the PX.

Overseas PX purchases are becoming increasingly difficult according to many GIs. Mostly the guns on offer are only available in places in the U.S. where they can be legally purchased and owned.

Many GIs, either officers or rank and file, are part of the gun culture. No surprise there. Guns are tools for these folks. Perhaps overly optimistically they seem to hope—and in some cases assume—that current stringent rules and regulations regarding overseas ownership, transport and trophy return will start to be relaxed.

Significantly, many of these same people do not really know exact rules and regulations or their current application where they are stationed—not so different from the general population. As with all things guns, lots of rumor and reluctance to talk or ask is currently out there. This works to the advantage of those in power, because if you don't know your rights it's pretty tough to demand them. And being under constant threat of penalty for not knowing the barrage of obscure rules your are subject to does nothing to enhance your freedom, and increases the control of those in control.

In addition, this often leads to uneven application and enforcement, which leads us back again to our introductory admonition. Make extensive inquiries if you are a GI contemplating any sort of private gun situation either to take away or bring home.

Chapter Thirty-Five
Egypt
World Rank: 38 • Firearm Freedom 36%

"Owning a gun in Egypt is possible, but first you must do many things!"

With that brief introduction we launched into lengthy discussions regarding private ownership of firearms in Egypt. A country torn by poverty, a heavy-handed government, political assassinations, massacres, plots and counterplots, and tough-to-understand Muslim fundamentalist foment. It is also a place with a strong gun culture including great numbers of gun-friendly citizens.

Five of us, including a cop/security officer whose rank I never understood, two of his deputies and a guide/translator also of obscure status sat around a restaurant table in the western desert oasis city of Farafra. Milky, sickly-sweet tea and fruit juice were the drinks of choice as we discussed guns and gun laws in Egypt.

Although officially introduced to us as a translator/guide, the English speaker's background and purpose were at best "unclear." We were, after all, in forbidden territory. Joining an armed military convoy was necessary for road travel into the region in which we currently found ourselves.

Levels of English proficiency demonstrated by the Egyptian translator suggested diplomatic training as did his frequent valiant attempts to avoid negative comments about persons or classes of persons. In many cases the man referred my often pointed, detailed questions regarding Egyptian law to the police captain and his two minions. Their sidebars in Arabic were incomprehensible to me, but I was always provided with some sort of innocuous, yet superficially detailed answer.

Our translator claimed he was a private legal gun owner who had gone through all of the procedure and paperwork he now described. The cops all carried concealed, but owned no personal weapons. Other than a few words of greetings, the cops spoke no English.

Egypt is about one and a half times the size of the state of Texas. It occupies the very top and far eastern corner of North Africa. The southern Mediterranean Sea laps its northern shores. Egypt is the place of the Suez Canal and pyramids. Israel borders to the northeast.

Armed Egyptian guard at the pyramids

Private citizens even in fascist, overly controlling Egypt can own some firearms legally. Paperwork, along with fierce restrictions, are tremendously eased by payment of bribes known as *baksheèsh*, which greases the skids for all kinds of economic activity in the "cradle of civilization." Here, a vistor chats with a machine-gun armed security officer, at a tourist site for the world-famous pyramids.

Although large in size, little of Egypt is usable or rich in any kind of resource. Intense farming takes place in the very narrow Nile River valley. Other vast tracts in Egypt contain some of the most inhospitable, uninhabitable desert on our globe. Not even a single blade of grass per square mile here.

After 30 years of bitter and costly warfare, Egypt and Israel signed a formal peace treaty on March 26, 1979. By so doing, the two cultures broke a cycle of bloodshed that served little purpose other than pauperizing both nations.

Egypt's Arab neighbors reacted with blind fury. Results of this breach are still evident in Egypt today. Armed soldiers stand 24-hour watches in many sections of Cairo. Road travel—private and commercial—into many sectors of Egypt is controlled by the military. It isn't because of fear of Israel that Egyptians convoy their trucks and cars. It's because of militant Islamic extremists. A machine-gun-carrying truck leads, with one in the middle and yet another machine gun in the rear. As many as an estimated 500 cars and trucks comprise a single military convoy.

Numerous military check points along all Egyptian roads are reminiscent of pre-Castro Cuba and of Yugoslavia before the big blow.

Average Egyptians make about $350 per month, or perhaps $4,200 per year. Unemployment is a high 13 percent. Ag production, including cotton, wheat, rice and numerous and varied vegetables account for the largest segment of the economy. Tourism is a very close second. A dollar or two at a time for entrance fees, collected from tens of thousands of tourists at hundreds of temple, museum and burial sites brings in many billions annually. They know how to do it. Egypt has been a major tourist destination for hundreds of years.

Exactly how much of Egypt's GNP is currently tourist related is obscured by the fact that past figures do not apply. The 9/11 terrorist incident in the U.S. dramatically reduced the influx of dollar-bearing tourists to Egypt. In addition, Islamic extremists have attacked and massacred foreign tourists in Egypt in at attempt to punish Egypt's government—explaining in part the many armed guards, metal detectors at every public building, and perhaps their sometimes-draconian gun laws.

Europeans on high fixed incomes could enjoy living in Egypt. Prices are reasonable, Egyptians have a great work ethic, they are very honest and there are some great seaside recreational areas and properties rivaling those in Mexico's Baja.

Moneyed Europeans willing to work through a third party could probably own just about any guns they wish. Experimental and design work might be possible. But before packing for Egypt, read on. Their culture is not our culture.

Basically, Egyptians have a common, two-part gun-ownership licensing certificating process similar to many other parts of the world.

First, one must qualify as a potential firearms owner by securing a gun-owner's permit/certificate from the local gun-compliance officer at a nearby police station. With permit in hand, Egyptians are free to attempt to secure specific permission for a specific gun. Permission to purchase is only extended on the basis of that person having a good reason to own. After purchase, the gun is registered to the new owner's name on their gun-owner's permit.

All of this would be burdensome, yet reasonably simple and straightforward if Egypt were a reasonable, simple, straightforward country. In terms of understanding Egypt, western culture is not a good place to start. Egypt, for us, is difficult. Little understanding through our cultural lens is possible.

First and foremost, Egypt is one of the most thoroughly and completely fascist countries left on Earth. Some may argue that point relative to Burma or North Korea. Those are actually socialist continues. Fascism is just as repressive but something different.

Fascist Egypt is characterized by the fact that most things and property are privately owned. Use and administration of that property is extremely tightly controlled by a pervasive, intrusive, inefficient system of rules, regulations and an extensive system of licenses and permits. Even more so than England or Germany, Egyptians require a permit to do or own absolutely anything. There might be exceptions for shining shoes, running errands, carrying luggage, cleaning windows, or owning a bicycle, but I doubt it.

Virtually every aspect of life in Egypt is heavily controlled by a web of permits and rules. Egyptian horse cart and bicycle owners are required to secure licenses. Licenses are required to fix shoes, butcher animals, interpret for tourists, sell coffee, serve food at restaurants and on and on and on. Although gun ownership is fairly tightly controlled, gun stores themselves are owned by private citizens.

In other countries with tight gun controls, the police or military run the gun shops. They also do in Egypt but indirectly by means of tightly prescribing exactly how the private stores should be operated. In all areas of commerce and general life, government oversight staffs are intrusive, abusive, numerous, troublesome and meddlesome.

Egypt also has a large standing army and a tightly controlled press, all additional indicators of a classic, fascist state as first envisioned by Mussolini.

Incredibly, 80 percent of the work force is employed at least part time by the government. "Work in the morning for the government and in the afternoon for yourself," we frequently heard. These government workers create no goods or services for the half day they work issuing permits. They simply interpret and enforce complex, detailed, and frequently obsolete and obscure regulations. They issue permits and, at times, share enforcement duties.

Only by constantly paying petty bribes, called baksheesh, can Egyptians ever hope to cut through their bureaucratic red tape and actually get anything done. This baksheesh/bribery system has been in place so long in Egypt it has become institutionalized. Egyptians cannot perceive life without it.

As a result, everything in Egypt relative to gun ownership is technically illegal, but nothing is impossible. Readers should keep this important fact of life in view when understanding Egyptian systems of gun ownership, qualification and licensing.

Start a quasi-legal quest for gun ownership by applying for a gun-owner's certificate at the local police station. Cost is about $175, almost one month's salary for an average Egyptian. Authorities quickly admit that this price is kept intentionally high to limit numbers of gun-owners' certificates actually issued, or even applied for. "We don't want everyone owning a gun," I was told.

Allow three to five weeks unless one has a criminal record, has a problem with a neighbor or the police captain just doesn't like you. Apparently a fairly thorough investigation is made, unless there is sufficient baksheesh for immediate issue. One exception may be those affiliated with prohibited religious/political organizations who supposedly cannot own guns under any circumstances. No one will venture a guess as to how much baksheesh these guys would have to come up with. Even though these groups are hated and feared, there is probably still a price they could pay to legally own a gun or guns.

Non-citizens of Egypt are generally not allowed gun-owner certificates. Our informants believe that this prohibition could be overcome by having a club or one's attorney apply for the certificate and then hold the gun or guns themselves.

Other than religious crazies, all restrictions are lifted in the case of payment of sufficient baksheesh. "How much baksheesh?" "Enough to get the job done," I was told.

Gun-owners' certificates in hand, Egyptians are free to purchase one rifle, pistol or shotgun. All these guns "reportedly" must be made in Egypt. Several other terms and conditions impinge on this one-gun limit other than payment of baksheesh.

Members of trap, skeet or pistol shooting clubs found in most larger cities can sometimes own far more than just one gun. Officials may require that these additional guns be stored at the club but sometimes they are kept at home. Club membership is from $3,500 to $5,000 per year, including use of the pool and golf course. Filthy-rich Egyptians are there but, again, these fees certainly discourage average citizens.

Ownership of any specific gun is always contingent upon having a good reason for owning that gun. Baksheesh may be a good reason.

Two teenagers were hunting pigeons and doves with an air rifle. Is a permit required for that air rifle? "Yes," they said, "and they must have a good reason for ownership. Their reason was to supply fresh meat for the market." Given the modest scope of the enterprise, I didn't think baksheesh was much of an issue, but even in this case we can't be sure if the kids had to cough up some baksheesh for an air rifle permit.

A gun-owner enthusiast told me military type, semi-auto rifles such as AK-47s or M-16s were completely forbidden. Yet another fellow said there were good, functional M-16s on offer at the big, tightly controlled gun store in Cairo. He owned one, he said. Perhaps his convincing need was application of enough baksheesh. Or perhaps he was a member of the military or perhaps this was all pure bravado to impress an American gun owner. We just didn't know.

Personal security in remote areas or regular transport of large amounts of cash, jewelry or gold often qualifies as a valid need when applying for permission to purchase a pistol. But not when there is a police or military check point already close at hand. What qualifies as "close at hand?" Perhaps baksheesh.

Anybody with a gun-owner's certificate can legally own a single-barrel shotgun. Apparently (and surprisingly) no baksheesh required.

Single-barrel, single-shot shotguns were not out on display in the hinterlands. I did see a number of pump-action 12-gauge shotguns that looked much like Mossberg 500s. These might have been made in Egypt, perhaps of pirated designs. Egypt does have a fairly extensive, sophisticated gun and ammunition manufacturing industry located in the city of Alexandria.

These shotguns were in the hands of what could have been local militia, temporarily stationed at various roadblocks and checkpoints along our route. We whisked by in our convoyed autos far too rapidly to be sure about exact make, model or manufacturer.

Perhaps Egyptian gun makers are producing a knockoff of a Mossberg 500, but what about M-16s reportedly on offer in Cairo? "Janes," the world authority on military weapons, does not list Egypt as an authorized user or maker of M-16s.

We do know that absolutely no hand loading is allowed on the part of any civilian in Egypt. As evidence, we are told that industries as mundane as fireworks manufacture are, even by Egyptian standards, extremely tightly regulated and licensed. No Egyptian gun owner or official with whom I talked had even thought of hand loading. Egyptian ammo is manufactured to high standards of the highest possible quality, obviating any need to hand load, I was informed.

Permission to purchase and own a pistol carries with it the automatic presumption that it will be carried concealed.

Several privately owned pistol, rifle and shotgun ranges are available near Egypt's larger cities. Ammunition can sometimes be purchased at these ranges for use at that range. Users must present their gun-owners' certificates to qualify for purchase of any ammo. Only ammo used in guns listed on the certificate can legally be purchased.

Ammunition can also be purchased at gun clubs and, of course, officially sanctioned gun shops. Quantities of ammo that can be legally purchased without baksheesh are tightly controlled. Only exception is ammo fired at gun ranges or clubs. This ammo is closely inventoried.

Neither the police nor our gun-owning interpreter were entirely clear about how much ammo could be purchased at the gun store and carried away home. They figured perhaps only 25 rounds per gun per year or some such similar figure.

Within reasonable limits (whatever that means without baksheesh), there is no limit to shotgun ammo that can be purchased. Prices for ammo are intentionally kept very high in an attempt to limit usage among less affluent Egyptians.

Hunters frequently and more easily meet the "reason to own" requirement, especially for pump shotguns and bolt-action rifles. Those going to the trouble and expense of securing a national hunting license are sometimes allowed more than one gun. Allowed hunting guns could include a shotgun, high-power rifle and a .22 rimfire rifle.

Doves, pigeons and some partridge-like birds are hunted. Big game comprises a few, mostly very scarce varieties of antelope. Small game might include some fox and cat-like critters. Varieties of these latter critters seem to blend into one another.

Absolutely everyone I talked with about guns in Egypt said incidence of illegal gun ownership was very, very high. "Anyone who wants an illegal gun can have one, but they are taking a horrible risk," I was told. Egyptian jails are exceedingly grim. Even baksheesh by the camel-load won't bail you out of a serious, illegal gun charge, they said.

All types of illegal weapons, up to and including heavy machine guns and mortars, are easily available, they claim. All that was needed was sufficient cash. Even this requirement was substantially waived in the case of local homemade guns and mortars.

How much cash for a genuine war trophy? Perhaps $1500 for a full-auto AK, $4500 for a fifty-caliber machine gun, and so on. Trench mortars and light machine guns are also commonly available. We don't know at what price.

At the time of my visit, local papers were making a big stink about an Egyptian millionaire who had been found in personal possession of two illegal, unregistered machine guns.

Origin of illegal guns in Egypt seems to be Yemen, fishermen (who get them God-only-knows-where) and from the U.S. and Russian governments. These latter weapons come via Afghanistan, I was told. The cops and the interpreter were equally nebulous on this one. Perhaps an urban myth, but one they truly believed. "Both the U.S. and Russians were smuggling guns into Egypt in an attempt to destabilize the government," they said.

All WW II left-behinds have been cleaned up. Incredible as it seems, given the millions of rifles, pistols and machine guns left behind, all have disappeared someplace.

Reportedly a black market in Egyptian AK-47s as carried by thousands of very poorly paid Egyptian GI conscripts also exists. Pay enough baksheesh and the soldier will sell his weapon. Large quantities of surplus military ammo are also available at relatively low prices from these starving Egyptian GIs. Origin is a mystery, perhaps Afghanistan. I was told this surplus ammo is of either Russian or American manufacture, "so it has to come from Afghanistan," they said.

Taken all together including all of their cultural anomalies, private firearms ownership in Egypt is simultaneously tightly controlled and fairly open. It is also fairly widespread. Those with sufficient funds own whatever guns they wish. Accumulating these funds in a third-world country such as Egypt is the trick.

As we go to press, Egypt is in the throes of a grassroots citizen revolt against the fascist nature of the nation and its 30-year dictator. This has led neighboring Arab nations to consider similar uprisings, and portends changes to the contents of this book, let alone all those nations and others. All of this points to the fact that *The Worldwide Gun Owner's Guide* represents a snapshot in time, a milepost in history, and a benchmark from which to gauge the march of time as an uncertain future becomes the increasingly distant past.

Chapter Thirty-Six
Crete
World Rank: 3 • Firearm Freedom 95%

Private firearms ownership in Crete, the autonomous Mediterranean island-province of Greece, is said to be the highest in the world. It's certainly true if we take their self-evaluations as evidence. Virtually everyone owns guns, they say. If nothing else, their account has a ring of authenticity, even if it isn't entirely true.

Estimates indicate 75 to 95% of families keep guns at homes. Some gun buffs reportedly have huge arsenals of guns and ammo, up to heavy machine guns, mortars and 20mm cannons. Estimates at the higher end are made by credible government officials. Other lower estimates are those regular citizens have come to hold and accept.

Like summarizing true and correct gun-ownership patterns in the U.S., no one really knows for sure. Citizens in both places tend not to give honest answers to sensitive questions such as those about personal possession of guns, many of which may be illegal. Interviews with Cretans make it immediately clear that they are no different, in this regard, than Americans. There are, however, abundant indications that estimates of extremely high gun-ownership levels are basically correct.

Crete is a semi-autonomous island province of Greece, lying south of Greece and Turkey out about 175 miles in the Mediterranean Sea. Greek law, including its stringent personal firearms rules and regulations, supposedly governs Crete. But, as we shall see, any Greek political writ, if run on Crete, is run with a decidedly Cretan flavor.

Large enough to not seem like an island, Crete is 160 miles long, east to west, and from 11 to 40 miles wide, north to south. Crete is famous among sun-loving European vacationers as a place of nice beaches, gorgeous women, pleasant climate and excellent, inexpensive wine and food. Their currency is the Euro.

Per capita income of Greek citizens living on the mainland is about $21,300. In part because Crete was not absorbed in Greece' destructive civil war immediately following WW II and because of its rich agricultural heritage and now extensive profitable tourist trade, individual annual personal incomes there are thought to run considerably higher. Perhaps $26,000 each, per year, for the 240,000 Cretan citizens. Tourism and agriculture are the two principal economic engines of their booming little economy. Smuggling comes in a perhaps not-too-distant third.

Child's drawing of WWII resistance

This grade-school drawing so clearly demonstrates how
children of Crete viewed the Nazi attack on their homeland.
Expecting the citizens to quietly roll over, similar to the
responses of people in much of the rest of Europe, Germans
launched the largest air assault of WWII—and the first
extensive use of paratroops in warfare. But using private
arms to capture more arms, citizens of Crete put up horrific
resistance which continued long after the last English and
Greek soldiers had been evacuated, captured or killed.
Imagine if the determined spirit displayed by this school
child's drawing ran rampant throughout the world, and the
effect that would have on the ambitions of tyrants. In too
many lands today, such a drawing might instead earn
condemnation, counseling, and government-drug-induced
stupor to quell such politically incorrect thoughts of
individual responsibility and resistance to oppression.

Cretans speak an easily recognized dialect of Greek. Modern Cretans speak Greek, English and German. Perhaps 80 percent of the population converses nicely in the latter two, making information gathering a bit easier than in most foreign countries.

Very significantly the question, "Which are you first—a Greek or a Cretan?" gives them reason to pause a moment before answering. Some can't or won't give a direct answer to that question. Cretans tend to be fiercely nationalistic as well as very, very independent. Citizens of Crete tend to depreciate American freedoms, claiming ours are only a shadow of their own.

Evidence of this independence can be seen throughout the island via graffiti on walls and monuments denouncing NATO, the U.S. and the European Community. Other somewhat petty acts of defiance abound. Citizens refuse to wear seat belts because their use was arbitrarily mandated from afar by those "who don't know what is going on here!" Speed limits are universally ignored. European community agricultural mandates issued from Brussels are a complete joke in the eyes of Cretan farmers. Drug sales rules involving pharmaceuticals are completely ignored. Buy what you want without a prescription across the counter at any drugstore on the island. And finally, smuggling for their active black market is said to be as common as olive groves on Crete. Olive groves occupy at least one half of all arable land.

Cretan philosophy, mentality and worldview—including their concept of private gun ownership—have been mightily influenced by their history. This history includes the fact that, on a terrifyingly regular schedule, their island has been overrun by world power, often for no really good reason.

As recently as May 20, 1941, Hitler's German army invaded Crete. Similar to the other portions of Europe populated by poorly armed, less determined and less nationalistic citizens whom the Germans had already conquered, they expected Crete to quickly roll over. To be a "piece of kuchen" for the mighty German paratroopers.

Instead, incredibly fierce fighting involving heavily armed local partisans, surviving elements of the Greek army, British, Australian and New Zealand relief forces erupted. Hostile independent Cretan partisans took huge exception to invasion of their homeland. Led and aided by warrior priests from the Greek Orthodox Church, they mustered in incredible numbers, extracting a horrible toll on the hapless, unsuspecting invaders.

Hitler expected both to draw the British Mediterranean fleet into Crete where his superior air force could destroy it, and to be able to dominate the Mediterranean Sea from the island. Neither expectation materialized. Winston Churchill, with full knowledge of the losses the

British Mediterranean fleet was suffering, withdrew the vessels as soon as they were able to take some of the soldiers off the island, stranding remaining armies but saving the fleet.

Ten days later, the Germans were victorious—if one does not count the loss of their elite paratrooper force, destruction of their air transport and delays relative to the invasion of Russia. As a result of Crete, the Germans were not able to invade England and they were five weeks late off the mark into Russia. Rather than taking Russia during nice weather, the German army found themselves forced to fight on during one of Europe's most severe winters on record.

Citizens of Crete did not consider the withdrawal of Greek and English forces as an indication that their war was over. Deploying deadly, effective guerilla tactics from their heavy mountainous interior camps, they fought on. By the time the Germans left in mid-1945, they had suffered as many or more casualties as during the initial invasion. An estimated 5,500 Germans were lost in the May 20th invasion and about 15,000 Allied soldiers were killed, wounded or captured. Only about 14,000 soldiers were transported before the fleet had to be withdrawn. Until 1945, some 8,575 Cretans (mostly partisans) lost their lives to German occupiers. Although that's not many in terms of total lives lost during WW II, Crete's relatively tiny interrelated population ensured that these losses affected everyone on the island and would be remembered in historic infamy.

Before the Germans it was the Turks. They occupied Crete from 1669 to 1898. After they left, Crete enjoyed its only period of independence. It was brief—from 1898 until 1913 when Greek-speaking Crete mostly voluntarily became part of Greece.

Cretan history explaining their almost fanatical eagerness to resist occupation and to remain free does not only go back to the Turks and 1669. As if it were yesterday, they recall the Venetian occupation from 1204 to 1669. Before that it was nationalistic Byzantine Greeks infused with religious fervor. They took the island back from the Arabs who had it from 824 to 961.

Before that there were Greek occupiers again, and before them the Romans. Every citizen of Crete has these events and dates firmly fixed in mind. They don't like being occupied and claim they would react violently to any government that tried to take away personal firearms with which they intend to resist any future occupiers. This neatly explains why the Greek government won't touch the issue of illegal guns on Crete with a ten-foot olive branch.

Information for this chapter came from a two-week personal visit to Crete. During that time I interviewed a citizen computer geek who at one time lived in California's Silicon Valley, a RentRooms/Taverna owner who spent 17 years in Toronto, Canada amassing a fortune so he could return to his beloved island, set up a business, and marry. Other information came from three talkative waiters, three elderly British survivors of the Battle of Crete living on the island, and an irrationally anti-American furrier who lives and works in the major city of Iraklio. There were also extensive conversations in German with the owner of a private WW II military museum. There one found sufficient British Brens and German MG-34s to make a gun buff drool.

Was their collective estimate that 75 to 95 percent of Cretan citizens owned guns accurate? We really don't know. Technically all were illegal. Every one of these folks started their conversations with the disclaimer that "I personally don't own any guns, but most residents do have guns in their homes. Some have lots and lots of guns including cases of ammunition," they said.

For avowed non-gun owners, these folks were tremendously knowledgeable. The computer nerd spoke accurately about differences between Steyr AUG, Kalashnikov and Armalite rifles. All, he said, were common in Crete. "Cretans can't be expected to defend their homeland with old relics and junk," he postured.

The non-gun owning furrier knew more about modern models of Smith & Wesson pistols than most American gun-store clerks! Some braggadocio, perhaps, accompanied the restaurant waiter's comments—perhaps detracting from their credibility.

All of the many tour books we accumulated mentioned something to the effect that national laws that conflict with local customs are simply disregarded. Also that guns are strictly regulated in Greece but nearly every household in Crete has at least one illegal firearm and many harbor small arsenals.

Probably these characterizations, as well as the assessment of the citizens who talked about firearms, are accurate. Here is more circumstantial evidence.

If there is a rural road sign in Crete that is not severely, completely and unrecognizably shot up by small arms fire, we either didn't see it or it was put up only a week ago. Ammo can't be expensive or scarce in Crete. For some strange reasons, citizens expend tens of thousands of rounds shooting up their road signs.

Some of the damage is easily recognized as the work of shotguns. Other damage is definitely 9mm in origin and still other damage is 30 caliber. Probably AK-47 7.62x39 rounds.

Like no other place in the world, small-arms fire is commonly heard in the evening, echoing across the valleys. Unmistakably it is from multi-round military shotguns, 9mm pistols and submachine guns, AK-47s and even the occasional heavy machine gun booming in the distance. All this immediately outside a popular tourist resort near Rethymno.

Completely legal ownership of some firearms is possible in Crete. Virtually every large city has at least a couple of gun stores. A few discreet rural shops are also out there, but these are not easy for outsiders to stumble upon.

Virtually anyone, even those with "light" criminal records, can legally own a single-barrel, double-barrel or bolt-action shotgun. Gun shops have a few, mostly 12, 20 and 9mm models. Ones on display were Italian or American. Semi-auto shotguns are not legally owned.

Single-shot rifles are also frequently permitted. These can be from .22 rimfire up through larger calibers such as 8x57 or 7.62x51.

When purchasing a legal shotgun or rifle at a local gun shop, first time buyers must pick out their gun, agree on price, take a bill of sale to their local police station and pay about $70 as a processing fee. Then they must wait five days for investigation and paper processing. If there is even a traffic violation, permission will only be given for a shotgun, not for a rifle. In all cases, buyers must convince the police of their need for a gun. Hunting and target shooting are valid needs. Self-defense is never accepted as a need. Hunting licenses are seen as evidence of an intent to hunt. Cost of a hunting license is a modest $11 annually.

As a legal matter there is no limit on the number of guns one may own. As a practical matter the police quickly conclude that applicants can only need and use a very few different models. This dramatically reduces numbers of police permissions given to one person.

Legal pistol ownership is possible but convoluted and difficult. Ownership of air rifles, I was told, is completely impossible in Crete. This is because air rifles tend to fall into the hands of kids who don't know how to use them. Incredible if accurate! Only one person seemed to know anything about air rifles, suggesting this information may be correct.

No one knew anything about dealers' and experimenters' permits. All assumed they would be expensive and not available to new residents on the island.

Pistol ownership is only possible for those who join a pistol club. All target shooting must be done at the club. Club membership is expensive and difficult, I was told. New members are only enrolled upon the recommendation of two existing members. Membership fees were said to be high, but no one seemed to know exactly how high.

There are also hunting clubs where game populations are encouraged and maintained for those who don't want to stumble around the hills of Crete hunting for sparse or non-existent game. Birds and deer, as well as badger and ferret-like small animals are hunted.

Permits to carry concealed or open are very, very rarely granted in Crete. There is so little crime officials virtually never see the need.

Transportation disassembled between the gun club and home is absolutely all that is allowed pistol owners. Rifles and shotguns can only be carried with valid owners' cards and hunting licenses between home and the range or field.

Security of shotguns and single shot rifles in the home is not an issue. Pistols, however, must be securely locked away. Significantly, Greek army officers on their bases carry pistols, but they have no magazines for their pistols—not in the gun and not visible on their belts.

Purchase of pistols and pistol ammo must be done through the club. All legal pistol ammo must be accounted for on a per-round basis. Shotgun and rifle ammo is sold only on the owner's purchase license. Numbers of rounds permitted each rifle and shotgun owned was unknown to our informants. They assumed it would be a box or two. Significantly, the question was considered to be unimportant because of large quantities of illegal ammo floating about Crete.

Reloading of pistol, rifle and shotgun ammo is done by various clubs. Apparently pistol clubs have official sanction to import powder, primers, bullets and shot. I was also informed that numerous small reloading factories existed out in rural areas wherein small arms ammo was reloaded for resale. Exactly where these small ammo factories get their powder and primers is a bit foggy. I was told both powder and primers were manufactured locally and that these were also smuggled in from Europe or former Yugoslavia. Either explanation seems implausible but yet possible. My guess is that larger .50 caliber or 20mm cannon ammo is always smuggled in from war zones intact. Reloading of this is probably seldom tried. At any rate, any shortage of ammunition on Crete is certainly not evident.

Silencers are apparently illegal but quite common on Crete. Cretans like to hear the noise of gunfire at celebrations, but will use silencers to hunt or to keep as a deterrent to invaders.

Local village machine shops turn out very nice silencers, I was told. Cretans are skilled, accomplished craftsmen. That rural machine shops turn out silencers and gun parts does not stretch credibility.

Crete is a very pleasant, easygoing place to live with nice two-season Mediterranean climate and luxurious beaches that appeal to most Americans. Property rights are enforced to a large degree. Resident permits for expats are said to be easy, mostly dependent on demonstrating an adequate living income. Cost of living on Crete is about 2/3 of the cost in the U.S.

Crimes of the burglary-robbery-shoplifting-rape-and-murder variety are virtually unknown. Home and automobile doors are seldom locked except by tourists from big cities. Nevertheless it would take an estimated two years of wise living with and among native Cretans till one is sufficiently trusted so that locals would openly demonstrate their guns or sources of supply.

So where do all of these many and varied illegal guns come from? Our informants looked at me like I was some sort of ignorant hick when I asked this question during my two weeks' investigation.

One obvious source is WW II battlefield pickups. Lake Voulismeni, in the heart of the resort city of Ayios Nikolaos ("the bottomless lake"— but actually only 210 feet deep) was supposedly a repository for small arms left by retreating Germans in 1945. Significantly no trace of any guns has been found. Also significantly, no trace of any workable guns has been found near Hania where most of the WW II fighting took place, or near Sfakia where the British evacuated some of their soldiers. Every gun and round of ammunition disappeared.

Although ownership is technically illegal, no civil authority on Crete will confiscate any war trophy held by any family so long as no breach of peace has occurred involving those guns. But modern day Cretans proudly go out of their way to explain that modern citizens hold modern guns. These reportedly are assault rifles, squad automatic weapons, submachine guns and modern, full-capacity pistols, they claim. "All," they say, brought in by commercial fishing boats or hidden in containerized imports of other goods.

Modern guns and ammunition flow in from countries comprising former Yugoslavia or Albania. This is plausible since steaming time from northern Crete to these chaotic nations is two to three days max on mostly calm, benign Mediterranean seas. Some German soldiers, for example, made the journey in 1941 in small sailing vessels using nothing more than hand-held compasses!

Black-market guns from Germany, originating in the former Soviet Union—as well as guns legally purchased in Switzerland and the U.S.—flow into Crete. Often these are sent by regular mail.

"They can't open every package," I was hectored. Again—it's probably true for a place that produces few manufactured goods. All automobiles, trucks, motorcycles, bicycles and air conditioners, as well as all spare parts, are imported.

"If we are ever occupied again, the Church (Greek Orthodox) will coordinate gun and ammo smuggling into Crete," our informants claimed. "Our clergy are often military officers and will assume their historic role as coordinators of the resistance," they continued. "They can do it, because the Church is so very wealthy in Crete" and "because we enjoy freedom," they went on.

Again it's a most plausible explanation. Museums throughout Crete are stuffed with statues and pictures of tough, bearded rifle- and pistol-toting priests who martyred themselves fighting Germans and Turks.

Why is self-defense not an issue and crime virtually non-existent in Crete? "Because we are a friendly, gentle, small, closed society where everybody knows everybody else among a population of only 240,000." I was told. "You murder, rape or steal and everyone will know who you are. How are you ever going to even get away off the island?" one especially nationalistic fellow lectured.

But what about Crete's notorious Sicily-like vendettas? Very occasionally a Cretan's fierce pride, sense of family honor, and/or defense of his property leads to a family feud called a vendetta. Some of these have gone on for years and years, eventually escalating into a cycle of retribution and revenge as each side brought more and more family members into the matter. Some vendettas have lasted 20 years or more, eventually killing scores of people. Whole villages have been emptied as a result.

The most notable feud between Sfakin Satzekakis and the Pendaris families started in the 1940s. It lasted till 1988 when about 150 had died. Only intervention by riot police sent from Athens allowed tempers to cool.

"We don't understand this stuff either," several citizens told me. Quite obviously Cretans are a friendly, open, gentle, peace-loving society, where this sort of thing seems not only out of context but totally impossible. It's certainly true if one is not perceived to be a threat to the peace and freedom of individuals there. Cretans are, nevertheless, independent and eternally vigilant lest they again be invaded and subjugated.

In this regard, it seems true that citizens of Crete are the most heavily armed citizens on Earth. Hitler and his generals believed they could overrun Crete in a matter of hours, suffering only light casualties in the process. Unlike the Cretans, citizens of Poland, France and Holland were not privately armed and they were quickly overrun. Memories may fade, but probably no one will make the same mistake again on Crete in the foreseeable future.

In the meantime, Cretans hold fast to their right to keep and bear arms
no matter what outsiders and their rules and regulations may suggest.

Chapter Thirty-Seven
Argentina
World Rank: 11 • Firearm Freedom 79%

I was seriously fearful that I was going to have a runaway. There, right
in front of me, available for immediate touching and fondling, was a
beautiful WW II vintage M-1 Thompson .45-caliber submachine gun
in good to very-good condition. Incredibly, it was for sale, over the
counter, for a mere $500.

The clerk took great pleasure pandering to my shocked surprise,
bordering on absolute gun lust. "We don't see things like that much
anymore," I finally managed to stammer.

It started innocently enough. "If Argentine citizens and legal residents
can secure permission to collect, own and fire assault rifles, machine
and submachine guns, where do they go to purchase them?" I asked
the Buenos Aires gun-shop clerk. All done in the line of duty collecting
information for this chapter on Argentine gun laws.

"To stores like ours," the clerk instantly responded as he fetched that
wonderful old collectors' gun from behind the back counter.

Private ownership of a great variety of firearms is permitted in
Argentina. Virtually every city of any size has at least one and perhaps
two or three stores selling guns and ammo. Like the U.S. of yesteryear,
ferreterias (hardware stores) tend to carry guns and ammo. Buenos
Aires, the capital, has three or four concentrated in one area near the
intersection of Uruguay and Paraguay streets. Consolidations or
groupings of similar shops are something of a throwback in history to a
time when sales of goods and services were grouped by type. This
suggests these gun shops have been around in one form or another for
a long, long time.

Business, at the time we visited, seemed very good. A steady string of
customers that would have warmed the cockles of any U.S. gun-store
owner passed through.

Argentina is not a wealthy country. It is, however, not a poor third-
world one either. *Per capita* income is around $12,400. This includes
an estimated 21 percent of the work force that are currently
unemployed. Perhaps 37 percent live below the poverty line (set by
the Argentine government and basically undefined.) Yet one of the

more pervasive current political problems involves the many illegal workers flooding into the country from Peru, Chile, Bolivia, Paraguay and Brazil. They came for what they consider to be high-paying jobs.

Argentina is a very large country (about one-third the size of the U.S.) lying on the eastern two thirds of South America. Chile borders on the west, Brazil and Paraguay as well as the South Atlantic on the east. Topographically the country runs from swampy, sleepy river-fed tropical lowlands and vast prairies on the northeast and south to the beautiful and rugged Andes mountains on the west. The country is rich with deposits of oil and minerals. Perhaps ten percent of the available land is farmed. Experts conclude Argentina could easily feed all of Europe if authorities in the EU ever decide to end agricultural subsidies there, allowing importation of inexpensive Argentine meat and cereals.

Guns in Argentina reflect world prices. Sako and Beretta models, expensive in the U.S., are also beyond the financial reach of many average Argentines. Gun shops in rural areas tend to stock thin inventories of rifles, shotguns and pistols, trending toward more inexpensive models. Many of these stores are more catalog-order points rather than stocking dealers. Within some relatively wide parameters, citizens and legal residents can order just about any gun or type of gun they can pay for. Lots of inexpensive Chinese and Turkish models we have never seen or heard of before are on display in these stores.

These shops also have or can quickly order a large variety of ammo. More than the U.S., Argentine ammo suppliers tend to shop worldwide for ammo. Several gun-shop owners said virtually any and all ammunition is available. A shop clerk claimed he could even supply .41 caliber ammo for an old Swiss Vetterli rifle he had in his rack.

Initially I assumed this to be some sort of antique rimfire round best left in collectors' hands. On reflection, the fellow probably had one of the Vetterlis that was originally sold as military surplus and later converted from rimfire to centerfire. Winchester .348 brass can be used to manufacture this round. This suggests Argentine gun people are a fairly sophisticated, knowledgeable bunch when it comes to firearms.

First-time Argentine gun owners start the process of acquiring firearms by applying for a gun-owner's certificate at their local office of the Ministry of Defense. Called the Registro Nacional de Armas, or RENAR, this is really not the police or military. This is an office only for gun owners. RENAR offices are conveniently located throughout the country in most medium and some small-sized cities. In some cases, Argentine gun owners must deal with their military, but this is for full-autos and assault rifles. RENAR holds itself out as a private organization.

Serious past abuses on the part of a vicious, autocratic military have so conditioned Argentines that they are extremely reluctant to deal with their military under any circumstances. For sure, hundreds and perhaps tens of thousands of mostly young, activist-type citizens were covertly rounded up and secretly and summarily executed between 1976 and 1983. Carlos Meném, a past president, pardoned those involved but a league of aggrieved mothers won't let the issue fade.

Application forms for a gun-owner's certificate are not long and detailed. However, securing necessary attachments can be a chore.

First, applicants must secure a document from the local police verifying that they have no criminal record. This is said not to be a particularly difficult document to obtain, unless the police choose to make a big deal about driving infractions or some other past minor brush with the law. Normally securing this document takes only a few days to a week, if there is no criminal record in one's background. Usually there is no cost for this document. Bribery among police and military people is not unheard of in Argentina, but it is uncommon.

Applicants must be 21 years old or older. Younger Argentines legally use their parents' guns but cannot legally own them. Not frequently, but occasionally, Argentine kids can be seen out duck or grouse hunting using a parent's firearm.

Second, citizens must secure a certificate from a medical doctor verifying that they have no mental problems or history of mental problems. Some severe physical handicaps may also preclude gun ownership. Gun shops keep current lists of medicos willing to issue these certificates. Costs vary, but are said to be nominal.

Third, applicants need a gun-handling-competency certificate issued by a certified instructor at a local gun club. Some very rural applicants may have problems with this requirement, but this is said to be a mostly routine matter. Cost of $10 for the certificate and training suggests that it really is a simple, routine matter.

The fourth and final requirement is considered by Argentines to be the most onerous. A document from their equivalent of their IRS must be supplied listing out how much tax money was paid the last two years and where the applicant worked. Gun-owner-certificate issuing authorities want to be convinced that you have a regular job and are dutifully paying taxes.

Given high unemployment levels and the fact that most Argentines deal extensively in the off-the-books or underground economy, this requirement could be a real stickler.

For example, only three of perhaps 20 hotel clerks at properties where we stayed officially registered us as guests or took anything except cash payments. An owner of a very ritzy custom leather shop in Buenos Aires extended a huge discount for U.S. cash payment on a full-length designer-type woman's leather coat. Hotels, shops or restaurants kept few if any records of our transactions unless we paid with plastic.

One hotel owner commenting about their economy said that if the average Argentine spent as much time and energy producing stuff and innovating rather than dodging government officials and the tax man, the country wouldn't be such an economic train wreck.

A gun-owner's certificate costs about 150 pesos and takes two weeks to come through, if all necessary attachments are in good order. Unlike other countries and bureaucracies, Argentine officials don't seem to look for excuses to turn down citizens who want to own guns.

Documented legal immigrants can apply for and receive a gun-owner's certificate as well as legally own firearms in Argentina. Importation is possible, but will take time before all paperwork is completed. Gun shops will work with expats who wish to bring their guns with them when they move to Argentina.

There is a sense that immigrants possessing firearms "development and engineering" skills would be welcomed into Argentina with open arms by the government, but no one knew for sure. These situations would be handled on a case-by-case basis, knowledgeable locals claim.

Gun-owner certificate holders can own bolt-action and single-shot rifles, pump, semi-automatic and double-barrel shotguns, and virtually any type of revolver or pistol they can pay for. Beretta, Smith, Colt, SIG, H&K and Ruger pistols are commonly seen in display cases. Double rifles and shotguns as well as drillings are a seldom seen anomaly, and too expensive for most citizens.

Once purchase of a firearm is completed at a gun shop or among cooperating private holders of gun-owner's certificates, the new owner takes or sometimes mails the receipt over to the RENAR office where that firearm is recorded to the new owner's license.

A separate gun card is issued for each weapon. Card in hand, the new owner may pick up the gun from the shop. Owners do not need any other permissions for these guns and they do not have to register .22 rifles. Argentine gun owners do not have to otherwise justify or receive any additional permissions for permitted guns. In other words, they don't have to provide a reason for ownership of this class of firearm. As a practical matter, they are free to own as many guns as they wish.

A separate permission is required to carry concealed. Bank couriers, judges or jewelry-store owners with good reason to carry concealed have little problem securing permission. Carrying concealed in one's home or business or on one's private property is apparently common. We noted several store owners who were carrying.

Argentine citizens currently complain bitterly about the proliferation of crime in their streets. From an outsider's perspective, the country seemed extremely peaceful and law-abiding. Like folks in Spain, Argentines seem to have a "lock things safely away" mentality rather than a "defend one's property with a gun" inclination. Three locks and a deadbolt on doors is common. Citizens in big cities were continually on the alert to remind us to lock our car, carry our cameras securely and to watch our money. We observed no real problems first hand.

It is often said no one can ever get more than a mile from a cow in Argentina. No way to know if that's true, but there really are lots of cows there and lots of real working cowboys managing those cattle.

Many of these guys pack what appears to be ancient Spanish knockoffs of Smith & Wesson revolvers. Illegal guns are said by gun stores and hunt-club folks not to be an issue or a problem in Argentina. Perhaps it's true because there are few places from which illegal guns could originate and perhaps because legal ownership is reasonable and easy.

Having made this observation, many Argentines believe most of the many cowboy sidearms are illegal. Are these guys grandfathered into their current gun laws? Or perhaps no one cares to question them. Argentina is a huge country with a great outback. We can easily imagine cowboys go weeks and even months way out in the bush without encountering anyone but other cowboys known to each other.

Ammunition sales requirements are a bit complex and the stuff can be fairly high priced. Most shot shells and metallics up to .38 caliber are not controlled. Buy as much .22 rimfire, .32 ACP, .25 auto, 9mm and 12, 16, 20, 28 or .410 ammo as you can afford. Purchasers do not have to show their gun owners' or registration certificates to buy.

Shotgun ammo sales are limited to rounds loaded with number five shot or smaller. Buck shot and slug rounds are reserved strictly for the police and military, or sold under special permit to security personnel and bank guards.

Both shotgun ammo and smaller metallics including .22s are made in Argentina. A box of 50 .22s sells for $2. Italian and Spanish ammo, principally shot shells, are imported. A box of 25 12-gauge shells sells for $5.

Large rifle and pistol rounds are available but expensive. Forty-five auto rounds in boxes of 20 sell for $20, with no restrictions on military rounds. Both .223 and .308 ammo are available but supposedly Argentines don't like .223s. "Too small," they claim.

Purchase of larger-caliber rifle and pistol ammo such as .22-250, .30-06, and 7mm mag, etc., are limited to 500 rounds per year for each caliber and rifle. Purchases of these larger rounds are recorded to the owner's gun-registration form.

What about assault rifles, submachine and full machine guns and such like? These guns are legally and fairly easily owned in Argentina, but ownership involves another layer of permissions. Silencers are not legal in any form in Argentina.

Those who want to purchase assault rifles or submachine-gun-type arms must secure a sanction from the military. This permission to buy is predicated on having what the army considers a "good reason to own." Supposedly it's not all that difficult to secure.

However, as mentioned, Argentine citizens have extensive past bad baggage dealing with their military. Most really loathe and fear having anything at all to do with military officers or personnel. Rather than owning military-type assault rifles and having to deal with their military, they make do with permitted lesser classes of weapons.

Defense of one's home or business, design and testing, or interest in collecting and studying assault weapons and submachine guns is frequently seen as sufficient reason for ownership. Citizens would often rather not own than be forced to deal with their military. Even so, private ownership is sufficiently common that larger gun shops carry most popular assault rifles and a few submachine guns.

Reloading pistol, rifle and shotgun ammo is common in Argentina, perhaps because factory ammo is extremely expensive, especially in odd calibers. Most gun shops carry or can order powder, bullets, shot and primers.

A special reloader's permit must be obtained from RENAR before components can legally be purchased. Folks at the gun shops did not recall how difficult, expensive or time consuming this additional certificate was. Since large numbers of Argentines reload, they felt securing necessary reloading certificates was a fairly routine exercise.

They also understood that some sort of yearly restrictions applied to amounts of components that could be purchased and held by Argentine reloaders. But no one could recall exactly how much these were. Apparently amounts were sufficiently generous that they were not a factor for legitimate hand loaders.

Argentina is definitely not a third-world country. They may lack a fully developed middle class, but standards of service, dress, cleanliness and technology seem world class, with a decidedly agricultural touch. Given the country's huge size and the vast remoteness of so much of it, living in peace and isolation would seem easily possible for those who wish to take advantage of Argentina's fairly reasonable gun laws.

Chapter Thirty-Eight
El Salvador
World Rank: 48 • Firearm Freedom 25%

Experienced international travelers refer to it as *The Suriname syndrome*, referencing a remote, far-off little country that may initially seem exotic. This is principally because few people have heard of it and fewer still can pinpoint its location with any degree of accuracy. A place that, when one looks closely, has little to nothing to recommend it. There's little to see and do in Suriname-syndrome countries.

Tiny Massachusetts-sized El Salvador—100 by 36 miles—perfectly fits this description. We include gun laws in El Salvador because these are very much like the gun laws in Crete where we also find extremely high incidence of gun ownership. Most of it is illegal, but conveniently overlooked or ignored by the authorities.

Like Crete, El Salvador's gun-ownership patterns reflect the fact that extremely serious and protracted fighting took place in the country.

Recent and frequently recurring killer hurricanes and devastating earthquakes have completely destroyed all of the older charming colonial-era government buildings, museums and cathedrals. El Salvador is located on the far western edge of Central America, with Guatemala to the west and Honduras to the north and east.

No matter by whose criteria, little charm remains in El Salvador. On the one hand, visitors see terribly poor, depressed shanty-town slums, carefully walled away from a few palatial estates owned by super-rich landowners and government officials. On the other there are brand new glitzy gleaming modern steel and glass shopping centers. Little reason exists, it seems, to travel thousands of miles under difficult circumstances to observe such.

Information for this chapter comes from a personal visit to El Salvador including San Salvador—the capital—conversations with Salvadoran nationals and from comments collected from gun owners in surrounding countries. There is also a bit of published material which is helpful if one is willing to read between the lines.

El Salvador's important history relative to politics, economics and gun ownership is relatively recent. Mutually exhausted by a long, brutal and seeming never-ending civil war, government forces and the FMLN

(Faribundo Marti Nacional Liberacion Front) representatives agreed to a UN-brokered peace treaty on January 16, 1992.

Both the North Americans and the Soviets (up until their empire went bankrupt) flooded the 8,124 square-mile country with tens of thousands of assault rifles, machine guns, pistols, mortars, heavy machine guns and explosives. Historians agree that the situation had degenerated into a standoff. Obviously neither side could actually win the war in a crisp, outright manner. Military historians claim one cannot understand these type wars without understanding the Spanish Civil War, especially true here. The war could not be won by either side and dragged on so long many citizens no longer understood the issues, while significant numbers of them were killed in the process.

An elderly man famously summarized the situation as his little village was cruelly shot up in the course of a fierce firefight. "You know," he was overheard to shout in anguish, "let whoever wins win. But please let the war be over!"

Out of a population of roughly six million, an estimated 75,000 died. At least twice that many fled the country. Most went to the U.S. Currently an estimated $1.5 billion annually is remitted back to El Salvador from those still living and working in the U.S.

This explains why visitors observe so many well-dressed Salvadorans in toney restaurants, bars and shopping centers who otherwise have no visible means of support. *Per capita* income is reliably estimated at $4,900. Salvadorans have a reputation for being very frugal and hard working, but this hardly explains some of their more ostentatious displays of wealth.

The war and its subsequent truce left tens of thousands of guns and millions of rounds of ammo scattered about the country. Possibly more than in Crete even including weapons dumped by evacuating British and Greek soldiers as well as those the Germans left.

According to the truce, the FMLN was supposed to hand in their weapons to the new central government in which they were no co-participants. As a practical matter, some—perhaps even most—of the heavy machine guns and mortars were surrendered. Most but certainly not all small arms and ammunition went underground, both figuratively and literally.

Enough AK-47s were eventually collected to fill at least two large warehouses in San Salvador. Those in the international gun trade vividly recall that existence of this relatively large supply temporarily drove world prices for good used AK-47s to about $27 to $30 each. Rumor has it that many of these guns ended up in Panama, Colombia or other parts of the world where they became part of a large pool of illicit weapons. Dark rumors abound that some politicians lined their pockets with profits from this temporary but lucrative line of business.

As part of the truce, land reform of sorts was implemented. All estates of over about 600 acres were to be purchased or appropriated from the previous owners by the central government. This land was intended for apportionment out to ex-soldiers and guerilla fighters as part of universal land reform. These new little farm sites provided convenient places in which to stash illicit weapons.

Peace and friendly accord proved to be a bit rocky. Former guerillas were invited to run for election and to otherwise participate in the government as bureaucrats. Some—mostly local—government officials managed to successfully do so.

On paper, El Salvador has gun laws much like those in Honduras and Guatemala. A gun-owner's certificate is issued by the local police in conjunction with the military, recording all weapons. Only those deemed to be of sporting or accepted security purpose are allowed.

Numerous gun stores located throughout the country cater to that trade. Sales to the extensive security personnel, both public and private, seem to generate most profits. Hunting is virtually non-existent in El Salvador. Some target shooting is done by the very wealthy who seem to live with or ignore the laws.

In practice, former guerillas do not want to confiscate weapons from former comrades. Government officials also do not want to confiscate weapons from their former associates. Everyone really truly dreads going back to war. They hope and pray hostilities will never resume. Probably they will not as long as this generation is alive.

In summary, everyone has some reason not to seriously upset the other guy by demanding their weapons, or by taking a hard-nosed posture about the issue. As a result, levels of private, but illegal, gun ownership in El Salvador are rumored to be some of the highest in the world. Yet, unlike Crete, sounds of gunfire are not heard every night in rural regions. Salvadorans do share their disdain for road signs with the Cretans. Most are thoroughly shot up.

Reloading is not done in Salvador. No components are imported. Surplus ammo is still extremely inexpensive and common.

Gun-store permits are said to be necessary but reasonably easily obtained for those with connections. It appears "connections" means ex-military people.

Crime in El Salvador is a serious problem. Well-armed criminal gangs are said to control some areas of the city and country. Salvadoran police are reasonably well-trained, well-paid and reasonably honest.

They do not hesitate to deal with well-armed gangs whenever they encounter them. Citizens enjoy talking about major police and gang shootouts. Specific exact examples are seldom given, however.

Bottom line: When misuse of illegal firearms becomes overt, the authorities do not hesitate to act. Until then, they seem content and pleased to allow sleeping dogs to lie.

Salvadorans we met are unclear about concealed-carry permits. Officially these are available from their gun-control people, at reasonably cost in time and money. Practically, Salvadorans just assume that the next guy in a crowd might be carrying.

Frequent signs at government office doors, restaurant, churches, and banks warn that "carrying firearms into these premises is forbidden." It is also common to observe outlines of pistols in pants pockets or underneath a shirt, or to see them openly displayed, stuffed behind a pants belt.

Rules of law and property are said to be in place in El Salvador. This may be relative. Wealthy people seem to have more property rights than the faceless majority on the bottom of the socioeconomic totem pole. Yet some recognition of property rights for everyone seems to be out there. Rules of law and property rights for everyone are said to be improving. This is a result of a lack of these rules being seen as an impediment to economic development.

Salvador's lowland tropical climate is hot, muggy, buggy and—some would say—oppressive. As mentioned, unless one enjoys endless surfing or beach bumming, there is little or nothing to see or do.

Most North Americans find little to recommend life in this tiny place, in spite of the fact that U.S. dollars go a long, long way. In reality, El Salvador is an expanded city state. Even their indigenous currency has disappeared; U.S. dollars are officially used since January 1, 2002 for all transactions.

Yet visitors cannot but be impressed by the national pride and passion of the many Salvadorans they meet. Large numbers have left to make their fortune and have now returned home. One does not easily leave their native place of birth and culture.

Like Crete, El Salvador's private gun situation is interesting but not particularly helpful unless the lessons of illegal gun ownership are included. Most U.S. gun owners would not enjoy similar uncertainty attached to illegal ownership. No matter that this ownership might include great numbers of interesting, historic, fun-to-shoot weapons using incredibly cheap surplus ammo.

Chapter Thirty-Nine
Ivory Coast
World Rank: 54 • Firearm Freedom 18%

That various countries world wide usually follow well-established cultural patterns when developing, enacting and enforcing their gun laws should come as no surprise to readers who have made it this far into this text.

Seems the world over, insecure politicians and bureaucrats usually see limiting private gun ownership as a means of securing their own tenure as bosses. What follows is very cultural. But throw some colonial baggage into this mix of culture and things get really weird.

We haven't looked at West Africa or a former French colony as yet, so we go there next. The Ivory Coast is an excellent place to start.

That's especially true given the fact that, until relatively recently, the Ivory Coast was held out as an unusually brilliant African success story. It is like few others in terms of property rights, economic development and stability, supporters claimed. A very nice, pleasant place where living was easy. That was before the revolution.

Something very marginally larger than New Mexico in land area, the Ivory Coast lies under the western bulge of Africa next to Liberia to the northwest. Ghana lies to the east. Ivory Coast is a seaside country, but does little maritime commerce.

Ivory Coast consists of a relatively narrow strip of dense tropical forest lying along the shore. Rainfall here is intense. A great patch of extremely fertile savanna characterizes the northern interior.

Without really realizing it, Americans heavily interact with Ivory Coast farmers. Virtually all of our raw cocoa used to produce chocolate, as well as many other chocolatey delights, comes from this country.

Until their civil war started in September of 2000, Ivory Coast was something of an economic African poster child. Everything is relative, of course.

Per capita incomes were estimated at $1,500. Growth in GNP and *per capita* income was modest but steady, and relatively large for Africa. Exact figures were obscured by the fact that most of the country's commerce was off the books, principally to confound the tax man. Nevertheless, faster growth than any other African country, resident experts claimed.

In addition to the makings for chocolate, relatively rich Ivory Coast was blessed with deposits of diamonds, iron ore, crude oil, manganese, bauxite and valuable cobalt. Living was easy, especially in the interior savanna. Plant seeds in the fertile soil and very soon there is something to eat. Unless interrupted by civil war, farmers expected three crops per year off the same piece of ground.

Under the correct terms and conditions, most sporting rifles (not including assault rifles), all shotguns and all pistols were allowed private citizens in Ivory Coast, including virtually all action types, calibers and gauges.

Absolutely no submachine guns or full machine guns were allowed under any circumstances although illegal gun ownership in this class is said to be common. Unlike many other places in Africa where native Africans have a deep seated fear and mistrust of guns and gun owners, thirty percent of Ivory Coast citizens are estimated to be gun owners. Silencers are illegal.

In 1973 then-President Houphouet-Boigny outlawed all hunting in his country. Stories regarding why have taken on the character of urban legends, but parts have a truthful ring.

As the story now goes, Houphouet-Boigny made a state visit to Kenya where he admired the tourist potential for animal watching the Kenyans had developed. On return to the Ivory Coast, the president was apparently dismayed and somewhat angered when several ranking ministers went out and shot a number of wild antelopes for use in a "welcome home" dinner. This was supposedly to avoid tapping a slender state budget for the price of meat for the celebration.

Rather than firing or otherwise dealing with these offending ministers, Houphouet-Boigny banned all hunting in Ivory Coast. He also ordered privately held rifles be turned in to the nearest police headquarters.

Now jump seventeen years ahead to 1992 and to a new president. He lifted the ban on hunting. Not really much of a concession since most citizens who wanted to hunt did so anyway. Poaching, using traps or guns, has always been a major activity in rural Ivory Cost. Miraculously all private rifles were still in good condition, stored at local police stations, and available for return to their owners. All one had to do was go to the police station and ask. The hook was that, although big-game hunting was again officially legal, with payment of a $250 yearly big-game fee, no one was officially notified.

Small game licenses, mostly for birds, were always available, at $50. Shotguns and pistols were not banned or confiscated during this period. Apparently Ivory Coast bureaucrats believed shotguns were not used for big game and pistols were never used for hunting of any kind.

Gun ownership in Ivory Coast definitely favors expat colonizers. Those wanting a legal firearm or firearms, including rifles (after 1992), pistols and shotguns must go to their nearest police headquarters. Fill out multiple forms and pay about $50. An inquiry is then made regarding the applicant's status as a law-abiding citizen. Apparently officials expected a great many expat applications. Right from the get-go, arrangements were made to check with the applicant's home country regarding any legal breaches. These countries could be France or the U.S., or theoretically any other place in the world. Seems the Ivory Cost was relying on the good records of more modern countries, or perhaps they expected only French expats to want to own guns. We can only speculate about this and other strangenesses.

Copies of one's local resident card and/or passport were attached to the applicant's papers, to prove legal residency. Hiring a runner or paper-gopher to handle this bureaucracy was common.

Approval for this gun-owner's permit, literally translated from its French title as a "right to carry," took one to two months. Procedures were materially speeded up by payment of a $10 to $20 bribe. All transactions in Ivory Coast are done in French colonial francs, translated to dollars for the purposes of this chapter.

Right-to-carry permit safely in hand, one is legally entitled to purchase a shotgun (any action, single, pump, or auto is okay) from one of the few state sanctioned gun stores located in either Abidjan (the capital), or in a very few of the other larger cities. This gun is immediately registered to the owner's certificate. Only shotguns are legally available over the counter at gun stores in Ivory Coast.

Ownership of pistols and rifles is permitted so long as one has what the bureaucrats consider a valid reason for ownership. In the case of rifles and shotguns, hunting and target practice are good reasons. Payment of a bribe increases chances of the reason being accepted. Long-gun permits are handled by the local police.

Pistol permits must be approved by officials at the treasury office in Abidjan. Local officials will forward the paperwork but it is often faster and requires fewer bribes to do it personally. Ivory Coast is a small country with relatively good roads to the capital.

Valid reasons to own a pistol include self defense, work in a crime-ridden area, customarily transporting large sums of money and—to some extent—an interest in target shooting. A right-to-carry permit for a pistol carries with it the right to carry concealed.

Taking delivery of legal pistols and rifles is convoluted and unique. All must be imported. Once receiving permission to own, permit holders go to an importing agent who will bring in their guns and ammo if such is included in the paperwork. Residents and past residents of the Ivory Coast from whom we received this information firmly believe that these rules and procedures were put in place to favor the home industry of the colonizer (France). As a practical matter, most guns and ammunition are now legally imported from the U.S., Belgium and Russia, not France.

There is no limit on the number of guns one can import so long as it is possible to convince officials of a specific need for each gun. Many officials are not particularly savvy about items they control. During the time when only small game and bird hunting was allowed, .22 rifles were permitted. This was intended to mean .22 rimfire rifles, but several expats successfully imported .22 hornet or .223 rifles.

After local or national approval (in the case of pistols,) a customs agent does the rest. Fees are about $100. Legal residents and those coming to the country to hunt can land with a gun and leave it in a secure customs warehouse while securing official approval. This is said to be a common means of bringing rifles, pistols and in some cases shotguns into the Ivory Coast. Expats claim this procedure is fairly straightforward and effective but very costly in the long run.

Shotgun ammo and, very occasionally, a few ruinously expense .22 rimfire rounds, can be purchased in country from the few approved gun shops said to be run by Lebanese.

All legal ammo is recorded to one's gun-owner's permit (permit to carry.) As a practical matter, some shotgun and .22 rimfire ammo can usually be purchased in the black market (often at local markets.)

Resident gun owners commonly import all of their ammo, either with the original gun or as separate later orders. Relatively large quantities of ammo—up to 3,000 rounds—are allowed. This can be a mix-and-match deal, but only for guns registered on one's certificate.

Importation is absolutely the only method to secure .308, .243, .30-06 or .270 ammo for rifles. Costs including customs fees are high, but by batching orders among cooperating rifle and pistol owners, not prohibitive. As mentioned, ammo is often imported with guns. There are no rules regarding firearms storage in Ivory Coast.

Some hand loading is done. Apparently this activity falls below the scope of Ivory Coast bureaucrats, perhaps because no powder, primers or bullets are available, not even on the black market. Primers, powder and bullets have sometimes been allowed for importation.

All of this importation procedure is said to be dreary and time consuming, but is claimed to usually work for those with enough money to pay fees and bribes.

Police ranges are found, we are told, in virtually every city with a police station. Local cops may not have enough gasoline in their trucks to respond to crimes but they have enough of an ammo budget to be banging away on their ranges at all times of the day and night. Private gun owners can use these ranges if they make prior arrangements with the police. Residents make a great fuss over the fact that they seem never to be out of hearing of incessant gunfire in the Ivory Coast.

Government officials in the Ivory Coast treat gun owners as something of a cash cow to be heavily used. Annual taxes for rifles are $150 each. Pistol owners must pay $100 each. This in addition to fees for a permit to carry, bribe money and customs import fees.

As a practical matter, these fees severely limit legal gun ownership to a relatively few wealthy expats and government officials. Sales among private individuals are allowed so long as all of their paperwork is completed along with receiving necessary approvals. Purchasing overseas and importing is almost always cheaper and easier.

A few competent, skilled gunsmiths are found scattered around the country. Before the civil war they principally made illegal weapons for local poachers and bandits.

Our informants—residents and expats—doubt that government officials would see or understand potential economic benefits of a gun manufacturing or development industry in Ivory Coast.

Absolutely no one will predict what gun laws in Ivory Coast will be like after the civil war ends if, in fact, it ever really ends. One thing is sure. The war is bringing in tons and tons of small arms and ammunition up through three-inch mortars. Ivory Coast may not be free of all these guns and ammo for the foreseeable future.

People who really know are not talking, but local speculation suggests that most illegal guns are coming from Libya. Most are Soviet made.

As in other impoverished and despotic lands, rogue, poorly paid soldiers and police often sell or rent their guns and ammunition.

While future Ivory Coast gun laws may be questionable, it is certain that these rules and regulations are very similar to ones in other former French colonies comprising West Africa. In that regard, their situation is simultaneously extremely confused and informative.

Chapter Forty
Ecuador
World Rank: 59 • Firearm Freedom 11%

With Ecuador we arrive at a country and society with private gun-ownership rules and regulations so convoluted, difficult and arcane they set a world standard.

Certainly every country's gun-ownership rules are a product of its culture and history. However, in the case of Ecuador, one easily detects more than a faint whiff of U.S. government meddling in Ecuadorian internal affairs. Strange both that the U.S. would meddle in this arena, and that official Americana would muck around in opposition to personal freedom and property rights.

In addition to apparent U.S. intervention, Ecuadorian officials are already so overwhelmingly paranoid about firearms that we see some very strange results. For instance, one sees venerable, ancient, extremely valuable antique firearms displayed in Ecuadorian museums that have been criminally vandalized of key parts thus rendering them safely inoperable. As a result, a great deal of their early history is ruthlessly destroyed.

Information for this chapter comes courtesy of in-depth interviews with two gun-store owners in Quito, Ecuador, a similar interview with a retired army colonel previously charged with enforcing Ecuadorian gun laws, as well as in depth visits to rural areas where some guns are still used on a subsistence basis. We also spent a great deal of time in Ecuadorian museums, observing their decimated gun collections.

First-hand observation of their police/security services and the weapons these people carried proved instructive. We observed thousands of pistol, shotgun, M-1 carbine, and—in a few cases—submachine gun-toting officers. Personally we encountered no first-hand evidence of fraud or crime, but noted these issues weigh heavily on Ecuadorians today.

Ecuador is that Nevada-sized country lying astraddle the high equator in South America. Their land extends from the Pacific Ocean on the west to Columbia in the north (of South America) to Brazil on the east. Ecuador's border with Brazil comprises some very wild, unsettled, unroaded, little-explored areas of the Upper Amazon.

Extremely high volcanic peaks run down the center of Ecuador. Only one season in this area, characterized by cool nights and warm days. Day length is consistently 12 hours year 'round.

Per capita income is about $3,700. Most citizens work in the ag economy, much of it subsistence agriculture. Fall off the central mountain spine to the east and it's the Amazon River Basin. There the economy is based on crude oil, tourism and subsistence ag. To the west along their Pacific coast it's lots of huge banana plantations, a kind of upland paddy rice combination, sugar cane and shrimp ponds. Hot and buggy in these tropical lowlands. Few gringos show their faces here.

Ecuadorians are legally allowed to privately own a total of four separate guns. Permission for the first two, assuming one is willing to pass sufficient paper, is reasonably straightforward. A pistol for self defense and a shotgun or a .22 rifle to hunt with is their gold standard. Securing sanction for the second two requires that one have some rock-solid reasons for ownership. These reasons must convince some army officers who themselves are convinced that no reason exists to own more than two guns, if even that many.

Four guns is, in most cases, the absolute maximum. As a result, Ecuadorian gun owners are likely to own one receiver with four or more sets of barrels for that receiver. Common shotgun receivers with sets of 12, 16, 20, 28 and .410 barrels and perhaps occasionally a set of rifle barrels are frequently owned by Ecuadorian gun enthusiasts. In this regard, Ecuadorian gun owners are much like European gun owners whose rules and regulations force them into similarly evasive maneuvers.

Target shooting, a second back up pistol for defense, or a second different shotgun with which to shoot trap or skeet or with which to hunt are sometimes considered valid reasons to own. Among dedicated persevering gun owners, a .22 rifle, double-barrel shotgun with accompanying barrel sets and a pistol are the standard.

Army officials sometimes issue collectors permits to those who want to own multiple guns. But this permit is very limited and limiting. Holders are required to keep all of their guns permanently under lock and key. They are not allowed to transport their guns to the range or even carry them out of their homes.

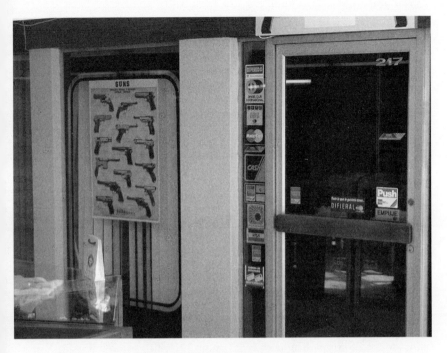

Ecuadorian gun store

Ecuadorian officials are extremely nervous about guns in
private hands. Like other South American countries, lack of
freedoms, economic woes and poorly run governments keep
the population in a more-or-less perpetual state of unrest.
Nevertheless, a few gun shops exist in major cities such as
this one in Quito, the capital. Prices unfortunately are
ruinously high. Credit cards accepted include the familiar
Amex, Visa, MasterCard and Diners Club, along with six
foreign service providers unfamiliar to most Americans.
Amex provided the "Push" sign for the front entrance.

As a practical matter they cannot shoot or ever use these collectors' guns. No purchase of ammunition is allowed for these firearms on their gun collector's permit.

Any type or style of revolver or automatic pistol limited to a ten-shot magazine is permitted. Normally only smaller "carbine" type .22 pump, bolt or lever-action rifles are allowed. Absolutely no semi-autos for civilians, and very few high power rifles are ever sanctioned. To complicate matters, permission for .22 rifles is only given if these are designated as carbines. Civilians in Ecuador can never own semi-auto rifles, especially military-looking ones. Even the police don't usually have these type firearms.

Shotguns between 12 gauge and .410 caliber are permitted. Uniquely, almost any action type including pumps, autos, bolts and double barreled shotguns are okay. Even short-barreled or military-type shotguns will be approved, both for ownership and importation, provided one takes care describing them. Employing politically acceptable correct descriptions of guns and ammo is something of an ongoing challenge for both importers and buyers.

As an example, only pistols in calibers .22 to .38 special are usually allowed. Mentioning the word "magnum" is always anathema. But at times, importation of .22 mag or .357 cartridges and guns is possible if they are designated as simple .22s or .38s. Importation and sales of nine-millimeter pistols is recently permitted which, according to the army colonel with whom we talked, has significantly increased incidence of crime. Bolt-action .222s or .223 rifles sometimes slip through as a result of being labeled simple .22s. Apparently semi-literate army recruits doing the checking do not notice differences.

Large bore combat-type pistol shooting enjoys some popularity among some moneyed Ecuadorians. Provided participants are willing to spend the money to join a club specifically formed for the purpose of engaging in combat-type shooting, permission will sometimes be given for .45 ACP and/or .44 caliber pistols. Specific ownership is a bit blurred. At times the club owns the pistols. Other times it's individuals.

Cost of club membership? From $200 to $1,000 to join plus perhaps $20 per month! Ecuadorians use U.S. currency. All figures are in U.S. dollars. As a complete aside, some U.S. ones, fives and tens have been in the country so long they are sufficiently ratty that one hates to put them in their pocket.

Similarly there are clubs formed to shoot trap and skeet. Both American and international-style shoots are available. Membership fees, ammo and costs for clay pigeons propel this activity into the realm of "only for the super rich."

Ammo and firearms cost roughly twice as much in Ecuador as in the U.S. Ecuadorian gun owners lament the fact that few young people are "getting into" shooting sports such as hunting, pistol target shooting and shotgunning.

Besides clubs and wide-open rural areas, military and police ranges are available to citizen shooters. Use of some of these may depend on developing a friendly working relationship with local police or army officers. Government corruption is not rampant in Ecuador, at least not to the extent of Mexico or Italy.

Control of firearms in Ecuador is done both by licensing citizen owner-buyers and by strict controls on importation from other outside manufacturing countries. Currently no civilian firearms can legally be imported from the U.S.! This because our very own State Department has decided that far too many civilian guns in Ecuador have been finding their way across the border into Colombia where they are supposedly being used by guerillas fighting the central government.

Yet the January 20, 2005 issue of El Pais, a popular Quito newspaper, carried a feature article pointing out that the Ecuadorian government had just taken advantage of a U.S. program to purchase 2,000 Ruger 10/22 semi-auto rifles with factory-installed and fitted silencers as well as 400 Mossberg model 500 12-gauge riot shotguns with nine-shot extended magazines. Total value of the deal was a reported $1.2 million. A great issue was made of exactly describing the guns in great detail in the newspaper story, including photos. Silencers, as an aside, are never legal for common Ecuadorian citizens.

Two threads characterize the actual processes of delivering a firearm to a private citizen. All gun dealers are licensed by the Ecuadorian army. They, in turn, apply for an import license and an import quota from the Ecuadorian military. Only a very few guns are manufactured within Ecuador, most by back-country artisans in primitive shops somewhat reminiscent of Khyber Pass gunsmiths in northern Pakistan.

Guns they produce are single-shot shotguns and very crude revolvers with unrifled barrels. It is not certain, because no one really knew, but it seems there is no way to make these homemade guns legal. Some ammunition comes from the black market but gun owners claim there is really little of that.

To an extent, numbers of guns allowed on an import license are tied to numbers of guns already sold by the shop. In theory at least, a shop can start the process of acquiring another import quota when they can prove substantial sales under a previous quota.

As a general rule, 25 revolvers, 25 automatic pistols, 50 shotguns and 35 .22 carbines are allowed at any one time on a single import license.

It usually takes from 31 to 45 days to secure the next import license. At times military authorities simply and arbitrarily shut down importation processes. Nothing can be done then but wait for a change of heart.

The cost of import licenses is said to be "modest." Modest, for an Ecuadorian making about $80 per week is probably about $20.

Processes of importing guns and securing an individual gun-owner's permit are closely linked in Ecuador. Individuals start their portion of the process by going to their local Ministry of Defense office. Those in remote areas mail to Ministry offices in Quito or Guayaquil or take the bus to appear in person. In many cases there are local convenient army offices that can handle the application.

The following documents must also be attached to individual forms requesting a firearms owner's certificate, starting with copies of a regular Ecuadorian citizen ID card.

Next, copies of a military service card. All Ecuadorian males must register for the draft. Because of ongoing severe budget restraints, relatively few men are taken into military service. But the registration card is part of the application process.

In theory, women can own guns in Ecuador but this being a basically macho society, it is often not that simple. More on this issue when we get to mandatory psychological examinations.

Copies of your police record are also needed. It must be absolutely clean or no permit will be issued.

Two separate, distinct, signed and notarized letters of recommendation and good conduct, executed by reputable upstanding citizens finish the set. Said certificates must include signer's exact address and phone numbers. These references will be contacted by army officials.

It takes about 15 days for an application to be suitably vetted and returned by the authorities. Cost is $12.60 per applicant. These gun-owners' permits must be renewed every two years.

After going through all of this and receiving approval to continue, applicants then must submit to a psychological exam administered by an army doctor. One gun-store owner claimed that this was fairly routine and that applicants could easily be coached up to correct, acceptable conduct and answers. Another was extremely bitter about this portion of the process, claiming applicants were frequently turned down for no apparent reason. This after going to all the time, trouble and expense of completing the first section of the application.

By implication it was suggested that single women who plead self-defense or wish to target shoot with pistols were frequently flunked by macho army psychological officers who did not take kindly to self-reliant women.

At this point import permits and gun-owners' permits for specific weapons intersect. Licensed gun-store owners may import some (with appropriate caliber and model restrictions) pistols, revolvers and carbines of specific make and model for qualified buyers. This takes a long, long time but frequently this is what happens.

Gun-store owners register a specific gun to a valid gun-owner's permit. This registration places that gun on the holder's permit and withdraws that gun from the store's official import inventory. Registrations are cross-checked against import and owner's documents by Ministry of Defense officials.

Gun-store owners complain bitterly about painstakingly slow processes by which army bureaucrats evaluate their import documents and sales records. Whenever import and sales records fail to exactly match, processes grind to an immediate halt.

Valid legal ownership implies the right to carry loaded, concealed, or whatever. Also, those with valid gun-owner's cards can privately buy and sell arms among themselves, so long as the guns are registered by military officials to gun-owner's permits, as appropriate.

Legal ex pats can own guns in Ecuador so long as they comply with all of the licensing processes and restrictions on models and calibers.

Ammunition sales in Ecuador are similarly convoluted. Supposedly, gun-owner's permit holders can purchase whatever ammo they wish in whatever quantity they can afford so long as gun-store clerks accept that the purchaser has a valid need and use. All this is tempered by the fact that the army seldom approves importation of more than 100 rounds of ammo per gun! Gun shops may, subject to official whim and outright caliber restrictions, apply to import additional separate quantities of ammo. Stores frequently check only the gun-owner's authorization card before selling ammo. They infrequently match a listed gun to caliber of ammo purchased, making the process slightly less convoluted.

But like all things Ecuadorian, it isn't that simple. It isn't for nothing that the Wall Street Journal, in conjunction with the Heritage Foundation, ranks Ecuador tie for 114 in their Index of Economic Freedom for the world's nations under the category of "mostly unfree!"

The Ecuadorian military has a division that assembles small arms ammunition from imported components. These folks enjoy a monopoly selling shotgun and some pistol ammunition to gun stores and shooting clubs. Occasionally permission is granted to some gun stores to import specific kinds of ammo not offered by the military.

Permission to import is only ever granted for what are said to be "critical needs," based on creative descriptions of ammo not otherwise available from the military.

Examples are 12-gauge 1-1/4 oz. loads of Number Six shot needed to control depredating seagulls and cormorants away from shrimp ponds, and for use in international skeet competition. Since the military does not manufacture this ammo and there is a good reason to own it, importation may be sanctioned.

Skeet and trap, target and combat shooting clubs often become channels of distribution for ammunition. Once established, these channels are said to be effective—however, they can be very expensive and as slow as an arthritic great aunt at times.

Permission to bring in reloading supplies is only rarely extended by Ecuador's military. Some claim there is absolutely no reloading while others say that through the years they occasionally reload pistol and shotgun ammo. Generally, it is just as easy and inexpensive to import loaded ammo. Why bother with components, one informant said.

There is no interest at all in Ecuador in original firearms design work, nor any indigenous industry in guns and ammo.

Illegal guns are thought to be only a minor problem in Ecuador. In years past, before tougher gun laws in the U.S. took effect, some few illegal guns may have come into the country via cargo vessels coming to Ecuador for sugar and bananas. Today a few illegal guns may possibly come in from Nicaragua. Although Colombia is said to be bristling with guns, very few find their way to Ecuador by that route.

An AR-15 is worth at least $2,500 in Colombia, an AK-47 $1,500 or a UZI $2,000 we were told. These high prices scare away Ecuadorians who have little to no use for such guns. Prices of these common assault rifles are inflated by access to easy drug money in Colombia. This is surprising since the street value of an AK-47 in not-too-distant Nicaragua is still only $30.

A few illegal guns are used by subsistence hunters in very remote areas. These were not thought of as being much of an issue. Travelers frequently see people in remote areas carrying .22 rifles or cap lock, muzzle-loading shotguns. Military people pass them on the road without paying much attention.

Ecuador is an extremely interesting, diverse, inexpensive place to live. Climate up in the high Andes is delightful. Double cheeseburgers are a dollar, and a ham and egg breakfast is also a dollar. Lots to see and do hereabouts, but paranoia about a few light civilian small arms falling into the hands of Colombian guerillas cancels out much of this charm.

Especially given that Colombians flush with drug dollars can and do shop worldwide for their guns.

All of this places virtually insurmountable burdens on anyone who wishes to target shoot, hunt, or protect their families, persons or property in Ecuador.

Chapter Forty-One
Poland
World Rank: 46 • Firearm Freedom 28%

Certainly the most shocked and disbelieving responses I received in the course of securing many shocked and disbelieving responses to questions regarding private gun ownership occurred in Poland.

Eventually we collected all of the necessary information by visiting a Polish gun shop in the city of Lodz, but we first put our questions to an English speaking University student guide at the Auschwitz memorial/museum/monument.

"I find the fact that anyone outside of the police and military would want to own a gun shocking," he said. "It's just not done in Poland. I don't know of a single person who privately owns a gun."

The fellow went on to say that he couldn't imagine any valid reasons for private gun ownership although he vaguely recalled an uncle, now long deceased who he thought was a hunter.

I pointed out that an armed citizenry was an effective deterrent to being overrun by hostile powers—an obviously frequent occurrence in even recent Polish history.

"Yes, but if anyone wants to occupy us, there is little our small nation of 45 million could do to stop them," he replied.

"Not an immediate given," I responded. "History suggests otherwise. What about the Warsaw ghetto wherein perhaps fifteen hundred determined Jews, armed only with pistols, captured rifles, grenades and a few submachine guns, held off the full prideful German army in all its fury for 28 days?

"Or what about the Warsaw uprising? Like the Jews in the Ghetto, these lightly armed Polish partisans held a very upset, determined German army in limbo for several months. Tragically, promised support from the Russian army never materialized, leading to the destruction of these brave but naïve irregular Polish fighters. (Both situations our friendly guide personally detailed to Auschwitz visitors.)

"And there is also Kibbutz Yad Mordechai in Israel near the Gaza wherein no more than 100 mostly amateur partisan farmers armed with personal weapons held off the entire Egyptian army including tanks, infantry, air support and artillery. The six days they delayed the Egyptians allowed formation of an Israeli army and ultimately the state of Israel itself!

"Or what about those lightly armed partisans on the Island of Crete who refused to capitulate and finally destroyed the German army entire paratrooper force?"

While later recapping the Crete imbroglio, German General Kurt Student said that the German army expected civilian citizen resistance on Crete to be similar to what they previously found in Poland, France and the Netherlands. 'Nobody got out their private weapons and took pot shots at our army,' Student said. Instead, his paratroopers landed in a maelstrom of hostile citizen small-arms fire.

"There are also examples of the Nez Perce Indian War, wherein incidents are on record of approximately 30 Nez Perce warriors stalling the advance of 630 or more U.S. pony soldiers (at the Battle of the Clearwater), or our American Revolution and, more recently and closer to home for Poland, the Russian-Finnish Winter War in 1939, as well as the Boer War, just to name a few."

"Yes, yes, you make excellent points," our young university student guide responded, "but please understand that there are other serious considerations in Poland. Any private citizen found with a firearm, either by the Germans during the War or later by Russian occupiers, was summarily put against the wall and shot. "We still carry that baggage," he pointed out.

"But (and this was a big 'but' in this fellow's eyes) unlike many of your examples, Poland has no natural, readily defended borders and terrain." This is an old, old, tired argument often raised even suggesting that the country of Poland had no historic reason to exist. Better to parcel out its bits and pieces to its neighbors, some historians and statesmen have seriously suggested.

Poland lies to the east of Germany, south of the little stand-alone piece of Russia on the Baltic Sea, and Lithuania, Belarus and the Ukraine to the east, and Czech and Slovak republics to the south. Relatively large for Europe, Poland is the size of the state of New Mexico. Poland profits immensely from its twelve-month ice-free ports on the Baltic Sea to its north.

Poles say they have few natural boundaries. However, Poland does have the Carpathian Mountains to the south and the Oder and Neisse rivers to the west. Internally there are a great many large rivers, worn hills, lakes, marshes and swamps that would make controlling the country by force a real headache, especially when defended by a highly motivated, mobile and elusive militia.

Seven months of the year maneuvering armor or extensive infantry on Poland's well-watered deep, mucky plains would be a challenge. Perhaps impossible.

Although our friendly yet shocked university student guide didn't know about them, there are some legal gun-owning Polish citizens, as opposed to what is thought to be substantial illegal ownership of leftover WW II weapons. Because Poles are so suspicious and tight-lipped, this ownership is subject to wide, often wild, and perhaps irrational speculation.

That's understandable, especially remaining from the Polish Soviet era, making any conversations and opinions regarding illegal guns painful. Only a private military museum owner/collector near Wejherowo who had a great yardful of Soviet-era towable 37-mm guns, mortars and T-34 & 55 Russian tanks would discuss that subject.

Information that follows regarding private legal ownership comes from interviews with gun-store owners and a military-surplus store owner dealer in the Polish city of Lodz.

Properly papered Polish citizens can legally own all kinds of pistols and revolvers. No restrictions on caliber or magazine capacity, so long as they can convince issuing authorities they have a valid security or target-shooting purpose for ownership. They are also allowed single- and double-barreled shotguns of any gauge. Pump and semi-auto shotguns are allowed only to those who can convince issuing authorities they require these guns for security purposes.

Bolt action and single-shot rifles are permitted for both hunting and for target shooting.

In all cases, new owners must convince the police that they have a valid reason for ownership. In the case of hunting, pistol target, shotgun clay pigeon and rifle target shooting, this is said to usually not be that difficult. Rural people have an easier time with both security and hunting arguments. Membership in appropriate clubs (hunting, target shooting or clay pigeons, etc.) help city people immensely, demonstrating one is serious about gun ownership. Cost for membership is from $70 to $150 per year. It's expensive for the average Pole making the national average of perhaps $12,000 per year, but not bureaucratically difficult.

Pistol target shooters may be required to leave their guns stored at the club. Shotgun and rifle owners have few problems keeping their guns and ammo at home; only that they be locked in a steel case secured to the wall and floor. Numerous steel gun lockers are on sale at what appear to be extremely modest prices, from $30 to $80.

Owners of pistols kept for security or target shooting are limited to two or three guns total. No limits on rifles or shotguns are enforced other than convincing authorities of a need and of affording them.

Visitors and ex-pats residing in Poland can legally bring guns into the country. Mostly these are hunters from Germany and relatively wealthy retiring ex-pats from the U.S. Our informants knew of several individuals who had imported guns into Poland but did not know the exact procedure.

Guns and ammo are extremely expensive in Poland, as a result of high import taxes and the fact that most guns are high-priced, hand-made Austrian or German models. Ammunition we observed came mostly from Scandinavia. As mentioned, *per capita* income is about $12,000. Relatively low but perhaps mightily obscured by the great numbers of Poles working in the black economy in nearby wealthy EU countries.

New modern Glock pistols are priced from $1,000 to $1,350 each. All rifles and shotguns in Polish stores are similarly high-priced.

Absolutely no machine guns, submachine guns, assault rifles or any other modern military look-alike rifles or shotguns allowed. Some silencers are apparently built in rural machine shops, but these are said to be highly illegal.

Polish citizens start their process of gun ownership by going to their nearest police headquarters where they fill out a "several page" gun-owner's application. Fees are $100. Permits, when issued are valid for three years.

Next the police satisfy themselves that this specific applicant has a valid reason to own. Apparently they are not usually overly concerned about this reason. As mentioned, club membership, need to hunt, or personal security usually are sufficient.

Upon submission of one's papers, the police check the applicant's police record. Not a difficult or lengthy process since, like all Europeans, Poles must carry a national-identity card.

Next a doctor's examination is scheduled. Although psychological testing makes up a bit of this process, Polish doctors mostly look for an absence of drug use, good eyesight and lack of physical impairments that might make gun handling difficult or unsafe for that individual. Cost of the exam is about $200 plus applicants must pay another $135 for a separate health certificate.

Concentration camp museum in Poland

Snow-covered Auschwitz, Poland, now a memorial to and
museum of atrocities committed here by Germany in WWII.
Our English-speaking guide made a great issue of his firm
belief that there was absolutely no reason for private
citizens to own guns. Standing at the very reason for such
ownership, and knowledgably lecturing about the place, he
could not connect the dots, and thought our views were
absurd. He told us that people in Poland could not even
legally obtain guns, demonstrating not only a severe lack of
understanding of the issues, but ignorance of the actual
situation in his own country. His English was impeccable
but his qualifications for the job left room for doubt.

Gun store in Krakow, Poland

Poland has about one gun store per major city. This reflects
the fact that while private gun ownership in Poland is
possible, it isn't easy. The shop shown here is in Krakow.
On the window you can see a sign advertising availability of
ammunition, and top-selling brands Smith & Wesson,
Beretta, Walther, Glock, Sig Sauer and Hechler & Koch,
quite an international mix of products.

All of this paper goes back to the local police. Approval takes about six weeks. On approval, new gun owners go to their friendly local gun shop to make a purchase. There are few gun shops in Poland. Larger cities may have one or two each, but few are seen in rural areas.

From the gun shop it's back to the police station with a receipt from the gun shop. This receipt allows registration of the gun to that specific gun-owner's permit. Back at the shop, new owners can finally pick up their purchase. Procedures as more guns are purchased are a bit simpler; however each gun must be registered to the person's gun-owner's certificate.

Private gun sales are permitted between holders of valid gun-owner certificates who go to their local police office to register the transaction. Black powder, replica rifles, shotguns and pistols built on 1850 or earlier patterns are exempt from all registration and licensing requirements.

No limit on amounts of ammo owners can purchase so long as they can sustain the high prices. All ammo except shot shells is sold one round at a time. Some Polish stores sell nothing but ammo. Single .22 LR rounds cost about $1 each, .308 and 7x57 rounds, for example, are $1.60 each. Cheaper boxes of 25 Finnish or Russian made 12-gauge hunting shot shells sell for about $8. Ammo is sold only for guns registered on the buyer/owner's permit. Officials check the stores' inventory and sales records regularly, we were told.

Absolutely no reloading is done, either by clubs or by individuals. Components are not available and authorities are said to be generally hostile to importation of components and to the concept of reloading.

Authorization of a pistol for security reasons implies the right to carry concealed. Judging by the large inventory of pistols in some Polish gun shops, quite a few pistols are being sold for personal security reasons.

Visitors driving around Poland see a great many deer grazing out in the fields, as well as the occasional fox. Deer blinds up on 16-foot stilts are common. Apparently it isn't just German hunters coming here for an inexpensive hunt, but Polish deer hunters as well, using the blinds.

As our Auschwitz guide pointed out, gun ownership is not common in Poland. Those who go through the lengthy, relatively expensive process leading to ownership often keep the fact very much to themselves. Incidents of violent crime are said to be infrequent in Poland. When there is crime, it tends to be minor like padding a restaurant bill or adding it up incorrectly, snatching an unwatched parcel, or other sneak-thievery such as pick-pocketing. At one time, car thefts were common in Poland. Like public drunkenness and prostitution, these sorts of events seem to have diminished dramatically as Polish society moves away from their Soviet-era-induced poverty to one where citizens have hope of a better life.

Pity, however, that the Poles have not seen the need to develop a well-armed citizen militia similar to Finland, Israel or Switzerland. It would go a long, long way toward ensuring their place in the world in a free and unencumbered manner.

Chapter Forty-Two
Lithuania
World Rank: 30 • Firearm Freedom 44%

Of all cultures worldwide, the three small ones comprising the Baltic nations probably have suffered most at the hand of cruel occupiers.

Start virtually any place in their history. Seventeen hundred and ten, for instance. Napoleon crossed Lithuania with his giant army and supply train on his way to battle the Russians. Napoleon's objective was Moscow, rather than anything or anybody in Lithuania. As a result of already past centuries of irrationally brutal Russian suppression, Lithuanian citizens welcomed the French as liberators.

But the hapless French soon suffered tri-parte disasters of disease, fatigue and military defeat. Napoleon seemed extremely interested in freeing the Lithuanians. As a kind of intersection of apology and explanation, knowing full well the absolute hell the Russians would soon inflict on helpless Lithuanians for their little part in the French invasion, Napoleon said, upon leaving Lithuania, "Unfortunately the Lithuanian people will not be free until they have rifles in their hands."

Recently discovered mass graves near Vilnius, Lithuania's capital, contain the remains of more than 50,000 French soldiers, dead from exposure and disease rather than hostile fire. Reportedly, Russian re-occupiers tried to duplicate these numbers using Lithuanian peasants. Depopulation was sufficiently severe that historians marvel Lithuanian culture even survived.

Geographically as well as culturally, Lithuania is a real anomaly. The country borders Poland to the south and the little, stand-alone piece of Russia known as Kaliningrad to the southwest. Large parts of the country, including some excellent harbors, border the Baltic Sea. Belarus, another mysterious little country, lies to the east. Driving across pint-sized Lithuania takes three hours north to south and perhaps four hours east to west. In so doing, one must be very cautious not to stray into hostile Russia or Belarus. Corridors are narrow and often ill-marked.

One could only wish that Lithuanians really understood the role of an armed citizenry in remaining free, especially for a tiny country with few natural barriers. Yet they do not seem to do so. Instead they place great reliance on the good will of the Russians, world opinion and on associations such as NATO and the EU.

Private gun ownership is allowed but not encouraged. Some clandestine weapons remain from WW II and the breakup of the Soviet empire but, like Poland, Lithuanians are heavily inclined not to keep and use guns. Recognized links between maintaining their freedom and a gun-owning, gun-knowledgeable warrior culture are virtually non-existent.

There are at least three large gun shops in Vilnius, Lithuania's capital, and several in outlying cities and villages. Local holiday schedules and language barriers made gathering information more difficult than virtually any other country. We were finally able to interview a gun-store owner in Zarasai (far eastern Lithuania) in German. Our German is borderline. His was not that good.

What follows is perhaps sketchy but the best available under difficult circumstances. Gun-owner's certificates are required for most of those who wish to legally own guns in Lithuania. Of the Baltic States, Lithuania is perhaps most liberal regarding firearms papers. Perhaps there is some faint recall of Napoleon's statement on the subject.

No papers are required for rifles and pistols (probably just single shot models) that use rim-fire ammo up to 6 mm. This is almost entirely .22-caliber guns firing rounds we call .22 BB or CB caps and perhaps .22 shorts. Not much military or defensive application here.

After that, with a gun-owner's certificate issued by the police, citizens can own as many shotguns, rifles and pistols as their personal finances will allow. Our informant owned seven guns. He knew of another man who also owned seven. Pump and semi-auto shotguns are allowed in special circumstances (perhaps security). Otherwise it's just singles and doubles.

Bolt-action and single-shot rifles are permitted in virtually all calibers. We observed .30-06, .270, 7.62x39, .22-250, 8x57 Mauser, .300 Win Mag and dozens of additional calibers in stores available for over-the-counter purchase. Some of this ammo would be classified by Americans as collectors' grade.

Oddly, gun stores in Lithuania tend to specialize. Some sell only ammo, others only pistols and revolvers or rifles or shotguns. There were only a few stores in a few cities, but the country is so small this is of little concern.

Judging by pistol ammo on display for sale, large-caliber pistols of virtually all kinds are permitted and commonly owned. Sales of ammo are one round at a time. Up to 200 rounds per day can legally be purchased, but retaining more than 200 rounds at home is a no-no. Police checks may be made of the stores' sales records, but not sufficiently often to constitute a problem. Ammo is sold only for guns listed on one's gun-owner's permit.

No machine guns, machine pistols, assault rifles, semi-auto rifles or silencers are ever authorized.

Securing a gun-owner's permit from the police can be rigorous— sufficiently so that many potential gun owners are discouraged away from the process. A check is made of the applicant's police record and a doctor's exam is required. The exam is for physical disabilities and eyesight. After this, applicants must pass a gun knowledge and safety exam. This exam is said to be exhaustive and very tough to pass. Although he owned several guns, our informant couldn't recall the price of this application, examination and testing procedure.

It takes from one week to one month. As is the case in many other countries, all guns must be registered by the police onto one's gun-owner's certificate. There is also a requirement that all newly purchased guns be left with the police for ballistics tests recorded against that specific gun. Private sales between certificated gun owners are possible so long as they take the gun to the police to have it officially removed from the seller's firearms-owner's certificate and recorded on the buyer's certificate. We don't know if costly ballistic testing must be redone at this time.

Apparently a reason for ownership must always be provided. In a mostly rural agricultural society such as Lithuania, this is not seen as much of a hurdle. Hunting and security are valid reasons, as is target shooting in the big cities. Joining one of the few in-country target-shooting or hunting clubs may help, but is not seen as being necessary. Passing the gun safety and knowledge exam is the hurdle.

Reloading is frequently done, using mostly homemade tools, using cheap but inferior Polish and Russian powder and Scandinavian primers. One can see Russian, Swedish, Finnish and American bullets and shot in store display cases. No license or other restrictions exist for those who wish to reload. Little help comes from printed literature or the gun store, and components and tools seem meager to crude. Little to nothing is published on reloading in Lithuanian.

Visitors do not see duck and deer blinds in Lithuania. However they
don't see many hotels or, for that matter, signs signaling that "this is a
hotel" either. A strange culture this, and stranger still that links
between gun ownership and freedom fail to be recognized.

Chapter Forty-Three
Latvia
World Rank: 29 • Firearm Freedom 45%

A great new gleaming and impressive modern museum, appropriately
identified as The Museum of Occupation 1940-1991, lies right across
the street from the national tourist office in downtown Riga. Riga is the
capital city of little (25,000 square miles) Latvia.

It's a tough monument to miss and Latvians definitely do not want you
to miss seeing it. Tremendous amounts of time and treasure are
invested here, especially for such a small country with obviously
limited resources.

Inside one finds large collections of documents, photos and displays
memorializing atrocities perpetuated by the Germans and Soviets on
this humble little collection of people. Like Lithuania, the Soviet
Russians simply issued a decree in 1940 ending almost 21 years of
independence. Then, within a year, as a result of the German invasion
of Russia, Latvia was occupied by the Nazis.

After WW II, Stalin simply kept the helpless little state, claiming it was
part of the Soviet sphere of influence. Spineless world leaders, tired of
war, cruelly went along with this hoax. Latvians who objected went
immediately to death camps. Another factor was that the Latvians
initially welcomed the Germans, because they hoped they would be
better than the Soviets. As a result, the U.S. and U.K. had little interest
in standing up for Latvia against the Soviets.

All of this is graphically set forth in their Museum of Occupation,
including a reconstruction of a Soviet barracks of the type used to hold
political prisoners awaiting death in the gulag. Details of the large,
cast-iron pot replicas used as common toilets by the severely crowded,
malnourished Latvian prisoners are especially grim.

Perhaps because Dresden and Berlin in Germany are less than a day's
drive away, Latvians could see the end result of German aggression
first hand. Exact numbers are elusive, but some historians claim more
civilians were killed during Allied bombing raids in those cities than in

Hiroshima or Nagasaki. It creates some sense of closure regarding German oppression, which isn't found with the Russians.

Older Latvians still can and do speak some German. Younger Latvians learn English in school as they make valiant attempts to become part of the modern commercial world. Members of the large left-behind Russian community in Latvia speak only Russian. Most just refuse to learn another language or to adapt to another, more vigorous and active culture.

Russians in Latvia, along with their attached culture, are perceived as being indolent, stupid and inferior. As a result, Russians in Latvia are treated as distant third-class citizens. There is little forgiveness or closure with these folks, perhaps reflected in the fact that their (Soviet) repression lasted several decades and was much more recent.

Does all of this impact Latvia's national gun laws? Fortunately we were able to find a young English speaking clerk in a gun shop in Riga, the Latvian capital. He handled our interview so crisply and succinctly that it almost seemed as though he had done this before.

Most Americans have no clue regarding Latvia's location. In spite of tremendous—almost unbelievable—economic strides, Latvia is not a major player in world commerce or economy. Think north of Poland, sandwiched between the Baltic Sea and Russia, Latvia is the third of the pocket-sized Baltic republics (the others are Lithuania and Estonia.)

Agriculture—principally dairy and livestock raising—has been Latvia's principal economic activity. Since independence, major highways have been built and great strides made toward industrialization. As a result, GNP and personal incomes have risen rocket-like. Including Russians who seem to prefer fishing to working and earn virtually nothing, *per capita* incomes are estimated at an astounding $14,500. Not to forget, they started virtually at zero 18 years ago.

Significantly, a $14,500 *per capita* income seems to be about the threshold wherein a society leaves its Third World subsistence living standard. At this point, citizens begin to think more about quality of life, including the environment.

Latvia does not have a gun culture to the extent of some countries. But for Europeans who generally seem irrationally fearful of firearms, Latvians are fairly liberal regarding private ownership.

Latvian citizens and resident aliens can own pistols, rifles and shotguns. Their resident alien designation is an important one. Many Russian ex-pats in Latvia fall in this category. Some eastern European countries even prohibit Russian speakers from owning either guns or real property! Latvia is a bit more relaxed in this regard.

Full machine guns are never authorized but under some circumstances submachine guns are allowed, for high-risk bodyguards, bank guards, private airport guards and the like. It is sometimes possible to convince authorizing agencies of this need.

There is no limit on the number of rifles and shotguns private citizens may own. Pistols are limited to ten per person unless one secures a special collector's permit. There is some thought that this special collector's permit allows citizens with extensive collections of WW II pickups to come in under a legal framework, and to provide for firearms design work similar to the Finnish experience to go forward.

At any rate, special collector's s permits are given in Latvia. All are issued on a case-by-case basis.

Application for a gun-owner's certificate is made at one's local police office. Applicants must be at least 21 years old and the cost is about $50. An immediate police check is made of the applicant's crime, alcohol, drug and driving record. Relatively minor violations do not count with the exception of drunken driving. This may be another effort to quietly freeze out Russian applicants who are collectively most likely to offend in this area.

At this time both knowledge and physical exams are scheduled. Doctors charge about $60 for their medical inspection. The knowledge exam will cost about $50. Background checks to determine if one has a history of drug use or alcoholism, as well as a psychological and physical fitness exam, constitute the medical portion of this procedure.

There are four hundred possible questions on the knowledge exam. These questions cover gun safety, ballistics, gun design, game habits and first aid. Of the 400 possible questions, only four will eventually appear on the final exam. All must be answered perfectly. Because applicants can study the questions before taking the exam, this portion of the procedure is not seen as overly rigorous.

At that point the new gun-owner's permit is taken to a gun shop along with an approval form from the police to purchase a gun or guns of a specific type. Approvals for those with a gun-owner's certificate are easily given for hunting and target shooting, including rifles, shotguns and pistols.

Permission for pistols for security reasons are a bit less routine but are frequently given. Latvians can legally own any pistols up to 9mm for both security and for target shooting. There is no requirement or necessity for joining a target-shooting club.

Membership in a hunting club is not necessary for ownership, but a great advantage if one is serious about actually bagging game. Hunting licenses cost from zero to about $20 depending on the quarry. Hunters who agree to go after wolves, for instance, may be paid a bounty as an encouragement, in addition to receiving a free hunting license. Bear hunting in the Baltics is a major activity.

Makes, models or calibers of rifles and shotguns are unrestricted with two significant caveats. No military look-alikes or assault rifles are allowed, and any semi-auto commercial shotguns or rifles, including .22 rimfire rifles, are limited to three-shot magazine capacity.

Serial numbers, make, model and a ballistic record of the gun are recorded to the gun-owner's file at the police office. Latvia has only three large cities including Riga, the capital. There are two stores in Riga that sell guns and ammo. That's all for the entire country. Applications for a gun-owner's certificate and registration of one's guns can be done locally, but all purchases must be done in Riga. It is a maximum three-hour drive from outlying areas.

Concealed carry is implied in a pistol permit, extended for security reasons. Silencers are never authorized.

Latvian gun owners must store their guns at home in a special steel gun cabinet. It's as if some sort of steel gun cabinet manufacturers' lobby got through to all of the Baltic republic gun-law writers. All require steel gun cabinets.

One sees a huge variety of assorted calibers and gauges of imported ammo on offer in Latvian gun shops. No restrictions on caliber or gauge are apparent.

Private citizens who wish to buy or sell private guns do so by taking their gun or guns, and their previously issued gun-owners' certificates to the local police where transfers of ownership are officially recorded. It isn't known if expensive ballistic tests must be rerun on these private guns being transferred.

All ammo purchases are recorded to the gun-owner's certificate. As is common in the region, only ammo for weapons on one's gun-owner's certificate can legally be purchased. Citizens holding only security pistol authorizations may purchase only 500 rounds per day. No lead bullets, hollow points, wad cutters or expanding rounds are allowed for security purposes. As a result, most Latvian pistol owners seek out authorization for both security and target shooting, since there are no restrictions on bullet composition or design used for target shooting.

Curiously, Latvian police cannot carry off duty. Opinions of residents of the three republics are that the Latvian authorities, including their national police, are the most corrupt. Our experience does not suggest such, but bribery in Latvia is said to be common.

No limit exists on amounts of ammo one may purchase for hunting or target shooting. Ammo is sold one round at a time and is moderately high priced. Especially for common .308, .22-250 or 7.62x39 cartridges, we observed prices in the range of $1.40 to $1.60 each. Records of ammo purchased are maintained in the gun shops should the police require them.

Hand loading is permitted in Latvia without bureaucratic hindrance or problems. Buy your powder, shot, bullets and primers off the shelf in the gun store. These stores also carry a large assortment of fireworks including rockets and firecrackers.

Reloading powder on sale is either a very cheap Russian variety or a very expensive Swedish one. Primers, bullets and shot are all international brands familiar to American reloaders.

There are said to be large numbers of illegal military-type guns and ammunition simply abandoned by the Russians when Latvia reasserted its independence August 21, 1991. These are said "not to be a problem." When used legally, the authorities tend to "overlook them," which sounds similar to Crete. Hold your breath and hope for the best.

Latvian gun ownership in general seems somewhat more relaxed than in many other places, especially in central Europe and England. Yet they do have their onerous gun-owners' certificates, as well as universal registration. To make matters worse, there are no legal assault rifles in private hands, and there is very little recognition of the role private firearms play in holding down violent crime and in keeping their country free.

Chapter Forty-Four
Estonia
World Rank: 28 • Firearm Freedom 47%

According to an in-depth as well as detailed Heritage Foundation analysis of 155 countries around the world, little insignificant Estonia is the fourth freest country on Earth. Results of this remarkable analysis were published in the January 4, 2005 *Wall Street Journal,* partly explaining Estonia's remarkable transformation from a moribund socialistic economy as late as 1990 to one of the most vibrant, growing economies on the planet.

Personal incomes have risen from just a few hundred dollars annually when they left the Soviet Union to the equivalent of $14,300 today. Estonia's growth rate is a remarkable and virtually unbelievable 6.0%

per annum—a rate that virtually any other country in Europe or the Americas has failed to exceed or even duplicate. Statistically, Estonia's population, gross national product and personal yearly incomes all seem to have recently fallen slightly. But knowledgeable people say this reflects better, more honest record keeping rather than economic retrenchment or malaise.

Estonia is on the move. Investment capital is pouring in. Bright lights are on. Store shelves and showrooms are stuffed with desirable imported and domestic capital and consumer goods. Citizens seem to be working two or even three jobs.

But all may not be well in this economic paradise.

A book of this nature on private firearms ownership in foreign countries may not be the platform for this, nor may it be remembered perhaps when the time comes, but based on their rapid accumulation of wealth and their draconian gun laws, my prediction is that Estonia will not long persist as a free country.

Any tiny country (such as Estonia with 17,462 square miles), having absolutely no natural defensible boundaries or terrain, must develop a warrior culture, evident from a universal military conscription and training for both men and women. Estonia is very similar to Israel, Finland and Switzerland in this regard. Because Estonia cannot support even a small standing army—not enough people and money—instead they should be thinking about a citizens' militia.

After six months of compulsory firearms, demolitions, escape and evasion, cover and concealment, and survival training, new trainees— including women—should be sent home with their assault rifles and a significant cache of ammunition. Nobody would mess with them under those circumstances. Guaranteed—in twenty years there would still be an Estonia.

But, it's not happening. Instead they are comfortable relying on treaties with the EU and NATO, UN guarantees and current friendly relations with their neighbors. Like Poland, Estonia threw up its collective hands in resignation, claiming there is little their tiny nation of 1.3 million could do to stop an aggressor anyway. Why even contemplate trying...

Besides, good rational Estonians respond, "who will attack us?" Weakened Russia? Finland, Germany, Poland, Canada, Mexico or any other currently ridiculous examples you wish to suggest? To be sure, these and other surrounding countries are not currently warlike and expansionist. However, these matters have a way of changing very rapidly. One would think there is a lesson from history. If Estonians are learning from history, we could not detect it during the considerable time we were there gathering information for this chapter.

So where, exactly, is this little place? It's the northernmost of the three Baltic republics, bordered to the west by the Baltic Sea, to the north by the Bay of Finland, to the east by Russia and to the south by Latvia. Lake Peipus, a huge inland fresh-water body, borders to the east. Great economic activity bustles here, as both the Russians and Estonians race to exploit their half.

While their gun laws seem restrictive and convoluted, there are at least four gun stores in Tallinn, the capital, as well as several reported in outlying areas. There must be some remnants of a gun culture in Estonia to support this many retail stores.

We visited three gun shops located within Tallinn. Two of them were staffed by English speakers. A Russian with absolutely no interest in helping clerked the third store. Not much information here other than the fact that we observed a great many modern pistols and revolvers in his display case, a tremendous variety of ammunition and semi-auto rifles and shotguns in his racks. There was also a rare Mauser schnellfeuer broom handle pistol for sale. Unfortunately we couldn't make the fellow understand that we would like to examine that pistol to determine the extent to which it was functional as well as its value.

Significantly, Russians in Estonia can legally own guns although, it is said, few do. This is because they don't commonly have sufficient income to afford such. Russians living in Estonia who do not speak Estonian (very much like Finnish) are not allowed to own real property. Other non-native, non-Estonian speakers including Americans, Germans, Finns and Swedes are allowed to own property. In fact, foreigners have bought up enough property to create something of a local land boom.

Feelings against Russian speakers run high to extremely high, bordering on irrational prejudice, even 18 years after independence.

Estonians willing to install a special secure gun room in their homes or garages, outfitted with steel doors and window bars, alarm systems, smoke detectors and heavy masonry walls can own as many guns as they wish and can afford. Others who want to make do with cheaper heavy steel gun safes are limited to a total of eight different guns. All must be carefully locked safely away, except for one that may remain conveniently located outside the steel box for use for personal security.

Estonians may own commercial rifles, shotguns and pistols without restrictions as to caliber or model. Military and assault rifles are okay so long as they have magazines limited to a three-shot capacity. This goes for semi-auto and pump shotguns too—only three shots allowed.

Pistols and revolvers of all types and calibers are allowed. Silencers are sometimes authorized for target shooting only, never for security use.

Estonia gun store

Estonia, the little Baltic country finally released from
Russian tyranny in 1999, needs to have many more guns in
private hands if it is to fend off potential aggressors in the
future. This is one of four gun shops the author visited in
Tallinn, the capital. Note the old blackened snow on the
ground as author Grupp dons a glove against the cold.

Uniquely, laser sights are absolutely forbidden. Pistol security authorizations include concealed carry. However, those carrying concealed must carry unloaded. Yes, it's strange, but reportedly part of Estonian law.

No live submachine guns or machine guns are allowed, even for extreme risk situations. Collectors are said to sometimes be authorized dewat full-auto military guns, but no one knew the exact procedure or the extent to which these guns were dewatted.

Unfortunately Estonian security suffers mightily as a result of subjecting gun owners to the all too common procedure of requiring a gun-owner's certificate and then registering all legal guns to that certificate. All a hostile, malicious occupier need do is capture records of Estonian gun owners. With these in hand it would be a simple exercise to go door to door collecting up Estonians' best means of resistance.

"But we will destroy these records," is the official response. Yes, but average citizens won't know for sure if their records are actually destroyed. With gruesome details of the horribly cruel gulag fresh in their minds, few Estonians will risk keeping guns. Penalties for being caught with an illegal gun could easily be worse than simply being put against a wall and shot.

Estonians who wish to own guns start at their local police office where they pay a filing fee roughly equivalent to $70. They complete the required papers, said not to be overly lengthy or onerous, and submit these with a copy of their national identity card to the police.

On the basis of one's identity card, a search is made of the applicant's criminal and social file. No drug users or alcoholics need apply. Reportedly a total of three speeding tickets is sufficient to revoke or deny a gun-owner's certificate.

Applicants then go for a medical exam that reportedly looks for mental problems and physical infirmities, and checks for illicit drugs and alcohol use. Applicants' eyesight must be okay and no debilitating physical infirmities are allowed.

Simultaneously, representatives of the police visit the applicant's home to verify that secure storage rooms and/or steel storage cabinets pass muster. Applicants must have lived at their current location for at least 36 months. One gun owner with whom we spoke owned five guns which he had to keep in another gun owner's steel case simply because he had not yet lived at his current address for 36 months.

After that, applicants sit for a written examination (in Estonian). This examination tests for knowledge of guns, mechanisms, gun handling, safety, ammunition and first aid. Many Estonians applying for their first owner's certificate attend special courses (about 36 hours) wherein they receive training calculated to help pass this test.

Police approval can be given in as little as one month, but completing one's medical examination and passing the test may require several months. Gun-owner's certificates, when issued, are valid for five years. At expiration, gun owners must go through the entire expensive and time-consuming process all over again.

Every legal gun kept and owned by Estonians must be registered on the gun-owner's certificate. Estonians need a reason to own each and every gun. Valid reasons include hunting, target shooting including sporting clays, and security. Each gun and reason for ownership must be approved by local police.

Hunting and target shooting are the single easiest reasons for ownership. Permission for these activities is said to be relatively frequent, routine and easy. Hunters must join a separate hunting club as well as secure a separate hunting license as a means of validating their seriousness. Cost of a hunting license is about $80.

Gun-owner's card in hand, new buyers head to their local gun shop where they select the rifle, pistol or shotgun of their choice. Then it's back to the police station for final authorization to purchase. Once given by the police, owners must register make, model and serial number of the gun or guns they are purchasing.

Ammunition is sold only for guns listed on one's owner's certificate. All popular and some pretty obscure calibers are available in Estonia. Sales for pistols kept for security reasons are limited to 100 rounds per purchase. Hunters and target shooters are allowed 1,000 rounds per purchase. Nothing prevents purchasers with sufficient funds from waiting five minutes and making another purchase.

Extremely high prices for ammunition, usually sold only one round at a time, seem to limit quantities sold more than any statutory requirements. Military surplus ammo as well as inexpensive Russian ammo is available just 300 miles away in Russia. Unauthorized importation is, however, very illegal. All ammo is registered into a permanent store record which may be checked any time by the police.

Gun stores in Estonia sell bullets, primers, powder and shot as well as some tools for hand loading. There is no special license or requirements to purchase these. The one restriction—Estonians are supposed to never reload except for their own personal use.

People with whom we inquired about doing firearms research and design work in Estonia did not know for sure. Most reasoned that Estonian officials were interested in virtually all industrial economic development. It would depend on whom in the government one talked with and how they presented their case.

Estonian laws provide for licensing gun shops. Owners claim the process is rigorous and includes rules concerning secure rooms, bars on the windows and knowledge of gun laws.

Non-citizens living in Estonia can bring guns into the country provided they are legally permitted to own these same guns in their country of citizenship. At times, providing that proof is difficult.

Estonian authorities do not consider pistols to be offensive weapons of much concern to society. Rifles which can damage and kill over much longer ranges are considered to be more of a threat.

Illegal weapons left behind by Germans and Soviets are extremely common. Perhaps five illegal guns for ever two legal ones, they estimate. However, these guns do not seem to be seen as a security or peace-and-order threat. Dangers from old, cranky, land- and anti-personnel mines, as well as unexploded mortar and artillery rounds seem more pervasive to average Estonians. As in Finland, young Estonian males make a game of going out weekends to search remote areas for left behind guns, ammo and other military paraphernalia.

Reportedly incidents of crime including petty stuff such as pick-pocketing and car theft are rare and actually decreasing in Estonia. Bribery of officials, though not unheard of, is rare. New laws crack down ruthlessly on government corruption.

Citizens make more money more safely and easily working than they might do turning to crime, we were told. Even Old Russian mafia types find regular legitimate employment as security guards!

Estonia is a remarkable place. In spite of some absolutely horrible history and baggage, they are doing a commendable job building a vibrant, prosperous economy. Federal budgets are balanced. Rules and regulations, citizens claim, are being set aside in favor of a more free and open society. Even taxes are scheduled to drop significantly in the near future.

We can do little more than wish Estonia well while also looking on in cautious amazement as they defy the inevitable gravity of history—neglecting to live securely in a world characterized by thieving, thuggery and dishonest neighbors. Even humble, now peaceable, Sweden once occupied Estonia. Time will tell. And it probably won't be a great deal of time.

Chapter Forty-Five
Brazil

World Rank: 47 • Firearm Freedom 28%

Perhaps more than any other country, looking at and behind Brazil's gun laws is intensely instructive. Not so much for what lies on the surface, but for the many hidden agendas, political cross-currents and international maneuverings that lie behind and beneath. No other country we have examined has suffered from international meddling with their gun laws to the extent of Brazil.

For starters, Brazil's society has become one of the most corrupt on Earth. It's almost as if grubby, semi-literate, urban Mexican street cops are running and enforcing day-to-day legal affairs. Not only are average Brazilians likely to suffer direct, often brutal attacks on their persons or property, as frequently reported in their own media and travel books and from expatriate citizens, but also Brazil has some of the most poorly defined and poorly enforced property-ownership regulations on Earth. Repeated articles in the *Wall Street Journal* document the travails of property owners in Brazil. As a result, the modern industrial economic breakout, that Brazilians so eagerly look for and desire, is in constant jeopardy.

Farmers, for instance, cannot borrow money for modern machinery, seed or fertilizer because they don't know when government sponsored squatters may lay claim to their homes and land. Profitable world markets are there for the taking, but few Brazilians benefit. That there are no human rights without property rights, and little to no economic development without human rights, is writ large in Brazil.

Brazil is by far the largest country in South America. Half of the continent is Brazil. From north to south one can drive almost 3,000 miles without crossing a border. East to west it's exactly 2,691 miles. The eastern half of the country bordering the Atlantic Ocean is not all that far from Africa when the great South American bulge is included.

Incredibly rich natural resources characterize the nation. Abundant metal deposits including iron ore, copper and nickel, hydro power, vast, rich, farmable ground, forest products, fisheries, navigable rivers and many other resources are all available if only an acceptable, workable economic mentality were in place. Brazil even has potential as a source of jewelry-grade diamonds and is a world-class source of numerous gemstones.

Against huge odds, some few modern industrial developments have been initiated. Consider Embraer, the folks who produce commercial, military and executive jet aircraft for aviation markets worldwide.

Also weep for Brazil's arms and ammunition industry. They were budding world-class players till the Brazilian National Congress passed their "Statute of Disarmament" in 2003, effectively chopping domestic gun and ammo sales. Amadeo Rossi S.A. at Sao Leopoldo had a fine international reputation for their pistols, rifles and shotguns—wiped out in one day by the stroke of a politician's pen.

Like ammunition maker CBC (Companhia Brasileira de Cartuchos) at Ribeirao, Rossi tried to make it on export sales alone. Soon, however, the twin demons of no trial domestic market coupled with foolish, onerous export regulations made doing business impossible. Employment at these factories, as well as several others, is dramatically reduced in an economy that needs more, not less, jobs.

Brazilian gun laws should be viewed in three stages. First, the era before 2003. Second, the time up to their recent national referendum on total gun and ammunition ownership October 23, 2005. Third, what follows—including international ramifications of Brazil's anti-gun referendum.

Before looking in detail at the situation of Brazilian gun owners, one other economic fact is of tremendous importance. As, or perhaps more important than in any other country, Brazilian *per capita* income is estimated at about $8,100. Significantly here, *per capita* is an average.

Rural peasant farmers might earn only $250 per year, not including cereals, vegetable and meat produced on their tiny plots. Brazil is characterized by vast outbacks with little central government control. Because rural peasants don't own the land they farm, especially able and ambitious ones cannot grow economically.

Affluent middle-class city dwellers are estimated to earn, on average, little more than $20,000 each annually. There are also huge numbers of city people living in abject poverty in large, crime-ridden barrios who don't even make $250 each per year—including work in the underground economy! These folks can't even raise a garden or pig to supplement their meager incomes. Crime in these poverty-strewn barrios is world class.

An estimated two percent of Brazilians are easily classed as "stinking rich." These citizens afford whatever they wish, including whatever guns as we shall see. Poor victims of crime are left essentially helpless.

Information for this chapter comes from personal travel within the region, numerous accounts published in our popular media and from interviews with hunters, residents and ex-pats.

Prior to 2003, guns and ammunition were readily available to all citizens in Brazil with minimal to no paperwork. Some reloading supplies, telescopic sights, imported guns and a few semi-auto assault-rifle-type guns were offered at numerous gun shops found in most places around the country. Assault rifles tended to be either surplus military or home-made affairs more reminiscent of submachine guns.

Tariff regulations and general economic restrictions favored revolvers, rifles and shotguns produced locally by firms like Rossi. Yet Brazil is, and was, a nation of smugglers. When the price was right, almost anything was forthcoming.

Crime rates, especially in the barrios, were extremely high. Egged on by international meddlers, politicians blamed easy access of guns and ammunition. Apparently members of Brazil's National Congress never heard of John Lott. In a mad, senseless dash to exhibit "leadership," Brazil passed their now infamous "Statute of Disarmament."

Following a common worldwide pattern, this statute provided for a system of gun grabbing and graft familiar throughout much—but certainly not all—the world. Given Brazil's socio-economic system, it was the poor, crime-ridden victims who suffered—not the rich.

First a prospective gun owner was forced to secure a complicated, costly gun-owner's permit. Then each and every gun purchased had to be approved by the local police and listed on the permit. Sales of ammunition and loading supplies were sharply curtailed, and allowed only for guns on the permit.

As a result, great numbers of gun shops throughout the country were forced to close, resulting again in costly economic retrenchment. Poor Brazilians, especially those in rural, primitive areas, had fewer jobs and virtually no place to purchase needed guns and ammo.

But this was only the start.

Selection of guns approved to gun-owners' permits was limited to those considered to have a sporting purpose. Rich Brazilians, able to pay bribes and to argue a self defense or business purpose were reportedly occasionally authorized semi-auto assault rifles. Where these came from is unclear, perhaps from government stocks confiscated from less well-connected citizens. Their '03 law specifies that all contraband weapons had to be destroyed within 48 hours. A rule, no doubt, promulgated to minimize graft and corruption.

There is also the concept in view that specific registrable guns were frequently not authorized to one's permit. So the police, knowing about that gun, could simply confiscate it. Frequently Brazilian police resold these guns and pocketed the proceeds.

In general only single- and double-barrel shotguns, and single- and bolt-action rifles useful for hunting were authorized under the '03 law. A very few pistols were permitted whenever the owner could demonstrate a self-defense need, or for target shooting. It is unclear the extent to which bribes and graft facilitated this approval. Again, the rank and file suffered. Bribe money was not a problem for the wealthy.

Gun-owner's permits themselves cost $135, just to file the papers. This does not include extensive costs for a required medical/psychiatric exam, gun-owner's-proficiency training course, an extremely intrusive and subjective background check, and expenses for several other supporting documents. These last documents reportedly included one's employment record and tax-payment history. Many or most Brazilians are tax avoiders, especially the rural poor. Providing a tax history is impossible for these folks.

This last requirement was seen as seriously onerous. Unless a bribe was paid to speed things along, permits took from two to three months to process.

Gun-owner's permits expired after only three years. Then owners were forced to start the difficult, expensive process all over again. It's not clear how much graft plays a part in the re-licensing process.

We do know crime increased rather than abated, and that black-market suppliers stepped in to fill the gap left by honest dealers.

Fairly substantial, reliable guns of a surprisingly high quality were produced in tiny, up-country machine shops. This proves again that modern machinists using modern machine tools to produce simplistic modern weapons is not rocket science and that these people will quickly step in to fill an economic void.

There was and is talk of up-country manufacturers of ammunition. If true, this would be a universal first. Production of workable, suitable, essentially home-made primers and powder has always been the Achilles' heel of the do-it-yourself gun business. In this regard, Brazil may be a worldwide example.

When the price was right, poorly paid members of Brazil's military and police reportedly sold their issue guns and ammo or imported illegal military surplus for general sale. Sources for black-market guns were reportedly Paraguay, Uruguay or Argentina. A vast and quickly growing underground industry started and developed.

Obviously and predictably, crime increased rather than decreased. It is said the very poor were relegated to selling drugs and women to the very rich, using the proceeds to purchase black-market guns and ammunition.

Time now for Phase Three. Rather than honestly acknowledging life as it really is, including failure of policy, members of the international gun-grabbing/demonizing community decided Brazil was a good place to flex their economic and philosophical muscle. Egged on by the UN and international anti-gun billionaire George Soros, Brazil's Congress put an initiative on their ballot which to make all sales and ownership of guns and ammunition illegal in Brazil.

Supporters, with essentially unlimited budgets, figured it would be an easy sell to uneducated, unsophisticated rural bumpkins. Additionally they hoped to spread their winning patterns about the globe after triumphing in Brazil. They did succeed in mobilizing most of Brazil's media and some of the U.S. and world media in favor of this gun grab.

Brazil's culture is frequently mirrored by and influenced by their extensive soap-opera system. Universally the soaps propagandized against private gun ownership, in anticipation of the October 23 vote. But it was all a waste of their money.

Voting is compulsory in Brazil. On October 23, 2005 well over two-thirds of Brazilian voters voted *against* the measure, just completely disappointing Brazil's criminal drug barons who reportedly intended to make gun trafficking an even larger profit center.

As in the case of Crete, no one really knows the true extent of private illegal gun ownership in Brazil. Certainly it isn't as high or as open as it is in Crete, but many pundits reckon that it is about the same number as voted "no" on the anti-gun referendum (perhaps 67 to 70 percent!)

Next time George Soros may have to do it the Brazilian way and simply pay cash on the barrelhead for each needed "no" vote. But this would certainly not alter general possession of guns and ammo in the country.

Brazil and her gun laws are an excellent study in the unseen and unsaid, as well as the law of unintended consequences. The law of unintended consequences teaches that strange and often unforetold consequences will result from fooling around with basic human rights. While we in America have a much different system and culture, lessons recently learned are many and enduring.

Chapter Forty-Six
Turkey
World Rank: 45 • Firearm Freedom 29%

Turkey is a huge (the size of Texas and Massachusetts combined), largely rural, land comprised of lots of sparsely populated outback. Because many Turks still live on farms or in small, rural enclaves and continue to till the soil, one would suppose that their gun laws would favor reasonably easy private ownership. Add the fact that Turkey has a large, fully developed gun- and ammunition-manufacturing industry and this assumption becomes even more persuasive.

But this does not take into consideration the fact that the Turkish government continues to fight an entrenched insurgency and that this is a nation historically characterized by government intrigue, anarchy, and frequent swift changes in political direction. Traditionally and historically Turkey has been an extremely autocratic society. This the result of the six-hundred-year rule of Ottoman sultans.

Turkey is undergoing one of the most rapid, intense industrializations of any country in written history. Large, modern factories producing a huge variety of world-class goods are springing up literally everyplace, many in rural regions close to large pools of willing workers. Modern four- and six-lane highways support huge numbers of trucks shuttling raw materials and finished goods about the land. The claim is made that a total of 200,000 cars and trucks per day cross just one bridge over the Bosporus!

Turkish agriculture is mechanizing, as people flee the farm for more stable, better-paying jobs in factories. As a result of all these currents and cross currents pulling at their society, Turkish gun laws are convoluted and difficult. Nevertheless there is a cadre of gun owners including at least some illegal ownership. Officials claim little to no illegal gun ownership, but consider the following:

As it currently stands, no civilian is legally allowed to own a rifle of any size, type or caliber in Turkey. Yet, during our 1500 mile drive about the country, there was ample opportunity to note road signs full of bullet holes. Not to the extent of Crete, where citizens must absolutely hate their road signs, but shot up nevertheless.

Some of the pock marks on the signs were definitely the result of .22 LR fire. Twenty-two-sized holes through the signs must have been the work of .223 class rounds and .30 caliber holes probably the result of

7.62x39 rounds. This in a nation where rifle as well as .22 rimfire ownership of any type or kind is officially prohibited.

What follows is, in its major points, correct. We can conduct gun-store interviews in English, German, and Spanish and to an extent in Swahili. Regarding Turkish gun laws, it was tough to find anyone who could and would talk to us. When they did, we found their information to be sometimes contradictory.

Private as well as government-run gun stores are located in most of the large cities. Some English and/or German is spoken by owners and clerks, but frequently we found these folks quickly tired of speaking to us and just quit. In the U.S. we tried some University students from Turkey, as well as a Turkish college professor. Add these to the four gun-store clerks with whom we spoke in Turkey and we still have what is probably only an overview, perhaps lacking in some precise details.

Turkey is that Mediterranean country lying to the north of the Mediterranean Sea, bordered by the Black Sea to the north, by the Aegean Sea, Greece and Bulgaria to the west, by Azerbaijan, Armenia, Georgia and Iran to the east, and by Syria and Iraq to the south.

It is a fertile, lush country with great natural resources. During Roman times the area now comprising Turkey was considered to be a bread basket. Two crops of corn, wheat, cotton, sesame, potatoes, cabbage, eggplant, barley, sugar beets or any other row crop are possible every 12 months. Additionally, Turkey is rich in crude oil, copper, iron ore, limestone, snow-covered mountains, forest products and an extensive tree-fruits industry. Think miles and miles of olive and fig trees.

Travelers and residents feast luxuriously on a great many kinds of cheese, olive-oil-soaked lamb stew, chicken, turkey and beef. Some few pork products are available but, this being a Muslim country, these are not famously available. Europeans quickly discover that it takes pork to make really good sausage, which is not available in Turkey.

Turks are, by and large, only tacit Muslims. They tend to leave worldwide Muslim politics to others. Turks produce and consume great quantities of relatively good wine. Thousands of acres of vineyards run in some areas of Turkey.

Turkey's economy has always been a rollercoaster. Since WWII—Turkey was mostly neutral and did not send soldiers—their economy has gone numerous times from stupendous, breathtaking gains to complete, soul-deadening bust. *Per capita* income, spread fairly evenly through their society, is estimated at about $7,400. This constitutes a dramatic increase, even looking back only five years.

The 2005 Index of Economic Freedom prepared by the Heritage Foundation and the *Wall Street Journal* rates Turkey as a "mostly unfree" country. They are tied with Guyana and Namibia for 85 out of a total field of 157. Few dispute the fact that, if given their freedom, Turkey would be an economic dynamo, quickly surpassing Europe.

While private rifle ownership is forbidden, ownership of a shotgun or shotguns is said to be very easy. Pumps, autos, tactical "black" models, doubles and singles are all permitted to private citizens. Business must be fairly brisk. Each of the gun shops we visited had at least 30 shotguns on their racks available for sale. These included 12-, 16-, and 20-gauge as well as .410s. Government gun shops run by the police and military sell only pistols. No shotguns for sale in these places.

Private gun shops inventoried absolute mountains of loaded shot shells, empty primed cases and wads. No powder or primers needed to reload were seen at any gun shops. We were told these were available for sale at both private and government gun stores but these items were neither on the shelf nor in lock-up vaults we could examine.

The ownership process is apparently as follows: Purchase both a shotgun and a hunting license from the private gun shop. Take the license and a receipt for the gun purchase (called a *factura*) to the local police where the police will provide a gun-owner's application form. This form will include places for certifying two medical exams—one physical and one mental, and also information leading to a police vetting of one's criminal record.

Financial information, including job history, must also be included with the application. All firearms purchased in Turkey are authorized on the basis of need. Hunting with a shotgun is seen as a valid need.

Cost of the application alone, without paying for medical reports or other documents, is about $80. It takes from one to two weeks for a shotgun authorization to come through once papers are submitted.

On the basis of the invoice from the gun shop, the shotgun is noted down on the gun-owner's permit. New owners are now authorized to pick up, take home, and carry their shotguns. We observed numerous hunters out in fields or riding along on their motorcycles. They hunt birds, some deer-like critters in the mountains, and wild pigs. Mostly the pigs are hunted by visiting sportsmen. If a Turk shoots a pig to control the vast herds roaming some areas, they either leave it for the vultures or gingerly move it away with their tractor.

Authorization to own and carry a pistol is much more difficult. Only semi-automatics in 9mm Parabellum or .32 ACP, or revolvers in .357 mag are permitted. Ammunition for any other pistols is not available in Turkey. Only pistols of Turkish design and manufacture can be legally owned by Turks. Imported shotguns of many different makes are available off the rack if one can afford them, but only Turkish-made pistols are permitted.

Cost of new Turkish pistols varies from a staggering $992 to $2,633. Gun owners complain bitterly about this price discrimination, calculated to keep buyers of limited means out of the market.

There is no legal ownership of .22 pistols. As near as we can tell, there are no legal sales of .22 rimfire ammunition in Turkey although we must wonder about wasting such shooting road signs.

Applications for a pistol-owner's permit cost about $380 and takes from one to four months to receive an authorization, we were told. But this is basically unclear. Also unclear is if the application money is refunded if the application is denied. Licenses, if granted, are good for five years including both shotguns and pistols.

Requirements for pistol ownership are much more restrictive than for a shotgun. Only citizens who handle a great deal of money, have stores with especially expensive merchandise—assumed to mean proprietors of some of the many gold shops, those guarding buildings or vehicles, or people in danger or working in tough districts or such like—can expect to secure a pistol authorization. It's unclear if women would even be allowed to legally own a pistol in Turkey. Women are not required to wear chadors and veils, and they can drive vehicles, but it would be a great surprise if they could secure a pistol authorization in this Muslim place.

Medical forms, business licenses, certifications, criminal checks— many of which are common to shotgun ownership—are also required of pistol applicants but are much more closely examined. Once we were told there is a "one pistol limit," once "two pistols," and once "as many pistols as the buyer could afford." Apparently Turks can really own multiple shotguns, but providing reasons for multiple ownership becomes increasingly difficult. Satisfying this "reason to own" requirement probably is the limitation for pistols and most likely for more than two or three shotguns as well.

All pistols absolutely must be purchased from a government office called the M.K.E. This is run by a combination of Turkish Army and police. M.K.E. offices are only located in Istanbul and Ankara, not terribly convenient in a Texas-sized land.

All pistol ammo must be purchased from the M.K.E. The limit is 200 rounds a year, only for guns authorized on one's gun-owner's permit. Probably 85% of the pistols sold in Turkey are 9mm Parabellum. Chances are also good that most of the pistol ammo sold by M.K.E will be 9x19mm or 9mm Parabellum.

While we are unsure if primers and powder can be purchased locally in private shops, we were assured these were always available at the M.K.E. stores. "At what price?" is the unanswered question.

A reloading authorization or permit is required, but easily issued to those who wish to reload either for their handgun or for their shotgun and who already have a valid gun-owner's permit. No one seemed to be able to tell us if limits applied to reloading components, although we were told only components used for authorized firearms could legally be purchased.

Private sales are possible involving both pistols and shotguns, but parties involved are required to go through the police vetting procedure. Transferring a pistol privately appears to be extremely difficult and tenuous. Selling a shotgun to a friend or neighbor is said to be easier, but both must go through Turkish bureaucratic procedure.

Judging by the huge stacks of cases of loaded shells in private stores, it would seem no practical limit applied to sales of shotgun ammo. We do know only rounds for an authorized gun—even a shotgun—are allowed. Turks can legally purchase slug and heavy buckshot rounds off the shelf as well as a great variety of sizes of fine shot, but only for shotguns listed on their personal gun-owner's permit.

We were scolded that absolutely no machine guns, machine pistols or silencers were ever authorized to private Turkish citizens. Strange, since what appeared to be a 9mm silencer was locked in a cabinet with some of their pistols at the M.K.E. store.

Modern Turkey is a strange combination of Filipino incompetence and Mexican petty extortion. Major crime is virtually non-existent although shopkeepers and restaurant people will try to add their bills up incorrectly for tourists. Police riding four to a car are everywhere.

The country is very rich in hard-working people, extensive natural resources and a wonderful climate, but it languishes economically— too much government for capital to flourish. Yet some rural Turks are still part of a gun culture. Turkish newspapers frequently carry pictures of farmers and livestock men packing shotguns.

Official paranoia regarding firearms is perhaps understandable given the Turkish decades-long struggle with Kurdish separatists and their history of autocratic government. But, at the end of the day, legal pistol and shotgun ownership in Turkey is limited while legal rifle ownership of any kind is totally impossible.

Chapter Forty-Seven
Czech Republic
World Rank: 19 • Firearm Freedom 65%

Brno, including its justifiably famous small-arms production and development facilities, lies within the Czech Republic, the next country for which we examine gun laws. The historic Brno works are mostly dormant now, suffocated by an oppressive Soviet regime and an only slightly less repressive post-Soviet Czech government.

Yet Czech gun owners remember. There are at least four thriving gun shops in the medium sized Czech city of Plzen (Pilsen). Using the fact that she owned and hunted with a custom .257 Roberts rifle made on a VZ 33 short Mauser action, my wife opened an enlightening conversation with the proprietor and his wife of the city's largest and best-stocked hunter-supply store.

Old Czechoslovakia, comprised of the current countries of Czech Republic and Slovakia, are in what is commonly referred to by Europeans as Eastern Europe. Americans, who look at a map rather than relying on tradition, might refer to the area as Central Europe.

Poland borders to the north. Slovakia to the east and Austria to the south. Germany also touches this South Carolina-sized country on the northwest. Takes about eleven hours to reach Prague, the capital, by car from the undersea England-to-France tunnel at Calais.

A union of the Czech lands and Slovakia was achieved Nov. 14, 1918, forming Czechoslovakia. March 1939 saw the country occupied by Imperial WW II Germany. After WW II, the Soviets controlled Czechoslovakia till 1989. Sad remnants of Soviet socialist autocratic rule persist to this day in the Czech Republic as demonstrated by their approach to private property law, the general state of the economy, and to private ownership of firearms.

Gross domestic product is an estimated $172.2 billion. *Per capita* GDP—the best, quick and easy way to figure wealth of a country—is currently about $16,800. Problem is that inflation and GDP growth threaten to about cancel each other out, effectively stagnating expansion of personal incomes.

Mostly, the country is about agriculture and forestry, with some primary metal, mineral and coal extraction. Czech industry is usually characterized as old and decrepit. Much of their factory machinery left over from the Soviet era justifies that characterization. A few new, modern investments from the West have spiked production of machinery and vehicles in a few instances.

Information for this chapter comes from several published sources, as well as a personal visit to the country and some of their gun shops. As mentioned, we interviewed the owner and wife of one of the larger gun shops in Plzen for almost two hours. Doing gun-store interviews has improved our German dramatically. Good thing. He spoke only German and Czech and she, Czech and a smattering of English.

Before purchasing any guns in the Czech Republic, one must secure a gun-owner's permit from the police. At current rates of exchange, the permit costs between $84 and $125. Not an insurmountable amount, given average *per capita*—not family—incomes of $16,800.

Prices vary because there are five different categories or levels of permits. At the more restrictive end of the spectrum there is more checking and testing, leading to higher costs.

Potential gun owners must pass a firearms proficiency, handling and knowledge test. The test is sufficiently complex and detailed that most new applicants choose to enroll in special courses offered by the police. These courses emphasize safe handling, ballistics and—for hunters—field craft.

Applicants must also submit to, and pay for, a medical examination supposedly designed to uncover medical, physical and psychological problems. Do the examinations really ferret out mental incompetents, the criminally insane, or just those with poor eyesight and obvious physical handicaps? Our informants were not sure.

Categories of permits are: A– For possession and use of antique-type guns; B– For ownership and use of sporting rifles, pistols and shotguns including target shooting and trap and skeet; C– Permits for hunting, including only rifles and shotguns; D– Pistol permits for police and private security guards; and E– Pistol permits to carry concealed.

New owners may request levels they believe appropriate, but the authorities are not obligated to comply—everything is done at police discretion. It's not a terribly high hurdle we were told, until one gets to large bore, semi-auto pistol permits for police and security guards.

It is unclear if the gun shops are acting as agents of the government when they inventory and sell pistols in Category D to police. Municipal police get their permits and pass their proficiency tests in the normal course of their training. Mostly, these people use 9x19mm pistols, or ones in .380 caliber.

Czech Republic gun store

Citizens in the Czech Republic have traditionally been gun owners. This large, prosperous store is one of four located in the western city of Pilsen where ammunition, pistols, rifles and shotguns are made available, though many restrictions impede purchases and the citizenry. Pilsen is the site of a huge "Liberation Festival" that honors American soldiers who reached the town near the end of WWII, and under the command of Gen. George Patton helped liberate it. Awards, monuments and parades in the beginning of May each year recognize the efforts made by Americans towards peace.

Private security guards are very closely vetted. Employees of a known, reputable private security firm have the best chance of securing Category D endorsements.

Category E endorsements—to carry concealed—are only issued on the basis of great perceived risk. These permits go only to bankers, jewelers, couriers and personal bodyguards. Violent crime in general is very low in the Czech Republic, arguing mightily against issuance of permits to those who feel threatened. As a result, permits in the last two categories are not routine.

Czech citizens can legally own as many guns as they wish and can pay for. These include rifles, shotguns and pistols. Rifles and shotguns must be of a recognized sporting type. No "black" assault-type rifles or shotguns are allowed. But Czechs can own sporting-type pump, semi-auto and lever action rifles as well as semi-auto shotguns and .22s.

No fully automatic machine guns or machine pistols are allowed. Silencers are also *verboten*. Keeping up to four guns of all types in the closet is okay; after four, owners must invest in a gun safe, which is subject to unannounced police inspections.

Every gun must be registered by the police to the owner. New owners usually pick out their guns at hunting shops, take information on that gun to the police, and then receive authorization commensurate with their authorization level to go back to the shop to take delivery of their gun. Not an especially difficult process, we were informed, once one has a valid gun-owner's permit, provided it is a Category A through C authorization.

Legal private sales are possible so long as each party has a valid gun-owner's permit and the gun is registered to the new owner's permit. All guns are registered to the person's gun-owner's permit.

Currently there is also an exemption for sporting rifles and shotguns with barrels longer than 23.6 inches (60 cm). These can be purchased over the counter without securing a specific authorization on one's gun-owner's permit. Of course, everyone must have a valid gun-owner's permit. Whether these guns are registered to the recipient's gun-owner's permit is unclear. Apparently with regard to sporting rifles and shotguns with sufficiently long barrels, one just presents a gun-owner's certificate and walks out the door with the gun.

All ammunition used for pistols and revolvers, and which could be used in shorter rifles and shotguns, must be sold only on the basis of one's registration for a specific gun. But ammo for non-registered rifles and shotguns is sold over the counter we are told. There seems to be some contradictions and perhaps loopholes here.

No restrictions impede amounts of ammo one can purchase, but all ammo sales are noted in a permanent shop record book. Gun-shop owners with difficult-to-secure store licenses are likely to dutifully report abnormal multiple purchases to the authorities.

At current rates of exchange, 25 12-gauge international skeet loads cost about $4.25 per box. Boxes of 20 .308 hunting rounds cost $30. Seven by 57 Mauser rounds, 20 to the box, cost about $33. Not a lot of ammo stockpiling gonna go on at these prices. One .22 LR round costs 4¼ cents. Like when I was a kid, .22 ammo is sold by single rounds if one wishes.

Eight or ten gauge shotguns are either not permitted or not available. Judging by pistols on display, almost any caliber or cartridge up to the big .50s is okay.

Reloading is permitted but, like most Europeans, most Czech gun owners do not understand the utility of this activity. Gun shops are legally restrained as to how much powder and how many primers they can legally stock. This appears to be a major constraint.

Legally the shop in Plzen we visited could only carry 1,500 primers at one time, and an unspecified but meager quantity of powder. Shops in Prague, we were told, carry virtually unlimited quantities and varieties of reloading powders, primers and bullets. All are easily available over the counter without papers. No powder, shot or primers, dies, presses or any other reloading supplies were obvious on the shelves of the gun store we visited.

Illegal guns are said not to be much of a problem or issue in the Czech Republic. The store owner and his wife did *not* wish to talk about this issue. A temporary glitch in our ability to communicate developed.

Because the Czechs have been extensively involved in warfare and armed conflicts for hundreds of years, it is tough to quickly dismiss this issue. Certainly illegal guns flooding out of Russia into Germany and England must cross Czech borders. Perhaps few or none stop there, or perhaps the Czechs have sufficient guns left from WW I and II. No way to really check this out was available to us.

Like Poland, the Czech Republic is a wild, hilly, rural-to-mountainous land, characterized by a great many isolated little villages. The Czechs have been overrun, sold out, and plundered down through the ages. Yet, unlike traditional Swiss and Finns, citizens seem to rely on some mythical treaties and future good intentions of others for security.

Yet, having said this, there must be a fairly large cache of gun owners and gun users in the land. How else to explain the fairly large number of surprisingly well-stocked gun shops we observed?

Chapter Forty-Eight
Slovakia
World Rank: 20 • Firearm Freedom 65%

Slovakia is the weak sister of the June 1992 split-up of Czechoslovakia. Travel writers and historians attempting to put a positive spin on things suggest that "when, in spite of great concessions on the part of the Czech Republic, differences proved to be irreconcilable, the two decided to peacefully go their separate ways."

In hindsight this was not a particularly smart move on the part of the Slovakians whose real *per capita* incomes fell to about $14,500, some $2,000 per person less than the Czech Republic. It only makes matters worse that inflation tripled and that unemployment has hovered around thirteen percent.

In addition to traditional agriculture and forestry, Slovakia's economy is based on tourism and some mining and manufacture. Manufacturing is tough. Many of their plants and equipment are old, worn, dated and decrepit—still dating from the Soviet era.

Western Europeans, eyeing Slovakia's rugged mountains and forests, open lands and generally excellent bargain prices, contribute mightily to their tourist economy. Evidently Slovakian police have taken lessons from Mexicans. Officers speaking impeccable English regularly and professionally shake down tourists motoring along their few freeways, establishing yet another modest profit center.

Slovakia is roughly twice the size of Maryland. It would be three times the size if it were all squashed flat. Logically the Czech Republic adjoins to the west. Poland is north and the Ukraine is east. Austria and Hungary border to the south.

Information for this chapter comes from several published sources and from personal visits to three sporting goods shops in Slovakia. In spite of expending a great deal of effort, we still have only a rudimentary picture of Slovakian gun laws. They do, however, seem to differ materially from the Czech Republic's gun laws.

Our information gathering process was complex. At the Russian pullback in 1989, citizens with no real identification either in the newly reestablished countries such as Slovakia and Russia itself, simply decided their citizenship by default. Many just stayed behind, essentially making no decision. Characterized by their assumption of jobs involving little thought, effort or ambition, we found Russian nationals principally as super lethargic small shop clerks.

Unlike most Europeans, where even young school children can lay two or even three common languages on the counter for personal interaction, stock answers for these Russian clerks is, if you don't speak Russian or the obscure national language, forget it. We got this reaction from these types of people in the Baltics as well as Slovakia.

As a result of encounters with Russian clerks in the few gun stores that exist in Slovakia, we can only report bits and pieces of conversation and a great deal of what we saw.

The medium large city of Trencin has only one shop that caters to hunters. It is also a bicycle shop. One would suppose that if gun ownership were common in rural areas, there would be more than this one shop.

This bicycle/gun shop stocked eight or ten fairly expensive hunting/target rifles ranging in size from .22 rimfire to perhaps .308 or maybe 8 mm. All were bolt actions or single shots. No semi-autos, no assault rifles and no shotguns. The Russian lady clerk was completely uninterested in communicating with us.

Her shelves held an amazing variety of rifle and pistol ammo. Most of it was Finnish Sako brand. Only a box or two of each, but there were at least 30 different sizes of ammo. It seemeed strange that no shotguns or shotgun rounds were on offer, in this the only store of its kind for miles and miles.

For a basic small Third World shop, they stocked a huge number of costly pistols. No .22s in sight, but there were a number of 9mm semi-autos including at least one Glock. There were at least six or eight revolvers, mostly .357s or .38s. There might also have been one .32 ACP Colt knockoff.

Meager as it was, we could conclude that there was some sporting/hunting rifle and defensive-pistol ownership in Slovakia. But not nearly as much as in the Czech Republic where we encountered at least four times as many gun stores.

This was the only gun shop in the region. It was a humble little jumble in amongst the bicycles. Yet their inventory was greater in value than probably all of the bicycles, bicycle parts and probably the store building itself put together! Only two possible hunters' supply/gun shops were in the nation's capital city.

Staffers in the Tourist Office in Bratislava, the nation's capital, were surprised and shocked when we explained that we were gathering information for a book on national gun laws and wanted to interview people in gun stores. Yet they did try mightily to help.

A clerk and two customers in the "U.S. Army Store"—a tiny surplus and outdoor shop—were also helpful. They didn't sell guns and no one there was a gun owner. Yet they tried valiantly to point us in the correct direction. Some of their limited information may even have been accurate.

They believed that pistols and revolvers were allowed for personal security, shotguns and rifles for hunting and target shooting. A paper from the police was required, but they had no idea what these cost, how difficult they were to obtain, nor how long it took to issue. Perhaps the paper was only for pistols. They didn't know. "Go to the only hunter supply store in the capital," they suggested. "It's only three kilometers down this same road, Number 55."

Street numbers in Bratislava bear little resemblance to those in the U.S. or any other place we could think of. Finding the shop took so much time that by the time we got there, the Russian lady proprietor was shutting down the shop (closing at noon) and extremely anxious to lock the door and get on her way.

From the front steps, observing what we could while speedily asking questions (again, in German) we learned that a gun-owner's permit from the police in Slovakia was only required for pistols and revolvers. No paper for shotguns. "Just buy it off the shelf," she said. We spotted several new semi-auto Italian and probably a Turkish model or two on the shelf. We assumed these were among those shotguns permitted to citizens without papers. Her German was worse than ours!

She was in too much of a hurry to tell us what was required to own a rifle. That there were from 30 to 50 hunting rifles in the store rack was not instructive. These were all bolt actions and single shots. We could not determine if there were any .22 semi-autos, pumps or others before she slammed and locked the door in our face.

So large and expensive inventory in a basically poor land would suggest easy ownership. But this was the only gun shop in the country's largest city, and only the second we could find out about. Perhaps all Slovakian gun owners had to do their business at this one shop, explaining their relatively large inventory. We never found out. We did manage to determine that reloading was not permitted.

"Assault rifles, full-auto machine pistols and machine guns, as well as silencers, were not lawfully owned," she said. There was no limit on the number of guns—assumed to mean sporting-type rifles, shotguns, and perhaps pistols—one could legally own, according to her.

Ammo can only be sold for the gun for which you have a permit. All purchases of ammo are recorded in a permanent log which is regularly inspected by the police.

This last store in Bratislava stocked at least 50 different pistols of various kinds and types. Some looked much like Colt Woodsman pistols, which we later found were inexpensive Chinese knockoffs. Others were obviously of Russian design and manufacture.

In spite of now having spent the better part of a week trying to gather information, this was all we could come up with. Tomorrow was Sunday, and Monday a holiday. Staying in the country three more days with the intent of dealing with an obviously cranky, uncooperative store clerk in the only gun store in the city seemed unwise and probably unproductive. We had appointments in Austria to keep.

Wars and other miscellaneous armed tumults have swept over this little land. At one time they obviously had a vibrant, growing, producing gun design/manufacturing industry as well as a gun culture. Perhaps like the Baltics, any Slovakian or Czech found with an illegal gun was summarily shot by occupying Russians.

Perhaps there are still a great number of illegal guns remaining from previous times. Or perhaps remaining poor Slovakians are uninterested in firearms, seeing no need for them. We might suppose occupying Russians destroyed both their gun industry and their gun culture. We just don't know. After coming over 10,000 miles, this is the best and only information we could put together for Slovakia.

Chapter Forty-Nine
Austria
World Rank: 24 • Firearm Freedom 55%

Austrian gun laws are some of the ones we should all sit up and take special note of. Should the Schumers, Clintons, Kennedys and Soros' of the world have their way, these will be the model.

Private firearms will be allowed but only under a strict permit system, only to the very rich, famous and politically well-connected. Common folk of limited means can forget it.

For centuries, Austria had a dynamic, even vibrant, gun culture. A fine double-barreled .458 Winchester mag rifle made entirely by hand in Ferlach, Austria occupies an especially prestigious place in my gun rack. Franz Sodia, the maker, went to his reward perhaps 30 years ago now, but still today citizens of Ferlach easily recall his place in the community.

"It's that big cement off-yellow building his factory used to occupy," they quickly inform. Now urbanization, industrialization and several brutal wars have taken their toll. Ownership of guns in Austria is fairly straightforward, but bring lots of cash and be prepared to spend lots of paper time on the project.

Austria is only slightly smaller than Maine. It is a beautiful, rugged, mountainous place mostly comprised of brilliant green, snow-capped eastern Alps.

Switzerland and Liechtenstein lie to the west. Germany to the north, Slovakia and the Czech Republic to the northeast, with Hungary directly east. Italy wraps and intrudes to the south. Reaching all these places is relatively easy. Under the EU, most of the ancient historic borders are invisible. Autobahns are excellent. Crossing is so routine most motorists fail to take note that they are now in another country.

Austria is comprised of an historic, rich society caught in a bit of a self-righteous time warp. Personal incomes are high—about $31,300 annually. But economic growth is now only 0.1% per year, if that. Innovation, commerce, manufacturing and development are ossified. Onerous rules and regulations prohibiting firing and failing, while favoring powerful unions and keep unemployment at perhaps 4.4%. At the same time, productivity and investment are low. Little new and innovative is going on in this land of the Viennese Waltz.

Information for this chapter comes from several published sources as well as an in-depth visit to Austria. We were fortunate to be able to interview several gun owners between practice rounds at the *Schützenverein Ferlach* range on the north edge of historic Ferlach.

A pleasant Viennese dialect of German is their first language. The gun owners/target shooters we interviewed also spoke excellent English.

Finding a place to shoot that is both safe and sanctioned is a real challenge in this crowded country. Membership in extremely pricey clubs is often the only practical solution.

At least in this particular instance, shooting is done inside a closed clubhouse-like building out through a narrow slot in the side wall. Their ultimate backstop is the side of a mountain, all situated right on the edge of a built-up urban area we might refer to as suburbia.

The sharp report of a large bore, high-velocity rifle greeted my wife at the exact instant she opened the front door of the range building. Quite a surprise—but no more so than finding several congenial fellow gun owner/shooters more than willing to answer questions about their firearms ownership situations.

Austrian gun laws are relatively simple and straightforward. Like many places in the world, the first requirement is securing a gun-owner's permit from the police. Issuance of this permit is not particularly subjective on the part of the authorities. New gun owners receive their permits on the basis of passing a gun-owner's shooters' test. Passing this test is neither easy nor routine.

New applicants usually take extensive courses leading up to the difficult comprehensive final exam. Course work leading to the exam includes in-depth knowledge of Austrian game species, breeding patterns, habitats, food sources, general biology, botany and ecological matters. One must also demonstrate an in-depth, working knowledge of ballistics, gun safety, gun design and history, gun handling, regulations and field protocol.

Cost of this vetting/licensing process is a whopping $2,760 at current exchange rates. Doing the course work and taking the test can consume the better part of a year in many instances. Additionally, Austrian gun owners must either join a shooting club, for those who want to target shoot with rifles or pistols, or for trap or skeet. Join an even higher-priced exclusive club if you want to hunt.

Cost of a shooting-club membership can be as low as $140 annually. Cost of a hunt-club membership is entirely dependent on how productive and well managed the hunting area is. It might be as little as nothing if you can contract with a willing farmer/landowner willing to take harvested game in exchange for your right to hunt. Or perhaps tens of thousands of dollars for a really good area with a reputation for producing outstanding trophy critters. Austrians emphasize that landowners own the animals, not the state as is the case in the U.S.

Only guns with a target, trap, skeet or hunting application are allowed. Semi-auto sporting rifles are okay but not of military type or design. No "black guns" of any type, and no pump or semi-auto shotguns. In summary, all legal guns must have only a sporting purpose.

Pistols can only be used when humanely administering the *coup-de-grace* to a wounded animal, never for hunting itself. Ownership of pistols is also allowed for target shooting and, in some instances, for high-risk security guards. At times, permits are also given to people in high-risk jobs—bankers, politicians, jewelers, and at times, druggists may fall in this category.

Pistol buyers must both convince the authorities of their special need for a handgun as well as subject themselves to an even more rigorous and costly psychological and physical examination. Emphasis here is on being a supposedly "responsible person."

Numbers of guns a gun-permit holder may have is not limited other than by price and that of convincing officers of a specific need. Every gun is tracked by a specific piece of paper. Owning pistols, rifles and shotguns may entail membership in several different very costly clubs.

Meeting hall at Austrian shooting range

Here we have an indoor shooting range located in the center
of Ferlach, Austria. Private gun ownership in Austria is
limited to a great extent by extremely high costs for both
guns and permits. Note the homey, club-like atmosphere,
and the old-world charm that pervades the meeting area.
Members' cased arms are seen in the foreground. Two of the
six people pictured in this image of the club are women.

All guns must be secured in one's home in a special gun safe. Police are said to regularly check gun owners' storage lockers, both to be sure they are secure and to be certain that permit holders' spouses do not know the location of the key or otherwise know how to access the guns in the safe.

Some ten percent of Austrian gun owners and hunters are women, out of a total of only 110,000 Austrian gun owners, in a population of over eight million. These gun owners, we were told, support one or two hunters' supply gun shops in almost every large city.

Emphasis in Austria, more than virtually any other place, is on costly, highly engraved, handmade guns with exquisite fancy hardwood stocks. Mostly Austrians own what we would term very high-end bolt actions and single-shot rifles, over/under shotguns, and extremely expensive custom target pistols.

Austria is home of the high-priced three-barreled guns we call drillings, since it is sometimes difficult to own both a rifle and shotgun.

Austrian gun owners take justifiable huge pride in the fact that theirs is the last place on Earth where one can purchase an extremely high-end handmade gun. That this limits ownership to the very rich does not seem to concern them.

Austrian gun manufacturers contribute to high prices by adherence to government regulations that require every gun in Austria to be proofed and checked for overall condition before it can be sold.

Purchase of ammunition is reportedly not limited to those who have a "paper" for that specific gun. Yet, Austrian gun owners ask why anyone would want to purchase ammo for a gun they don't own! Perhaps for illegal guns they own, but ammo is so godawful expensive in Austria it seems no one would ever buy very much under any circumstances.

Single rounds of .308 target ammo cost roughly $2 each. Figure on $.65 each for standard 12-gauge hunting loads. Since no one of those with whom we spoke shot .22s they could not give me that price.

Silencers are never permitted, because gamekeepers need to know where and when game is taken by the sound of the shot. Silencers, when used, are assumed to be for the terrible, despicable act of poaching unpaid-for game.

Obviously there is no legal ownership of machine pistols or machine guns—no sporting purpose to these, as far as Austrians are concerned.

Reloading is permitted without special licenses or permits. But Austrians categorize reloading as a curious hobby of little actual practical value! Some gun stores sell components over the counter. There is also a cottage industry in Austria producing single rounds at a time of old, obsolete ammo for antique guns. These rounds are said to be extremely precise and extremely expensive. In Austria one can only imagine what "extremely expensive" means!

The only other restriction we encountered was one limiting—at the top end—the caliber size of pistols you may own. Pistols in .22 rimfire are okay, but it seems as though anything above .45 caliber is not okay, along with .22-caliber rifles in anything but bolts and single shots.

Perhaps there is a problem with illegal guns in large cities such as Vienna, but out in the rural villages they are not a problem, our informants reckoned. We would have liked to talk to game managers/landowners in this regard, but no one was available.

As mentioned going in, gun ownership in Austria—as a practical matter—is the prerogative of the moneyed class. There are many costly rules and regulations, but mainly the high price of guns and ammo after you have the needed super-expensive papers is the deterrent.

When these hospitable fellows in Austria asked if I would like to touch off a few rounds at their range, I declined. At roughly $2 per hole, I just couldn't bring myself to it.

Chapter Fifty
Liechtenstein
World Rank: 10 • Firearm Freedom 80%

Saying gun owners of Liechtenstein are worried is like claiming King Kong is just another monkey.

At least if one accepts the assessment of the owner of the country's largest gun shop, Liechtensteiners are *very* concerned about their guns, a concern shared to some extent by gun owners around the world. But it seems in Liechtenstein a recent bias against gun owners is extremely serious—quickly and needlessly moving their society from being one where guns were freely owned to one of great repression.

Newly proposed legislation driven by extreme pressure from the UN would, if implemented, dramatically reduce the ease and ability of private gun ownership in Liechtenstein. In that regard, citizens there resemble those in the U.S., where the NRA is frequently forced to sound the alarm regarding evil events at the UN. The problem is that Liechtenstein is too small for anything similar to an NRA, and it's probably too late in the game as well.

The Principality of Liechtenstein is a tiny—two-thirds the size of Washington, D.C.—protectorate sandwiched between Switzerland, Germany and Austria. The country consists of one low valley nestled in amongst majestic, towering Alps. We managed to drive every main road in the country the Sunday afternoon we arrived, while waiting for the stores to open the next morning.

That illustrates one of the largest problems facing gun-owning Liechtensteiners. Their country is so small and densely populated that, other than small-bore rifles and pistols in their barns, garages, parlors or basements, they have little to no place to shoot. What once may have been a gun-owning society may be reverting to a "we don't care about firearms" society because there are so few places to shoot.

Liechtenstein is closely associated with its immediate neighbor, Switzerland. They use Swiss francs as currency, rely on the Swiss for most foreign relations, follow a great deal of Swiss law, cherish their freedom and independence and—like the Swiss—remained scrupulously neutral in WW II. Unlike Andorra, which doesn't have its own post office, sales of rarely-used postage stamps in Liechtenstein contribute to a major national profit center. The colorful stamps are purchased by collectors and never again see the inside of a post office!

Apparently, citizens who shoot trap, skeet or larger bore centerfire rifles or otherwise practice with guns must use ranges in Switzerland. There is no real border control between the two countries. Whether Liechtensteiners could legally take their guns into Switzerland is unclear. It may be necessary to join expensive shooting clubs.

Used to be that Liechtenstein gun shops—where taxes are minimal to non-existent—did major business selling guns and ammo of sometimes questionable legality across borders to neighbors in Germany and Austria. Purchasers avoided more stringent rules and regulations in their home countries. But not any more.

Currently the proprietor of Liechtenstein's only remaining full service gun shop says he can not legally sell even a screw from a gun sight to a German or Austrian. Naturally he is disappointed over this loss of commercial opportunity.

As in Switzerland, freedom has been kind to Liechtenstein. *The Wall Street Journal* "Index of Economic Freedom" does not rate the country separately, apparently melding the tiny principality with Switzerland, ranked #15 for personal freedom in the world.

Personal incomes in Liechtenstein are extremely high. Their economic growth rate—in spite of having little to no industry—is virtually unbelievable. Personal *per capita* incomes are roughly $25,000. Real economic growth is estimated at 11 percent annually with little to no inflation! Their birth rate, however, is cautionary. At 1.04 percent, it is well below the replacement rate. This explains why hordes of German and Austrian guest workers pour over the border every workday.

Their information office was closed when we first pulled into Liechtenstein early one Sunday morning. Perhaps the fellow with whom we spoke standing by the locked door was not an information-office employee. Yet he immediately, without concern or hesitation, gave us the name and street address of the largest, best-stocked gun shop in the little land. Ominously it was the only one remaining. Later the proprietor told us there had been six or eight gun shops, but new laws passed in 1999—with the promise of more to come—had discouraged all of the shops out of business except his. There is also urbanization of societies around the world, giving citizens less reason and place to shoot—thus discouraging if not limiting gun ownership.

Tragically, this last operator of Liechtenstein's last gun shop was discouraged and fearful of what the future might bring. Of all the interviews held so far, his was the most reluctant. The man saw 30 years of work building his business evaporating at the hand of a capricious and irrational government.

"Perhaps you are a leftist journalist who hates guns and who will turn around and write drivel about private gun ownership in Liechtenstein," he kept saying. It took a long, long time to convince him we really understood his situation and were on his side. Understandable, and truly sad for a man with so many years invested, who now saw his livelihood arbitrarily gutted by greedy, self-serving, uninformed, unelected UN bureaucrats.

Currently, citizens of Liechtenstein can still own rifles, pistols and shotguns including "black" shotguns and semi-auto assault rifles in any quantity they can afford. We observed some really nice AUG assault rifles in .223 caliber in the gun-store rack, as well as lever-action rifles, semi-auto shotguns and rifles, and .22s. It was just about the same selection one would find in a well-stocked American gun shop outside Washington, D.C. or Chicago.

"Since 1999 there is a list of guns private citizens are not legally permitted to own," he said. It's unclear what this list includes exactly since his German dialect got a bit hazy and colloquial at this point. We assumed these to be machine guns, machine pistols, mortars and heavier modern guns. None of these on offer in his store, of course.

New gun owners are required to fill out a relatively simple one-page gun-owner's application at the police office in the local city hall. Even driving to the central office in the capital, Vaduz, is not much of an inconvenience in tiny Liechtenstein. Applicants must demonstrate they have no overt mental or physical problems that would make them a danger to society. References, including an employer, must be listed. A sworn statement affirms the applicant knows of no legal reason why permission to own a gun should be denied.

Cost of the application is about 50 Swiss francs, or about $38.50 at the time. It takes from three to five days for the police, who generally know everyone in Liechtenstein, to complete their checking. A paper is then issued allowing virtually unlimited purchase of rifles, pistols and shotguns. There's one copy for the applicant, one for the gun store and one for police files. Serial numbers of pistols and assault rifles must be registered with the police after purchase.

Judging from the large assortment of revolvers and semi-auto pistols in the display case, virtually any pistol is legally available, even shotgun pistols, which must also be registered. We observed a very nice Israeli semi-auto in .50 Action Express!

Other than the fact that they just aren't available in little Liechtenstein, there is no limit on size. Eight and ten gauge shotguns are okay, but not manufactured or imported. Pistols in .22 are okay. Our friend in the gun store had several for sale. Often these were of Spanish, Austrian, Israeli and Brazilian manufacture, and included many models that were not familiar.

Ammo is bought in any quantity by anyone who is a citizen. Since the country is small and places to shoot extremely limited, sale of ammo to citizens does not constitute a major profit center for the store, the owner pointed out. Yet he had an amazingly large inventory of ammo.

All ammo sales are recorded in a purchase book. This book must remain open to police inspection, but our friend the gun-shop proprietor suggests that in a country where everyone knows everyone else, the police seldom come by to inspect.

Silencers are never permitted. They have been illegal for "eternity plus three days," he says, using a clever German figure of speech.

Apparently there really are a few hunting opportunities in little Liechtenstein, perhaps for red deer and birds up in the surrounding mountains. We had no idea regarding exact national boundaries, so perhaps there's more territory than we might have first supposed. Shotguns and rifles are allowed hunters, but probably not pistols.

Pistols are legal for target shooting and for self defense. Permits are currently issued for concealed carry. These require more explaining and justification in front of the police. The police, who know virtually everyone in the country, already know who can qualify and who really needs a concealed-carry permit.

Reloading is permitted without papers or hassle. As is the case with many places in Europe, that activity is not held in high regard. At least not by the gun-store owner who would rather sell more profitable loaded ammo. Powder, primers and bullets and shot are freely traded over the counter if one can find a store that handles them.

We saw no reloading components or tools in this fellow's inventory. Unclear whether such could be brought in from Switzerland. Again, there are no border guards or check points going back and forth.

We were told that, because of new gun laws in Switzerland in the Canton of Bern alone, 150 of 300 gun dealers have gone out of business since 1999. If true, there are probably many factors leading to this current situation.

Assault rifles in the rack in the Liechtenstein store were priced at about $3,200 to $3,500 at current rates of exchange. Boxes of 100 .22 LR ammo cost 10 francs or about $7.70. Twenty rounds of .308 ammo were priced at $15.50. Twenty .300 Win Mag rounds cost $43 and a box of .50 caliber pistol ammo was $28.46 for twenty.

Illegal guns are said to be virtually non-existent in the country. Too small and rural, "where everyone knows everyone else," he said. Additionally, till recently, there has been no need or reason. Crime is also virtually non-existent.

Historically gun ownership in Liechtenstein has been very easy and open. Since crime—other than charging dramatically too much for hotel rooms and for burgers at McDonalds—is virtually non-existent, there is no reason to clamp down on guns. So why is the government listening to freedom-suppressing bureaucrats at the UN?

It's a question over which Liechtensteiners are agonizing. Not to forget this is the first place of many that, when we asked about gun stores in town, clerks in the Information Center didn't go into virtual apoplectic fits. The guy at the closed information center may actually have been a passing citizen. Nevertheless he instantly knew where to send us, including names and addresses.

Perhaps, we might speculate, that enacting tough gun laws in Liechtenstein might give the UN autocrats a place to point as being the one place in the world where tougher gun laws did not also lead to increased crime.

Or perhaps it is much simpler. Just perhaps Prince Alois, who now rules Liechtenstein with considerable autocratic authority, simply has decided that—like Austria—only the elite like himself will be allowed to have guns. And, perhaps he is trying to curry favor with fellow autocrats at the UN.

Time will tell. In the interim, Prince Alois is creating great unneeded angst among some of his subjects. Even those who don't own firearms see much of their precious independence, freedoms and neutrality being destroyed as a result of current politics.

Chapter Fifty-One
Luxembourg
World Rank: 4 • Firearm Freedom 90%

Doesn't take long to thoroughly look around a tiny country such as Luxembourg. The capital, Luxembourg City, is really the only large city. Blood, guts and feathers—the entire country is only half the size of our diminutive state of Delaware.

In many regards, Luxembourg is a microcosm of the problems and difficulties facing anyone doing research on gun laws in foreign places. The view there regarding gun owners, guns and gun ownership seems frightfully typical. The first fellow we asked about gun shops in the country, in his tourist office in the main train station in Luxembourg City, simply refused to answer. He just walked away.

Three additional information office employees also had little to say. It might even be accurate to conclude that all three went into virtual apoplexy over questions about existing gun-shop or hunter-supply outlets. These folks immediately clustered into tight little defensive groups. Speaking only in French, which we only peripherally understood, they cast furtive, suspicious, almost terrified glances in our direction. Finally they agreed among themselves that no one they knew or cared to know would voluntarily own a gun.

They did admit that perhaps they might maybe know the general location of a gun shop or two, but nothing specific. They flat out refused to make any phone calls on our behalf, leading us to believe that gun ownership in Luxembourg might be virtually non-existent. Strange, since Luxembourg is an extremely rich country—*per capita* income is $58,900, and they're frequently overrun by their neighbors.

After a lengthy search through Luxembourg City's western suburbs we finally located a shop that at one time *probably* had some guns, ammunition and hunting supplies on offer. It, however, was locked up tight by order of the police. Permanent seals, signed by the chief of police, closed off all of the entrances. Perhaps they went bankrupt. No way to know given our limited French and event more limited understanding of their official documents.

A rumored second shop probably did not actually exist any longer. Its reported location now lay under what was a recently constructed freeway cloverleaf.

In this one instance, letters to the Luxembourg embassy in Washington, D.C. asking for leads or general information were productive. Governments typically do not wish to address the highly politicized subject of private gun ownership, but the Luxembourg embassy supplied names and addresses of three large gun shops.

Correspondence with these three eventually provided enough information to complete a reasonably accurate chapter on their gun laws. In the whole world, New Zealand is the only other country where government officials materially assisted with our information gathering.

The Wall Street Journal and the Heritage Foundation rate Luxembourg as the fourth freest country on Earth, explaining high individual wealth and general prosperity. Luxembourg is characterized by good enforcement of property rights, relatively low net taxes, and—in general— a lack of permit-requiring, paper-producing bureaucracies.

Tiny Luxembourg lies to the north of France surrounded on the north and a bit south by Belgium and bordered on the east by Germany. The nation seems to be booming. Visitors see a great number of newly built highways and roads as well as many currently under construction. A proliferation of building projects, evidenced by numerous construction cranes, dots the horizon.

Citizens speak French and German with a smattering of English here and there. It's a different culture, but one that many American gun owners could thoroughly enjoy, especially living in the rural, rolling, tree-covered hills.

Of the 440,000 citizens, there are an estimated 2,000 hunters, 4,000 sport-shooters and about 1,000 people who mostly collect but seldom shoot their guns. Among these collectors there are "more than several" who have collections exceeding 250 guns! Given patience securing permits, getting to know issuing authorities and willingness to spend sufficient money, just about any small arm is legally owned in Luxembourg, including machine guns and machine pistols.

There are few to no crimes with firearms in Luxembourg. The few gun crimes that do occur invariably involve illegal guns brought into the country from the east over their extremely porous border.

Specifically, one goes through the process of legally owning a gun or guns in Luxembourg by applying to the local police for a gun-owner's permit. This application must include the category or categories for which one wishes to purchase and own a gun. As mentioned, these

include hunting, target, trap and skeet shooting—including pistols—
and collecting. Gun-owners' permits cost about $22.50, and take
about three months to issue. Renewal must be done every three to five
years and takes only about three weeks. Collectors renew more often
than hunters and sport shooters.

Gun ownership is individually personalized. First-time novice permit
holders are only allowed .22 LR rifles and pistols! After a couple years
without incidents or problems, they can eventually expand to virtually
any caliber and type of gun including assault rifles, machine guns and
machine pistols.

Applicants for gun-owners' certificates must have a clean record,
proven employment, a national-identity card and proven place of
residence, and must produce a certificate of liability insurance. We
know insurance companies in Luxembourg regularly issue these
certificates but not at what cost.

All guns are listed on the gun-owner's permit. In many cases,
principally in the case of collectors, this list can become quite lengthy.
Collectors are even required to list down the bayonets they hold in
their collections! There is no limit on the number of guns that hunters,
sport shooters or collectors may hold and own.

Additionally, hunters must apply annually for hunting licenses and
sports shooters must verify they were active target shooters by
demonstrating that they were at the range at least twice during the
course of the previous year. Membership in a hunting club or sport-
shooting club with a shooting range and/or a trap and skeet field can
be extremely costly. Apparently those too old and unable to continue
shooting on a regular basis at their club would lose their target-
shooting license and be forced to liquidate their guns.

No semi-auto or full-auto guns are permitted hunters or sport shooters.
Only collectors may have these.

The eight gun shops in the country carry an extensive inventory of
ammunition. No limit exists on the amount you may purchase if you
can pay for it, but dealers are required to record all ammo sales and
only sell ammunition for the guns on your permit. Those purchasing
huge quantities of ammunition may catch the attention of the
authorities and may have to answer questions regarding their needs.

Reloading is permitted. Components are on offer or can be ordered
from most gun shops, but—like most of Europe—reloading is not
commonly undertaken by citizens of Luxembourg. Perhaps it's a
reflection on their culture or perhaps their great personal wealth.

Non-citizens must live in Luxembourg for a year or more before
applying for a gun-owner's permit, a hunting license or hunting-club

membership. Importation of gun collections is permitted if you can demonstrate you are a responsible person, knowledgeable regarding firearms and can withstand the required paper blizzard.

Police in Luxembourg pretty much know everyone. As in New Zealand, good citizens have little problem dealing with these folks, who have probably known their family for generations.

Luxembourg is a very nice, friendly, comfortable place. In spite of initial reactions of those outside the culture, a reasonably large, fairly free-and-easy gun culture exists in the country. This is helped because little gun crime exists in the country and perhaps also because Grand Duke Henri, the constitutional monarch, is himself a gun owner, shooter, collector and enthusiast.

Chapter Fifty-Two
Afghanistan
World Rank: 35 • Firearm Freedom 39%

Information for this section on gun laws in Afghanistan comes from only one—perhaps credible or perhaps not so credible—source... since it's unlikely that any normal person would travel to this chaotic, war-torn land to verify facts. As a result, this summary could be a bit off or perhaps even incomplete.

One hundred percent certain, though, this information and analysis is definitely not the last word. National gun laws worldwide are changing. In Afghanistan they will probably change dramatically!

Gathering information on any aspect of the country of Afghanistan, whether it be economic or social, is tremendously difficult. One does not just fly into the country, check into a hotel, go down to a tourist agency office and then pop into a local gun store to ask questions. Only those heavily protected by either the U.S. military or Afghan government should contemplate travel to this chaotic land. Resident foreigners are still commonly kidnapped, assassinated, tortured and harassed in Afghanistan. Not necessarily in that order.

Our generous American information source worked as an instructor, armorer and gunsmith on a three-month contract with a private American company setting up a small-arms repair shop and gun-repair training facility in Kabul, the capital. In this regard he was in a perfect central position to know about and comment about Afghan gun laws.

Osama bin Laden, the Taliban, and our continuing military involvement have placed this country firmly in the American mind.

But, other than knowing Afghanistan is "over there someplace," most Americans cannot accurately place it on a world map.

It's little help to point out that Texas-sized Afghanistan is nine time zones east of New York. China borders on the east. Pakistan on the south and Iran on the west. The Hindu Kush mountain range—no small pile of rocks—splits the country east to west. With the exception of the somewhat favorable southwest, the country is smothered by high snow-capped mountains and cut to shreds by deep, often impenetrable valleys.

Per capita incomes are an extremely modest $800. But economic growth, hyped by a sudden influx of dollar-laden foreigners, is about 7.5%. Inflation, on the other hand, is at least 10.5%, indicating that the farther they go, the behinder they get.

While these statistics seem bleak, they must be tempered by the fact that average Afghanis have little to no use for government statisticians. Only an estimated 36 percent of these folks can even read and write.

Afghan gun laws are quickly summarized by noting that there aren't any. Our informant believes there may be some on the books, maintained by the Ministry of Interior, but currently no gun laws are being enforced. The only exception occurs when obviously wealthy—usually foreigners—are overly blatant about carrying machine guns or submachine guns and assault rifles in public places.

On such occasions, the Afghan police or military may use this behavior as an excuse to shake down the owner for a bribe. As a result, more easily concealed, smaller, collapsible submachine guns and large-bore pistols are eagerly sought by residents. Prices of such, we are informed, spike up to stratospheric levels as a result. Just about everything, including .454 Casulls, .50 AE and more common .40 S&W pistols are available. Small Czech .380 submachine guns are especially popular, but often very difficult to find for sale.

Some of the many weapons available are inferior back-shop Khyber-Pass knockoffs. Most, however, are high quality guns from original industrial-nation manufacturers. These include Israel, Brazil, Switzerland, Austria, the U.S. and, of course, Russia.

Ammo for even extremely exotic guns is available, but only if purchasers are willing to search it out and then bargain like Turkish rug merchants. No restrictions on quantities, sizes or bullet types. Prices, if one does not bargain, may exceed an unlimited budget!

Apparently little or no ammo is manufactured in Afghanistan. Some very small-scale reloading may occasionally occur. But most ammo is imported or has been imported by various militaries. Wide availability of surplus ammo has kept prices low and perhaps manufacturers out.

As an excellent—perhaps far out—example, our informant salvaged a 23mm cannon from a Russian MIG lying upside down in a local bone yard. No ammo was in the plane hull, but he was able to purchase all he needed to try out the gun down on Tool Street in central Kabul.

Tool Street, we are told, is the place to go for historic, exotic weapons. Ground-mount machine guns, heavy machine guns, anti-aircraft guns, submachine guns, 20mm guns, 155 Russian field pieces and others from all over the world are there for a price. Our informant gunsmith has pictures of a beautiful 1950 manufacture Kalashnikov AK-47 he purchased on Tool Street for $150. RPG-7 tubes are about $500 each. Rockets, depending on type, cost between $250 and $400.

One real oddity of Afghan gun availability stands out. Common .22 rimfire guns and ammo are generally unavailable in Afghanistan. Perhaps it's a situation where contending parties saw need only for heavier guns and ammo. Or perhaps in this one case the central government has been successful controlling import of .22 rimfire guns and ammo to—like Tanzania—control poaching.

If so, they are far too late! There are no birds, no rats, no deer, no nothing in the form of wildlife in that rural, rugged and desolate country. Only feral dogs and vultures are said to roam about.

Silencers for 9mm pistols and submachine guns are ubiquitous in Afghanistan. Both back-shop models and sophisticated, well-engineered factory models from France, the U.S. and Finland, are commonly found.

Any gun laws on the books are currently ignored. This ignorance, we are told, is officially sanctioned by the government to encourage citizens to arm and resist crime, as well as kidnapping and extortion. There is no limit on numbers, kinds or types of guns one may own.

Reportedly, American gun collectors would be drooling over historic and rare makes and models on offer. Some of these, including Mauser pistols and Martini rifles, would even be legal in the U.S.

Air India has fairly regular flights into Kabul from Delhi. There are some tourist-grade hotels. Conditions are improving, but western visitors are still targeted by criminals. Currently travel to Kabul to take advantage of their wondrous bounty is not a viable option.

Chapter Fifty-Three
Iceland
World Rank: 37 • Firearm Freedom 37%

Gun owners in Iceland really have their underwear in a bundle. And it isn't because there is no tree larger than four inches on which to hang a target.

It's because gun laws in Iceland are a dramatic microcosm of what happens when government bureaucrats think about and act in regard to privately owned firearms. It suggests that rational, reasoned thought by this class of people is probably an oxymoron. It's true the world over, but painfully evident here.

Slightly more than half the 300,000 Icelanders live in Reykjavik, their pint-sized capital. There are few real cities outside of the capital. Mostly there are only villages populated with from 100 to 200 hardy souls scattered about this Kentucky-sized island nation. Police in Iceland do not carry side arms. Crime is very minimal and people generally are meticulously law abiding.

Visitors see some farm houses, barns and churches strung out along the round-island ring road. But even these are relatively few and far between. Some wags accuse Icelandic map makers of including sheep feeders on their maps in an attempt to "bulk up" points of interest.

Because of its sparse population and basic rural character, reasonable men might expect gun ownership in Iceland to be common and basically unencumbered. It is somewhat common, but definitely not unencumbered. Their rules and regulations leading to legal gun ownership are unique and—we could even say—a bit dodgy.

With *per capita* incomes of $31,900, Iceland is a fairly wealthy nation. One of the current signs of success is becoming a licensed legal gun owner/shooter/hunter—something of a current fad among the newly rich. As a result, interest in gun ownership is steady to expanding.

This flies in the face of some significant obstacles. Gun owners, hunters and shooters, for instance, all must be licensed. Aspiring new gun owners must first take a comprehensive course in gun safety, function, capabilities and general design, including a section on game, environment and habitat if you will seek a hunting license.

Start by going to the local police station—of which there are sufficiently many scattered about rural Iceland. Fill out a form requesting enrollment in a gun/game course—then wait until 15 to 20 applicants are also ready to take the course. Anyone with any kind of criminal record is forever barred from legally owning a firearm.

With 15 to 20 applicants waiting, police will contract with a suitable private instructor. Cost for the first "gun portion" of the course is a whopping $250. Throw in the "game management/environmental section" leading to a hunting license and the price jumps an additional $170. Even by European standards, this is extremely high priced. This is the land of $6.50/gallon gas and $22 hamburgers.

The firearms course consists of three four-hour evening classes as well as a two-day weekend field session. Novice trainees will fire perhaps 25 rounds in both a shotgun and rifle during the course of this weekend field session. After completion of the course and upon receiving a sign-off by the instructor, the student is instantly issued a gun-owner's permit.

There is no written test at the conclusion of the course, nor any other examination—medical, mental, financial or otherwise. However the course instructor does take note of any handicaps or obvious mental problems that might disqualify a potential gun owner.

Those completing this portion of the procedure can now legally buy and own certain .22-caliber rifles and/or a shotgun. But only .22 bolt-action rimfire rifles, or lever action or pump-action .22s are allowed. Absolutely no semi-auto .22s are allowed. Pump, double or single-shot shotguns are allowed on what is referred to as an "A" permit.

Currently the Icelandic gun bureaucracy is having an absolute hissy fit regarding correct classification of .17 rimfire rifles and .22 rimfire mags under an "A" designation. Icelandic gun owners seem more amused than stressed regarding this imponderable dilemma challenging the bureaucracy. Perhaps because "A" permits are only a stepping stone.

Having been issued an A permit, new gun owners take their card to their local gun shop, of which there are many more than one might initially suppose scattered about the island. Then they are allowed to purchase only the sanctioned .22 rifle and/or shotgun of their dreams. Then it's back again to the police with the receipt, where the gun is registered to that gun-owner's card. Then go back yet again to the gun shop to take actual physical possession.

While this procedure certainly would not appeal to American gun owners, it is not quite as cumbersome as one might first suppose in tiny, personal Iceland where most folks are on a first-name basis. (Even the names in the phone books are organized by first name. Many cop shops scattered about the island's villages are generally filled with friendly, accommodating people. Bureaucratic glitches are uncommon. At least at this point.

A-type licenses are a kind of learner's permit. After one year, assuming no change in one's criminal status, holders of an A license are automatically upgraded to a "B" license. The B-license holders are allowed to purchase and keep semi-auto shotguns as well as centerfire rifles up to size .300 Win Mag. Those wishing to hunt their guns rather than just target shoot must also have a hunting license.

All pump and semi-auto shotguns must be plugged to a three-shot maximum capacity. No military semi-auto shotguns are allowed. Shotguns are permitted in any gauge, including 28, .410 and 10 mag. Eight gauge guns are okay except no one in Iceland has them or the ammo for sale.

Duck and goose hunting is extremely popular. Hunters from around the world come to hunt waterfowl in Iceland. They can bring their personal shotguns if their guide has secured the necessary permits.

Permitted rifles are all bolt actions or single shots. Absolutely no semi-auto rifles—big or small—are allowed, especially assault rifles. In some isolated instances, gun collectors are allowed to own and keep semi-auto rifles, but never to take them out of their homes to the range or to actually shoot them. Absolutely no full-auto guns are permitted.

Total number of shotguns and rifles one may own is not controlled, but after three pieces a very heavy, very specifically defined rugged gun safe is required. This safe must be inspected by the police before being placed in service.

Guns of caliber larger than .300 Win Mag, in the .458, .375, .416 class are permitted on a C-level license, but only after the owner has left the island three times to hunt overseas! Apparently new-rich Icelanders are traveling to Poland, the Baltics and Africa, among others, to hunt. So the bureaucracy makes this amazing concession just for them.

There is an "easy to acquire" E-type license for those who wish to hand load. Simply take the quick, easy, relatively inexpensive evening hand-loading class. Gun shops in Iceland carry a fairly large selection of reloading components, tools and equipment. Primers, bullets and powder are about the same price as in the U.S., after adding a bit for postage. There is no limit on amounts of powder, primers, bullets and shot one may purchase. No records are kept of these purchase.

Icelanders mostly reload rifle cartridges. A new little Icelandic factory, HLAD SF, both reloads shot shells and produces some very nice clear plastic rounds of its own from scratch. All of these, say the four gun owners we talked to, were so inexpensive it currently didn't pay to reload shot shells. It's cheaper and easier to buy from HLAD.

Virtually all common European rifle rounds up to .300 Win Mag are available at Icelandic gun shops. We observed .223, 7.62x39R, .308,

.22 Hornet, .22 rimfire LR & Mag, 30-06, 30-30, .270, and 7x57 as well as many others.

Purchasers must show their gun-owner's card, but can purchase any cartridge completely independent of rifle and shotgun sizes listed on their gun-owners' permits. Perviously, gun owners could only possess 500 rounds total. Recently the bureaucracy changed this to 5,000 rounds. There appears to be no means of verifying these amounts to the Icelandic authorities. No official record is kept of purchase.

Pistols are covered under a very difficult to acquire and expensive class D gun-owner's permit. Very few citizens shoot, much less have access to, a pistol in Iceland. Cost of a class D pistol sanction is about $170. Basically it works as follows:

B-level license holders who have been at this level for several years, and who have also not run afoul of any rules or regulations, may join a pistol club. Pistol-club memberships are sufficiently pricey that few gun owners join—high enough that our informants did not belong, and really didn't know how much they cost. This not withstanding, there are several active pistol clubs on the island.

After joining a club and being a member for six months, the club will apply to the police for a level-D sanction, on behalf of a member who wants to target shoot with a pistol. Upon approval, the club—not the individual—will apply for permission to import and keep a pistol. Gun stores in Iceland do not stock pistols. This pistol is never owned or kept by the individual who, nevertheless, has to personally shell out the *Kroner* to pay for it.

After permission is granted, a pistol will be imported in the club's name. If that isn't enough, no semi-auto pistols are allowed for target shooting. Only revolvers.

Additionally, the bureaucracy has decided double-action pistols are really semi-autos in disguise. These are all strictly forbidden too! Apparently, common double-action target revolvers are custom modified to single action only. This is to comply with the rules regarding double-action revolvers.

No pistol ammunition other than perhaps .22 LR is available in gun shops. Even this is uncertain, as .22 pistols reportedly are never sanctioned. Pistol clubs handle and sell .38, 9mm and .45 pistol ammo for their member target shooters. Some clubs also reportedly handle pistol reloading components for their members.

Other wild idiosyncrasies characterize Iceland's bureaucratic rules and regulations. Silencers, for instance, are not specifically prohibited. But altering a rifle barrel to accept a silencer is severely proscribed. Apparently these bureaucrats have never encountered or heard of threaded hillbilly-type friction caps used to effectively mount silencers without altering or changing a rifle in any manner!

Finding a place to shoot in rural, remote, sparsely populated Iceland is not challenging. Even as little as 20 miles out of Reykjavik, the land is so thinly populated shooting would not be a problem.

Shooting clay birds has apparently taken off dramatically in almost a faddish fashion. Icelanders who traveled to Mexico, Argentina or parts of Africa find that, if they practice a bit before hand so they can actually hit the birds, the experience is more enjoyable.

Little, friendly but difficult-to-reach Iceland, located way up almost on the Arctic Circle in the North Atlantic between Canada, Greenland and England is truly unique. Its people are wonderful, the scenery is spectacular and unique, the benign climate is unique and, of course, Iceland's gun laws enforced by bureaucracy are completely unique.

Nevertheless, their gun/hunting/shooting culture seems to thrive. No less than six to eight customers at any one given time could be observed in the largest gun shop in Reykjavik when I was there.

Chapter Fifty-Four
Albania
World Rank: 2 • Firearm Freedom 96%

In some places in this world the besotted hand of anti-gun-rights UN bureaucrats is obvious, in others less so. Unfortunately, tiny Albania has become the poster child for UN gun banners. They have even produced a foolish, contradictory, inconclusive 120-page tome celebrating their actions as they willy-nilly run about spending unlimited funds on studies and procedures they themselves admit lead to very uncertain, illogical conclusions but which, if implemented, will lead to a disarmed, dispirited, subjugated citizenry.

In this regard, we can be extremely thankful for the alert and vigorous actions of our National Rifle Association. Early on, the NRA folks identified the risk of allowing these UN anti-gun-rights bureaucrats any kind of policy making traction in the United States.

Our study of Albanian gun laws is only interesting in regard to the great atrocities perpetrated on unsuspecting citizens by the weenies at the UN. In this one instance, we learn exactly what these rabid anti-gunners are thinking and what end they have in mind for all freedom-loving, self-reliant gun owners throughout the world.

Logically one would conclude that Albania deserves a respite. They suffered mightily under communism, having the dubious distinction of being one of the poorest countries in the world. Since renouncing communism in 1991 their *per capita* GDP has risen to a still paltry $4,900. But 47 years of trying to be the best, most thoroughly pure communist society on Earth took a deadly toll. Currently they suffer, perhaps not quite as badly, from hordes of locust-like European Union and UN bureaucrats having little to no concept of personal responsibility and private property. To their intense credit, even Albanian officials pay this UN bed-wetting, thumb-sucking horde minimal to no real attention unless driven by bribery and coercion.

Locate Albania on a map straight east of Italy's boot heel, across the Adriatic Sea. This sea forms Albania's extensive and porous western border. Greece borders to the south, Macedonia to the east and Montenegro to the northeast. Albania is slightly larger than Maryland.

The critical date for Albanian gun owners occurred during March of 1997. This was a time when several Ponzi-type get-rich-quick schemes, seemingly supported by the new democratic government suddenly and predictably, went T.U. Rioting and looting broke out throughout the land. Citizens with a lingering communist mentality who couldn't know the difference between public and private property looted government warehouses.

Albania, at that time, bulged with warehouses crammed full of small arms and ammunition, allegedly on call should evil capitalists invade. Albanians, often under the approving eye of government bureaucrats, summarily looted these warehouses loaded with assault rifles, web gear, uniforms, pistols, light and heavy machine guns, ammunition, mortars, anti-tank rockets, rocket-propelled grenades, hand grenades, explosives and other military gear. UN bureaucrats had a virtually terminal hissy-fit over the fact that so many citizens now privately held so many "unregistered" guns and ammunition.

Currently these same UN gun-control advocates still spend a great deal of time, money and personal energy attempting to estimate how many guns and munitions still remain in private hands. They make endless, foolish studies regarding how many suicides, levels of poverty, incidents of domestic violence, mental illnesses, robberies, murders and incidents of fear and uncertainty have resulted from so many guns being in such wide circulation. Most of these analyses are framed by the statement that we can never really know the actual number or the real impact, but we charge ahead anyway.

Most reasonable estimates suggest that, of the 1,200 military depots looted, about 652,000 weapons, 1.5 billion rounds of ammunition, 3.5 million hand grenades, 3,600 tons of explosives and one million mines were taken. At least 330,000 weapons (or roughly half converted to private ownership) are still in private hands. That's in spite of extensive private surplus-munitions sales they have made all over the world, several extended national amnesty turn-in periods, some efforts at confiscation, normal wear and tear along with everyday consumption. Still, everyone in Albania who wants a gun has one. The discomfort this brings the UN bureaucrats is, to say the least, gratifying.

Albania's gun situation is made even more complex by the fact that both officially on the part of the government and unofficially on the part of good citizens who buried materiel in their back yards, there were tons and tons of guns and ammo left behind from World War II.

Minimally, 330,000 guns of all types, plus whatever was left from WW II, in a population of 3,600,000 suggests that at least ten percent of Albanians are gun owners. Because Albania has some tradition of gun ownership, one could even suggest that these ten percent are likely gun-owner gun-collecting enthusiasts.

The UN Undersecretary General for Disarmament Affairs, headed by Jayantha Dhanapala, operating on the basis of surveys, statistics and conjecture that he admits are irrelevant or purely whimsical, Albania has implemented gun rules and regulations. These make converting any illegal guns to legality or even owning most sporting weapons difficult to impossible. On the bright side, even the UN bureaucrats admit these regulations are poorly administered or enforced.

Mr. Dhanapala, for instance, places great stock in data his office had developed regarding the frequency with which Albanian citizens knew about a gun crime, were personally fearful, trusted the police, contemplated suicide or whatever. He skillfully manages to cherry pick respondents' thoughts about gun crime, selectively reporting only those that fit his pre-conceived notions. "Do you think firearms in the home improve or worsen family relations," is one of his favorites.

Obviously many of these issues have little to nothing to do with private gun ownership. Yet, in spite of markedly better data gathering, along with dramatically higher levels of private, non-sporting gun ownership, crime rates are falling in Albania, at times dramatically. Of course, the concept of more guns, less crime, completely eludes those who work for the UN.

Information on Albania comes from an attorney who spent three years there as a missionary in rural regions and then a year in big cities as a Fulbright Scholar. This fellow also questioned friends and colleagues there by e-mail on our behalf. We also have a long published report and analysis issued by the UN specifically on the gun situation. Some gaps in our data persist but, by inference and past experience, most of the information on Albanian gun laws can be assembled.

Start with what we know for sure or can infer with some certainty. Reloading is not popular or easily undertaken in Albania, other than perhaps shot shells, there's just too much cheap, surplus military ammo floating about. Importation of powder, bullets and primers from Italy, a principal trading partner, is certainly possible, especially when dealing with ultra-corrupt, easily and cheaply bribable government officials guarding the border.

Sport and subsistence hunting is undertaken in the rough remote northern mountainous areas of Albania. As a result, some use of either imported or reloaded shot shells may occur. Albania's indigenous arms and ammo manufacturing industry is *kaput*.

We also know that all legal firearms must be registered with the Albanian Ministry of Defense. Only guns with an approved sporting purpose are permitted. Apparently, other than some limited issue for private security guards, government officials and businessmen, this precludes legal ownership of pistols. We are unsure, but judging from the fact that illegal pistols reportedly sell on the street for about five times the cost of an AK-47, it is a valid assumption. Perhaps in dirt-poor Albania, both trap and skeet as well as legal target pistol shooting are seldom if ever undertaken.

Legal gun ownership starts with an application for a gun-owner's permit at one's local cop shop. Statements accompany the application indicating: lack of criminal record or court indictment, lack of any physical or mental impairment, financial capacity, and a great deal of additional personal data. You assert that you do not owe any money, are a certified member of a local hunting organization, and include a statement from local police verifying you're not involved in any vendettas and are a citizen in good standing. Obviously some of these documents would be very expensive and time consuming to gather. Some must even be done through the local courts. Applicants must be 22 years or older. Apparently women can apply, but are seldom legally sanctioned to own firearms, this being a mostly Muslim society.

UN antis take great pride in having pushed Albanian authorities into these draconian difficult anti-private-gun-ownership measures. We can easily assume this is what they have in mind for U.S. gun owners.

Costs of actual permits to own a pistol are 600 Lekes (about $6) and 1,000 Lekes (about $10) for a rifle. Licenses are issued by a committee of police chiefs supposedly within 30 working days. Gun-owner's permits are issued for an indeterminate period of time, and officially sanctioned permits may be revoked at any time, solely at the discretion of the police without cause or explanation.

On issuance of a gun-owner's permit, holders may go to any of the several gun and hunters' supply shops located in major cities about

Albania to purchase a specific gun. Then the police must sanction purchase of that specific gun for an approved sporting purpose. Oddly, this gun technically remains the property of the state!

Unknown at this point is how many guns citizens may legally own, probably only one or two. One limit is the need to convince issuing authorities of another need for a sporting purpose. Probably only single-shot or bolt-action rifles and double- or single-barrel shotguns will be sanctioned. Official regulations are silent concerning shotguns. Certainly no semi-autos of any kind would be legally allowed.

Legal ammo purchases from hunter supply stores are only permitted for guns registered to one's gun-owner permit. We don't know what restrictions on quantities apply.

One July 2005 government report indicates that 1,683 legal hunting rifles were imported from Turkey. One can validly assume that these were both sporting rifles and that they moved relatively quickly into private hands in Albania. It's inconceivable that merchants in poor Albania would hold expensive inventory any length of time.

Ironically, given all the illegal guns floating around Albania, there is some opinion that some more modern assault rifles and pistols are moving into the country illegally. "It's the fishermen and their damn boats," the UN weenies whine.

At the insistence of the UN, several gun amnesty/turn-in programs have been attempted. Because these programs were designed and funded by socialists who understood nothing about free-market incentives and private property, they all failed. The UN types refused to buy the guns because "it would send the wrong message." Guns are a scourge, they maintain, not an item of value!

Ninety percent of the guns surrendered were old, rusty, derelict WW II models. What few good weapons and ammunition that came in were generally improperly inventoried. Often they were quickly resold out the back door by destitute government officials in desperate need of a payday. Naturally, the Albanian government lost interest in collecting or even controlling illegal guns, much to the anguish of the UN folks.

Possession of weapons in the north Dibeb and Elbasan regions is traditionally considered the right of every male 18 years of age or more. This tradition was maintained even throughout the long, long communist era. UN staffers attempt cherry-picked focus groups and national surveys to prove otherwise, but there is still a strong element of a gun culture in Albania. Some Albanian government officials even told the UN that Albania doesn't have the prison capacity to rigorously enforce gun laws.

We conclude this analysis of Albanian gun laws with a verbatim quote from the UN gun law report:

"Of course there are also those who will not be convinced to part with their unregistered guns, whether by greater stability, lotteries, education and awareness-raising programs, development projects or police raids. While all interviewers put criminals into this group, ordinary citizens were also included. For example, here one would include those for whom a gun was regarded as necessary for providing personal and family security or tradition. These people would go to considerable lengths to ensure that their weapons were not discovered, with weapons collectors noting that people no longer simply hiding guns under their beds but in more ingenious or awkward to reach places."

Of course humans are personally responsible for their own property and safety. It's what our Second Amendment is all about. After two major wars and one horrible occupation, apparently the Albanians have learned. Obviously UN officials have not. Thank God for the National Rifle Association—that they were on to this idiocy in time to choke it off.

Those who wish to read the entire UN report on guns in Albania can do so on the web at saferworld.org.uk/publications.php?id=115.

Chapter Fifty-Five
Cyprus
World Rank: 49 • Firearm Freedom 24%

Rumor has it that the tiny island nation of Cyprus, lying in the far eastern Mediterranean Sea, is wide open for private gun ownership, as well as being an island paradise characterized by miles and miles of unspoiled, untrammeled beaches. A close look however finds the gun part to be less than accurate.

The part about being an island paradise is true. Tens of thousands of Europeans not only flock to vacation destinations on Cyprus, but also purchase glamorous yet relatively inexpensive beachfront vacation homes. Most come complete with balconies overlooking hurt-your-eyeballs-pretty blue ocean framed by white sand beaches.

In spite of an almost old-world colonial charm, this is not a third world country. Everything on Cyprus is neat and clean as well as functional.

Per capita annual income for the free and independent southern two-thirds of the island is a relatively high $20,300. A more economically

retarded Turkish-occupied portion to the north musters up only a
measly $7,135 each. Free Cyprus ranks 20th in the *Wall Street Journal*
Index of Economic Freedom, explaining its citizens' relative wealth
and the European stampede to purchase property. Cypriots respect
property rights.

Shelves in free Cyprus stores are fully stocked, traffic lights work,
toilets flush and there are functional sewers and running water.

However, rumors regarding private gun ownership on Cyprus are
materially incorrect. These rumors probably originated with
speculation on the part of United Nations weenies in Albania who
objected to the fact that the shipping documents for surplus military
small arms from Albania both originated and disappeared in Cyprus.
Also, UN types are particularly notorious for not favoring free-market
economic growth. Most of the really loudmouth, corrupt UN
bureaucrats seem to come from more despotic nations.

Gun laws for residents and citizens of Cyprus are really very simple.
While not on the level of Vietnam, China, Japan or Mexico, they can
easily be characterized as "the answer is 'no,' what's the question?"

As a result, we interviewed only one gun-store owner/manager—in the
largest gun shop in Larnaca, the south's principal city. No need to
inquire further—his information was neither complex, convoluted nor
difficult to follow. Like most Cypriots, he spoke excellent English.

Citizens as well as resident foreign nationals, of whom there are an
estimated 50,000 in their winter homes, can legally own double-
barreled shotguns and that's all. Absolutely no pistols, rifles (even .22
rifles!) and, of course, no assault rifles, submachine guns or pump,
semi-auto or even single-barrel shotguns. Private citizens can own air
rifles only in .177 size. Twenty-two caliber air rifles are prohibited (too
dangerous)—a fact that Cypriot gun owners find exceedingly strange.

Sixteen- and twenty-bore guns are permitted but 99% of the shotguns
legally held are 12 bore. Twenty- and sixteen-bore ammo was on offer
at the gun shop, but mostly the wall was stacked with 12-gauge shells.

Maximum shot size permitted is number two lead. Absolutely no slugs
or buckshot rounds are allowed. Private citizens are completely
prohibited from owning or using gun powder or primers, so there is no
hand loading here.

All ammunition is made by local, in-country factories. On the other
hand, all shotguns are imported. No guns are locally manufactured
unless it is completely clandestine. A great number of Czech, Russian,
Italian, Belgian and American shotguns were on display in the store.
Prices on all seemed similar or only slightly higher than in the U.S.

Private citizens can own a total of ten different shotguns. Special licenses are infrequently available for more, but these entail installation of costly security cameras, alarm systems and special metal gun safes. As a practical matter, ten shotguns per person is the limit.

Strangely, new shotgun owners or those adding to their collections do not have to give a reason for ownership—common in other restrictive countries. This avoids process abuse which is common elsewhere.

Although a great many shooting and hunting clubs are available, club membership does not appear necessary for shotgun ownership. As a result, gun owners can spend more of their hard earned cash in the gentlemen's clubs, of which there are many in Cyprus. Those who wish to hunt for some of the numerous game birds on the island must secure a separate hunting license and perhaps join what can be a pricey hunting club. Especially true if one wants to get out on some good hunting country where the game is well managed and abundant.

There are some remote wild mountainous areas on this country, 1-1/2 times the size of Delaware. Generally the land tends to rolling, sandy, rocky-to-rugged dry hills. A few nice tree and brush covered regions containing abundant game can also be found, mostly in the west and highland center.

British soldier trainees use a remote, far west, tree-and-brush-choked region on a small peninsula for maneuvers and small-arms practice.

Acquiring a new hunting license is not easy on Cyprus. Cost is about $100 per year. There are three mandatory training sessions lasting about one evening each. Doctors, gunsmiths, ecologists and zoologists are the teachers. At the end there is a fairly rigorous exam. Let your license lapse at the end of the year, and the test must be repeated.

Of the estimated 750,000 inhabitants of Cyprus, approximately 55,000 are hunters. Nobody can guess what part of the 50,000 foreign residents are hunters, but it is thought to be a relatively high number. Recent laws regarding applications for foreigners obtaining a gun-owner's permit were softened a bit to accommodate them. Other than sunning, swimming, drinking and golfing, there isn't much to do on Cyprus. Hunting is popular.

Again, as a practical matter, it appears that foreigners cycle through Cyprus on a fairly predictable schedule. They seem to tire of the seclusion and limited activities, soon becoming anxious for other things. We encountered several foreigners who moved to Cyprus from Europe or the U.K. and then, after a couple of years, moved back.

Securing a gun-owner's permit and a permit to purchase a shotgun is fairly easy and definitely more straightforward than in many countries. Issuing authorities may reason that being able to afford pricey, handmade side-by-sides and under-overs may sort out the pissants. New owners do not have to secure a hunting license or join a club, although doing these things is said not to hurt.

First go to the police station in your home area. Male citizens must document their military service. Non-citizens and women just have to present suitable ID. At present a passport does nicely. Everyone—male and female over the age of 18—can apply. Computer searches of the applicant's record—or lack thereof—are then made.

Assuming no blemishes, it takes about 24 hours for this police check. Applicants then fill out police forms requesting permission to purchase and own a shotgun. This part of the process moves very quickly, we were told—never more than a day or two.

Form in hand, newly authorized applicants trot down to their local gun shop, of which there are a surprising number on the island, to pick out a shotgun. From the store, the shotgun goes immediately back to the police to be registered. Registration costs $100 per gun! This comprises permission to own that specific shotgun. Although initially costly, unlike hunting licenses, shotgun permits last as long as the original owner holds the gun.

Owners can purchase and hold up to 250 shot shells, or ten boxes of ammo, at one time. Purchase records are maintained by the gun shop and sales consummated only on the basis of a valid gun-owner's permit for a specific gun.

Cyprus, according to our informant at the gun shop, does not have a gun culture similar to the ones on Crete, or in the U.S., Germany or anyplace else. Gun ownership is becoming more popular but, because only shotguns are permitted, it is more subdued.

What very few illegal guns end up in the south usually arrive, they reckon, from the Turkish-occupied north. Surprising, since guns are not readily available anywhere in Turkey, and the border seems reasonably well enforced. Cyprus may be a transshipment country for military small arms, but it seems certain few are landed there. If nothing else, there seems to be no market. Like Crete, fishermen could easily bring in black market guns, but nobody seems to want them.

People on Cyprus are very patient, friendly and honest. Surprising, given the hordes of folks trooping through their pansy patches. Gun laws there are actually a relic of British occupation—being, of course, not something the average, free westerner could easily live with.

Chapter Fifty-Six
The Netherlands
World Rank: 15 • Firearm Freedom 75%

What sort of gun laws could we expect in a country characterized by legal, licensed, organized prostitution, and one where the authorities conveniently overlook marijuana sales and use in numerous coffee houses set up about the country for that specific purpose?

As compared to other parts of central Europe, gun ownership rules and regulations are reasonably liberal—perhaps even enlightened—in the Netherlands, but only by that comparison. Their gun laws are, to say the least, extremely complex. Yet, based on numerous (more than a dozen) personal visits to the country, in-depth interviews in English with a large gun-store owner/operator and shooting-club operators, as well as correspondence with gun owners, we can make some sense of their situation, perhaps even summarizing it in logical order.

It isn't because two-thirds of the Netherlands lies below sea level that it's difficult to describe the country's geographic location. It's more nearly because it is an otherwise plain vanilla little land without many distinguishing features. The Atlantic Ocean's North Sea borders to the west. Germany lies to the east and Belgium to the south.

Historic economic activity, including trading, shipping, warehousing and insurance, have created a generally wealthy class of people. *Per capita* incomes average about $29,500. Perhaps 60 percent of the Dutch speak fluent English. As traders, they are hell on wheels. The author once encountered a Dutch cooking oil salesman working for Unilever in Damascus, Syria who could and did sell his product in Dutch, English, French and Arabic!

In general, Dutch citizens and some residents are permitted to own a total of five different guns. These can be any mix or match of pistols, rifles, including semi-auto assault rifles, and shotguns including pumps and semi-autos.

There is a limit on the size of centerfire rifles allowed, but those who demonstrate an ability and interest in large game hunting outside the country are fairly easily allowed larger rifles such as .300 Win Mags, .338 Win Mags, .458 Mag and even .375 H&H rifles. The only caveat is that aspiring shootists must join a suitable safari big-game hunting club to demonstrate their sincerity and interest.

Amsterdam gun store

Firearms owners in small, crowded Netherlands are limited
by space for marksmanship opportunities, but like any
other country, they find a way. This is the storefront of the
only gun shop in Amsterdam.

Shooting range in Amsterdam

Amsterdam's only gun store features an indoor range, and
as you can see, a range is a range wherever it is situated.
This clean, well-kept facility has 10 shooting points and
electrically operated target pullers.

Shooting clubs are ubiquitous in the Netherlands. If one is patient, it isn't particularly difficult to find or even form a club dedicated to one's special interests. Average yearly cost for club membership is about $40 per person.

The Dutch allow hunting with a pistol. A situation unique throughout much of the world, pistols are either judged as overly dangerous for private folk or are strictly tools of personal protection and nothing else.

Recent changes in Dutch gun law now require that purchasers of military-type assault rifles such as AK-47s can no longer legally change their operation from full-auto to permitted semi-auto. These rifles must now all leave the factory as semi-autos.

No rules regard magazine capacity other than a two-round limit in semi-auto and pump shotguns and rifles used for hunting. Pistol hunters must limit their handguns to five rounds. Owners blasting away on the range can have magazines of whatever capacity they wish. Sporting-clay shooters, for instance, seldom have magazine blocks in their pumps or semi-autos. All firearms held by private owners must be locked away in a gun safe when not being used.

Of pistols permitted, .45 ACP is the maximum size unless one secures special sanction for larger bore target shooting. There is another special permission for collectors who wish to accumulate and shoot more than five guns. Generally this permission is said to not be overly difficult to secure. We talked to one man who probably had 150 working pistols in his collection. But this sanction is usually limited to guns of a specific class or design. WW II rifles or pistols, Lugers, Mausers, trap guns, WW I guns, short-barreled pistols or whatever—all can qualify as long as there is a club dedicated to such. Obviously this class can be quite broad!

While being mostly alien to Americans, this clubby business is popular throughout the world. Clubs can form for just about anything. Knitting, hooking carpets, owning, driving and mechanicking vintage autos, shooting .50 caliber pistols or whatever. Where no club exists for a special interest, two or three citizens can easily form one.

An organization in Holland called KNSA keeps track of shooting clubs, including how often one actually practices on the range, or members get together to discuss firearms design and history, go hunting, what they got hunting or even their scores at the range. Most of this would seem intolerable to average gun owners used to much more freedom, but the Dutch simply go on with it.

All this seems fairly simple, easy and perhaps even a tiny bit enlightened, until it comes to securing that first gun-owner's certificate. Then things get very complex, quickly. Yet, an estimated 100,000 residents and citizens are hunters and sport shooters in the Netherlands. This out of a total population of about 16.5 million on a land area only twice the size of New Jersey.

First, aspiring Dutch gun owners must join an appropriate club. Eventually they may join four or five different ones, but start with one. Applicants to gun clubs must be 18 years of age. Ironically, while shooting is considered to mostly be a man's sport, the KNSA record keepers now offer a subsidy to women's shooting clubs, an attempt to attract more women shooters.

Applicants to a shooting club—sporting clays, pistol, .22 rifle, large-bore rifle or whatever, apply on an introductory basis. Neophytes are then allowed to shoot the club's guns on the club's range three different times on a trial basis. If after this the newbie wants to continue, club members must approve of the new member. Then newcomers must round up three different letters of reference.

With these three trial sessions behind them and the three reference letters in hand, new applicants can—unless they are complete jerks—expect full membership to be extended. Now it gets even more hairy.

Using club rifles, pistols or shotguns, new shooters must shoot a minimum of 18 times during the next twelve-month period. At the end of these twelve months, newbies can request, from the club, an authorization for a weapon license. This is for a single pistol, rifle or shotgun. Assault-rifle and even full-auto ownership and use are possible, as we will see, but not this early in the program.

If and when the club issues a certificate of proficiency, this paper is taken to the police who do a computer background check on the applicant. Strangely, no medical examination is required. Apparently the assumption is that club members would have identified any mental or physical impairment during the first year's trial period.

It takes about two weeks and costs about $15 per person for a police paper. After a first-gun license is issued, it takes only a few minutes at police headquarters to secure additional authorizations up to the common maximum of five. All gun licenses must be renewed with the police annually at a cost of $15 for each gun.

However, only one gun is permitted that first year. On securing a permit, it is taken to a gun dealer and exchanged for a gun, along with about the same amount of cash we would expect to pay for similar guns in the U.S. Quite a number of gun shops can be found about tiny Holland. Many establishments combine club, shooting range and storage with their role as retailers of guns and ammo.

After this, several additional requirements come into view. Shooters must by law practice on their club range at least 18 times a year. Not to forget, big brother KNSA is keeping track! Fail to do your required 18 in any one year and you will receive a warning from the police. Fail a second year in a row and your gun-owner's permit is revoked!

With this as a start, now spanning several years, Dutch gun owners work themselves up into either a collection, or five-gun status.

Reloading is common in Holland. It's surprising, since most Europeans don't reload, and surplus ammo is cheap in Holland. Perhaps they reload because of the high expense of shooting 18 times per year. We don't really know.

In Holland, reloaders are allowed to inventory up to three kilos (6.6 pounds) of powder. No special license or club membership is needed for citizen reloaders, but regulations for component retailers are strict.

Everything gun is imported into Holland! Guns and ammo come from Italy, Switzerland, Sweden, Russia, the Czech Republic, Finland and, of course, the U.S. Ruger rifles and pistols, for instance, are common and popular in the Netherlands.

Loaded ammo, bullets, primers and empty cases are only sold on the basis of being used for guns on one's gun-owner's certificate. Twelve-gauge skeet rounds cost $35 per hundred, .22 LR ammo is $35 per thousand, 9mm rounds run about $200 per thousand.

Possession limits on ammo are typically Dutch. Most ammo is purchased and held at one's club—often at a steep discount. Ammo held at home is reckoned by household, assuming three people at home. Private gun owners can hold up to 10,000 rounds *per house*! Primers are included in this count. It also seems these 10,000 rounds can include shot shells and large-bore rifle rounds as well as .22s!

As mentioned, Dutch gun laws are extremely complex and detailed. We could go on and on. Full-auto assault rifle and perhaps machine-pistol clubs, for instance, provide for private ownership of these guns to members dedicated to owning and firing such. Supposedly the Dutch words for these clubs are "places where grown men enjoy changing money into noise."

Silencers are allowed private citizens only for air rifles, but are common among police and military target-pistol shooters. We did not see silencers on large-bore hunting rifles as is common in the U.K.

Shotguns in .410 and .28 gauge are not allowed for hunting, only for clay-bird shooting at the club.

All of this applies only to persons who are Dutch citizens. Yet ownership of multiple passports is said to be very common in Holland, implying that just about anyone who wants to own a gun in Holland

and is willing to withstand the lengthy, convoluted process can legally own and use just about any gun they wish.

Illegal guns are thought to be so common that most Dutch gun owners won't even attempt an estimate. Apparently everyone who really wants a gun can have one if they will settle for an illegal gun. These illegals are not only WW II weapons, but very modern designs arriving from Russia, Romania, the Baltics, the Czech Republic, Albania and many others, in spite of fairly stringent laws regarding illegal guns. European borders are now so porous that inflows of anything cannot really be stopped or even controlled to any great extent.

At any rate, residents of the Netherlands do enjoy a certain amount of gun freedom. Not as much as we would be comfortable with, and their rules are awfully picky, but they can own guns.

Chapter Fifty-Seven
San Marino
World Rank: 6 • Firearm Freedom 88%

Perhaps San Marino is not actually a separate country. They don't have their own currency, electing to use Euros instead. Citizen residents speak Italian rather than a separate, distinct language. Few people know where to find the tiny 24-square-mile republic and San Marino is not listed in the "Wall Street Journal Index of Economic Freedom."

But gun owners have got to be wildly enthusiastic about the place. A great large storefront sign for Armeria G.M.B. right on the country's only main thoroughfare greets folks as they drive into the nation.

San Marino lies on the north central eastern edge of Italy facing toward, but not directly on, the Adriatic portion of the Mediterranean Sea. Italy completely surrounds this most ancient of still existing republics. Historic Yugoslavia lies across the ocean to the east.

Armeria G.M.B. is the largest but definitely not the only gun store in the country. Here we have a delightful, interesting gun shop extremely reminiscent of ones in our own country back in the sixties and seventies when freedom still reigned.

Piat mortars (deactivated but without visible damage,) two-inch trench mortars, 50-round Thompson drum mags, German potato-masher grenades, and various assorted interesting stuff decorate their shop windows.

Inside one drools over assorted Mauser rifles and pistols often with matching shoulder stocks, a great many both common and historic Lugers, Garands, M-1 Carbines, FN assault rifles, SIG AUGs, tactical shotguns, dewat MG-42s, as well as thousands and thousands of similarly interesting and spectacular rifles, pistols and shotguns. Prices in Euros are about similar to ours in dollars. Euros traded at $1.37 when we were in San Marino.

Inventories of surplus ammo, reloading dies, powder, primers, shot and bullets rival anything else one can discover in the world. Armeria G.M.B. has a most extensive inventory of what must total hundreds of pounds of reloading powder. Bruce Hodgin would just beam.

"We sell to Italians who can't find quantities, prices and selection like ours in their own country," the super friendly, knowledgeable, articulate clerk patiently explained.

Firearms ownership is common and easy in The Republic of San Marino. Gunstore folks estimate at least one firearm per household on average. "Some collections stretch into hundreds of pieces," we were told. Full-auto machine guns and pistols are technically illegal but are also common. That Armeria G.M.B. sells ammo belt-linking machines probably says a lot about local machine-gun ownership. As long as no mischief results, officials tend to turn a blind eye.

Two licenses regulate legal gun ownership in San Marino. Those having a hunting license can purchase sporting-type shotguns and rifles over the counter without further registration or paperwork. Sporting use is very broadly defined and includes many semi-auto high powered rifles. The only restriction on these semi-autos is a ten shot capacity. Magazine capacity limitations do not apply to .22 rimfire rifles, or to other rifles and shotguns used for target shooting.

It appears as though the only purpose of this license is to notify the authorities (police) that one is a gun owner. San Marino gun shops will sell to anyone who can prove they can legally own the gun they purchase in their own country of citizenship.

Securing a hunting license is not particularly easy, and very European in nature, unlike the U.S. where we simply walk into Walmart and plunk down our credit card. Cost of a hunting license is minimal in San Marino, but new hunters must take extensive classes on game management, stalking, shooting, ecology and field craft—culminating in a difficult, comprehensive test that must be passed before a hunting license is issued.

Those wanting to own and legally possess pistols and some tactical rifles and shotguns must secure an owner's permit from their local police. Everything in San Marino is local. Permits are so cheap and quickly given that gunstore clerks could not recall prices or how quickly they were actually issued. If not for a couple of dollars and in a couple of hours, certain within a week to ten days, they estimated.

With gun-owner's certificate and/or hunting license in hand, citizens can purchase as many pistols, rifles and shotguns as they wish. However only pistols on an approved sporting or personal list can be bought. This test is extremely broadly defined. Snub-nosed revolvers and tiny auto pistols are not on the list, but may be easily purchased by those who have a security reason for ownership. Simply receive a separate sanction from the local police. Most other pistols including all kinds and types of Lugers, Mausers, Walthers, Berettas, Glocks, SIGs, etc., are on the list of pistols approved on a gun-owner's certificate.

San Marino rules and regulations require that no pistols be legally privately held in 9mm Luger (Parabellum)—9x19mm! Some very strange twists and dodges result.

What are probably thousands of WW II collectors' pistols as well as many new Glock, SIG, Beretta models supposedly have been re-chambered to 9x21mm (9mm *largo*.) No markings on the barrels or obvious tool marks suggest that such transgressions have actually occurred on any of these extremely valuable collectors' pistols. Yet both the gun-store clerks and the gun-shop tags suggested these pistols are actually now 9x21s rather than 9x19s. There are no restrictions on pistol magazine capacity or the number of mags one may own.

Shooting military-surplus ammo is illegal in surrounding Italy, but nobody cares what is fired in what guns in San Marino. Huge quantities of bulk ammo including surplus of all sorts is on sale at Armeria G.M.B. Sale of all ammo is uncontrolled. Buy as much of whatever caliber as you wish. No records are kept and there is no requirement to purchase ammo only for guns one actually owns.

Sporting pistols, rifles and shotguns are not registered to owners. No permission to purchase is required and there are no storage requirements, onerous or otherwise.

Dewats are entirely unregulated. Residents purchase as many as they wish. Apparently, a lively, profitable trade exists for this class of firearm. The only requirement is that machine guns, submachine guns, mortars and such are *supposed* to be deactivated according to Italian specifications. Two very quick observations in that regard: Guns we saw were obviously very lightly dewatted and it is very unclear if they were actually done to Italian specifications.

Large magazine capacity SIG AUG, FN assault rifles and such like are permitted on one's owner's certificate. We observed one U.S. Garand fitted with a 20 round box magazine. It appears that all one needs is a gun-owner's certificate. No recording or registration is made, and there is no limit on the numbers one may purchase.

Silencers are not specifically forbidden, but it is said to be best not to have one in possession unless owners have a very good reason for ownership and are otherwise above suspicion. Having made that point, we were told that at least two other gun shops in San Marino had silencers for sale.

There are absolutely no restrictions on hand loading. As a result, a brisk and certainly profitable trade with Italian gun owner/reloaders is carried on. We looked at some very interesting approximately five pound (2.0 Kg) containers of REX powder made in Hungary.

Some European countries place restrictions on replica and original muzzle loaders as well as swords and bayonets. These don't exist on muzzle loaders or edged weapons of any kind in San Marino.

There is, however, a strange restriction on shotguns—anything over 12 gauge is forbidden. Black tactical-type shotguns are permitted and, in a strange Italian twist, there are a number of interesting yet obscure 24, 26, 28, 36 gauge and 9mm shotguns and ammo available.

Other than very large anti-tank rocket-type weapons, there is no restriction on cartridge size of rifles or pistols.

Reportedly there are thousands of illegal guns in private hands in San Marino, mostly scarfed up after WW II ended, of German and British origin. "American soldiers didn't fight here in east Italy" we were told. Only British with mostly Gurkha troops, so we saw Thompsons, Brens and Stens but not M-2 carbines and M-3 grease guns.

San Marino would be a very nice place to live for folks with incomes of at least $4,000 per month. The climate and gentle rolling terrain are about perfect. The place is tidy and extremely clean and neat.

Officially their *per capita* incomes are $34,600. Annual growth rates are 7.5% or more. Unemployment is nil. We observed a great number of Ferrari, Maserati, and super-expensive Mercedes cars on their roads.

Embedded in Europe where unemployment frequently reaches ten to twelve percent, San Marino's unemployment rate is an unbelievably low 2.6%. Attracting sufficient Italian guest workers does not seem to be a problem.

The country is nicely snuggled into picturesque rolling hills. Homes and stores absolutely drip prosperity. This demonstrates what can be done economically, even when surrounded by economic squalor, ignorance and indifference, if only people are left free to rise and fall on their own initiative and abilities.

So is it any accident that most of these small, well-run, pocket-sized countries that have *not* built up large bodies of rules, regulations and bureaucracies are extremely prosperous? They stand as a testament to the direct relationship between freedom and quality of life.

Chapter Fifty-Eight
Italy
World Rank: 36 • Firearm Freedom 38%

A petite yet Sophia-Loren-style 5'3" lady clerk in a typical Italian gun store held up a poster-sized sheet of paper covered with 10-point type. This poster, which almost totally covered her, was a summary of *most* of the rules and regulations pertaining to hunting—in that particular Italian state!

Her point was well taken. Nothing is ever simple and easy—without massive, detailed rules and regulations—in Italy. Especially private gun ownership, which is extensively covered by both state and federal regulations. As a result, readers more familiar with some gun regulations in other specific Italian states may take issue with the accuracy of the following information.

Our information is based on several interviews with gun-store clerks in small cities in some but not all of the 17 Italian states. It is the best average understanding practically possible given the fragmented and convoluted rules and regulations in Italy. It isn't just guns—copious rules and regulations smother every segment of their society.

Of the two, state regulations seem to often be more stringent than federal. For instance, in many places in Italy it is forbidden to own more than three pistols and/or six rifles. In the place where we interviewed our first gun-store proprietor, there was no limit on total numbers of shotguns and rifles one could theoretically possess. Yet there was *probably* a six-pistol limit. Italy's 17 states or administrative districts include Sicily which, it is said, operates virtually as an autonomous district. Our present analysis does not include Sicily which, we were led to believe, is something of a Wild West frontier-type situation.

Machine guns and submachine guns as well as gun collections containing unusually large numbers of guns including assault rifles and pistols can only be sanctioned by a special federal permit. This special permit allows for display of the guns but does not include the right to shoot or use them for anything but display. No ammunition can legally be purchased or even held in the same location for any of these guns.

Italian gun-store owner

The proprietress of a gun shop in Arqata, Italy, is holding up a sheet of paper with the detailed regulations relating only to hunting! Private ownership of firearms is similarly regulated with thousands of picky, detailed, often onerous requirements, which vary from region to region. None of these rules have any affect on the robust organized crime enterprises that make this nation their prosperous home. Italians in general tend to ignore these regulations, but not quite to the extent of some other countries.

Apply at the national police special firearms branch that handles these matters and expect at least a three months' wait. Exact price of these permits remains a mystery. Judging by prices for other permits and sanctions, probably thousands of dollars. No one knew details and procedures with certainty.

Hunting firearms are seen as somewhat different than "sport" or trap, skeet and target firearms, by Italian authorities. No military type guns, long or pistol, are allowed for either sport shooting or for hunting. Sporting type semi-auto rifles and shotguns are allowed for hunting so long as magazine capacities are limited to five rounds.

Oddly, hunting authorities in Italy have a great deal of discretion over what kinds of firearms and especially what size of cartridge one may own and hunt with. In many places, .300 Win mag rifles are okay, but .458 Win mags are not. Shotguns larger than 12 gauge are prohibited, both for hunting and for "sport." Only way to know for sure is to take the local hunting course.

Italians do sanction a great number of fun-sized 20 through 36 gauge shotguns as well as a little 9mm shotgun. Ammo for these is currently made by Fiocchi, among others. Some of this is exported to the U.S.

Although many manage to do so, hunting licenses are difficult and expensive to obtain. First-time applicants pay a fee of about $250, but this isn't all there is to it. They must sign up for a class—or classes—often taught by university professors and/or professional foresters. These classes include extensive detailed instruction on hunting techniques, hunting protocol, game identification, sex and maturity of game, ecology, field craft and tracking techniques as well as tagging and reporting procedures. Hunting licenses must be renewed annually, but the renewal process is said to be much easier and less convoluted in subsequent years. One does, however, need to be familiar with changes in hunting regulations.

A second, perhaps marginally easier path to private gun ownership in Italy is available.

Italians specifically translate this method as "making a demand." This is the procedure for applying for a gun-owner's permit. These applications actually start with the national police, who quickly kick the application back down to the local police, who do an extensive background check on the applicant.

Both the public doctor and one's private doctor must sign off on the application. Checks are also made of the applicant's employment history, property ownership, income and status as a taxpayer, as well as general standing in the local area.

Cost of a gun-owner's permit? I am not making this up! Our informant in one gun shop immediately reached for her pocket calculator and started pecking away. "You need to pay everyone," she told us in some exasperation. Including special documents, tax stamps, doctors' fees, legal copies and whatnot, the price will be up around at least $200 a year. This does not include the expense of a hunting license, which many Italian gun owners believe somewhat simplifies the process of gun ownership. Apparently some official effort is made to control gun ownership by keeping the price high to very high. At the least this is what many Italians believe.

Takes about one month to receive the first permit. Both hunting licenses and gun-owners' permits must be renewed annually. She reckoned it would only take 20 days to renew.

All guns must be sanctioned by the local police who list them by serial number on one's gun-owner's permit or hunting license. Do new gun buyers take their recently purchased guns to the police shop for registration or do they simply receive a receipt from the gun shop which is used to record the gun to their gun-owner's permit? Apparently the answer is "yes." It may work both ways depending on the state and whether the new purchase is a pistol or long gun.

Pistols are allowed on one's permit with some limitations as to caliber, size or magazine capacity. Parabellum 9mm cartridges are prohibited, for instance, but 9x21 *largo* handgun cartridges are okay. As in San Marino, it seems that many pistols in Italy have been or are chamber lengthened for this round.

Permitted pistols are specifically listed on a sport and hunting list published by the central government. Only pistols deemed "not for war" are sanctioned. These can include a great number of both revolvers and semi-automatics of calibers from .22 LR through .454 Casull and might also include some with full-capacity magazines. The only blanket prohibition is for 9mm Parabellum.

Ammo purchases are similarly convoluted. Only rounds for guns listed on one's license or permit can be legally purchased. Quantities are limited by police in a strange way unique to Italy. You go to the police and negotiate a number-of-rounds sanction, and that's how many you can purchase. Police then may continue to approve that number, up the quantity, or cut it back, depending on their whim of the day.

Then it's off to a special store called an *armoria* licensed to retail ammo. An *armorias* is said to be present in virtually every city of over 5,000 people. Legal gun ownership, including pistols, must be fairly common in Italy. Most larger cities seem to have one or more gun shops and *armorias*. Prices there are high to very high. A box of fifty .22 LR, for instance, sells for about $3.50. Twelve-gauge shotgun shells—a box of 25—range from the cheapest at $8 to $23.50 for exotic heavy shot rounds. NATO 7.62mm rifle rounds are prohibited, but .308 Winchester rounds are okay.

Reloading is only permitted under a separate Italian "demand" (license). Components are only retailed in a very few specialty stores that operate under a separate, difficult-to-obtain store license. An Italian store owner cannot ever inventory more than 25 kg of powder and a limited, set number of primers at one time.

Many Italians slip over the border—which is unregulated in any fashion—into San Marino where they can get reloading powder and primers in quantity at greatly reduced prices without any restrictions.

Italy is not a particularly wealthy country. *Per capita* incomes run about $27,700. Cost of living, especially for vehicles and fuel, is very high by our standards. Price breaks for anything—including shooting supplies—are eagerly searched out. Only slightly larger than our state of Arizona, Italy is the long, thin, 1,000 miles long "boot" stretching out into the Mediterranean Sea.

Permits to carry and their attached right to purchase a smaller pocket pistol are possible, but not necessarily easy. This depends entirely on one's circumstances and relationship with the police. Again, apply at the local cop shop, and list a specific weapon as well as precise reasons for ownership and carry.

Dewats are fairly freely owned and traded. No license or registration is required. Perhaps due to their popularity and the fact that the Italian authorities are not sanctioning a great many more, prices have zoomed out of reach of average Italians, they complain.

As one would easily suppose, living so close to the Balkans, as well as Eastern Europe, and given the ravages of two world wars, illegal guns are everyplace. Boat-owning Italian fishermen must have an extremely lucrative business bringing in current models along with cases of military surplus ammo. With only a few easily made minimal contacts, Italians can purchase just about anything in the military gun line they wish. AK-47s are said to be most common and popular. But others in great quantities are also available.

Italy is constrained by the fact that, unlike many other places in Europe, residents generally speak only Italian. Their roads are poorly marked, drivers demonstrate an almost suicidal propensity to accidents, and cost of living is stratospheric. Include the fact that this is not a particularly gun-friendly place, even if one takes the necessary time to unwind their convoluted regulations.

It is, however, a unique colorful place, inhabited by lots of very friendly people.

Chapter Fifty-Nine
Chile
World Rank: 31 • Firearm Freedom 43%

Firearms-retarded Canadian officials are not the only ones who crab over more easily accessible firearms in a bordering country, blaming their own soaring crime rate on their more freedom-loving neighbors.

Other than some very mild attempted bunko and petty thievery of the price-tampering and bait-and-switch variety, there is little to no crime in Chile, and virtually no violent crime to speak of. There is also a very, very low incidence of illegal guns. Nevertheless, what few illegal guns are discovered are instantly attributed to smugglers who bring them in from much more gun-relaxed Argentina, principally through Chile's free-trade zones located in the far north and south.

Chilean gun owners themselves attribute this low incidence of illegal guns to the fact that they haven't had a war in more than 200 years— actually about 120 years counting the Revolution of 1891—and to the fact that average citizens can, with relative ease and inexpensively, own a few (but not many) firearms.

It isn't because there is absolutely no gun culture or interest in guns in Chile. While checking out the situation during our extended stay in Santiago we were able to spend considerable time in three different gun shops. When required, we had the services of an able interpreter who had previously lived in the U.S. for 12 years.

All these gun shops experienced steady traffic including considerable observed sales throughout their opening hours. There was enough business that at times it was difficult to carry on a coherent interview. Six clerks in the largest shop were very busy handling customers.

Between 35 and 40 expensive pistols and revolvers, and about 20 rifles and shotguns were inventoried here, suggesting brisk turnover.

Perhaps Chilean police need something to obsess about. But problems with crime and illegal guns seem minor—at least compared to places like Mexico, Panama and Columbia.

Chile is that strange string bean sliver of South American land stretching along the Pacific coast from Tierra del Fuego in the far south to Bolivia and Peru in the north. France and England together about equal Chile's land area. But the country averages only about 112 miles wide by an incredible 2,700 miles long! Chilean maps are commonly laid out in three separate long and narrow cumbersome sections.

Average income is about $10,700 and rising nicely. Unemployment is very low. All this easily qualifies the country as middle to upper-middle class. Cost of living in Chile is reasonable to low except, it seems, when purchasing some guns and ammunition. A box of 25 shells of common 12-gauge ammo costs about $10. Fifty .22 LRs will ring up to between $9 and $22, depending on type and grade. Shotgun ammo is manufactured in Chile but that's all. No centerfire rifle or pistol or even .22 rimfire ammo is manufactured here.

More inexpensive Walther .22 LR pistols start at about $400. 9mm Glocks, H&Ks and SIG Arms pistols run from $600 to $1,200. Inexpensive American-manufactured import .22 LR bolt-action rifles were $250. A utilitarian 12-gauge single-barrel shotgun made in Russia was also about $250. Many doubles and pump shotguns were considerably higher. Perhaps these high prices can be attributed to the fact that everything except 12 ga. ammo is imported. Chileans are dealing in a world-class gun-and-ammo economy on less than world-class personal incomes. Yet, personal incomes are rising at an approximate six percent per annum rate, which keeps everyone happy.

Prices for guns and ammo, one could conclude, were high to quite high as compared to the U.S. Compared to any economy where the average income is less than $1,000 per month, prices were restrictively high. Nevertheless, average Chilean citizens were in the shops kibitzing, fantasizing and buying.

Chile is notorious for being a place stuffed full of paper-pushing, paper-shuffling, tree-killing, deal-stifling bureaucrats. But to our surprise, gun ownership is reasonably straightforward and fairly easy. A gun-owner's permit is required and each gun must be registered to the owner. Minimum age is 18 but few receive their first gun-owner's certificate at this age, principally because of the driver's license and doctor's-certificate requirement. These are not regulations average American gun owners could tolerate but are fairly workable when viewed from the perspective of many other countries.

A maximum of seven guns can be legally owned by any one citizen. Non-citizens can own guns but must comply with the same limitations and ownership-certificate requirements.

A maximum of two of these seven guns can be owned for self defense. These might include certain pistols and shorty pump shotguns. The other five firearms must qualify as sporting, either for target shooting or hunting. As a curious anomaly peculiar to Chile, only one semi-auto pistol or semi-auto hunting rifle is allowed per household. Semi-auto rifles are OK if they are not classified as assault rifles. Semi-auto shotguns are also sold and owned but, again, only one per household.

No full-auto rifles, machine guns or machine pistols are allowed under any circumstances, not even for collectors, inventors or historians. There is no way to make this class of firearm legal.

All gauges of shotguns from 10 through 20, as well as .410s, are permitted although securing ammo for 10s and 16s is said to be tough. Buyers may have to wait a year or more until supplies are imported.

We were told that the largest rifle cartridge permitted was a .308 Winchester or 7.65 Argentine Mauser. That means .375 H&H or .458 Winchester rifles, for instance, are forbidden. But on looking through one shop's order catalog, we noted a .416 Rigby for sale!

Perhaps rifle-size sanctions depend on how one holds their mouth when talking to the authorities. We do know that, under some special circumstances, up to a 12-gun total will be sanctioned. This is entirely at the discretion of one's local police. Contrary to some international supposition, principally among leftists, Chilean police enjoy a very good standing among average citizens. They have an excellent reputation for honesty, integrity and competence. Nevertheless, having any government authority making decisions about what gun is needed and appropriate is undesirable to say the least.

Pistol size is not restricted, we were told, but the largest pistol on display and in the order books was a .40 S&W. No .45s on display.

Securing a gun-owner's permit is relatively different and relatively easy in Chile. Gun stores issue them.

Prospective new gun owners must gather several documents which are then presented to a gun-store clerk. The first requirement is a current national-identity card which everyone is required by law to carry. Every time you do a credit-card transaction in Chile it is necessary to note down the passport number in the case of foreigners or the national-identity card number in the case of nationals.

Next, applicants must have either a national driver's license or a doctor's certificate attesting to their physical fitness and sanity. It's one or the other. It's obviously much simpler, easier and less costly to come up with a driver's license. Third, evidence of a permanent place of residence. In this case a tax notice, utility bill or similar will do.

Fourth, you need a hunting license or a shooting or hunting-club membership certificate. Gun shops sell hunting licenses. Prices vary dramatically according to the game sanctioned, time of year, place of hunting and so on. Club membership fees are said to be modest.

Finally you must take and pass a gun-owner's test. These tests are administered and graded by the gun shop. Newbies pick up a study manual from the gun shop containing likely test information on

Chilean gun laws, gun safety, firearms operation, first aid, gun mechanics, game laws and game habitats and seasons.

When ready, new gun owners sit for a test in their favorite gun shop. Cost is about $30. These tests are said to be rigorous but reasonable.

Upon successful completion of the test and successful completion of all one's papers, the gun-store-issued permit is taken to the local police. There, for about $12 more, the police schedule a visit to the applicant's home. This verifies the applicant really is who they say they are and actually lives there. In a complete switch from many other countries, there is no requirement regarding firearms storage. It's interesting to note what exactly worries authorities about gun ownership. In Chile it is apparently not about theft.

This last portion of the exercise takes about a week or less. Permits are valid for five years. Renewal, if the applicant's record is still clean, is easy to automatic—with payment of another fee, of course.

With police-validated authorization in hand, new or existing gun owners go to their local gun shop where they can purchase up to their allotted seven firearms (or twelve in special circumstances.)

Registration of each gun is done at the gun shop. Upon purchase, a special laminated card is issued for each gun. Registration papers are sent by the selling store to the police, who keep permanent files.

Ammunition can only be purchased for guns for which the owner has a registration card. A maximum of 1,000 rounds can be purchased and legally held for any one gun used for sporting, hunting or target shooting. Self-defense type weapons, however, are restricted to 500 rounds purchased and/or held per gun.

It is very unclear how gun stores verify amounts of ammo expended and held for each individual gun. If the firearm is a .22 target or hunting pistol, a 1,000-round limit applies. When it's classed as a self-defense gun, it's only 500 rounds. Is the goal to stop Chileans from getting into protracted firefights? And, again, other than limiting daily purchases, one wonders how this rule is enforced.

Silencers are never permitted under any circumstances. Reloading is not done in Chile. Components of any kind are not for sale in any shops, and cannot legally be imported.

Almost every larger city in Chile has at least one shop where guns and ammo can be purchased. As mentioned, we visited three in a working-class neighborhood in Santiago. Several more shops were said to be located in the city's wealthier neighborhoods, implying that guns are often purchased by wealthier members of society.

Other than being something no American gun owner could live with, Chilean gun laws really don't tell us very much. Theirs is a fairly wild, spacious, basically rural, wide-open country, not characterized by a very high *per capita* gun-ownership pattern or a high crime rate.

Chilean authorities will fairly easily and quickly issue a gun-owner's permit for self defense when a citizen feels threatened. Perhaps that is why violent crime is so rare, or perhaps Chileans are just basically law-abiding people.

Chapter Sixty
Falkland Islands
World Rank: 16 • Firearm Freedom 70%

The tiny British colony of the Falkland Islands is one of the most incredible places in the world. But don't take our word for it—consider the thousands of cruise-ship visitors each year who promptly decide that one day ashore is absolutely not enough and who quickly return for a more in depth visit.

Used to be sheep raising and wool were the only pillars of the colony's economy. Since the 1982 conflict, it's tourism (in a dramatically expanded fashion) and squid fisheries. Both are booming so frantically that average incomes for the 3,200 permanent residents have zoomed to well over $26,000. Negative unemployment rates force recruitment of visiting workers from Chile, St. Helena and the Philippines.

A whopping 55% of the permanent residents, 1,774, are licensed gun owners—a stat from the colony's chief of police who makes do with a total of nine line officers. Incredibly there has never been a recorded case of gun crime on the Falklands.

Let's quickly review. More than half the residents of the Falklands privately own guns, putting a firearm within easy reach of absolutely everyone *and* there has never been a single incident of gun crime on the island in recorded history!

During the two weeks we spent on the islands researching their gun laws we kept track of vehicle registration plates. The highest we observed was in the 880 range. Maybe there are more vehicles out on the remote farms, but even at 1,000 licensed vehicles, licensed gun owners dramatically outnumber licensed vehicles.

Our 1,000-vehicle estimate may be close to accurate! Only one gas station in the entire colony, which is about the physical size of New Hampshire plus Delaware. The Falkland Islands are located in the deep South Atlantic about 250 miles southeast of the southern-most tip of South America. They are quite close to the Antarctic.

Getting to the Falklands requires dedication, with only one flight in and out per week via Punta Arenas, Chile. The Falklands are actually a group of about 200 islands. Two major big islands—East Falkland and West Falkland—comprise most of it. Some islands in this group are little more than small piles of partly exposed rock or tidal flats.

Rifles, shotguns and pistols are all permitted and commonly owned by colony citizens. This an English colony where pistols are sanctioned. Yes, and we were told on several occasions that we (the Falkland Islanders) may be an English protectorate, but we are very different, with different rules and regulations, and not limited to private ownership of pistols.

Fully automatic ground-mount machine guns, machine pistols and especially FN assault rifles with full-auto capacity are commonly owned illegally and held by Falkland Islanders. Especially those out in remote farms or stations, referred to by the locals as "camp."

Our friendly police chief knows about these guns but is completely unconcerned. "Most hold them as souvenirs of the 1982 conflict with Argentina," he said. "In many cases, ammunition for these guns is severely limited and farmers who have them have absolutely no larcenous intent." As a result, the chief spends zero time worrying about them. The small-town limited-population atmosphere with the everyone-knows-everyone-else-and-is-happy-about-it syndrome is part of this place's charm.

We spent a great deal of time driving the roads on the Falklands—not an easy chore. Only one partly hard-surfaced road runs from Stanley, the only city—a village actually—out to the Mt. Pleasant airport, the only international airport, which is also a British military base.

All roads in the colony have been constructed since 1982. Good ones are gravel. Not so good ones are mud. All are poorly marked to not marked at all. Because all roads are recent, even maps from the tourist office are incomplete. This makes navigation about the colony tricky, especially since the only petrol is back 93 miles in Stanley (located on the east side of East Falkland.) There is little to no traffic in the sparsely populated interior. Folks experiencing road problems or vehicle breakdowns face either a very long walk or a very long wait.

Yet we were able to visit four or five remote interior farms. Incredibly residents always invited us in for coffee or tea. When this happens, (1) don't forget to remove your shoes upon entering the house, and (2) do not be so rude as to forget to sign the guest book.

Our conversations usually turned to gun ownership in the colonies. Not one of the several couples we coffeed with actually admitted to illegal gun ownership. Yet all pointedly alluded to such. Is this a situation similar to Finland, Crete and Switzerland where citizens collect up military firearms in anticipation of another foreign occupation? Not likely in the Falklands.

Even though Argentine officials continue—even at this late date—to make irrational hostile noises, Falkland Islanders probably don't have armed or overt resistance on their minds. Last time Argentina occupied for 74 days there was no armed resistance and little to no sabotage.

There was no need for sabotage. The Argentines did it to themselves. They completely failed to feed, house or clothe their men. Many conscripts did not even know where they were. Deaths in their ranks from exposure, accidents and even starvation were common. Daily orders including rules relative to occupation were virtually never passed on to the soldiers. Nobody knew the plan, what was going on or what was required or expected. Chaos among the Argentine army was so severe Falkland Islanders could not believe it. No need to add to something already terminal.

Rules for securing a gun-owner's permit are simple. Go to the only police office on the island, located in downtown Stanley across from the post office and the one and only bank. Ask for a gun-owner's firearms license application. Pay about $65. They already know who you are, who your father was, and how well you fit into the colony's tightly knit social structure.

Gun-owner's permits are often issued on the spot. No tests. No vetting. No character references. Even most of the colony's medical histories are common knowledge, much to the chagrin of some citizens.

Bring the gun-owner's permit to the Falkland Islands Company gun store, located about three blocks up the harbor. It's the only one in the colony and apparently the only place to arrange imports of firearms and firearms-related items. Pick out the rifle, shotgun or pistol you want, either from their limited inventory or place an order to import.

Importation of a specific firearm takes from six months to a year. This is because all guns, ammunition and components must be transported by specially designated military vessels.

Importation by the Falkland Islands Company gun shop, while slow, is done without further restrictions. Personal importation of a specific firearm may raise questions such as why you want it, and for what specific use, making it a bit more rigorous. This is the point where the process becomes a whole bunch less free and more arbitrary.

Import permits for specific firearms cost about $35 at the police station, and permission will only be granted when the applicant can provide good, valid reasons for such. For instance, ownership of pump and semi-auto shotguns already on the islands is permitted, but may not be extended for importation without a good, convincing reason.

There is no limit on the size and number of guns which a person can legally own. Large pistols in the range of 9mm and above are discouraged. Yet target and recreational shooters who have formed a club can and do own pistols in the .44 magnum class. One shop clerk told me that her "partner" had a legal .44 S&W mag which she enjoyed shooting, but was really an "over the top" model and caliber.

Firearms for personal protection are never sanctioned. No snakes, wolves or other predators on the islands require use of a sidearm.

Larger rifles in the .300 Win mag class are okay for those who can convince the firearms officer that they intend to practice ultra-long-range target shooting. A purely notional affair, since howling winds across the Falklands seldom settle at less than 12 to 15 knots.

Hunting for upland geese, ducks, rabbits, rats and feral house cats is a logical, legitimate reason for ownership. There are no game seasons or licenses on the Falklands. Everything is left to the landowner to decide.

Having a rifle or shotgun to take to South Georgia, Chile, Africa or England with which to hunt is usually an easily acceptable reason for ownership. Like most island dwellers world over, Falkland Islanders eagerly take extended vacations off their beloved islands, perhaps as a break from "island syndrome." Well-traveled citizens are common rather than the exception, especially since prosperity.

Similar to the U.K., silencers fail to excite anyone, yet all are permitted. One sees them on offer in Stanley's only gun shop without so much as a blink of the eye.

Ammunition can *only* be purchased for guns listed on one's license. All guns are listed to the gun-owner's permit. Those without a .308 Win. on their license, for instance, are said to be unlikely to fire their surreptitiously held FN assault rifles! There's no limit on number of rounds a person can purchase or hold. The Falkland Island Company tries to keep a large supply of ammo on hand at all times. Sales of 2,000 rounds would be no problem, we were told.

There are no restrictions on shotgun gauge. Yet, like so many places in the world, 16-, 20- and 28-gauge ammo may be impossible to buy over the counter and very time consuming to import. The Falkland Islands Company gun shop will import obscure ammo for customers to the best of their ability.

Gun collecting as a hobby is permitted. At least one resident has a reputation as a hard-core gun buff/experimenter and tinkerer. You want to collect strange and unusual guns? Go talk to the chief. He is a really nice guy, having a reputation as a listener.

Hand loading in the colony is pretty much in limbo. Getting the components is the issue. There are no restrictions. Several clubs hand load for members who have gun-owner's certificates, or they allow members to use their machinery and components. Their only gun shop does not stock components but "will try" to special order them.

Club membership can and does include many different shooting, hunting and travel-hunting-type activities. There are several in existence, one of which at least has among its members some world-class target shooters. These are friendly, gregarious people who generally enjoy each other's company. Expense for club memberships is unknown. Probably modestly high like everything else in the colony.

These, again, are not gun laws to which Americans would be accustomed or to which they would peacefully submit. They are nicely workable for Falkland Islanders in a place where virtually everyone is a gun owner and where there is absolutely no gun crime. There has to be a lesson in that.

Chapter Sixty-One
Communist China
World Rank: 61 • Firearm Freedom 2%

Like everything else Chinese, gun laws and gun ownership in communist China are both very simple and extremely complex. Lots of lessons here for those of us forced to deal with gun banners.

Simply put, communist China's gun laws are straightforward. Private legal possession of any rifle, shotgun or pistol is completely and absolutely forbidden—no way for a private citizen under any circumstance to own a gun. Those caught with private firearms face a three-year jail sentence. Even replicas are *verboten*.

No sense pursuing questions about multiple gun ownership, reloading, membership in shooting clubs, legal hunting, caliber and model-type restrictions, hunting licenses, storage rules or anything else on our list of questions. Nothing "gun" is legally sanctioned to private citizens in communist China. This should not imply that either private gun ownership or a gun culture does not exist here.

To the complete amazement and consternation of communist Chinese authorities and international gun banners, a large, growing and active gun culture exists amongst all of this prohibition. This due in part to communist China's glorification of firearms as a means of revolution, theirs being one of the largest arms and ammunition manufacturers in the world, and to a State that venerates competitive shooting.

Citizens here attach great honor and importance to the fact that their first Olympic gold medal in 1984 was won by Xu Haifeng in the 50-meter pistol competition. And that the official national shooters—usually from their army—won five of 51 possible gold medals in this year's Olympic shooting event in Beijing.

Other major factors contribute to communist China's growing gun culture. In spite of the fact that they will never legally own a firearm, all freshmen receive marksmanship training during their first year at college. Used to be that this was viewed as a defensive measure. Now it's seen as high recreation.

Lax enforcement of laws and rampant bribery, coupled with large-scale theft from numerous arms factories, contribute mightily to the pool of illegal guns available to private Chinese citizens. One fellow in Shanghai was recently busted with 600,000 rounds of illegal ammo in his possession. This is not a misprint. Over half-a-million rounds, which he reportedly was peddling over the Internet. This earned him 12 years in the grey stone hotel!

Stealing from communist Chinese factories is a well-established, well-entrenched and well-known tradition here. Distribution of Bibles, for instance, is forbidden by the communists, but Christians prohibited from legally distributing Bibles have quietly set up huge Bible printing operations. Supposedly for export, great numbers of these Bibles walk out the back door, accomplishing these folks' original objective.

Industrialization of communist China has contributed to illegal gun ownership. Super accurate, long-range target rifles are difficult to manufacture from scratch in simple village machine shops. But simple pistols and not-so-simple submachine guns and assault rifles are relatively easy to manufacture with modern machine tools.

Authorities assign blame for much illegal ownership to these village shops that are currently producing both guns and ammunition in fairly large commercial quantities. And to the fact that, under their economic liberalization programs, significant numbers of the people have become wealthy. If not wealthy, then middle class. Like Denmark, this new middle class looks to gun ownership as a kind of important, and fun, status symbol.

A lady member of the communist Chinese politburo once explained that allowing folks to accumulate wealth by liberalizing their economic system would eventually destroy communism in China. She even said this might lead to legal gun ownership. Although increased wealth is obviously eroding Chinese communism the jury is still out on legal private gun ownership. *Per capita* incomes have rocketed to a healthy $5,600, and they are continuing to rise—much faster than communism is disappearing.

Information for this chapter comes from several personal visits to the Chinese mainland, working there, published papers on gun ownership and several key interviews with government, military and police officials. There are, of course, no gun stores in communist China to visit. It is said that more people here speak some English than all of the remaining English speaking peoples of the world combined!

A huge country, China shares borders with (clockwise from the north) Mongolia, Russia, North Korea, Vietnam, Laos, Burma (now Myanmar), India, Bhutan, Tibet, Nepal, Pakistan, Kirgizstan and Kazakhstan, with eastern shores on the East China and Yellow Seas, and southern shores on the South China Sea. Much of its land mass comprises harsh, impenetrable and non-productive mountains. Most of the population lives on or near the seaboard.

As readers might suppose, communist China's draconian gun laws date back to Mao Zedong's murderous regime. Americans generally concur that collective communism cannot succeed given an armed population. Mao, who brought death to as many as 60 million of his own defenseless people to solidify his rule and crush any vestiges of freedom, knew that as well.

Communist societies routinely ban private gun ownership to subjugate the masses—prevention of which is a main reason America encourages gun ownership—but in communist China it wasn't quite that simple. Left-behind guns from the civil war that ended October 1, 1949 must have been something of a factor. Yet, in general, dirt-poor peasant Chinese did not own firearms. Nobody out in the country did. They were too poor. Those they picked up were quickly sold.

When Mao instigated his so-called Great Leap Forward in 1958, peasant farmers had no means of resistance. At a conservative estimate offered by the communists themselves, at least 20 million died cruelly of starvation. Not a new world record for one leader, but close.

Gun ownership among the far less numerous but somewhat more wealthy intellectual city dwellers was, if not common, not uncommon. At the time of the Great Leap, this class of people was not horribly affected by Mao's criminal governance. Mao did not need to institute new restrictive gun laws at that time.

Mao's murderous campaigns were divided into two parts: The "Great Leap," calculated to murder peasants, and a second component undertaken in 1966 known as the "Cultural Revolution" directed toward wiping out teachers professors, engineers, factory owners, skilled craftsmen and other such like. These guys tended to have some private firearms tucked away.

As a result, Mao promulgated communist China's first harsh gun laws in 1966. He had to disarm his subjects or his murderous enterprise might have grounded out. The communists' gun laws have been strengthened since that time, but all essentially date from Mao and his "Cultural Revolution."

After pro-democracy demonstrations in 1989, even common replica guns became contraband. These replicas must have been extremely popular in communist China as government authorities report confiscating and destroying hundreds of thousands of them. Exports of look-alike "air-soft" guns from the communists to America are huge.

Absolutely any possession, import, private export, or private manufacture of firearms and ammunition was prohibited. Officials admit that many parts of this prohibition are ignored, especially out in the provinces. Yet draconian penalties await those officially caught with anything gun.

So has all this tyranny produced a gun-crime-free nation where bank, payroll, stores or persons are never held up at gun point? Where mass killings by a gun-wielding nut on a rampage are unknown? Where drug-hyped criminal gangs never shoot it out? Is this the kind of utopian society gun banners lust for?

In spite of propaganda to the contrary, western gun owners already know the answers. While only reluctantly admitting that these sorts of crimes frequently occur, communist China's officials are also extremely quick to gloss over and minimize any official gun-crime reports. No sense publicizing the fact that their policies are an obvious failure unless, as has happened recently, the crime is so notable it can't be swept under the rug.

As mentioned at the start, there are many places and methods by which subjects even in rigorously controlled communist China can secure guns and ammo. Like drugs, guns will always be supplied to people who feel they need them and who have money to pay. Both gun-ownership patterns and confiscation records in communist China authenticate the truth that rapidly emerging newly rich middle-class Chinese subjects are willing to pay. Which leads to several additional gun anomalies peculiar to communist China.

Credible rumors and outright reports circulate that high-ranking army officers with access to some sporting type guns—principally shotguns—organize hunting and/or shooting events in remote areas of the dictatorship (what the *New York Times* prefers to call *a one-party system*). Bored with golf, affluent businessmen slip into the countryside for bird or even larger game hunts, or just to shoot bottles!

As has been the case in Russia post 1989, military officers sometimes turned a blind eye to gun "borrowing" or even thefts from some of the huge number of arsenals spotted about the country. This is likely facilitated by extremely poor recordkeeping, sometimes perhaps intentionally poor.

Officials seem to recognize and accommodate their rapidly growing active gun culture by sanctioning and establishing shooting ranges about the country. These are definitely not your average range as we westerners understand them.

Shooting ranges in communist China are owned and operated by the Red Chinese army—and not for army use, but for use by recreational shooters. All guns and ammo are controlled by the military. Mostly they have military-type firearms at these ranges.

Those who wish to shoot select a weapon or weapons from the house arsenal. These range from heavy ground-mount machine guns to AK-47s, PPsh41 submachine guns, and Tokarev pistols. Occasionally one sees U.S. military firearms such as M-16s or BARs.

Visitors can select shotguns with which to shoot clay birds, but most customers seem to prefer cacklin' away with full-auto assault rifles or machine guns.

You step up to the counter and pay cash for boxes or belts of appropriate ammo. After the officer loads the gun it is the customer's right to blaze away at paper targets till the ammo is expended.

Tourists, as well as Japanese, Chinese and American businessmen like myself seem to be the principal customers. On days I visited, a steady flow of folks moved through the range. Doesn't take long to convert lots of money to noise on full-auto!

By western standards, cost of ammo was modest and shooting some of these exotic weapons was definitely fun. This is as good as it legally gets for communist Chinese subjects. But one must wonder, what does the future hold?

Chapter Sixty-Two
Australia
World Rank: 21 • Firearm Freedom 60%

Australia's component for this book started over lunch with our local chief of police. Not an anti-gunner in the slightest, he mused. "I wish you would find out what is really going on in Australia. I hear that private ownership of firearms is completely impossible and that, as a result, their crime rate is soaring dramatically!"

While Australian state gun laws have, for the most part, been co-opted by their national authorities, some slight state variations appear at the margins. Nevertheless, after four weeks in Australia during which time we interviewed three pistol-club member/shooters at their club, two gun-store clerks in their shops, two skeet shooters at their local range and several farmer/ranchers, we can provide illuminating information.

Bottom line? Gun ownership, for many makes and models, is possible but not easy or convenient in Australia and crime is increasing in some categories but from a very, very low base. Average citizens with whom we spoke did not seem to be overly concerned with crime in their society. For example: walking through Kings Cross, Sydney's notorious red-light district in the middle of a jet-lag-induced wakeful night did not seem even slightly threatening.

Perhaps because Australian authorities have dramatically cleaned up their country's more nefarious districts, additional crime is not yet a major political issue. Compared to previous visits to Australian big-city red-light districts, the situation is much subdued. Tough to even determine one is in a tough neighborhood.

Evenly spaced, virtually territorial street walkers who once dominated major intersections and business entrances are less obvious. Bordellos no longer advertise with flashing lights and blazing marquees.

Excluding Alaska and Hawaii, Australia is roughly the same size as the U.S. Instead of 48 contiguous states, they make do with seven including the island state of Tasmania. Tasmania is where, in 1992, a deranged man with a rifle went berserk, killing 37 people.

As a result, Australia's relatively relaxed, enlightened gun laws were suddenly and dramatically toughened, leading to a compulsory $500 million gun buy-up scheme. A plaque in the Darwin Military Museum makes the claim that, given huge numbers of weapons found in civilian hands, it is surprising that more massacres did not occur.

Maybe the surprise is that, as Australia's evidence and museum demonstrated, the presence of firearms does not create deranged people. Coincidence is not causation, but irrational anti-rights types perpetually miss this point.

Since there is no up or down in outer space, it's inaccurate (though popular up here) to say Australia is a large island in the Pacific Ocean, at the bottom of the Earth. Climate and seasons are reversed from what we in the northern hemisphere experience. *Per capita* income data puts Australians at about $30,700.

Like many countries, Australian police have a local dedicated firearms officer. It is with this officer that one starts the process of legal firearms ownership. Enjoying a reputation for generally being honest and incorruptible, we were frequently told that they can and do often "tailor" written rules to fit local conditions. Frequently this tailoring leads to significant relaxation of their laws when local conditions warrant. Because these officers can arbitrarily decide if an applicant really needs that specific gun, it can also lead to arbitrary abuse.

New gun owners complain bitterly that an application for a firearms license—which eventually should lead to a gun-owner's permit—an applicant must simultaneously lay out about $1,000 for an approved gun safe—before knowing if the application will be approved! As part of the application process for a firearms license, a local officer will inspect the safe to be sure it is of proper weight and strength and that it is correctly secured to the wall and floor.

Initial applications take from two weeks to nine months to process. Cost is about $35. During this time police run a check of a background and medical records. At age 16, Australians can apply for their own license. From ages 12 through 15 kids can shoot or hunt with an adult. This adult must never be so far away that they cannot immediately control a younger shooter should the need arise.

After the wait, police notify applicants by mail if they are approved. Successful applicants must then sign up for an approved training course. Reportedly these training courses are rigorous and all-encompassing, often given at a local community college. Cost is about $150 for six lessons spanning four weeks. Tests given at the conclusion of the course are notorious for being difficult to pass.

If you pass the course and submit proper paperwork, you now wait for your firearms license. Licenses are issued in classes. Class A is easiest to acquire. Class C&D are extended only in special circumstances. Class H licenses are only for pistol-club members.

Class A: Air rifles, air guns and paintball firearms; .22 rimfire rifles (not self loading); single- or double-barrel shotguns (not self loading or pump action), including receivers.

Class B: Muzzle-loading firearms (not being handguns); revolving-chamber rifles; centerfire (not self loading); break-action shotgun/rifle combinations. All other firearms that are not class A firearms (not being prescribed firearms, handguns, self loading or pump-action shotguns), and includes receivers.

Class C: Self-loading rimfire rifles with a magazine capacity no greater than 10 rounds; self-loading shotguns with a magazine capacity no greater than 5 rounds; pump-action shotguns with a magazine capacity no greater than 5 rounds; and includes receivers.

Class D: Self-loading rimfire rifles with a magazine of more than 10 rounds; self-loading centerfire rifles; self-loading shotguns with a magazine capacity of more than 5 rounds and pump-action shotguns with a magazine capacity of more than 5 rounds; and includes receivers. Class D licenses are rarely issued.

Class H: All handguns (including air pistols).

A special collector's category exists for deactivated machine guns and machine pistols, of which there are very few in Australia. Permits to carry are very, very infrequently extended and then only to opal and gold bullion couriers.

Class A & B Firearms must be secured by attaching and locking to part of a building or in a locked cabinet constructed of hardwood or steel securely attached to a building or in a locked steel safe securely attached to a building (unless safe mass, when empty, is 330 lbs. or more) or stored in a locked steel and concrete strong room.

Class C, D & H Firearms must be stored in a locked, steel safe, securely attached to a building (unless safe mass when empty is 330 lbs. or more) or stored in a locked steel and concrete strong room. A cabinet or safe must be made of material of sufficient thickness to prevent it being easily broken, opened or destroyed, and must have fittings and locks that prevent it from being easily forced open.

All firearms, including air rifles and pistols, are registered to the owner. Ammunition must be stored separately from firearms or in a locked container.

Note that few to no semi-auto or pump-action rifles or shotguns are permitted, including .22 rifles unless applicants are members of a trap or skeet club or farmers or ranchers in remote locations. Depending on the sanction of the local firearms officer, semi-auto or pump shotguns with a five-round maximum capacity may sometimes be allowed.

Some remote farmers and ranchers can also own semi-auto or pump rifles and shotguns again provided they can convince their local firearms officers that they have a legitimate and valid need. Some farmers and ranchers can also secure special sanction for .22 semi-auto rifles. Semi-auto high-power rifles are seldom ever sanctioned no matter what the reading of license class.

There is no limit on the number or size of shotguns or rifles a person may own. Four- or eight-gauge shotguns are OK if one can only find the guns and ammo for sale in Australia. Yet permission to own a .50 cal. and BMG rifle—even a single shot—is not specifically forbidden, but as a practical matter never sanctioned. Australians can own bolt-action, break-action, lever-action and pump-action rifles without demonstrating special need (not including semi-auto .22 rifles).

Pistol ownership is permitted as long as one is a member in good standing of a pistol club. Cost is about $130 per year *and* pistol owners must prove they are actually engaged in target shooting. Police check to be sure that there are at least six practice sessions or matches per year. Fall below that standard and lose your pistol-owner's permit!

Theoretically Australians can own multiple pistols. However, their rules require use of the first pistol in six events per year and, for each additional pistol, four events per year. This requirement effectively and severely limits numbers of pistols a citizen can legally own. Also note that a gun-owner's permit is required for air rifles and pistols.

All legal pistols must have barrels at least 120mm (long (4.75 inches). Semi-autos—even .22s—are OK as long as the magazines are modified to hold no more than ten rounds. Maximum caliber for target pistols is 9mm unless one is a member of a cowboy-action shooters club. Then just about any pistol, up through .50 cal. S&W, is permitted.

Although the government is starting to open some common land for general hunting, virtually all hunting in Australia is done on remote, isolated, thinly populated private land. In some cases, hunting licenses are necessary but usually, we were told, hunting takes place in areas so remote that no one is around to check. And, the regulations also require that the hunter have written permission of the landowner on their person while hunting. Other than some very specific, unlikely circumstances, hunting with a pistol is never permitted in Australia.

Shooting someone, even in desperate self defense, is virtually never done in Australia—because ammo and guns must be locked away separately. And shooting anyone carries tremendous burden of proof as well as liabilities.

Registering one's rifles and shotguns with the local police usually costs about $35 to $50 each. Depending on state laws, registrations are valid from five years to forever. Those moving to another state have 30 days to re-register their firearms in their new state of residence. Pistol registrations are often separate. Cost is $65 per pistol, valid only five years at most.

Private citizens can trade or sell guns. But all transactions must be done through a licensed dealer or club, including appropriate paperwork, authorizations and registrations. Because silencers were not permitted, but were legal in New Zealand, Aussies often went to New Zealand to purchase one.

Once Australians have their gun-owner's card, ammo purchases are relatively unencumbered. Purchase as much ammo as you wish, in whatever caliber. Even pistol ammo can be sold to card carriers who own no pistols. Cost of ammo is about the same as in the U.S.

Australian gun owners and shooters tend to be reloaders. As long as one has a gun-owner's permit, they can legally purchase powder, bullets and primers in whatever sizes and quantities. Theoretically reloaders are not supposed to have more components on hand than they will use in one year. Component prices, most of which are imported, seem similar to the U.S.

Importation of makes and models of firearms not usually found in some of the many local gun shops is possible. Using catalogs or the Internet, Aussies locate a seller, secure sanction from their local firearms officer and have the gun shipped into the country. Currently large quantities of guns and ammo come into Australia from China.

Depending on whom you ask, illegal guns are either a tremendous problem, or "I have never seen one," as one competitive pistol shooter explained. A friendly military historian/author still had his father's WW I Steyr Hahn 9mm pistol. However, he had it so deeply hidden, and he so infrequently visited it, the fellow didn't know if it was a semi-auto or a revolver!

Is there an extensive gun culture in Australia? Hard to say. They have gun shops in virtually every city and village, but few homeowners, farmers, ranchers or urban folks with whom we spoke would admit to owning guns. Yet Australians do have some gun shows. They have a very few indigenous gun magazines and seem to import very few gun books and magazines.

Only very limited manufacture of powder and ammo there. Apparently no primers or bullets are currently manufactured in Australia, although rumors of some production of .223s and required powder float about.

A friendly (all Australians are friendly to very friendly) fellow visitor to the Darwin War Museum remarked that he saw no reason for citizens to own military-type arms—while reviewing displays commemorating

64 Japanese bombing missions over Darwin. For at least 18 months at the start of WW II, Australians feared invasion was imminent.

"It's not about kangaroo hunting," I cheerfully pointed out. But the message was certainly lost and I didn't pursue the matter with folks as friendly and gracious as these.

Chapter Sixty-Three
Malta
World Rank: 17 • Firearm Freedom 69%

It's very important, when evaluating the island country of Malta's gun laws, to keep in mind that this is a very, very small country. Not as tiny as San Marino, Andorra or Morocco but miniscule by any reasonable standards. The country of Malta is actually smaller in size than the American city of Philadelphia—only about 122 square miles! An estimated 400,000 people live on the 8x15-mile island.

Evidence remaining from WW II suggests that a supreme effort was made to clean up their rocky soil, and achieve some food self-sufficiency, but generally it's wall-to-wall people, roads and houses. Precious fresh water comes largely from desalinization. Folks here quickly learn to live in each other's back yards. *Per capita* income is about $7,300, suggesting this is not a rich country—but not a third-world one either.

Notwithstanding the general lack of open spaces to hunt or shoot, Malta has a fairly active gun culture. At least seven gun shops are listed in their island-wide phone directory, as well as a number of shooting clubs and ranges.

Malta lies about 60 miles south of the eastern tip of Sicily in the northwestern reaches of the Mediterranean Sea. Tourism is, as far as one can tell, the only major industry. Virtually everything is imported.

Information regarding Maltese gun laws comes to us via a personal visit that included in-depth interviews with a shooting-range operator and a gun-store owner/manager. English is fairly common among Maltese. Good thing, as native Maltese is a conglomeration of Italian, Latin, Spanish and Turkish. Not something an outsider might already know or quickly pick up.

The gun-store owner is a gregarious, friendly retired police officer who has worked with the American FBI. The shooting-range operator would have much rather spoken to us in Italian but we muddled through in English. He was also very friendly and helpful.

The most curious anomaly in their rules is that air rifles are included in the same registration and licensing categories as shotguns. Not very many countries require licensing of air guns.

Only shotgun hunting is undertaken on the island. Private individuals are permitted rifles of many different kinds and types on the assumption that they will be taken other places hunting (e.g. Africa.)

The quickest and easiest way to become a new legal gun owner in Malta is to secure a shotgun license. Do this by attaining the age of 18 years, joining a shooting/hunting club, studying their hunting, shooting, gun safety, gun operation and game habitat protocols, and then successfully pass a test on these subjects administered by the Maltese Environmental Planning Authority. Cost of a club membership is about $40 a year and usually includes a place to hunt and shoot.

Assuming a passing grade on one's test and a year's paid-up club membership, the local police will do an in-depth new-gun-owner's interview. This is mostly to decide if there are physical infirmities or obvious signs of mental instability. A paid-up gun-owner's insurance policy costing about $50 must also be presented at this first interview.

When test scores, insurance and club-membership evidence is all in order and assuming a good first interview, one's application is sent to police headquarters for further vetting. The first interview takes about one day. Assume at least a month to complete the second phase for each class of license, at police headquarters. There will probably be additional licenses and sanctions in the future, all taking at least a month wending their way through the Maltese bureaucracy.

Maltese police at their headquarters run an extensive record check to be sure there are no major criminal convictions on one's record. Interesting that here in the shadow of Mafia HQ on nearby Sicily a record of past traffic infractions, restraining orders, complaints, etc., not effectively adjudicated, will not count against aspiring gun owners.

Shotgun licenses, referred to as Target Shooter B licenses, also include ownership of air rifles and black-powder muzzle loaders. No limit on the number, size or type action of shotguns that may legally be owned. Pump and semi-auto shotguns must have no more than a three-round capacity unless one elects to own under a special tactical shotgun category. These are sanctioned under a special separate license selling for an additional $5 per gun per year.

Ownership of shotguns is usually only the first step for gun owners on Malta. After this it is somewhat easier to secure what they refer to as Target Shooter A and Collector A licenses. Both take a month or more to secure. At this point the procedure becomes extremely interesting.

In an apparent effort to accommodate those holding large numbers of military weapons left over from the many wars that have raged over Malta, a sanction exists for these guns. It closely mimics gun laws in San Marino and Luxembourg and is one American gun owners would greatly appreciate.

Under a Maltese Collectors A category, one can legally hold any and all guns made before 1946, including ground mount fully automatic machine guns, machine pistols and even 20mm cannons, we were told. The shooting range owner thought this category did not include full-autos, but the retired police officer/gun owner was sure it did. We quizzed him very closely on this point. These pre-1946 guns are all registered, are supposedly never to leave one's house, and are supposedly never to be fired although rumors circulate that some are fired on indoor personal ranges.

Maltese having this category of license can own as many guns as they wish and can afford. Important to note that Collector A license holders can also hold an additional ten modern guns. These guns can be rifles, pistols and semi-auto assault rifles (with payment of an additional yearly fee of $5 each.) No modern full-autos on this ticket.

Maltese gun shops separate out pre-1946 guns and modern guns in their displays. We saw many exceedingly nice collector-grade WW II Mausers, Walthers and Lugers on offer in one of their gun shops. Prices were similar—but not competitive—to U.S. prices. Judging by the relatively large inventory of rifles, pistols and shotguns, both modern and pre-1946, business in the shops must be brisk.

Modern pistols and rifles of all types and calibers including semi-auto hunting rifles and assault rifles are allowed on what is referred to as a Target Shooter A license. This license combines with the Collectors A license to sanction a maximum of 20 modern guns per person, not including shotguns, which are not limited, and collectors' guns which are also not limited in number. There is no limit on magazine size, caliber or action, except no pistols with barrel length under 3.5 inches are allowed.

Pistol shooters/owners must join a pistol club, providing a shooting range. The club then recommends its members for pistol ownership as part of the process of securing a Target Shooter A license. This eliminates a police approval to justify purchase of any pistols one may wish. All shooting on the range is recorded by date, time and number of rounds fired.

All guns held by private individuals, including collectors' guns, must be registered with local police. Other than tactical shotguns and semi-auto assault rifles which carry an annual registration fee, there is no annual fee. However, general licenses, including Collector A, Target A and Target B, must be renewed annually at a cost of roughly $75.

All guns and ammunition must be locked in separate storage lockers. Yet these storages are not inspected by the police when assured that citizen-applicants understand the laws regarding gun storage.

In some regards their registration scheme is unique. Pre-1946 collectors' guns are registered at local police offices. New guns purchased at gun shops are registered by the shop to one's license. It is the shop's responsibility to notify the police that a new registration has been made. Individuals trading a gun take it to a local police office where it is held till a new owner picks it up and has it listed on that owner's license. Maltese make a great issue of the fact that women can and do own guns.

All legal sales of ammunition and components are recorded in a permanent record book maintained by each retail gun shop. Bullets, primers and powder are available at the many gun shops around tiny Malta. Like assembled ammunition, all purchased components are recorded in the shops' record books. No silencers are permitted.

There have been two voluntary gun amnesty/registration drives on Malta, wherein illegal gun owners could legally register their mostly pre-1946 firearms. The first in the summer of 1960 was viewed with some suspicion and alarm. When these guns were not confiscated as a result of this amnesty registration, a great number of additional people came forward in 1985 for a second amnesty. As a result, illegal weapons are said not to be much of an issue in Malta. As an aside, their peace and order situation seems especially laudatory as evidence by huge numbers of carefree tourists frolicking about the island.

Ammunition is sold only for guns on one's permit. Apparently ammunition can be purchased for pre-1946 collectors' guns which, in theory at least, are never to be fired. At a maximum, a limit of 5,000 rounds for pistols or rifles can be purchased or held at any given time. No limit on shotgun ammo, although a maximum amount of reloading powder can be stored at home. Maltese are said to commonly reload shot and pistol ammo, but seldom rifle ammo.

Importation of reloading components and entire guns is said to be an issue on Malta. This primarily because such a large volume is imported. No one seems to check to see if some of the packages contain guns and ammo. Inspections of imports are said to be infrequent and cursory. Even pre-1946 full-autos such as German Mauser Schellfeurers can be brought in on one's collector's permit. We inquired specifically to this point.

Hunting birds and rabbits is said to be popular on Malta. As an aside, we did not observe any hunters or any of the reportedly white rabbits and partridge they are said to pursue. Also, nothing squashed on the roads. We did drive many remote small winding rural roads.

As a result of their pleasant, even mild, Mediterranean climate, nice local scenery, history and rock bottom low prices, many European ex-pats make Malta their retirement or winter home. Those there long enough can and do start the process of legal gun ownership and collecting. Yet neither of our informants knew exactly how long this took or know other than starting the paper process similar to regular citizens, to go about becoming an ex-pat with guns.

Given Malta's close association with European Union and UN gun-hating weenies, and its dense population and small size, it is a huge surprise that their private gun laws are as permissive and friendly as we find them. Might be fun to live there and build a collection of exotic WW II assault weapons.

The downside, of course, is that they lack space to even raise carrots much less shoot. So that pipe dream stays on the back burner.

Chapter Sixty-Four
Russia
World Rank: 23 • Firearm Freedom 59%

Russia absolutely must be in the book, I was frequently admonished. That Russia is the largest country in the world, while also being one of the most mysterious, argues mightily for inclusion.

On the other hand, getting any accurate information is extremely difficult, not helped a bit by the average Russian's natural propensity toward suspicion, mistrust, and their incredible arrogance. Russia is also one of the most expensive places on Earth in which to travel and work, starting with $400 just for visas for two people.

The last observable sign in English, German or Spanish welcomed us to the Moscow International Airport. God help those, I say reverently, who didn't already know that's where they were. Out in the cities and rural areas, English/German/Spanish is as scarce as raw whale blubber. Good English is even scarcer.

Sorry for the cliché. But we decided it was necessary to bite the bullet, pony up the considerable cash, budget the time and go to Russia for information on their gun laws for inclusion in this book you are holding. Information which follows is the end result of gun-store interviews and observations carried out during the course of this visit.

Russia, or more accurately, the Commonwealth of 21 Independent States, is nothing at all like we had envisioned or were previously led to believe. Visitors quickly discover that most of what they knew about the country is not true.

For starters, we were not prepared for the incredible wealth and level of economic activity we observed in their large cities as reflected by huge, snarly traffic jams caused by tens of thousands of big black Mercedes, Audis, large Toyotas, Volkswagens, Chryslers and other huge land yachts as well as freeway, apartment and shopping center construction. Chaos everywhere.

Even Russian gun shops reflect great wealth. Super expensive English, German, Italian and Austrian double rifles and shotguns were on display, in numbers and variety unseen in most of the rest of the world, including Germany and England.

Traditionally we in the west have supposed Russia to be a society with dramatically plummeting birth rates and life expectancies, characterized by rampant alcoholism. Statistically this has been true. Yet, at this writing, Russians are waiting hopefully and expectantly for their next census which they earnestly trust will show a dramatic reversal of these trends toward higher birth rates and greater longevity.

Liquor stores, bars, taverns, strip joints as well as illicit drug use seem much more open, common and notorious in Poland than in Russia, especially when one factors in Russia's very rural areas.

But enough of political/economic comment. It's Russia's gun laws in which we are really interested. One last fleeting observation, which really reflects on this entire volume. According to Russian guides we met, their *per capita* income is currently $540!

This would, of course, include some dirt-poor villages without paved streets. But, according to UN and World Bank data, *per capita* income should be about $16,100! Like all economic data in this volume, these figures are subject to many, many different interpretations, analyses, time of day taken, how responders held their mouths, and many other imponderables. All these figures—or any other economic data, for that matter—really show is how Russia might compare to the rest of the world. Take your pick. Is it economic data from bureaucrats we trust, or what is observed out on the streets?

We do know that there are large numbers of very expensive guns in the racks of Moscow and St. Petersburg gun shops that somebody must be buying. Russian gun shops are hives of activity with dozens of clerks and scores of busy customers scurrying about. Also, Russian gun shops do not seem to carry inexpensive domestic guns popular in the west, such as Baikals, which—according to one gun-store clerk—"no one here wants."

Russians can legally own a total of five rifles and five shotguns and that's absolutely all. Those who want another gun past these five each must sell a gun before taking ownership of another. Private sales of guns are permitted so long as you go through necessary procedures at the police station.

Absolutely no private legal ownership of pistols is allowed. Some gun shops sell imported and domestic pistols and ammo to police, government and sanctioned security people, but never to private folks. There are, however, enough illegal pistols out there for anyone who is determined to have one, we were told.

Semi-auto hunting and target rifles and shotguns are permitted as long as they are limited to a five round capacity. In the case of .22s, ten round magazines are sanctioned.

Semi-autos can include Kalashnikovs but only with five round magazines. Russian gun shops traditionally offer acceptable five-round mags, for a great profusion of different rifles and shotguns. Typically, as is true in most of Europe, these guns tend to be models with detaching magazines we seldom see here in the west. Even models of bolt-action rifles frequently have detaching magazines. Yet we were also informed that it is not particularly difficult to find full-capacity mags out on the street.

Machine guns, submachine guns and silencers are also not legal for private ownership. Russia is a very sophisticated society with a number of good machine shops and a great manufacturing capacity. It is also fair to say that some Russians can be greedy folks, on the lookout for any opportunity, some of which may not conform to code. Apparently some of their shops turn out clandestine but acceptable silencers and full-capacity magazines, only available on the street.

Owning the few guns they are permitted is surprisingly straightforward. Not acceptable, by our standards, but straightforward! New, first-time gun owners in Russia must be at least 18 years old. They also must own shotguns only for at least five years without legal mishap or incident, before transitioning to rifle ownership. Unlike many European nations, no requirement exists that new gun owners must join a sporting, shooting or hunting club, but many do join such clubs.

Cost of club memberships and hunting licenses are sufficiently modest and insignificant that folks we talked with didn't know what they were. Perhaps $90, one fellow speculated.

Many Russian gun clubs allow members to target shoot, trap shoot and even hunt birds and small game with their own club rifles. It's a way of interesting and familiarizing new people with gun ownership without going through procedures and expense of private ownership.

Unlike many other overly restrictive countries, Russians are not required to take courses, and then pass tests relative to gun function, game management, ecology and first aid before being issued a gun-owner's permit.

Gun ownership starts with a visit to the local police office where one registers the intent to own a gun. Officers start the process by checking new applicants for obvious physical infirmities. We were told with an absolute straight face that anybody with three fingers or three toes—or more—could legally qualify. Perhaps a commentary about cold winters in Russia—we don't know.

From the police office it's to the doctor's office for additional physical, mental, psychological and drug-screening. Cost is about $135 at the cop shop and perhaps $65 for the drug/psychological and physical exams. Gun shops will handle initial applications at the cop shop for another $135–270 total.

It takes about one month the first time. When your gun-owner's permit comes through from the police, take it to the gun shop where your newly purchased shotgun or, five years later, a rifle, is listed on your permit. New owners must then take their gun back to the police where it is fired three times and the bullets captured and kept on file. Since these bullets are not cataloged, gun-shop people thought this process was at best an exercise in futility, or at worst, blatant harassment. Subsequent ownership permits for additional guns take only about 15 days, provided nothing bad has popped up on your record.

Apparently Russian police also try to capture and keep the pellets from a fired shotgun. We are uncertain regarding this procedure but, given other Russian strangenesses, especially among their bureaucracy, this requirement did not seem particularly bizarre.

No limit on bore size of shotguns exists. Eight- and ten-gauge shotguns are permitted but not common. Most shotguns we saw in stores were 12, 16 or 20s. Like many other European countries, 16-gauge shotguns are popular in Russia. This the result of an ownership-size compromise where total numbers of guns permitted are strictly controlled.

Although our informant didn't know of any .50 BMG rifles or ammo being sold in Russia, he did mention .338 Lapua, .500 Jeffrey and .416 Rigby and similar. In other words, no restrictions on rifle size in Russia.

Ammunition can only be purchased for guns on your license, which must be shown at the time of purchase. All ammo purchased is listed in a record book. There is no limit on numbers and amounts of ammo one can purchase. However only 400 rounds at any one time can be legally transported in one's private vehicle unless a special transport permit is secured. No indication of how complex and time-consuming securing this permit may be.

Reloading is possible for shotguns, but not for rifles. Many gun shops in larger cities sell shotgun primers, powder and shot but currently, we were told, it is more costly for components with which to reload then purchasing new factory ammo.

An estimated 25 to 30 gun shops are said to be in Moscow, the capital, ten to 15 in St. Petersburg and three to four in every other large to medium city in Russia. As one proceeds eastward into Siberia, where guns are used much more frequently as tools, incidence of gun shops is said to diminish. Expensive regulations regarding shipping are said to add mightily to costs of gun ownership in Siberia.

All private guns must be kept in a secure, suitable safe, along with ammo. New owners are advised to expect an on-site inspection, but these inspections are far from certain. Plan for an inspection, but don't have your feelings hurt if it doesn't happen, we were told.

Very light duty, small-caliber air rifles are not regulated. Above seven joules of power, air rifles face similar restrictions as shotguns and rifles. They must be recorded on one's gun-owner's certificate. Air rifles can only be used for target practice. They are never allowed for hunting, to take any game or carried in the woods or field under any circumstance.

And that's about it. Tremendously restrictive as we might have previously supposed, but not particularly complicated.

As mentioned, security data on Russian gun laws was one of the more difficult and expensive portions of this project, not made easier by reason of the fact that few Russians speak English and everything, including guns, ammo, hotels, food and transportation, are ridiculously expensive.

Chapter Sixty-Five
Conclusion

Now, what have we learned from all this? Quite a lot actually. Neither the bleeding-heart anti-gun-rights liberals nor the died-in-the-wool cold-dead-finger conservatives may relish some of the findings, but at least now the debate can take place in the light of day.

- Every nation studied has a gun culture, gun laws and gun buffs.

- The idea that America stands alone on gun freedoms is a myth.

- Contrary to popular belief, America does not have the greatest firearm freedom, ranked only 9th out of 62, with an 83% firearm-freedom rating.

- Nations that have guidelines and access to firearms that exceed what U.S. citizens have set a good example and can be emulated.

- Perpetuation of the myth that America is unique regarding guns, by the media, anti-rights activists, politicians and the UN, is harmful to freedom and does a gross disservice to the world's gun owners.

- For the first time in history, the world can see what its gun laws are.

- Prospects for the world's access to improved gun rights are good.

- Even the most repressive gun laws contain the seeds of freedom and respect for some level of gun rights. Those seeds deserve nurturing and removing the obstacles for growth.

- A law that says you can only have firearm X if you jump through flaming hoops is a guarantee that you can indeed have firearm X. What's needed then, from a legal and cultural standpoint, is X + 1 and a fire extinguisher.

- People from diverse backgrounds both here and abroad can at last learn about their homeland's approach, and have a basis from which to improve conditions. To quote Steve Maniscalco, "If you knew all your rights you might demand them."

- The days of criticizing and attacking America for having the best gun rights are over.

- The most repressive world regimes are exposed and can get attention they sorely need, for improvement and restoration of human rights.

- Where citizens face the greatest repression, a robust underground economy helps fill the void.

- The black market for civilian guns is discreet and apart from other criminal activity.

- Government efforts to deny peoples' rights have a predictable effect on the black market—it supports growth.

- While many foreign nations contribute to the effort to disarm innocent people, others support and encourage wise, healthy gun ownership and safe use.

- Nations with the best gun laws have parallels with better economies, better respect for the rule of law and private-property rights, and the freest markets.

Gun laws reflect cultures of various countries. Cultures change slowly, if they do at all. In spite of popular perception, gun laws throughout the world are not changing rapidly or dramatically. In places like South Africa where major shifts have occurred, concurrent rapid changes in gun laws were seen, but by and large, the international picture is more stable than you may have been led to believe.

Like it or not, guns are going to be with us for the foreseeable future, that's just the way it is. For one thing, the world's governments and leaders are adamantly opposed to giving up *their* guns, from sidearms to nukes. We have seen how the major source of illegal guns is the military and the police, who themselves are armed to the teeth and are not about to allow themselves to be disarmed.

The myth of civilian guns being the supply pool for illegal weapons is just that—a complete myth. If nothing else, civilian guns have never been manufactured and distributed in tens of millions as is true with AK-47s, M-16s, FN FALs and SKS carbines. There just aren't sufficient numbers or caches of private guns to pervasively infiltrate even small countries. The criminal syndicates and black market operators rely on boatloads of supply, not the inconsistent pickings of some general populace.

Despotic countries that try to limit availability of civilian guns often add to their own troubles by putting more and more uniformed or plain clothes gun-toting officials on the streets. In too many countries, individuals in the military and police are the principal sources of illegal guns! Poorly paid, desperate enforcement people are known to sell their stolen or government-supplied guns for cash, adding dramatically to the pool of illegal weapons. Doctor, heal thyself—let the government that seeks to disarm its citizens lead by example and first disarm itself.

Endless, fruitless and costly campaigns to disarm the innocent are hypocritical and immoral. They are wasteful, ultimately ineffective and doomed to failure. Continually pursuing that course borders on insanity, but at least it's expensive, and diverts scarce law-enforcement resources towards managing the innocent and away from where they're really needed—disarming criminals first. Government proposals that leave the power brokers fully armed and leave the populace defenseless "for their own safety," are suspect at best and openly tyrannical at worst.

Many American anti-gun proposals have their origins in the practices of repressive regimes overseas. It's well past time to curtail that and adopt instead some of the more freedom-oriented practices. America can look to the nations that outrank her for ideas. The Swiss stand out as a model from which we can learn and grow.

The virulently anti-Second Amendment London *Economist* magazine rates countries such as the U.S., Finland, Switzerland and New Zealand as being at the top of the list for having a sound body of law, with corresponding respect for property rights. These, as we have seen, are wonderful places for private gun owners. It is easy to conclude that governments that trust their people with the factors of production also trust them with firearms. Invariably the freest countries have the best, most vibrant, rapidly expanding economies.

In all cases of private gun ownership there is a great element of personal responsibility and integrity. Societies that lose these traits and come to rely on government for anything really important seem to lose their ability to own guns and to use them responsibly. Switzerland is a country whose citizens display great personal responsibility and integrity. Neighboring France, riven by socialism, is the opposite. Predictably, France's private gun ownership rules and regulations are picky and tortured, while the Swiss enjoy and encourage enormous personal latitude in this regard.

The world's governments should provide for efficient, easy methods of private firearms ownership. The Swiss understand the formula, support the shooting arts and sports, encourage training for all citizens all year long, and no one accuses them of being warlike—just the opposite— the well-armed Swiss are peacemakers.

Perhaps, like the police in New Zealand, it is time for our own FBI, BATFE, local law enforcement and others to rethink some of their ban-enforcement strategies. Mexico and our own local gang bangers have demonstrated how flawed that approach is.

Take up instead the challenge of teaching safe, responsible gun ownership and educating our citizens. *That* would make the world a safer place. Discount deeply the "news" media's incessant bleating to the contrary, knowing that ignorance is rarely a viable strategy for progress. Sure, go after bad guys as one component of an overall plan, and it gives the authorities a sense of purpose. Bad people though, government types included, who want guns will get them. History provides an unbroken record of that fact. So do the smart thing— open the gates and welcome in the good guys, with open arms.

--

Keep in mind that many influential groups do not want the information in this book widely available to the people of the world. It undermines strategies and policies designed to disarm the public and accumulate power solely in the hands of the "authorities" and ruling classes. We anticipate efforts to demean and denigrate this research and its highly talented extremely accomplished author Larry Grupp. We expect to hear claims that will cast aspersions on the conclusion that all nations have some level of gun rights, and that this is a good thing. Bring a thoughtful and critical eye to such claims. Read the book and decide for yourself whether the U.S. is the only nation that cherishes the fundamental human right to keep and bear arms.

--

To recap the opening remarks:

The Swiss general said he could put a million men with rifles in the field on 24-hour notice. So the German general arrogantly asked, what would the Swiss do if I sent five million of my best heavily armed men swarming across your borders? Came the wry reply—each Swiss citizen-soldier would fire five times and then go home.

That's how peace is maintained in this best of all possible worlds.

Peace through strength.

About Larry Grupp

Author Larry Grupp has 42 books and a long list of magazine articles to his credit. These cover a great variety of action topics including hunting and fishing, military history, weapons analysis and their place in military history and paramilitary actions, to political analysis and governmental affairs. Grupp has spent a significant portion of his career visiting actual battle sites, places of significant economic and social tumult and militarily and politically important locations throughout the world.

At age 14 Grupp secured his first Federal Firearms License, which he has held for 58 years, leading to a lifetime of interest in guns, hunting, shooting, firearms collecting and retail sales.

Nine years ago, author Grupp embarked on a great saga of assembling and analyzing rules and regulations relative to private gun ownership in countries around the world. This was partly in response to his distaste of the patently false claims made by anti-gun-rights activists, promoting a false notion that U.S. citizens are the only ones in the entire world that can freely and easily own private firearms.

Information he compiled for this book comes straight from the sources. It had to—it was not available from any other place—not at the UN, not the U.S. State Department, and not from any national gun owners' associations.

INDEX

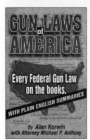

GUN LAWS OF AMERICA
Every federal gun law on the books, with plain-English summaries
by Alan Korwin with Michael P. Anthony, 352 pgs., #GLOA $19.95.
Like a complete gun-law library in your hand! The first and only unabridged compilation of federal gun law—everything Congress has done on guns and the right to arms, and **every law is clearly described in plain English!** Covers citizens, dealers, collectors, Militia, National Guard, manufacturers, global disarmament, "proper" authorities, types of guns, the lost national right to carry, National Transportation Guarantee. Good laws, bad laws, 70 pages of juicy intro, and plain-English summaries make it so easy. Widely endorsed.
"Outstanding" –former Arizona Attorney General Bob Corbin.

SUPREME COURT GUN CASES: Two Centuries of Gun Rights Revealed
by David Kopel, Stephen P. Halborook, Ph. D., Alan Korwin, #SCGCC $17. These 92 Supreme Court gun cases prove they've said a lot—200 years of decisions confirm an individual right to keep and bear arms. You get 44 key cases unedited, the rest carefully excerpted. Each has a detailed plain-English summary, main passages highlighted. The cases *"assume or are consistent with the proposition that the 2nd Amendment is an individual right."* –Kopel. *"Superb... Groundbreaking."* –The Goldwater Institute. This out-of-print classic now delivered as a fully searchable CD or by email.

Traveler's Guide to the Firearm Laws of the Fifty States

TRAVELER'S GUIDE to the Firearm Laws of the 50 States
by Attorney J. Scott Kappas, 68 pgs., #TG $13.95.
Because you are subject to arrest for simply traveling from state to state with a personal firearm, some sort of guide has been badly needed for years. This excellent book covers all the basics for armed travel: vehicles, glove box, open carry, permits, loaded or not, weapon types, even Canada and Mexico and more. An indispensable tool if you want to travel armed and know the basic rules at the next state line. Ranks each state on its relative freedom too. Before you pack your bags and go, get and read this book. **Includes the Nationwide CCW Reciprocity List!**

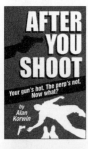

AFTER YOU SHOOT
Your gun's hot. The perp's not. Now what?
by Alan Korwin, 160 pgs. #AYS $14.95.
Dangerous legal loopholes facing innocent people after self-defense are described, with solutions proposed. Calling 911 after surviving a criminal assault erases your right to silence, your right to have an attorney present, and compromises your 5th Amendment guarantee against self incrimination—into a police recorder while you're traumatized and shaking from adrenaline. Suggests law and criminal procedure changes, how to handle the aftermath, the model used by police themselves, plus the controversial "Adnarim" statement.

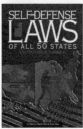

SELF DEFENSE LAWS OF ALL 50 STATES
by Mitch and Evan Vilos, 576 pgs., #SDL $29.95.
State-by-state deadly force comparison chart; When can you use deadly force—in your state; What gets innocent gun owners arrested; The biggest myths about self defense; Can you "rack one in" your 12 gauge to stop a threat; For every gun owner—not just CCW permit holders; The line between your rights and the rights of predators. With true-life examples and plain-talk summaries. Know your state.